Quest for the Human

Quest for the Human

An Exploration of Saul Bellow's Fiction

Eusebio L. Rodrigues

Lewisburg
BUCKNELL UNIVERSITY PRESS
London and Toronto: Associated University Presses

Associated University Presses, Inc.
4 Cornwall Drive
East Brunswick, N. J. 08816

Associated University Presses Ltd
69 Fleet Street
London EC4Y 1EU, England

Associated University Presses
Toronto, Ontario, Canada M5E 1A7

Library of Congress Cataloging in Publication Data

Rodrigues, Eusebio L., 1927-
  Quest for the human.

  Bibliography: p.
  Includes index.
  1. Bellow, Saul—Criticism interpretation.
I. Title.
PS3503.E4488Z83   813'.52   80-66707
ISBN 0-8387-2368-3

Printed in the United States of America

For Merlyn with love

Contents

Acknowledgments

I wish to express my deep gratitude to Professor Robert F. Lucid of the University of Pennsylvania who directed me to the fiction of Saul Bellow and guided the writing of the dissertation out of which this book has sprung.

I am grateful to my colleagues in the English Department of Georgetown University, especially Roland Flint, John Hirsh, Jason Rosenblatt and Thomas Walsh, for their valuable comments and suggestions. To Srinivasa Rao of La Salle College and Professor Michael Stieg of Simon Fraser University I owe a special debt of gratitude for their insightful criticism.

I also thank Georgetown University for a summer grant and for help toward part of the publication costs.

I would like to thank the following for permission to quote from published works:

Introduction

Saul Bellow seeks fictional answers to fundamental questions about human existence and action in our day: "Why were we born? What are we doing here? Where are we going? In its eternal naïveté the imagination keeps coming back to these things."[1] His novels, from *Dangling Man* (1944) to *Humboldt's Gift* (1975), are imaginative responses to the challenge of being human in today's complex and chaotic world.

This essay attempts to understand these acts of creative discovery. Criticism, especially criticism of the works of a contemporary writer, should begin as an act of understanding before it proceeds to judgment. The process of arriving at a valid interpretation, and thus at the true meaning,[2] of a contemporary novel cannot be reduced to a formula. The reader has to immerse himself in this fictional universe before he can map its geography and act as a guide. "People do not read attentively and are not willing to undertake hard work," complains Bellow.[3] David Lodge in *The Language of Fiction* describes the process of understanding thus: "It is my own experience that the moment of perceiving the pattern is sudden and unexpected. All the time one has been making the tiny provisional notes, measuring each against one's developing awareness of the whole, storing them up in the blind hope that they will prove useful, and then suddenly one such small local observation sends a shock like an electric charge through all the discrete observations heaped up on all sides, so that with an exciting clatter and rattle they fly about and arrange themselves in a certain meaningful order."[4] To continue Lodge's metaphor, the moment of perception is also a moment of vision that lights up the complete fictional world that is the novel.

A critical grid imposed over such a world would distort and falsify it. I have therefore deliberately avoided using any particular critical methodology, relying instead on my intuitions and on my sensibility to look at theme, structure, and language in Bellow's novels. Bellow's dominant theme, as stated above, is the onward and upward quest for the human. Man today, even more urgently than in the past, has to discover who and what he is. "The great question," writes Bellow, "seems to be

9

when will we seek new and higher forms of individuality, purged of old sicknesses and corrected by a deeper awareness of what all men have in common?"[5] Each of Bellow's eight protagonists (who are different manifestations of contemporary man) travel in search of humanness, the search gathering momentum, height, and complexity as one fictional stage succeeds another.

Bellow had to use and develop fictional forms to dramatize this search. This essay will attempt to understand how each novel is put together and will also illustrate Bellow's use of increasingly complex fictional modes in his later novels. I offer no definition of structure, but accept Bellow's suggestion that art has "something to do with the achievement of stillness in the midst of chaos."[6] Bellow himself cannot explain how the artist achieves this stillness, this form, this order: "I don't say that the novelist knows what order is, but he relies on his imagination to lead him toward it. In a work of art the imagination is the sole source of order. There are critics who assume that you must begin with order if you are to end with it. Not so. A novelist begins with disorder and disharmony, and goes toward order by an unknown process of the imagination."[7] In "Skepticism and the Depth of Life" he has said: "The integrities upon which good workmanship depends, and the act of creation itself, interest critics and scholars very little."[8]

Besides looking at theme and structure, this essay will also consider Bellow's use of language. I come with no theory of linguistics or of stylistics. There is, it seems to me, a vital connection between the thematic and structural complexity of the later fiction and the vigor and range of the language Bellow has used. The reader who travels through Bellow's fictional cosmos gradually develops a growing awareness of the "language" of Bellow's fiction—its rhythms, its semantics, its vocabulary, its grammar.

This essay has been deliberately titled "Quest for the Human," for it seeks to make the reader aware of a threefold quest for humanness. It will examine each of Bellow's eight novels to demonstrate that the Bellow protagonist is always in search of the human. The novels clearly suggest that they are projections of Bellow's own arduous climb toward true humanness. Each novel marks a stage of the Himalayan ascent, the quest and the humanness manifesting themselves in richer and increasingly complex forms. This essay itself assumes the form of a quest, for it is a journey through and an exploration of the fictional universe that Bellow has created.

The quest begins in the foothills with *Dangling Man*.

NOTES

1. Saul Bellow, "Distractions of a Fiction Writer," *The Living Novel,* edited by Granville Hicks (New York: Macmillan, 1957), p. 13.

2. In a letter dated May 4, 1918, Joseph Conrad wrote: "A work of art is very seldom limited to one exclusive meaning and not necessarily tending to a definite conclusion. And this for the reason that the nearer it approaches art, the more it acquires a symbolic character." See G. Jean-Aubry, *Joseph Conrad: Life and Letters* (New York: Doubleday, Page & Co., 1927), 2:.203.

3. Chirantan Kulshreshtha, "A Conversation with Saul Bellow," *Chicago Review* 23, no. 4, and 24, no. 1 (1972): p. 8.

4. David Lodge, *The Language of Fiction* (New York: Columbia University Press, 1967), pp. 80–81.

5. Saul Bellow, "Buñuel's Unsparing Vision," *Horizon* 5 (November 1962): 112.

6. *Writers at Work,* Third Series, p. 190.

7. "Distractions of a Fiction Writer," p. 6.

8. Saul Bellow, "Skepticism and the Depth of Life," *The Arts and the Public,* edited by James E. Miller, Jr., and Paul D. Herring (Chicago: University of Chicago Press, 1967), p. 23.

Quest for the Human

1 *Dangling Man*

Dangling Man (1944), Bellow's first novel and clearly not a fictional achievement, is significant in many ways for an understanding of his mind and art. It relays the bewilderment of a number of young American intellectuals during the early 1940s. It announces with emphatic assurance a break with the fiction of the immediate past: neither the Hemingway code nor the Hemingway mode will do for Bellow. The basic premise on which all his fiction rests—that it is marvelous to be alive—is set down here together with themes that Bellow will later explore in greater depth and complexity. *Dangling Man* indicates the general direction, thematic and structural, Bellow is heading toward a novelist, and marks the first stage of his creative quest for the human.

Joseph, Bellow's protagonist, is forced by a conspiracy of circumstances to reexamine the values by which he has lived. His former beliefs have collapsed and cannot protect him from the chaos that threatens to overwhelm him. The image of the torn awning of the neighborhood corner store that does not afford any shelter from the wind and the rain haunts him. He sees himself as a man dangling, suspended between two worlds, one dying, the other refusing to come into existence. His state is one of demoralization and utter confusion. He cannot understand his strange behavior, the ugly explosions of temper that erupt out of him. Nor can he come to terms with the interior darkness that has invaded his being. In a desperate attempt to dispel this darkness and to understand his condition, he decides to keep a diary. It is his way of talking to himself about himself, it is a form of release and self-therapy.

Bellow's use of the form of the diary-novel in *Dangling Man* is an act of significant choice. It proclaims his rejection of the Hemingway manner. "Most serious matters are closed to the hardboiled," notes Joseph. "They are unpracticed in introspection, and therefore badly equipped to deal with opponents whom they cannot shoot like big game or outdo in daring."[1] "It is awfully easy to be hard-boiled about everything in the daytime, but at night it is another thing," writes Jake Barnes, the hero of *The Sun Also Rises*.[2] The Hemingway hero deliberately suspends the functioning of his mind; he refuses to plunge into his self and to understand his secret despair. Tight-lipped and stoical, he wants to achieve grace under pressure; life for him takes on heightened meaning only when it is in danger of extinction. He freezes all his internal fears and leaps with a sense of relief into vigorous action. The Bellow protagonist will let loose a compulsive flow of words trying to relieve the torments of his inner life, vainly seeking a grace beyond that of mere gesture or action.

The use of the diary as a fictional device together with the deliberate break from Hemingway suggest that Bellow realized that the prevailing forms of American fiction were not adequate to nourish his creative sensibility. He found what he needed in nineteenth-century Russian and twentieth-century French fiction. Behind Bellow's *Dangling Man* stands Sartre's *Nausée*, and behind both these works looms Dostoevski's bitter and savage *Notes from Underground*. Keith Opdahl and John Clayton spell out in detail the parallels between *Dangling Man* and these two novels.[3] Bellow's literary indebtedness to these two writers, especially to Dostoevski (Kafka hovers somewhere in the background), is evident. He may not have been consciously imitating Sartre or Dostoevski. Perhaps Bellow found himself drawn toward these novelists who had used sophisticated versions of the journal form to capture the contradictions, paradoxes, and exasperations involved in the act of reaching toward the human in their time. It was natural for Bellow to seize on the form they had used and to adapt it in order to dramatize the lacerating questions about the human that obsessed him in the early 1940s.

A novelist need not be a technical innovator, suggests Bellow, nor does he have to invent a form for himself: "There is no need for every writer to keep up the pretense that the art of the novel begins with him and that his originality is total, pure and god-like."[4] In *Dangling Man* Bellow tried to compel the form he inherited from his predecessors to serve his own creative needs. He brought to the making of *Dangling Man* the rich awareness of an artist, not the cool mind of a thinker. Writing about the young Bellow who had come to New York from Chicago in 1942, two years before *Dangling Man* was published, Alfred Kazin tells of his delight in meeting someone who was intellectually brilliant ("full of the Great Books and jokes from the Greek plays"[5]) and also convinced about his talent for the novel. "It was refreshing," writes Kazin, "to be with a man who believed himself headed for power in the novel."[6] *Dangling Man* is the work of a novelist who is acutely conscious of the form he is using, even though he cannot as yet control it. Bellow uses a number of compositional strategies to achieve structural coherence, while allowing his novel to appear as a casual linear record of haphazard entries and unconnected incidents.

The novel focuses on what happens to Joseph, the diarist-hero[7] (who never reveals his last name), between December 15, 1942, and April 9, 1943, his last civilian day. A slack narrative line stretches through these diary entries of about five months. When the diary opens, Joseph, waiting to be drafted, is free and unemployed. The novel tells of his dangling through his days of enforced freedom until finally, out of an exacerbation generated by the strange events, moods, and encounters he records, he decides to volunteer. This decision brings both the diary and the novel to an end. Both sources of unity are obviously too weak to supply the novel with structural consistency. The narrative pace does not compel the diary material together. And Joseph, a thinking, brooding, passive figure, who drifts rather than acts, is not a source of focal power, unlike Underground Man, whose compelling voice is a unifying force that forges the two almost disparate sections of Dostoevski's novel together.

The problem of time, however, a crucial problem for any novelist, is handled with craftsmanlike skill. *Dangling Man* communicates a sense of Joseph's aimless drift through a period of five months, but the careful reader can detect Bellow's control over time. Behind the five months recorded in the diary stand the events of the past, and the fragments of the past have to be pieced together as in a jigsaw puzzle for chronological coherence. Joseph's present dangling does not arise illogically or abruptly, but is the result of certain past events for which a temporal, if haphazard, index has been provided.

Quick flashes light up the story of Joseph's past before December 15, 1942. Certain incidents trigger his thoughts. Or else there are deliberate acts of recall. Thinking of the Joseph of a year ago, Joseph releases this information about himself: "Joseph, aged twenty-seven, an employee of the Inter-American Travel Bureau, a tall, already slightly flabby but, nevertheless, handsome young man, a graduate of the University of Wisconsin—major, History—married five years, amiable, generally takes himself to be well-liked. But on close examination he proves to be somewhat peculiar" (18–19). The encounter with Jimmy Burns in the restaurant tells us that Joseph had joined the Communist party in 1932, but was soon disillusioned. He has been married for six years now. In 1940 he had a brief love affair with Kitty Daumler, which he broke off when she hinted that he should leave his wife, Iva. In the winter of 1941 the first symptom of his present state manifested itself when he lost his temper with his landlord. In March 1942 he resigned from the travel bureau in order to respond to the call for induction. Since that day he has been dangling, awaiting the final summons.

In order to understand the condition of Joseph when the diary opens, the reader has to be aware of the Joseph that was. "You used to be an absolutely reasonable guy," his friend, Myron Adler, tells him (105). Joseph was a calm, cool, even-tempered intellectual who had come to terms both with himself and with the world around him: "In the last seven or eight years he had worked everything out in accordance with a general plan. Into this plan have gone his friends, his family, and his wife" (20). Keenly aware of his own being and its importance to him, he had looked at himself and found himself not wanting. He had looked at the world around him, agreed with Hobbes that existence could be "nasty, brutish and short" (38), but was glad that he had discovered a "colony of the spirit" (27), a circle of friends who got together to insulate themselves against the dangers and crudities of the world around them. Joseph thought that he had found the right answer to the question: "How should a good man live; what ought he to do?" (27)

Dangling Man places before us a Joseph who discovers that his answer is inadequate. His general plan cannot defend him any longer from the terrible assaults of the world outside him and the world within him. The props that have shored him against collapse give way one by one: "I began to discover one weakness after another in all I had built around me" (39). His marriage is a failure and, after he visits his in-laws, he realizes the bleak truth that "babble, tedium, and all the rest were to be expected; they came with every marriage" (16). The two-year love affair with Kitty Daumler gradually fizzles to an end. More important, Joseph discovers that the colony of the spirit that he firmly believed in no longer keeps its covenants against spite and cruelty.

It is the Servatius party in March 1942 that shatters Joseph's faith in a protective community of friends. Bellow's fictional talent, his ability to charge an incident with quick life and to convey the graphic actuality of character and situation, reveal themselves in this brief episode. The party is dramatically presented through the naked, bruised sensibilities of a Joseph ready to experience a moment of truth. Joseph, with Iva, comes in late and immediately the heat and stridency of the party bursts upon him. Minna Servatius, the hostess, is drunk and unsteady. The gathering has broken up into small groups and there is a great deal of chatter, but no real conversation. There are the usual outsiders who do not fit into the inner circle of friends, which is itself split and fragmented. Harry Servatius neglects everyone to spend the whole evening talking to and dancing with one woman. Robbie Stillman tells his usual, stale comic stories. Joseph is bored and irritated. Twice Minna attempts to pull the party together. She badgers George Hayza into recording a facile surrealist poem he had made popular some years ago. Everyone is embarrassed. Her second attempt is a disaster. She insists that Abt Morris, who is still in love with her, should hypnotize her; he does so reluctantly. Joseph witnesses the degradation of Minna and the rage, spite, and savagery that manifest themselves in Abt when he has Minna completely under his power.

Joseph now becomes aware of the real nature of the meetings of the colony. Unlike ancient ritual gatherings and annual festivals wherein pent-up feelings of scorn, hatred, and desire were released in a form of communal therapy, the Servatius party was a bitter exhibition of modern savagery: "We did these things without grace or mystery . . . assassinated the Gods in one another and shrieked in vengefulness and hurt" (31–32). Joseph and his friends are not a colony of the spirit, but a "tight little bunch," "all fenced around" (37), a group that trample on each other in order to assert their weak individual selves. With the help of an outsider, Jack Brill, Joseph sees for the first time the cruelties and the petty meannesses that lurk beneath their seemingly civilized behavior. He experiences the sharp point of the Hobbesian truth that he had heretofore avoided: "One was constantly threatened, shouldered, and, sometimes invaded by 'nasty, brutish, and short,' lost fights to it in unexpected corners. In the colony? Even in oneself. Was anyone immune altogether? In times like these? There were so many treasons; they were a medium, like air, like water; they passed in and out of you, they made themselves your accomplices; nothing was impenetrable to them" (38). It is Joseph's first real insight into human nature.

Even more of a shock is the fact that his innermost self, into which he retreats as a refuge against the onslaughts of the outer world, betrays him. He who thought of himself as a mild man, a good man, discovers corruptness within him. Joseph is horrified at the crude malice of Etta, his fifteen-year-old niece, whom he spanks, and is even more horrified the next day as he reflects on the fact that Etta resembles him closely, and that "a similarity of faces must mean a similarity of nature and presumably of fate" (50). His horror is intensified as he recalls an incident in his childhood when his friend's mother, Mrs. Harscha, had seen the Mephistopheles in him, something rotten and diabolic behind Joseph's handsome exterior.

Dangling Man presents a Joseph who struggles between a past that has been shattered and a future that has not come into view: "I, in this room, separate, alienated, distrustful, find in my purpose not an open world, but a closed, hopeless jail. My perspectives end in the walls. Nothing of the future comes to me. Only the past, in its shabbiness and innocence. Some men seem to know exactly where their opportunities lie; they break prisons and cross whole Siberias to pursue them. One room holds me" (61). Joseph's room is an appropriate physical analogue for his psychic imprisonment. His dangling days shuttle between stretches of "narcotic dullness" (13) and times of intense, frantic self-questioning. Neither the world nor his own condition make any sense: "Jeff Forman dies; brother Amos lays up a store of shoes for the future. Amos is kind. Amos is no cannibal. He cannot bear to think I should be unsuccessful, lack money, refuse to be concerned about my future. Jeff, under the water, is beyond virtue, value, glamor, money, or future. I say these things unable to see or think straight, and what I feel is less injustice or inhumanity than bewilderment" (56). Joseph's malaise is of the spirit.

Joseph's dangling can be seen as an effective metaphor for the plight of a number of young New York intellectuals during the 1940s. Having lived through the trauma of the depression and then fired by the promises and enthusiasms of communism in the early 1930s, these young men gradually lost all political and social faith as they experienced in succession the disillusionments of the Moscow Trials, the Spanish Civil War, Munich, and the 1938 Nazi-Soviet pact. After Pearl Harbor and America's entry into the war, with Soviet Russia as one of its allies, the younger generation was more confused than ever about the real implications of the international struggle and the reasons for supporting or opposing the war. In 1943, *Partisan Review*, the radical journal of the time, ran a series of essays entitled "The New Failure of Nerve," which analyzed the crackup of the American intellectual under the stress of war, and warned him against switching from reason to faith as a solution to social and human problems.

It would be a mistake, however, to read *Dangling Man* as a "document in the cultural history of the forties,"[8] even though its early reviewers seized on its contemporary relevance. Delmore Schwartz opened his review in *Partisan Review* thus:

> Here, for the first time I think, the experience of a new generation has been seized and recorded. It is one thing simply to have lost one's faith; it is quite another to begin with the sober and necessary lack of illusion afforded by Marxism, and then to land in what seems to be utter disillusion, only to be forced, stage by stage, to even greater depths of disillusion. This is the experience of the generation that has come to maturity during the depression, the sanguine period of the New Deal, the days of the Popular Front and the days of Munich, and the slow, loud, ticking imminence of a new war.[9]

Edmund Wilson, in an oft-quoted statement, hailed *Dangling Man* in 1944 as "one of the most honest pieces of testimony on the psychology of a whole generation who have grown up during the depression and the war."[10]

Dangling Man does communicate a faint sense of the political and social anxieties in American intellectual life during the 1940s. It is, in a way, a crystallization of the ideas and the controversies that were featured in the *Partisan Review* between 1940 and 1944.[11] From the perspective of the 1980s, however, it is clear that Joseph, with the basic assumptions he starts from, with his attitude toward the war, and, above all, in the light of his tangential involvement with communism, is more significant as the first sketch for the Bellow protagonist in search of the human rather than a representative dangler of the 1940s.

For Bellow does not dramatize the disillusion with communism as a major reason for Joseph's dangling. The incident at the Arrow suggests that Joseph himself was one of those "earnest eccentrics" he refers to, who merely talked about "socialism, psychopathology, or the fate of European Man" (22), but were not committed to any form of action. Later, he interprets his angry outburst against Comrade Burns as an expression of his disgust with the party: "For the insolence of Burns figured the whole betrayal of an undertaking to which I had once devoted myself" (26). Still later, Joseph reveals the tenuous nature of the commitment to communism when he tells *Tu As Raison Aussi* that he never enjoyed being a revolutionary and that he "regarded politics as an inferior activity" (92). The problem of Bellow's protagonists will be nonpolitical, for the ultimate problems of the self cannot be solved by political means.

Joseph dangles for many reasons and in many ways. Bellow places his rather abstract, isolated hero in the midst of a crowded rooming house to make us see him as a human being, not as a mere mind. He takes great pains to make the rooming house come alive by using realistic detail, setting forth its cooking odors, its roaches, and its odd inhabitants. By introducing Mr. Vanaker, Bellow provides a character who can function as parallel and counterpoint to his protagonist. Joseph cannot really understand the sudden explosions of anger that burst out of himself, but he does realize that Vanaker's irritatingly eccentric behavior—Vanaker coughs perpetually, he leaves the door ajar when using the toilet, he invites the blind Mrs. Kiefer to the movies—is Vanaker's way of calling attention to himself. When Vanaker leaves, Marie, the maid, discovers the following articles in his closet: "Bottles, of course . . . picture magazines with photos of nudes, gloves, soiled underwear, the bowl of a pipe, a grease-stained handkerchief, a copy of *Pilgrim's Progress* and a school edition of *One Hundred Great Narrative Poems*, a carton of matches, a felt hat, a necktie with some matter dried into it" (124). Here is the paraphernalia of loneliness. Joseph's tantrums and Vanaker's eccentricities issue from their human need to compel others to acknowledge their existence. Like Joseph, Vanaker, too, dangles, but in grotesque fashion. The casual reference to Bunyan suggests that both Joseph and Vanaker are pilgrims on their way to the craters of the spirit.

Bellow uses this structural strategy throughout *Dangling Man*. Random characters and apparently unrelated incidents that bob up in the diary form a meaningful pattern when linked up with other incidents. The Christian Scientist episode, recorded on March 5, is cleverly designed to be both a casual happening and an important contrast to Joseph's dangling. Like Comrade Burns, whom Joseph accuses of being an addict, the Christian Scientist is a dedicated woman who does not dangle because her life has a passionate, powerful focus: she has found "an ideal construction" (93). But this commitment to a cause has ravaged her face and her being so that "she had lost all sense of her whereabouts" (108). She serves as a powerful contrast to Joseph just as Vanaker is an important parallel.

Bellow's compositional tactics are those of juxtaposition. He exploits the devices of parallelism and of contrast to offset and to highlight the predicament of his protagonist. Joseph dangles, but his dangling has to be seen in the context and against the background of the activity of other figures in the diary. Joseph is diametrically opposite in character and temperament to Amos, his brother, a prosperous, self-made man, who has married into a rich family and who, with his wife, Dolly, believes in the gospel of money and success. The contrast between the two brothers (a device Bellow will exploit in his later novels) is vividly established, the sensitive, hesitant Joseph as against the crude, successful Amos.

Bellow also places Joseph in the center of a group of friends to establish other contrasts and tensions and to extend the novel's meaning. The Servatius party reveals Joseph's disillusionment with his friends and with their attitudes to life. Later diary entries explore his relationships with each of his friends and present the solutions they have surrendered to. Joseph drifts away from most of his friends, who take different paths and pursue different ends. Jeff Forman, in love with excitement, is killed in an air crash in the Pacific. Robbie Stillman becomes an officer-engineer, while George Hayza expects a naval commission. One of Joseph's best friends is Abt Morris, who was inordinately ambitious at school and decided he would become an outstanding political philosopher. Abt's great plan, his construction, has failed, for he is no Locke; instead of dangling, however, he goes to Washington and establishes himself firmly in the bureaucracy.

While Joseph dangles, his friends gradually change. Myron Adler, who tries to help Joseph get a job, is a pragmatist who becomes successful and prosperous. Alf Steidler has his own solution: he pretends he has a bad heart, tells the psychiatrist he is a deadbeat, and gets turned down by the army. With his dreams, his pathetic memories and delusions, his corny jokes, Alf bounces merrily away from the hard reality of existence. He turns into a music-hall figure: "My line is getting by," he tells Joseph (87). The only solution that attracts Joseph is that of his artist-friend, John Pearl, who goes to New York and works for an advertising agency, a job that allows him freedom to paint. John Pearl's is the way of the imagination, a solution that Joseph can respond to but cannot adopt for himself.

It is the war that gives direction to the lives of many of Joseph's friends, and it is the pressure of the war that forms another pattern in *Dangling Man*. The Farsons discover that it solves their domestic conflict. Joseph's friends commit themselves to the war without a qualm. Amos is unconcerned, but worried about his personal well-being and economic safety. He advises Joseph to make use of the war for personal advancement by becoming an officer-candidate, but Joseph rejects the idea: he would rather be "a victim than a beneficiary" (56). It is the culminating impact of the war that has set Joseph adangling, both physically and spiritually. He considers the war a tragedy and looks upon himself as a "moral casualty of the war" (13). But he supports it in his own way: "I support the war, though perhaps it is gratuitous to say so. . . . But as between their imperialism and ours, if a full choice were possible, I would take ours" (56). Perhaps the key to Joseph's attitude is his reply to Steidler that he is "willing to be a member of the Army, but not a *part* of it" (89).

The neat conclusion to *Dangling Man*, one which has generated some critical controversy,[12] is a resolution that is both structurally and thematically right. In formal terms, it provides a decisive end to the drifting story of Joseph: he drops into the army, where the dangling will presumably stop. It is also a thematic solution, albeit a temporary one, to Joseph's agonizing desire to know himself and to participate in the doings of the world he inhabits. In order to interpret the meaning of the ending, one has to appreciate the basic assumptions Joseph starts from, understand his attitude toward the war, and examine closely the nature and the direction of Joseph's quest for the human.

Joseph is the first of Bellow's protagonists to initiate a search for the human. He goes forth to meet the Socratic demand: "But I must know what I myself am" (80). This cry for self-knowledge suggests that Joseph, dangler though he be, is yet another, a more modern, more subdued version of the typical American hero who continually seeks to define himself. The quest for the human subsumes the quest for the self, and both quests demand twentieth-century answers. Joseph tells *Tu As Raison Aussi* that he would like to discover his "real and not superficial business as a man" (110). It is not a simple problem which can be dismissed by the assertion that since one is a human being nothing human is therefore alien. Nor is it a question of achieving mere identity, or of realizing the self in the depths of one's self, and letting the world go by. For, like Thoreau before him, Joseph discovers that the world and the individual self are inextricably intertwined; the world is within him, so that he cannot tear himself from it without damaging his inner self: "I was involved with them; because, whether I liked it or not, they were my generation, my society, my world. We were figures in the same plot, eternally fixed together. I was aware that their existence, just as it was, made mine possible" (18). The world can and does pollute the self but, as Joseph tells *Tu As Raison Aussi*, it is impossible to pretend to be alienated from this complex, chaotic world because it is woven into the very texture of the self: "The world comes after you. It presents you with a gun or a mechanic's tool, it singles you out for this part or that, brings you ringing news of disasters and victories, shunts you back and forth, abridges your rights, cuts off your future, is clumsy or crafty, oppressive, treacherous, murderous, black, whorish, venal, inadvertently naïve or funny. Whatever you do, you cannot dismiss it" (91).

Joseph is hopelessly bewildered, torn between reason and faith, between affirmation and despair. He confronts the typical American dilemma: how to harmonize the imperatives of the singular self with the overwhelming need for community. He knows that his self craves pure freedom; he also knows that "goodness is achieved not in a vacuum, but in the company of other men, attended by love" (61). Endowed by his creator with an anthropologist's sensibility, Joseph is constantly aware of the animal in man. On a streetcar he sees a woman with a "pointed, wolfish face" (70). He has at one moment a ghastly vision of Chicago reverting to its primitive condition: "It was not hard to imagine that there was no city here at all, and not even a lake but, instead, a swamp and that despairing bawl crossing it; wasting trees instead of dwellings, and runners of vine instead of telephone wires" (64). What infuriates and maddens Joseph really is his inability to penetrate the mysteries and the paradoxes of human nature. On January 4 he broods about but cannot understand the reason for man's cold indifference toward his fellowmen: "I do not like to think what we are governed by. I do not like to think about it. It is not easy work, and it is not safe. Its kindest revelation is that our senses and our imaginations are somehow incompetent" (56). Joseph cannot reconcile Hobbes and Jacob Boehme, the horror of "nasty, brutish and short" with the occasional feeling of transcendence he experiences: "But for all that, Joseph suffers from a feeling of strangeness, of not quite belonging to the world, of lying under a cloud and looking up at it" (21). His hunt for the human is complex and difficult: it compels him to take into account the related problems of limits, freedom, responsibility, reality, and death.

Joseph sets forth on his journey to the human having lost faith in the world he has lived in, a world made up of politics, his family, his wife, his mistress, and his friends. Nor is he sustained by the superior world of books he had earlier lived in. Joseph, the diary provides the evidence, has read Diderot and the philosophes of the Enlightenment, he quotes from Goethe, he has read Joyce, Dostoevski, Thoreau, Villon, Baudelaire, and Spinoza. In his dangling state he finds he cannot turn to the wisdom derived from books, those "guarantors of an extended life" (8), to help him in his search. He can only read the newspaper, full of the world's doings, "their businesses and politics, their taverns, movies, assaults, divorces, murders" (18), and the comics, which he has always enjoyed reading. *Dangling Man* pointedly suggests that the quest for the human cannot be achieved by way of the intellect alone, from knowledge and wisdom derived from books.

What buoys Joseph up and prevents him from toppling into despair are certain values he clings to. Joseph refuses to let go of the basic assumptions he, and his creator, start from. He begins with a Miranda-like wonder at the miracle of human existence, the brave new world he has been born into: "In a sense, everything is good because it exists. Or, good or not good, it exists, it is ineffable, and, for that reason, marvelous" (21). Even in moments of dark despair, Joseph never relinquishes this faith in human existence. During the second exchange with *Tu As Raison Aussi*, when he is at the end of his tether, Joseph maintains: "You can't prepare for anything but living. . . . I'm saying that there are no values outside life" (110). Linked with this calm affirmation is Joseph's refusal to look upon the times he lives in (he is a history major) as a "condemned" age, a special era of anxiety, despair, and doom. "In all principal ways," writes Joseph, "the human spirit must have been the same" (18).

But Joseph's confidence in the worthiness of the human quest is deeply shaken by his gradual realization of the alien quality of the landscape around him. No local colorist, Bellow goes beyond Dreiserian documentary. Chicago, with its ugliness and its occasional beauty, is presented through the impressionistic Joseph who interprets the human dimension of the city sights he sees: "The street had been blown dry (it had rained the day before), and it presented itself in one of its winter

aspects, creased and with sidelocks of snow, all but deserted" (16). On
his way to Kitty he hears strange sounds as he walks through an
Eliotesque street: "Low, far out, a horn uttered a dull cry, subsided;
again. The street lamp bent over the curb like a woman who cannot turn
homeward until she has found the ring or the coin she dropped in the ice
and gutter silt" (64).

His friend, John Pearl, appalled by the treeless wastes of South
Brooklyn, complains about its "unnatural, too-human deadness" (101).
Joseph can understand his friend's horror for he too is shocked by the
lack of the really human in the "too-human" (the term is out of
Nietzsche) environment around him. Unlike John Pearl, Joseph accepts
the city as a natural environment for twentieth-century man. But he
cannot accept the implications of what he sees from the third-floor living
room of the Almstadts, the "ranges of poor dwellings, warehouses,
billboards, culverts, electric signs blankly burning, parked cars and
moving cars, and the occasional bare plan of a tree" (17). This bleak
landscape, Joseph tells us, created by man for man, proclaims a terrible
message about man's inner life and his very nature. "Where was there a
particle of what, elsewhere, or in the past, had spoken in man's favor?"
(17) Joseph has no answer to this question, for he is reluctant to
denounce the human spirit as vile and ugly.

Joseph does not really solve or explore any of the problems that assail
him. Pondering the nature of the freedom he enjoys, he discovers that it
is not the pure and authentic freedom that every human being yearns for.
He thinks about human limits. That modern man, compelled by the mad
desire to assert himself in various directions, rejects the idea of a limit to
what he can be, disturbs Joseph. He is profoundly shocked by the
Werthers and Don Juans, the Napoleons and Raskolnikovs, and also by
present-day "debaters in midnight cafeterias who believed they could be
great in treachery" (60), who are maddened by the dreams of greatness
that drive them onward, terrified lest they fail to achieve their
immoderate desires. He tells the uncomprehending Kitty that "a man
must accept limits and cannot give in to the wild desire to be everything
and everyone and everything to everyone" (67).

The brief encounter with Mr. Fanzel raises another important question
that Joseph cannot answer. Terrified by the economic insecurity
generated by the war, Mr. Fanzel charges Joseph fifteen cents for
stitching a button to his coat, a service which he had formerly performed
gratis as an act of kindness. Bellow transforms this simple incident into a
fable (with a moral tacked on) about the limitations of capitalism and the
business ethic. "Look out for yourself, and the world will be best served"
(72); "if everybody takes care of number one, the general welfare is

assured" (73)—such is the business wisdom of Mr. Fanzel who has to stifle his impulses of charity in order to protect his own interests, but not those of Joseph, who is deprived of his meagre breakfast. Joseph recognizes the futility of laissez-faire, which may satisfy the economic but not the true self, and which does not automatically ensure the general welfare of mankind. He remembers Mr. Luzhin in *Crime and Punishment*, who vehemently refuses to accept the idea of tearing his coat in half and sharing it with another, for then both would shiver in the cold. Should one then be responsible for another? What is the extent of human responsibility? The Fanzel incident leads Joseph to complex questions about man's responsibility for his fellowman. In his later novels Bellow will elaborate on these themes and questions which Joseph casually alludes to in his diary.

It is Joseph's obsession with death that comes through quite powerfully in *Dangling Man:* "Without warning down. A stone, a girder, a bullet flashes against the head, the bone gives like glass from a cheap kiln; or a subtler enemy escapes the bonds of years; the blackness comes down; we lie, a great weight on our faces, straining toward the last breath which comes like the gritting of gravel under a heavy tread" (77). Joseph hails death as "*the* murderer" (81) and indulges in an uncharacteristic rhetorical outcry:

> Who does not know him, the one who takes your measure in the street or on the stairs, he whose presence you must ignore in the darkened room if you are to close your eyes and fall asleep, the agent who takes you in the last unforgiving act, into inexistence? Who does not expect him with the opening of the door; and who, after childhood, thinks of flight or resistance or of laying any but ironic, yes, even welcoming hand on his shoulders when he comes? The moment is for him to choose. [81]

Vividly he imagines his own death during battle: "How will it be? How? Falling a mile into the wrinkled sea? Or, as I have dreamed, cutting a wire? Or strafed in a river among chopped reeds and turning water, blood leaking through the cloth of the sleeves and shoulders?" (82). Death shocks Joseph. As his dreams about the concentration camp and the war and the recall of the moment of his mother's dying testify, he feels emotionally shattered as he experiences death vicariously. Intellectually, he cannot accept the idea that death is the "abolition of choice" (98), nor can he come to terms with its absolute suddenness or the implication that it marks the utter end of any quest for the human.

Bellow does not succeed in dramatizing Joseph's intellectual quest. No dramatic conflict animates Joseph's search, which is carried on in the form of brooding. In a review of André Gide's *The Counterfeiters*, Bellow states: "And as human isolation increases while education and abilities multiply, the most vital questions and answers become the internal ones. Sadly enough, the number of intelligent people whose most vital conversation is with themselves is growing."[13] *Dangling Man* establishes, once and for all, the fact that Bellow's novels issue from one single, unitary, and unifying consciousness. The limitations of such a perspective are evident, the lack of breadth, of diversity, and of drama. It will be revealing to see how Bellow attempts to overcome the inherent limitations of this perspective, turns it into an asset and amplifies it so as to achieve depth, extension, complexity, and drama.

In *Dangling Man* the narrative thread is too weak to bind all the incidents and events together. Nor does the novel have the intellectual thrust that can compel all the ideas and themes into a kind of order. The themes of freedom, death, responsibility, and limits issue out of Joseph's consciousness in desultory fashion. It is the reader who has to see the pattern that arises when these themes are related to Joseph's quest for the human. In the *Paris Review* interview, Bellow refers to the difficulty of writing an American novel of ideas: "To call therefore for dramatic resolution in terms of ideas in an American novel is to demand something for which there is scarcely any precedent."[14] In *Dangling Man* Bellow attempts with some success to dramatize three important moments of Joseph's brooding.

In order to reduce its abstract quality, the first moment is cleverly sandwiched between Joseph's irritation with Amos at the Christmas dinner and the grotesque comedy of the tussle with Etta. Joseph climbs to the attic and listens to a Haydn divertimento for the cello played by Piatigorsky, listens beyond the music to the solution the music suggests. The adagio speaks to him of the inevitability of human suffering and humiliation, and the need to accept them with grace, a virtue he does not possess. The music goes on to suggest one answer to the human dilemma: faith, surrender to God. Joseph plays the record again and this time rejects the religious solution as one not valid for himself. For it would involve the surrender of human reason, which Joseph, who has read Diderot and the philosophers of the Enlightenment, is not willing to sacrifice: "Out of my own strength it was necessary for me to return the verdict for reason, in its partial inadequacy, and against the advantages of its surrender" (46). The device of using music to project internal conflict was probably suggested by E. M. Forster's *Howard's End*, a novel that uses Beethoven's Fifth Symphony to dramatize different attitudes to life.

The other two moments are the long conversations Joseph holds with

Tu As Raison Aussi, the Spirit of Alternatives. Bellow borrowed the device of the dialogue from Diderot, who used it to project two incomplete versions of himself in *Rameau's Nephew*, a work from which Joseph quotes (84). Not so colorful or so sprightly a figure as Rameau's nephew, the Spirit is a disembodied voice who suggests rather than states. Unlike Joseph, the Spirit knows who he is and, in the course of a lively exchange, flavored with irony, asks many needling questions that prod Joseph toward a solution.

During their first encounter Joseph accuses the Spirit of denying the validity of reason and of relying on the unpredictable heart in the manner of Pascal. Joseph expounds at some length on the recurring historical need for a plan and a program for man to face the chaos of life. He has not really forgotten his earlier discovery that plans are foolish (27) and dangerous, and can "consume us like parasites, eat us, drink us, and leave us lifelessly prostrate. And yet we are always inviting the parasite, as if we were eager to be drained and eaten" (59). Restating his earlier solution to an interested listener, who is also a persistent questioner, Joseph realizes that any "exclusive focus, passionate and engulfing" (93), will surely ravage any human being (this abstract idea is concretized in the episode of the Christian Scientist with her ravaged face). Another problem that hits Joseph for the first time is that of the nature of reality: he becomes aware of the tremendous chasm that can exist between the ideal construction one desires and the actual reality one lives in.

Before his second meeting with the Spirit, Joseph stumbles on a spiritual discovery: the highest ideal construction is for him not a construction, but that which "unlocks the imprisoning self" (102). He now sees human life as a continual struggle toward achieving freedom, which he interprets as a "giving" of one's self, instead of a living unto oneself, but how and to whom and to what he knows not yet. Bellow's later work will attempt to substantiate and dramatize the way one can give one's self and achieve a measure of true freedom.

The second meeting with *Tu As Raison Aussi* leads Joseph to a temporary solution. He reiterates his belief that all men are on a quest. Earlier he had written: "We are all drawn toward the same craters of the spirit—to know what we are and what we are for, to know our purpose, to seek grace (102)." Joseph now paraphrases Spinoza's proposition in *Ethics*: "No virtue can be conceived as prior to this endeavor to preserve one's own being." This preservation of one's essential self is not a simple matter: "Chance must not govern it, incident must not govern it. It is our humanity that we are responsible for it, our dignity, our freedom" (111). Joseph has arrived at the first stage of his journey to the human. He is now aware of the complex nature of his quest. He knows that he himself has not attained true freedom which he links with full comprehension. He realizes that though he does not have, as yet, a "complete vision of life" that can illumine his spiritual darkness, he has to follow his destiny. Whereupon the Spirit, in a pointed parody of Hemingway's "a separate peace," asks gently whether he has "a separate destiny" (112). Joseph doesn't answer and, faint with fear, collapses into bed.

The response, which Joseph knows he has to make but doesn't to the Spirit's question, is that he cannot cut himself off from the fate that threatens the vast majority of mankind. Before Joseph can discover his own destiny, he has to face the brutal fact of a war that has turned everyone into dangling men. The Spirit tells him of the need for the survival of the self even before one can set out to know one's self: "When and if you survive you can start setting yourself straight" (110). Joseph has no illusions about the war. He knows that it is a misfortune, a mere incident in human history: "A very important one; perhaps the most important that has ever occurred. But, still, an incident. Is the real nature of the world changed by it? No. Will it rescue us spiritually? Still no. Will it set us free in the crudest sense, that is, merely to be allowed to breathe and eat? I hope so, but I can't be sure that it will. In no *essential* way is it crucial—if you accept my meaning of essential" (111–12). Joseph supports the war in his own way, preferring "our" imperialism to "theirs" (56). The war is also, as the Spirit puts it, "the vastest experience of your time" (109), and, despite Spinoza, Joseph cannot "claim the right to preserve myself in this flood of death that has carried off so many like me" (111).

Joseph decides to give himself up and volunteers into the army.[15] Bellow does not make Joseph arrive at this crucial decision on March 16, the day of the second talk with the Spirit. He allows a ten-day interval to elapse so as to make Joseph's surrender on March 26 a little more dramatic. Joseph walks the black rain-swept streets of Chicago after an ugly quarrel with Iva and after shouting furiously at the pathetic Vanaker (both irrational outbreaks of temper) and in an alley near his rooming house he witnesses a scene that stirs him deeply: "A steel ring on a rope whipped loudly against the flagpole. Then, for a moment, a car caught me in its lights. I stood aside for it and followed its red blur. It was gone. Something ran among the cans and papers. A rat, I thought and, sickened, I went even more quickly, skirting a pool at the foot of the street where a torn umbrella lay stogged in water and ashes. I took a deep breath of warm air" (121). Here is a moment of epiphany. What he sees proclaims his own condition and impels him to a decision. The flapping steel ring, the unseen rat, the torn umbrella in the water and the ashes tell Joseph that he is trapped, unprotected, dangling in the wind. The carlights provide instant illumination. The gulp of warm air Joseph himself interprets as a breath of relief at having arrived at a decision.

The proclamation at the end of his diary,

> I am no longer to be held accountable for myself; I am grateful for that. I am in other hands, relieved of self-determination, freedom canceled.
>
> Hurry for regular hours!
> And for the supervision of the spirit!
> Long live regimentation!

is Joseph's delayed response to *Tu As Raison Aussi*. Joseph's cries are not expressions of weak, hysterical surrender. They are ironic cries of genuine, but temporary relief. He surrenders to army discipline with a full understanding of what he is doing. "*C'est la guerre. C'est la vie*" (105): behind the playful conjunction of these two epigrams which Joseph (under the influence of the Spirit with a French name?) had earlier offered Myron Adler is a deep truth. The army offers Joseph a reprieve from a state of dangling and an involvement in the inevitable. Joseph's future is now open, and he sees it as a series of perhapses: "Perhaps the war could teach me, by violence, what I had been unable to learn during those months in the room. Perhaps I could sound creation through other means. Perhaps" (126). After the war the quest for the human will continue, provided, of course, Joseph survives.

Dangling Man is, in many ways, not only the story of Joseph's dangling but also a skeletal parable about the spiritual confusion of modern man as experienced by a sensitive intellectual in the 1940s. Lacking the sustenance of religion, disillusioned by the limited visions proffered by communism and by capitalism, living not in heavenly cities but in an ugly, crowded megapolis, forced to undervalue himself despite being assured by history that the self is his most precious possession, having lost the ancient certainties about action and behavior, and unequipped with any new assurances about himself and about human nature, haunted by death and painfully aware of millions of his fellow human beings hunting for the same goal, this modern man dangles precariously, clinging, however, to a slim thread of hope and faith in human existence and refusing to plunge into despair.

It would not be too difficult to seize on the limitations of *Dangling Man* and tear the novel apart. Its texture is too thin, and lacks sensuous, rendered detail. It is all surface with few plunges into depth and complexity. Its form is parsimonious, ascetic, and contains few riches of character and incident. It is the work of a writer who is quite self-conscious about his style: "Three o'clock, and nothing has happened to me; three o'clock, and the dark is already setting in; three o'clock, and the postman has bobbed by for the last time and left nothing in my box" (11). The reader becomes aware of Bellow the stylist behind Joseph the diarist in this deliberate use of balance and repetition: "The worlds we sought were never those we saw; the worlds we bargained for were never the worlds we got" (18). It is Bellow the stylist who describes Kitty Daumler's breasts as "the world's most beautiful illustration of number, tender division of the flesh beginning high above the lace line of her nightgown" (66).

Bellow's use of symbolism is all too obvious: the scene that drives Joseph to his crucial decision has a symbolic function; the death of Mrs. Kiefer just after Joseph decides to volunteer suggests the death of Joseph's older self; the black rain that falls bespeaks the human condition; and what Joseph sees on the kitchen sink at the Almstadts is a highly rhetorical indication of his own condition: "A half-cleaned chicken, its yellow claws rigid, its head bent as though to examine its entrails which raveled over the sopping draining board and splattered the enamel with blood" (17).

"I think it fair to judge a writer in part by the way he breaks through his first defects, the stiffness of his beginner's manner, his romanticism, his early thicknesses or thinnesses. In writing, as in personal history, what a man overcomes is a measure of his quality," Bellow comments on Dreiser.[16] Instead of dismissing *Dangling Man* as a failure, it would be more profitable to regard it as a seminal work, a signpost pointing to Bellow's strengths and limitations, and to the fictional path he will take. Bellow focuses on a single, introspective figure, concentrating on what happens to him within and without, and introduces other figures for variety and contrast. He is not primarily interested in narrative, though some episodes are vivid and dramatic. Conflict is centered within the intellectual who struggles with his problems and tries to resolve them within himself by himself.

As a novelist, aware both of his medium and of the direction of his talent and temperament, Bellow will surely try to overcome his limitations. As a craftsman, he will exploit different methods and techniques to dramatize his basic concern, the quest for the human. This quest can very easily be dull, static, and monotonous if it is merely an abstract push toward knowledge by and in a single mind. It will be interesting to watch Bellow develop as a novelist, to observe how cleverly he will disguise his limitations, and transform them into fictional assets.

NOTES

1. Saul Bellow, *Dangling Man* (New York: Signet, 1965), p. 7. Hereafter page numbers will be cited in the text.

2. Ernest Hemingway, *The Sun Also Rises* (New York: Charles Scribner's Sons, 1926), p. 34.

3. Keith Opdahl, *The Novels of Saul Bellow* (University Park: Pennsylvania State University Press, 1970), pp. 29–31; John J. Clayton, *Saul Bellow: In Defence of Man* (Bloomington: Indiana University Press, 1971), pp. 57–59, 61–69, 77–81.

4. Saul Bellow, "A Personal Record," *New Republic* 130 (February 22, 1954): 20.

5. Alfred Kazin, "My Friend Saul Bellow," *Atlantic* 215 (January 1965): 52.

6. Ibid.

7. Bellow used the term "diarist-hero" in "Two Faces of a Hostile World," *New York Times Book Review* 61 (August 26, 1956): 4.

8. Charles Eisinger, *Fiction of the Forties* (Chicago, 1963), p. 345.

9. Saul Bellow was one of *Partisan Review's* protégés during the early 1940s. Two of his early short stories were published in this journal, "Two Morning Monologues" in 1941 and "The Mexican General" in 1942. An excerpt from *Dangling Man*, "Notes of a Dangling Man," appeared in 1943. The May-June 1942 issue has the following note: "Saul Bellow, a young Chicago writer, is now in the Army. Colt Press is bringing out his first novel, *The Very Dark Trees*."

10. Edmund Wilson, *The New Yorker* 20 (April 1, 1944): 70.

11. *Partisan Review* published at that time many articles about the war and its international implications, about dissent, radicalism, and the failure of nerve in America. The journal was a popular form. André Gide and Stephen Spender both wrote journals, extracts from which appeared in *Partisan Review* in 1939 and 1940. Spender's journal opens thus: "I am going to keep a journal because I cannot accept the fact that I feel shattered that I cannot write at all." (*Partisan Review* 7, no. 2 [1940]: 90). A significant diary-journal first published in 1940 was Walter Morris's *American in Search of a Way* (New York: Macmillan Company, 1942).

12. See Opdahl, pp. 47–48 and p. 171, note 6; and Clayton, p. 117.

13. Saul Bellow, "Gide as Autobiographer," *New Leader*, June 4, 1951, p. 24.

14. Alfred Kazin, ed., *Writers at Work:* The Paris Review Interviews, Third Series (New York: Viking Press, 1967), p. 193.

15. Joseph's attitude toward the war is surely that of Bellow. Almost all of Bellow's protagonists are willing participants in the war. Augie March is carried away when America enters the war and goes about making a speech about the Dostoevskian ant heap that would result if the enemy won. He undergoes a painful operation for inguinal hernia before signing up with the merchant marine. Tommy Wilhelm gets himself drafted and becomes a G.I. in the Pacific. Henderson becomes a captain and wins the Purple Heart, while Moses Herzog is a communications officer in the navy.

16. Saul Bellow, "Dreiser and the Triumph of Art," *Commentary* 11 (May 1951): 502.

2 *The Victim*

The search for humanness gathers momentum and complexity in Bellow's second novel. *The Victim* (1947) presents Asa Leventhal's slow, reluctant struggle toward the human, a struggle staged in the secret arena of the self and on the hot, crowded streets of New York. Bellow tells the story of another journey to the craters of the spirit. But this time the story is thick with color and detail, packed with character and incident. The narrative pace is slow and moves to a deliberate, insistent, almost hypnotic rhythm. The structure is not linear as in *Dangling Man* but a nuclear holding together of themes, ideas, images, and events in a state of dynamic balance. And the language Bellow uses with its dark cadences and its powerful resonance amplifies one man's bewilderment into mankind's tragic cry for light.

The opening paragraph prepares the reader for a work with many overtones and levels of meaning:

> On some nights, New York is as hot as Bangkok. The whole continent seems to have moved from its place and slid nearer the equator, the bitter gray Atlantic to have become green and tropical, and the people, thronging the streets, barbaric fellahin among the stupendous monuments of their mystery, the lights of which, a dazing profusion, climb upward endlessly into the heat of the sky.[1]

Both sentences, one short, making a statement about New York heat, the other long, intensifying the sensation of heat and multitude, vibrate with meaning. The new York/Bangkok juxtaposition is not a mere simile but widens the geographical range of the novel. The fellahin reference and the phrase "monuments of their mystery," which takes in both pyramids and skyscrapers, supply a temporal dimension that stretches from the remote Egyptian past to the tumultuous New York present. It is as if we plunge into a world where both time and space are shifting and unstable. The words convey a sense of urgent, involuntary, meaningless, and painful movement: a continent slides, people throng the streets like animals in a jungle, lights climb upward endlessly (the two adverbs, each with the first syllable stressed, enact the slow, arduous effort involved). There is a confusion of color and the numerous lights, strangely, do not illumine the scene but seem to have an unending quest of their own. By placing Asa Leventhal's story in this symbolic setting, Bellow heightens its significance.

Reduced to its essentials, *The Victim* is the story of an education. Asa Leventhal, an editor of a small trade magazine in New York, is a good man, unambitious, happily married, with a comfortable job; he has emerged from poverty, and has attained a measure of stability. Into his placid, unremarkable life suddenly appears Kirby Allbee, who claims that Asa was responsible for the loss of his job. He repeatedly accuses Asa of having ruined his life out of malice and revenge. The ordeal Asa undergoes in his several encounters with Allbee forces him to look into the hidden recesses of his self, consider the values he has lived by, and examine the nature of his relation to the world he lives in. During the same period, a summer of upheaval and discontent, Asa is compelled to break out of his insulated world and assume responsibility for his brother's family. Mickey, his nephew, is ill with a rare bronchial infection and it is Asa who decides to send him to a hospital, despite the reluctance of his sister-in-law, Elena, who would rather nurse him at home. These two narrative strands determine and delimit the area in which Leventhal's initiation will be enacted as he is propelled inexorably toward a new comprehension of what being human entails.

It is extremely important that the reader align his perspective with the narrative slant of the novel in order to reduce distortions of interpretation. The sufferings of Asa Leventhal are channeled to us not by an objective narrator but by the sufferer himself, though he is not quite a Jamesian central intelligence. Bellow abstains from his right of entry into the other characters: he limits himself to Asa's consciousness and thereby deliberately restricts our direct experience of all the other characters, including the mysterious Allbee. He also eschews first-person narration. By placing him both within and behind Asa's consciousness, Bellow requires the reader to be a witness, a participant in Asa's thoughts and fears, and an understanding and discriminating judge. For though Asa has the experience, he is not aware of its entire meaning.

It is not strictly true, however, to say that *The Victim* is told from the point of view of Leventhal. Two chapters, the second one and the last, are related by a narrator who is at first omniscient but who shifts imperceptibly into the Leventhal perspective. The first paragraph of the second chapter describes the appearance of Asa Leventhal objectively: his figure is burly, his features large, his thick hair and eyes are black. We are told about the intelligence he does not use, and about his impassiveness, a characteristic he shares with almost every Bellow hero. The rest of the chapter lays bare Leventhal's past, sketched and summarized for us by an apparently objective impersonal narrator. We learn about Asa's humble origins, his selfish father and his mother, who had died in an insane asylum, his efforts to get a decent job, and the simple details of his marriage. These facts are related casually and briefly, with no emphasis on any particular event. Leventhal gets a place with Burke-Beard after a difficult period of job hunting. He marries Mary despite knowing of her brief affair with a married man. The chapter ends with a highly significant paragraph:

> He said occasionally to Mary, revealing his deepest feelings, "I was lucky. I got away with it." He meant that his bad start, his mistakes, the things that might have wrecked him, had somehow combined to establish him. He had almost fallen in with that part of humanity of which he was frequently mindful (he never forgot the hotel on lower Broadway), the part that did not get away with it—the lost, the outcast, the overcome, the effaced, the ruined. [26]

What is implied is that the hurried look at the past, the telescoping of events, has been presented by a narrator who has deliberately limited himself to the Leventhal view of the past. It is as if Leventhal himself were coolly and neutrally looking at his past and telling us about it objectively. Bellow is thus able to introduce a Leventhal who has drifted through a past that he can summarize compactly and casually, because it offers no real meaning to him. Structurally, the second chapter is important, because the rest of the novel will reveal how Leventhal, like Joseph, has misread his own past and will be compelled to see it in another light and revalue it. The chapter ends neatly with a dip into Leventhal's state of mind before coming events break up the complacency he has settled into and force him to realize that he has not gotten away with it at all.

The narrative ordering of the novel also needs to be perceived. *The Victim* consists of twenty-four chapters that present the travail of Asa Leventhal. The last chapter, one in which the omniscient narrator once again intrudes, and which, like the second chapter, is detached from the time-sequence of the main narrative, is a kind of coda, a revelation of what happens some years later. The first chapter, a retrospective look at the events of a single afternoon when Asa visits his sister-in-law on Staten Island, is a deft piece of strategy. It establishes the world in which Asa Leventhal moves, and plunges us without delay into one set of events in which he is involved. Deliberately pitched in a low key, it prepares us for the turbulent drama into which Asa will soon be hurled. By placing this chapter before the second, which sets forth the past, Bellow avoids the neat pattern of sandwiching the present between past and future. Chapters 3 through 23, projected through Leventhal's consciousness, present the anguish and the turmoil Asa has to undergo before he can obtain a new awareness of what it means to be human.

The two sets of events in which Leventhal is involved, the Allbee and the Mickey stories, are not fused together into a single narrative strand. Each story is presented in alternate chapters. Thematically, however, they coalesce and dissolve into each other. The story of Mickey's death and its effect on Asa Leventhal, told in a few brief scenes, projects a dimension of the dominant theme of responsibility that informs the novel, and also broadens Leventhal's rather limited personal world. The story of Mickey's death lacks dramatic impetus. Mickey is taken to hospital, where he dies. This bare event is used to explore and present Leventhal's sense of guilt and dread, the reasons for his basic suspicion of other people, and the gradual dawning of the sense of responsibility and love in him. Bellow uses the events around the death of Mickey to dramatize Asa's reaction toward Elena, toward Philip, his older nephew, and toward his brother, Max. Asa's involvement with all three leads him to a better understanding of himself and of his fears. What begins in chapter 1 as mere family duty ends with a warm embrace in chapter 20.

Asa's initial attitude toward Elena is one of noninvolvement. He has always kept himself aloof from his brother's family, and he goes to Elena as to a stranger. He misreads every move Elena makes, and consistently misinterprets her behavior. He cannot understand her fear of hospitals; her slovenliness irritates him; he convinces himself that she holds him responsible for Mickey's death. Leventhal cannot open himself to the Italian exuberance of Elena, which for him betokens madness: "He observed that her eyes were anxious, altogether too bright and too liquid; there was a superfluous energy in her movements, a suggestion of distraction or even of madness not very securely held in check" (15). All through the Mickey crisis his dread of his sister-in-law is intense; he sees a bitter, accusatory look on her face on the day of the funeral and explains it away as a product of her madness. It is Max who later reveals how wrong Leventhal was in his suspicions about Elena and her mother: "You mean I was mistaken about Elena." "I sure do. And about the old lady" (242). Asa comes to realize that his wild misinterpretations of the behavior of Elena's mother—he sees her as a Sicilian Catholic, full of hatred because her daughter has married a Jew—are unjustified. "It's as clear as day to me that she thinks the baby's death was God's punishment because Elena married you" (211), he tells Max, who sees his mother-in-law as just a harmless, old, cranky widow. Leventhal begins to understand that his confused view of Elena and her behavior is the result of some flaw, an inner darkness, within himself. He sees the parallel between Elena and his own mother, who, according to his father, had died in an insane asylum. Asa has never investigated the truth about his mother's madness, but has always dreaded "the manifestation of anything resembling it in himself" (54). The reason for his jaundiced view of Elena, Asa realizes, is buried deep within his self and needs to be dug out: "If he were wrong about Elena, thought Leventhal, if he had overshot the mark and misinterpreted that last look of hers in the chapel, the mistake was a terrible and damaging one; the confusion in himself out of which it had risen was even more terrible" (211). Like Joseph, Asa becomes disturbingly aware of treasons hidden at the center of his decent, humane self.

Through his involvement with Philip, Asa slowly tries to reach out to yet another human being. His early gestures toward his nephew—the gift of a quarter, their brief exchanges about haircuts and food—are awkward and stilted. Asa reads a reproach in Philip's eyes accusing him of past neglect. After the Manhattan excursion, however, uncle and nephew are drawn toward each other and Asa makes the most human gesture he is capable of at the time: he passes his hand over Philip's short hair to show his concern and affection for him.

Asa's attitude toward Max also undergoes a change. When Mickey falls ill, Asa resents the fact that Max's rightful burden has fallen on his shoulders. But, at the funeral, when he sees Max in tears, all rebukes drop away. The brothers gradually come together, and in one scene, instead of shaking Max's proferred hand, Asa clasps and embraces him at the moment of parting, feeling "faint with the expansion of his heart" (213).

Out of the Mickey crisis a different Leventhal emerges, one who is capable of tears, love, and some sense of responsibility. He is now aware of the inexplicable darkness that lodges deep within him and affects his judgment. His condition is parallel to that of Joseph after he discovered that there was a corruptness within him that he could not account for. The Mickey story, despite its thinness of dimension, is important in that it equips the reader with some insights necessary for an understanding of Leventhal's struggles as he plunges into the Allbee ordeal.

Bellow allows the two narratives to meet at two tangential moments: Allbee makes a scene at the restaurant where Philip and Asa go to eat, and Max visits Asa at his apartment when Allbee is present. A deeper level of thematic unity is achieved by having these two ordeals fuse together in Asa Leventhal's consciousness, where they are subsumed by the term "showdown":

The word itself was an evasion, and he, not the doctor, had

introduced it. But it was a comprehensive word; it embraced more than Mickey's crisis, or Elena's, or his own trouble with Allbee. These were included; what had been going on with Allbee, for example, could not be allowed to continue indefinitely. But what he meant by this preoccupying "showdown" was a crisis which would bring an end of his resistance to something he had no right to resist. Illness, madness, and death were forcing him to confront his fault. He had used every means, and principally indifference and neglect, to avoid acknowledging it and he still did not know what it was. [141–42]

It is the Allbee turmoil that compels Asa to excavate into his innermost self to uncover some bitter truths. It is a difficult task: "His large eyes stared as though he were trying to force open an inward blindness with the sharp edge of something actual" (183). It drives him to a deeper perception of the mystery of human responsibility and of the human condition. The Allbee story is punctuated by a series of collisions between Leventhal and Allbee and is climaxed by Allbee's attempt at suicide in Asa's apartment. Every successive encounter shocks Asa out of the comfortable cocoon world he has built around himself. The novel charts the grudging, reluctant progress of Leventhal from a state of confusion to a kind of perception.

Allbee injects himself like a virus into Asa Leventhal's life at a time when Asa feels weak and extremely vulnerable. Mary, who has supplied him with confidence, is away at Charleston. His nerves are unsteady, and he feels threatened by a vague menace around him. Bellow introduces the reader to Asa's hallucinated, heat-drenched consciousness before presenting the first encounter with Allbee.

The first meeting is not dramatic, but it sets the tone for the subsequent encounters. The impact of Allbee registers itself on two distinct, though overlapping levels. Leventhal cannot understand why the mere sight of Allbee disturbs him so profoundly. He experiences an oppressive feeling when he realizes that Allbee is watching him. The derisive grin on Allbee's face and the harsh eyes call to mind an actor. Leventhal is surprised that he can recall Allbee's name so readily, despite his poor memory for names and despite the fact that they had met only a few times. As they sit talking on the crowded park bench, Leventhal suddenly feels that "he had been singled out to be the object of some freakish, insane process" (36). On the more conscious level, however, Leventhal feels mere contempt when Allbee holds him responsible for his dismissal from *Dill's*. Allbee had been on the staff of the weekly and had recommended Leventhal, who was then unemployed, to Rudiger, the editor. Leventhal had insulted and infuriated Rudiger, who had fired Allbee. Allbee now accuses Leventhal of having deliberately planned his dismissal from *Dill's*.

The first encounter betweenf Asa and Allbee, like the opening paragraph, has several overtones of meaning. Bellow introduces the image of theater and acting here, a key image that will be used to explore the meaning of humanness. The curious smile and the deeply ringed eyes of Allbee the actor, his strange accusations and his strange name, intimate a complex fictional existence. The fact that he reminds Leventhal of the seedy drunks on Third Avenue indicates strongly that Allbee is one of the lost, the outcast, the ruined, the ones that had not gotten away with it as Leventhal thinks he himself has. Allbee is an apparition out of Leventhal's past that Leventhal thought had been buried and forgotten. The shifting planes that constitute this encounter are evident during this exchange between the two:

> "I haven't thought about you in years, frankly, and I don't know why you think I care whether you exist or not. What, are we related?"
> "By blood? No, no . . . heavens!" Allbee laughed. [34]

Allbee's cynical laughter is a provocative challenge to Asa Leventhal, who will be compelled to acknowledge the terrible reality of this ghost and the inexorable truth that they are, indeed, kin to each other.

The preposterous accusation of Allbee forces Leventhal to recall and investigate the two incidents mentioned by Allbee—the party at Williston's where Allbee had insulted Asa's friend, Harkavy, with some anti-Semitic innuendoes, and the interview at *Dill's*. Leventhal is distinctly disturbed when he remembers his own Allbee-like behavior when he was down and out and hunting for a job. During those months he had been "despondent and became quarrelsome once again, difficult, touchy, exaggerating, illogical, overly familiar" (44–45). The interview with Rudiger was like a moment of insanity when Leventhal felt possessed by a force he could not control. Leventhal accepts his mistake, but can find no fault with himself: he had not acted out of malice and revenge. During the second encounter, Allbee magnifies his accusation against Leventhal, monstrously charging him with total responsibility not only for his own ruin, but also for the death of his wife, Flora:

> "You try to put all the blame on me, but you know it's true that you're to blame. You and you only. For everything. You ruined me. Ruined! Because that's what I am, ruined! You're the one that's

responsible. You did it to me deliberately, out of hate. Out of pure hate!" [74]

Shocked, and troubled by guilt, Asa sets out to discover the truth for himself. His friends, Harkavy and Williston, help him admit to the possibility that he cannot be completely free from blame for Allbee's dismissal. Williston makes Asa realize that it was the stormy interview, not Allbee's drinking, that led to Allbee's loss of the job. Leventhal is amazed to discover certain facts he did not know before and had not taken into account: that Allbee had a brilliant career before him, that he was considered intelligent, well read, charming, not a drunk, but a wonderful husband. That a person with such promise is now such a wreck of a man disturbs Asa profoundly. He gradually comes to acknowledge that he is somehow responsible for Allbee's decline: "He saw that it was necessary for him to accept some of the blame for Allbee's comedown. He had contributed to it, though he had yet to decide to what extent he was to blame" (109).

The several encounters with Allbee force Leventhal to reconsider the moral mathematics which he has lived by and blindly accepted. Bellow gradually accelerates the pace and the significance of these meetings. The first four are casual and glancing. After the initiatory encounter in the park, Allbee materializes like a ghost in Leventhal's apartment, in a restaurant, and on the corner of Eighteenth Street. Allbee complains about more than his own condition; he is full of complaint about the cruel facts of the human situation which Asa has refused to confront. Allbee voices the bitterness that twentieth-century man experiences in today's urban jungle with its savage struggles for survival. The individual is no longer in control of his destiny and of his self: "The day of succeeding by your own efforts is past. Now it's all blind movement, vast movement, and the individual is shuttled back and forth. He only thinks he's the works. But that isn't the way it is. Groups, organizations succeed or fail, but not individuals any longer" (68). Even more terrifying, according to Allbee, is the injustice of the human lot, the cruel and sudden fact of death and the terrible unevenness and unfairness of divine justice, the general wrong under which mankind labors.

The fifth encounter is crucial. Allbee moves into Leventhal's apartment and into his very being. Bellow introduces more clues that suggest that Allbee is more than Kirby Allbee. The marks beneath Allbee's eyes remind Leventhal of the bruises under the skin of an apple. Leventhal experiences a strange, close consciousness of Allbee. He breathes in the odor and feels the weight of Allbee's body. It is an experience parallel to the one Asa had experienced at the zoo: when gazing at the animals he had been powerfully aware of the odor of Allbee, an odor that was both oppressive and intoxicating. The experience is like the slow approach of death, for the apartment reminds him of the airless room in which Mickey had lain. Allbee presents a strange sight to Leventhal after he emerges from the shower. Leventhal looks at the yellow hair on Allbee's head, and then observes Allbee's feet with a strange feeling of aversion: "The insteps were red, coarse, and swollen, his toes long and misshapen, with heavy nails" (148). They are the feet of an animal.

When Leventhal returns to his apartment after Mickey's funeral, he feels momentary fear and indignation on seeing Allbee, but he cannot get himself to drive Allbee away. Allbee virtually takes possession of Asa's apartment, which is soon full of dirt and disorder. The apartment, like Joseph's room, becomes the physical analogue for Asa's soul, which is now in a state of turmoil and confusion. Leventhal is furious when he discovers that Allbee has invaded his private life and read Mary's intimate letters. But he still cannot compel himself to throw Allbee out of his apartment. He experiences a strange mixture of emotions when he is with Allbee. He feels drawn to him and yet repelled by him; he feels oppressed in Allbee's presence and yet welcomes it too. Almost against his will, Leventhal finds himself helping Allbee: he lends him money, and puts Allbee to bed when he is drunk and has passed out.

Leventhal's tolerance breaks down when he discovers that Allbee has brought a prostitute into the apartment and has slept with her in his bed. He forcibly ejects Allbee and tries to put his apartment in order. His ordeal is not yet over. Allbee returns when Leventhal is asleep and tries to commit suicide by turning on the gas oven. Leventhal awakes and experiences an intense moment of terror. It is as if the "showdown" he has been awaiting has come: "His terror, like a cold fluid, like brine, seemed to have been released by the breaking open of something within him" (245). He confronts his fault at last. He confronts Allbee, who in murdering himself would have killed Asa. Allbee runs away and disappears. Leventhal's ordeal is over. He feels strangely calm: "In spite of the struggle, the revolting sweetness of the gas like the acrid sweetness of sewage, the numbness in his neck, and, now, the sight of blood, he did not seem greatly disturbed. He looked impassive, under the cloud of his hair (246–47).

The two ordeals affect Leventhal profoundly. He looks unperturbed at the end of the Allbee upheaval, but he has changed. Allbee believed that one could be born again and become a new man. "We're mulish; that is why we have to take such a beating," Allbee had told Leventhal.

"When we can't stand another lick without dying of it, then we change" (200). Asa does not realize the extent of the change within him, nor does Bellow summarize and reveal Leventhal's altered awareness of what it means to be human. It is the reader who has to decipher what the two ordeals have inscribed on Leventhal's being.

Unlike Joseph, Asa Leventhal is not an intellectual. Bellow does not endow him with a speculative intelligence that can grapple with the metaphysical and social problems that confront man. It is Allbee who poses some of these problems. It is Schlossberg who offers Leventhal some valuable insights about the human. Bellow introduces speculative discussions, dreams, and epiphanic sights in order to elevate the story of Leventhal's ordeals into a fable about the predicament urban man finds himself in today.

Asa is a person who does not think clearly but does feel strongly. All through the novel there are repeated and recurring references to the agitation in Asa's heart: it pounds, runs hot, beats agonizingly, quickens, beats swiftly, jolts. When he is told of Mickey's death, Asa feels "a clutch of horror at his heart" (156). When he talks to Max, "the blood crowded to Leventhal's heart guiltily" (207). Asa cannot "clarify his thoughts or bring them into focus" (201). Then what good was thinking, he asks, in despair about ever finding an answer. Asa's heart is the source of his unaccountable fears and sensations of doubt, dread, and guilt. At the end of his ordeal, it is Asa's heart that tells him that the showdown is over and that he has somehow made it. He feels faint with the expansion of his heart after leaving Max. And, after he has driven Allbee and the woman out of his apartment, and as he caresses the picture of his wife, Asa experiences the "remote, jubilant speeding of his heart" (243).

It is because Asa's heart is so sensitive and vulnerable that he, unlike his friends, becomes keenly aware of the problems of responsibility. The theme of responsibility, merely touched upon in *Dangling Man*, is dramatized in *The Victim* and supplies it with an enclosing unity. The question that echoes all through this dark novel is: how far is one responsible for one's fellow human beings? Allbee poses the problem in the context of a world that is a terrifying crowded place, choked with people who insist the world is made for each one of them:

> Who wants all these people to be here, especially forever? Where're you going to put them all? Who has any use for them all? Look at all the lousy *me*'s the world was made for and I share it with. Love thy neighbor as thyself? Who the devil is my neighbor? I want to find out. Yes, sir, who and what? Even if I wanted to hate him as

myself, who is he? Like myself? God help me if I'm like what I see around. [172]

Using the exasperated accents of twentieth-century urban man, Allbee asks the same question that the biblical lawyer had posed to Jesus (Luke 10:29). Asa Leventhal washes his hands of the problem and irritably asks, "Why me?" (76) when Allbee confronts him with his accusation. The epigraph from *The Thousand and One Nights* suggests that ignorance about the consequences of one's actions does not absolve one of responsibility. Like the Arabian trader who unknowingly flung the date stones that killed the Ifrit's son, Asa could maintain that his part in Allbee's ruin was accidental and unintentional. Asa, brooding about the problem and his plight, widens both into the predicament all mankind finds itself in:

> In a general way, anyone could see that there was great unfairness in one man's having all the comforts of life while another had nothing. But between man and man, how was this to be dealt with? Any derelict panhandler or bum might buttonhole you on the street and say, "The world wasn't made for you any more than it was for me, was it?" The error in this was to forget that neither man had made the arrangements, and so it was perfectly right to say, "Why pick on me? I didn't set this up any more than you did." Admittedly there was a wrong, a general wrong. Allbee, on the other hand, came along and said "*You!*" and that was what was so meaningless. For you might feel that something was owing to the panhandler, but, to be directly blamed was entirely different. [77]

Bellow does not present any answer to this problem of injustice. Leventhal senses that there is a general wrong in which all mankind is involved. But he also notes that man is not responsible for these arrangements and they are beyond his control. But, as between one human being and another, between an I and a Thou, the need for responsibility does exist. In crowded, competitive New York Leventhal finds it difficult to acknowledge any responsibility for others. The Mickey ordeal instils in him a feeling of love and a natural sense of responsibility for his brother's family. The Allbee ordeal makes him painfully aware, at least, of all the Allbees of this world, the lost, the outcast, the ruined, who are also part of humankind. Schlossberg tells Asa that because one is human and therefore involved in mankind, payments have to be met. Asa himself hesitantly proffers the suggestion that to be human is to be accountable in spite of many weaknesses.

Other themes that Bellow ingrains into the texture of his novel are the

ubiquity of suffering and the reality of evil in human existence. In
Dangling Man Joseph referred in passing to the "general malignancy"
(DM, 98) that infects this world, and was aware that "trouble, like
physical pain, actively makes us aware that we are living" (DM, 55). The
experiences of Asa Leventhal force him out of the unreal, comfortable
world into which he has withdrawn himself, and hurl him into the dark,
savage, real world opened up by Allbee. Mary, his wife, had acquired
the "firmness of her own confident strength?" (54) only after the anguish
of deliberately breaking away from her married lover. Looking out of his
window early one morning, Leventhal witnesses a violent Dostoevskian
scene. A husband furiously chases his wife in the shadows to beat her.
Another woman forcibly restrains him, while two soldiers, who had
apparently been with the two women, stand watching. Here is an
epiphany for Asa. He witnesses a primitive scene charged with passion,
fury, tears, and laughter, a scene that makes him realize his absolute
ignorance and lack of experience of the cruel world outside. He feels
that "he really did not know what went on about him, what strange
things, savage things. They hung near him all the time in trembling
drops, invisible, usually, or seen from a distance" (89). It is only after he
has been forced to experience upheaval and turbulence that Asa feels
that he, "like everybody else, was carried on currents, this way and that"
(86). At one moment he feels he is in a kind of hell: "It came to his head
that he was like a man in a mine who could smell smoke and feel heat
but never see the flames" (226). Toward the end of his ordeal Asa
discovers that his life has lacked depth and a certain dimension of
meaning because he has kept himself away from real suffering: "Both of
them, Allbee and the woman, moved or swam toward him out of a depth
of life in which he himself would be lost, choked, ended. There lay
horror, evil, all that he had kept himself from" (241).

Linked up with the insistence on suffering as a way to the human is
the necessity to accept the reality of the human situation, above all, the
reality of evil in this world. Allbee breaks up the moral calculus by
which Asa has lived, a neat and simple construct whereby man is
responsible for his own fate, suffering is always deserved punishment,
and God is "the department of weights and measures." The inexplicable
death of Mickey, the anarchy he sees all around him in teeming New
York, and the nightmarish experiences he goes through, all confirm the
truth that Allbee drives into Leventhal's consciousness: "We do get it in
the neck for nothing and suffer for nothing, and there's no denying that
evil is as real as sunshine" (132).

The Victim records Bellow's questions about human existence, its
mystery, its unanswerable agonies, its paradoxes of evil and suffering,

without any surrender to a feeling of despair or *nada*. The title itself is Bellow's metaphor for modern man. It is not merely Allbee who feels he is Asa's victim, or Asa who is persecuted by Allbee, or Mickey who is yet another innocent victim. It is man himself who feels he is the eternal victim of the human condition.

In order to transform the story of Asa Leventhal into a fable about the human condition, Bellow uses devices that intensify, heighten and unify the elements that compose the novel. *The Victim* operates on two planes simultaneously, the realistic and the symbolic, that shift and dissolve into each other. Bellow creates an atmosphere that generates, contains, and reconciles the inner and outer turbulence of his protagonist. All events are enacted in a radiant, surreal darkness (as if the world of an el Greco painting had sprung to life) that establishes a powerful sense of unity.

Malcolm Bradbury refers to, but does not elaborate on, Bellow's attempt to step up the meaning of *The Victim*: "The stylization is all in the direction of mythic and psychological intensification: the tale becomes a tale for all men."[2] Bellow achieves this heightening, this intensification, by charging his style with a tense, electric life. His use of deliberate rhythm, of recurrent image and color, creates a magic spell.

The expressive use of language allows Bellow to conjure up a nightmarish city for his protagonist. New York, poured through the lens of Asa Leventhal's consciousness, is Eliot's unreal city, is Baudelaire's "*cité fourmillante*." The summer heat is heavy, suffocating, tenebrous, an intolerable burden. Even in the early morning the streets look deadened with heat and light. The sun shines relentlessly, deforming all objects with its merciless glare. Leventhal feels dazed by the sights and sounds of New York:

> The street was glaring when they emerged. The lights in the marquee were wan. There was a hot, overrich smell of roasting peanuts and caramel corn. A metallic clapping sound came to them from a shooting gallery. And for a time Leventhal felt empty and unstable. The sun was too strong, the swirling traffic too loud, too swift. [96]

The city is alive with mechanical life: cars and cabs whip endlessly by; buses wait at the curb with threshing motors and groan as they crawl by; there is a hard encircling rumble of trucks and subterranean trains.

It is as if New York, like Joseph's Chicago, had reverted to a dense, tropical jungle. Bellow introduces primitive touches to secure this anthropological dimension. An electric fan looks like a hovering fly; an umbrella flung open at the top of the subway stairs reminds Leventhal of a bat opening its wings. From his bed Leventhal can see the long "defile" of the street. From his window he sees the naked display of barbaric emotions. He realizes that "cannibalistic things" can happen in New York. These touches combine with the thronged zoo and the animal references to convey an impression of teeming, competitive life struggling for survival. The restaurants and subways are choked with people; the parks are dense with thirsty crowds that seek escape from the cruel heat; the ferry is jammed with passengers. Everywhere throng the barbaric fellahin.

New York is also a huge cauldron into which different immigrant races have been thrown together but have not melted into a unified society. There are the German Punts, the Puerto Rican Nuñez and his Indian wife, the Filipino busboy in the cafeteria. Bellow makes us aware of ethnic resentments that keep people apart. Anglo-Saxon Allbee resents the Jewish takeover of New York, where the "children of Caliban" have generated an Egyptian darkness. Leventhal, as a Jew, resents the Catholic funeral that his nephew is given, and cannot abide the priest, who is a Pole. Asa remembers his father's bitterness at the hordes of Italian and Irish children. New York is in a state of flux and social confusion where everyone lacks identity. It is crowded with souls "each concentrating on its destination" (63). They have no common goal in this huge metropolis for they have lost their roots. Leventhal reacts immediately to Allbee's taunts about "you people," but lacks an awareness of his Jewish heritage and its strengths. The bonds of community have been rent and no new ties have been established in the new world.

The introduction of the crowd scenes and of the immigrant theme is not a naturalistic tactic but an expanding device to widen the significance of Leventhal's plight. He senses the terrible pressure of people upon his consciousness: "There was an overwhelming human closeness and thickness, and Leventhal was penetrated by a sense not merely of the crowd in this park but of innumerable millions, crossing, touching, pressing. What was that story he had once read about Hell cracking open on account of the rage of the god of the sea, and all the souls, crammed together, looking out?" (163–64) What Leventhal experiences here is the overriding need for human community, together with the overwhelming desire to get away from the suffocating, agitated mass of mankind that could stifle one's sense of the self. In such a context the paradox of responsibility is impossible to resolve. Bellow introduces the crowd motif to deepen our awareness of Asa Leventhal as one lost in an area of darkness stippled with light. After he drives Allbee out of his apartment Leventhal sees another epiphanic scene:

> Instantly he heard the tumultuous swoop of the Third Avenue train rising above the continuous, tidal noise of the street. People were walking among the stripes of light on the pavement, light that came from windows opening on carpeted floors and the shapes of furniture; they passed through the radiance of the glass cage that bulged before the theater and into shadows, tributaries that led into deeper shadows and led, still further on, into mighty holes filled with light and stifled roaring. [239]

This recognizable New York street night scene with its sights and sounds, the people, the pavement, and the carpeted floors in the shops, expands into a metaphor for the mysterious darkness mankind moves in because of Bellow's use of images of the theater, the ocean (tidal, tributaries), and animal allusions (holes, cages, stifled roaring), and the light/dark references.

The light/dark motif is used repeatedly to create a diaphanous pattern of meaning. The key is provided by the image of the lights in the opening paragraph stretching yearningly into the black sky. Later references reinforce this sense of the impenetrability of blackness. Leventhal remembers that the tungsten in the bulbs of the jail-like flophouses appeared "like little burning worms that seemed to eat rather than give light" (68). After his second encounter with Allbee, Leventhal looks at the street and sees almost nothing but is "only aware of the featureless darkness and the equally featureless shine of bulbs the length of the block" (76). Emerging from the subway after seeing Max off, Asa's eyes move "from the glare of the cars flowing up in the street to the towering lights that stood far ahead, not quite steady in the immense blackness" (213). Chapter 18 opens dramatically with a four-word, four-syllable sentence with three syllables stressed, "the dark came on" (185), a sentence that forces the reader to be aware of the two-dimensional darkness in which Asa Leventhal is benighted. These images of the ineffectualness of light invading darkness dramatize the inexhaustible mystery in which mankind lives and moves, and suggests that man, like light, climbs upward into an impenetrable, unknowable darkness.

Another significant feature in *The Victim* that gradually but compellingly assumes the importance of a rhetorical figure is Bellow's use of color. The colors heighten and transform the realistic scene: "There was still a redness in the sky, like the flame at the back of a vast baker's oven; the day hung on, gaping fierily over the black of the Jersey shore" (28). After Asa drives Allbee out of his apartment and opens the front-room window, he sees an avenue of color: "The long lines of lamps hung down their yellow grains in the gray and blue of the street" (246). The colors are almost apocalyptic, ancient blacks, primitive reds, menacing tropical greens, and, above all, yellow. It is as if all characters and events, seen through a glass darkly and mysteriously, were bathed in a strange, transfiguring light. Black is a dominant color, but the one used in symbolic and charged fashion is the unearthly yellow. The insistent recurrence of yellow, which the reader gradually realizes is an item of significant repetition, creates a hypnotic effect. It is as if the lights were playing tricks with our vision, so that a comb, a sink, water, wash hanging out to dry, all seem to take on an atabrine tinge. Harkavy has yellow hair, while Benjamin, the insurance agent, has a drop of yellow in his black eyes. Significantly, Allbee is associated a number of times with this color: his hair, after it has been washed, is yellow; his face is yellowish and, at the end, there is a "yellowish hot tinge" (237) in his bloodshot eyes. Bellow casually lets slip the significance yellow holds, early in the novel. Leventhal reflects on the ferry to Staten Island:

> The notion brushed Leventhal's mind that the light over them and over the water was akin to the yellow revealed in the slit of the eye of a wild animal, say a lion, something inhuman that didn't care about anything human and yet was implanted in every human being too, one speck of it, and formed a part of him that responded to the heat and the glare, exhausting as these were, or even to freezing, salty things, harsh things, all things difficult to stand. [52–53]

Yellow is not a mere coloring agent that provides a decor, but a pointer to an element in human nature, to the animal in man, to something wild, fierce, and inhuman within him that demands to be recognized.

The animal references in *The Victim* form another binding device that Bellow uses. Leventhal had the tendency to reduce people to a nonhuman level. "Goddammed fish!" he exclaims when he is annoyed with Mr. Beard (13). "What kind of fish is this?" he asks himself during the first encounter with Allbee (31). Later, Allbee's face makes him think of gills and "for an instant he was no more human to him than a fish or crab or any fleshly thing in the water" (73). Leventhal gets his first inkling about the interrelatedness of animal and man during the visit to the zoo. It is here, when gazing at the animals with Philip, that he becomes so strongly aware of the presence of the nonpresent Allbee, that he can both see him and smell the odor of his hair and skin. Allbee, with his strange feet, strongly projects the animal in man, invariably associated with yellow. Bellow makes Leventhal himself expound this idea to Allbee: "They say you go to the zoo to see yourself in the animals" (131). During a later encounter Allbee tells Leventhal not to forget that man is an animal, and stresses the paradox of humanness: "Nature is too violent for human ideals, sometimes, and ideals ought to leave it plenty of room. However, we're not monkeys, either, and it's ideals we ought to live for, not nature" (180). Still later, Allbee fingers Leventhal's black hair and says, "It's like an animal's hair. You must have a terrific constitution" (198). Allbee's statement about Leventhal's constitution prepares the reader for Leventhal's recovery after the ordeal. All the animal references combine to suggest that man, in general, and Leventhal, in particular, have to come to terms with the animal in man, with the inhuman that lodges at the center of the human.

The crisscrossing, swirling waves of feverish movement, color and animal reference enabled Bellow to create an aura that could include both the realistic milieu of New York and the metaphysical plane on which the trauma of Asa Leventhal is enacted. It is because of this atmosphere that Allbee can function both as a character in real life and as "an anarchistic principle" in the words of Bradbury.[3] As a real character, rooted in plausible psychology, Allbee would have anchored the story to the naturalistic level. By submerging him in this magical atmosphere, by never allowing any event to be seen from Allbee's point of view, and by making us see Allbee only through Leventhal's blurred eyes, Bellow can invest Allbee with many meanings. Allbee is a mysterious figure that appears and disappears in strange fashion. We never learn the truth about the strange bell that rings before Leventhal meets Allbee, the note that Leventhal finds in his mailbox informing him that Allbee would be in the park at nine, the key to the apartment that Allbee appropriates. Allbee is the accusing finger that points out to Leventhal the sins of his past. He is also Leventhal's preceptor who teaches him about responsibility, about injustice, about evil, and about the human condition. Allbee is also a real human being. Bellow has taken great pains to distinguish between Allbee's truly human moments and those when he acts as Leventhal's tormentor and teacher. When the conversation centers on his wife and the tragic smashup she was involved in, there is a sincere ring to Allbee's words: "When he had announced his wife's death, he had sounded wrathful, but Leventhal had felt himself come nearer to him or to something clear, familiar or truthful in him" (72). At their final meeting when Allbee refers to Flora, Leventhal sees a sensational, terrible look of pain that rises to Allbee's eyes. Allbee betrays his false self by the perpetual smile he puts on, which Leventhal sees as an insane element in his makeup, and by the harsh glint in his eyes.

Allbee is in many ways Leventhal's Dostoevskian double. One can sense the heavy pressure of Dostoevski on the creative sensibility of Bellow during the composition of *Dangling Man* and *The Victim*. Bellow has himself acknowledged the many parallels between *The Eternal*

Husband and his novel: he apparently became aware of his debt to the Dostoevski novel only after it was pointed out to him.[4] His unconscious debt to Dostoevski can also be seen in the use of yellow both in *Dangling Man* and in *The Victim* (yellow is a revealing item in *Notes from Underground*) and in the nonexistent mice in his apartment that fill Asa with dread. The mice have been imported from Svidrigaylov's dream in *Crime and Punishment*.

Allbee is indeed Leventhal's double. The very term is used when Leventhal thinks of the strange eyes of Allbee: "He had a particularly vivid recollection of the explicit recognition in Allbee's eyes which he could not doubt was the double of something in his own" (151). "I often used to wish there were two of us," says Allbee when introduced by Leventhal to his brother, Max (206). At one time, Leventhal is overwhelmed by a suffocating sense of closeness to Allbee:

> But suddenly he had a strange, close consciousness of Allbee, of his face and body, a feeling of intimate nearness such as he had experienced in the zoo when he had imagined himself at Allbee's back, seeing with microscopic fineness the lines in his skin, and the smallest of his hairs, and breathing in his odor. The same sensations were repeated: he could nearly feel the weight of his body and the contact of his clothes. Even more, the actuality of his face, loose in the cheeks, firm in the forehead and jaws, struck him, the distinctness of it; and the look of recognition Allbee bent on him duplicated the look in his own. [144]

When Allbee touches Leventhal's hair (the reader has to remember Leventhal's brushing his hand over Philip's hair as a gesture of affection) Leventhal feels paralyzed under his touch. He tries to exorcize the spell of confusion and despair that Allbee casts on him. The pressure of Allbee on Leventhal's consciousness slowly increases: "At this moment Leventhal felt Allbee's presence, all that concerned him, like a great tiring weight, and looked at him with dead fatigue, his fingers motionless on his thighs" (201).

Bellow does create Allbee as Leventhal's double, but, as we have seen, he assigns Allbee a number of other roles. Bellow borrows the idea of the double, handles it deftly, but does not charge the relation between Allbee and Leventhal with psychological tension in the manner of Dostoevski. Asa's fears of rejection, his feelings of guilt and insecurity are not explored in depth nor are they all projected onto Allbee. Bellow underplays these fears and does not uncover their psychic roots, just as he deliberately avoids enlarging on the sexual anxieties of Leventhal. The identification of the prostitute with Mrs. Nuñez sends a momentary thrill of horror through Leventhal. Bellow however avoids a situation in which Allbee sleeps with a woman that Leventhal desires. Leventhal later silently apologizes to Mrs. Nuñez for his suspicion.

Allbee is more than Leventhal's double. Leventhal has to discover not only that Allbee exists (32), but that he exists within him. Like Blake's Albion, from whom his name derives, Allbee is the embodiment of all men. He is the power of blackness (his wife is significantly named Flora, goddess of spring) lodged within Leventhal, a force he has refused to acknowledge earlier. Allbee is the animal within man, the inhuman within the human that man has to acknowledge. After the prostitute is driven away, Allbee excuses himself to Leventhal using a phrase with theological overtones: "I know I have a fallen nature" (236). The phrase "a fallen nature" has to be linked with the reference to the marks beneath Allbee's eyes as bruises under the skin of an apple. Leventhal has a faint idea of what Allbee stands for when, just before he drives him out of the apartment, he shouts to Allbee: "You're not even human, if you ask me" (238).

That Allbee is not quite human is insisted on by the repeated references to him as an actor. "An actor if ever I saw one" (31) is the thought that strikes Leventhal when he first sees Allbee. Leventhal feels an element of performance in Allbee's behavior all through the several encounters with him and complains to Williston that Allbee is always play-acting with him. During their meeting at the restaurant, Allbee puts on a spectacular performance: "He was playing to the crowd and, standing there, his head hung awkwardly forward; he could hardly keep from laughing at the sensation he was making. And yet there was the usual false note, the note of impersonation in what he did" (97–98). "For Christ's sake, stop this damned clowning," Leventhal shouts during their fifth encounter (148). It is rather strange that when there is the possibility that Shifcart may offer him a job as an actor, Allbee says he does not want to act (202). For the truth is that he is a bad actor.

Allbee, as actor, has to be placed in the context of the imagery of acting and the theater, which, as Malcolm Bradbury rightly points out, is strong in the novel.[5] Bellow uses it as another binding device. Minor detail about theater and acting is thickly strewn about: there is a theater opposite Leventhal's apartment house, the Boris Karloff film he sees with Philip in set in a theater, a linotypist sells Asa a theater ticket he does not want.

It is in chapter 10 that the references to acting are linked up with the idea of genuine humanness. During the cafeteria discussion among Harkavy's friends, Leventhal listens to the wise words of old Schlossberg, whom he feels drawn to. Schlossberg maintains that it is bad to be less than human and equally bad to be more than human. Both states are a rejection of real life. Caesar, who wanted to defy death and be a god, is an example of the more-than-human. Livia, who murders her husband in the play, and then, as actress, communicates no feeling at all, is less-than-human. Good acting, affirms Schlossberg in a dramatic speech pungently flavored with Yiddish, is what is exactly human. One senses a meaningful pun on the word "acting," the implication that to be human is to act properly. In *Dangling Man* Alf Steidler escaped from being human by turning into a music-hall figure. Allbee, who at the end of the novel is associated with a once-famous actress, is not a good actor because he has made the mistake of not choosing dignity, which, according to Schlossberg, every human being and every actor must have. Allbee has finally come to terms with the human condition and is enjoying life. But Leventhal can detect the signs of Allbee's decline behind the mask that Allbee wears: "Allbee did not look good. His color was an unhealthy one. Leventhal had the feeling that it was the decay of something that had gone into his appearance of well-being, something intimate. There was very little play in the deepened wrinkles around his eyes. They had a fabric quality, crumpled and blank" (254).

Leventhal himself had been a bad actor. At their first meeting, Allbee rightly accused him of "bad acting" (33). According to Williston, Leventhal had "acted up" during the interview at *Dill's* (84). It is significant that Leventhal instead of Schlossberg, who is a born actor, picks up the business card of Shifcart, the talent scout. For he has the potential to become a good actor. The ordeals he has been through and the lessons he has learnt signify a beginning in that direction. Allbee says that Asa hasn't changed when they meet in the final scene. But Asa has changed. Significantly, though this detail is thrown in casually, Mary is pregnant. Leventhal has lost his sense of dread, his face has softened, his health is better, he looks younger.

Asa has learnt that one way to the human is to accept what life offers, as Max and Mrs. Harkavy do. Another is to accept the precious gift of creaturely existence and be what one is, in the manner of Harkavy. Schlossberg tells Leventhal to appreciate the greatness and the beauty of just being human, but he does not supply answers to the questions, what is human? what is good acting? *The Victim* does provide hints and guesses that can lead to an answer.

Leventhal, at one point, realizes that codes and rules are required, human nature being what it is: "Would we have to be told 'Love!' if we loved as we breathed? No, obviously. Which was not to say that we didn't love but had to be assisted whenever the motor started missing" (77–78). He agrees with Schlossberg that man, unlike the animal, can transcend his limits because of the mind and the imagination. But Schlossberg underlines the bitter truth that man is limited because he is subject to death and has only one lifetime in which to realize his true self. These revelations about human possibilities and human limitations reinforce another basic notion that hits Leventhal twice, but which he does not quite grasp. After a dream, in which he forces his way through a crowd at a railway station and is pushed out into an alley, Leventhal awakes in a state of great lucidity, a feeling of both relief and happiness: "It was supremely plain to him that everything, everything without exception, took place as if within a single soul or person" (151). On the day after the birthday party, Leventhal has another moment of extraordinary illumination: "He had the strange feeling that there was not a single part of him on which the whole world did not press with full weight, on his body, on his soul, pushing upward in his breast and downward in his bowels. He concentrated, moving his lips like someone about to speak, and blew a tormented breath through his nose" (226). What Leventhal dimly realizes, but cannot articulate, is the truth that he is not alone in his suffering. The world and the crowd that pass and press through him communicate the message that he and his afflictions form part of the human condition, in which all men can be seen as victims.

In the final chapter, the coda, Leventhal is no longer bitter about the human situation which he now sees as a "shuffle, all, all accidental and haphazard" (248). At the start of life, man assumes, that a promise has been made to him:

> In thinking of this promise, Leventhal compared it to a ticket, a theater ticket. And with his ticket, a man entitled to an average seat might feel too shabby for the dress circle or sit in it defiantly and arrogantly; another, entitled to the best in the house, might cry out in rage to the usher who led him to the third balcony. And how many more stood disconsolately in the rain and snow, in the long line of those who could only expect to be turned away? but no, this was incorrect. The reality was different. For why should tickets, mere tickets, be promised if promises were being made—tickets to desirable and undesirable places? There were more important things to be promised. Possibly there was a promise, since so many felt it. He himself was almost ready to affirm that there was. But it was misunderstood. [249]

Bellow probably took the image of the theater ticket from the famous scene in *The Brothers Karamazov* where Ivan offers to hand back God his ticket. Leventhal now realizes that most people are full of bitter complaint about life, not content with what life has offered them, desiring what they do not have. He has still no solution to this problem, only a vague hope, a feeling that mankind has been promised a better form of existence. Leventhal is content with this promise and has somehow accepted his own place in the theater of life. "What's your idea of who runs things?" asks Leventhal of Allbee. There is no reply to his question, the bell keeps on ringing, the lights go off, and in the darkness, "an usher showed them to their seats" (256).

Structurally the novel appears to be flawed. Chapter 10, which contains the cafeteria discussion, and chapter 21, which focuses on the discussion at the birthday party, seem to belong neither to the Mickey nor to the Allbee story. The final chapter appears to be tacked on as an afterthought. Thematically, however, all three chapters are essential. They constitute Bellow's attempt to inject ideas into his work, an extremely difficult fictional task that Bellow had then still to master. In *Dangling Man* the ideas stick out awkwardly. In *The Victim* Bellow incarnates some of the ideas in flesh and blood, especially during the scenes of confrontation between Leventhal and Allbee. Schlossberg, however, is a choric mouthpiece deliberately introduced to express the positive values about the human that Bellow could not dramatize.

The thematic resonance and the structural resilience of *The Victim* did however allow Bellow to hold together in a precarious, trembling balance a number of themes, images, characters, incidents, and even ideas. All these elements pour from and are related to the title, the novel's central metaphor. The second epigraph amplifies this image and prepares the reader for the vision that the whole novel will offer:

> Be that as it may, now it was that upon the rocking waters of the ocean the human face began to reveal itself; the sea appeared paved with innumerable faces, upturned to the heavens; faces, imploring, wrathful, despairing; faces that surged upward by thousands, by myriads, by generations.

One can immediately distinguish herein the human face of Mickey and then of Allbee, of Asa, and then the oceanic faceless crowds of New York. And finally, as in a comprehensive blur, the barbaric fellahin that all through the ages make up the tragic face of mankind.

The de Quincey essay "The Pains of Opium" from which this epigraph has been taken must have made a profound impact on Bellow's sensibility. Nightmares and the death of a child are recorded in this essay which also has the sentence "Thick darkness came on."[6] The essay tells of the torments experienced by de Quincey on renouncing opium: the horror dreams full of Oriental-animal images ("Under the connecting feeling of tropical heat and vertical sunlights I brought together all the creatures, birds, beasts, reptiles, all trees and plants, visages and appearances that are found in all tropical regions"),[7] the tyrannic dream of the human face, the thought of death enforced by the endless days of summer. The end of all this suffering leaves him "agitated, writhing, throbbing, palpitating, shattered."[8] But it is finally a state of catharsis And the second to the last paragraph of the de Quincey essay can perhaps be used as an extra coda to *The Victim*, for it captures the final condition of Asa Leventhal:

> Jeremy Taylor conjectures that *it may be as painful to be born as to die.* I think it probable: and, during the whole period of diminishing the opium *I had the torments of a man passing out of one mode of existence into another.* The issue was not death, but a sort of *physical regeneration* and I may add, that ever since, at intervals, I have had *a restoration of more than youthful spirits,* though under the pressure of difficulties, which, in a less happy state of mind, I should have called misfortunes.[9]

NOTES

1. Saul Bellow, *The Victim* (New York: Signet, 1965), p. 11. Hereafter page numbers will be cited in the text.

2. Malcolm Bradbury, "Saul Bellow's *The Victim*," *Critical Quarterly* 5 (Summer 1963): 127.

3. Ibid., p. 122.

4. Jay Nash and Ron Offen, "Saul Bellow," *Literary Times* (Chicago, December 1964), p. 10.

5. Malcolm Bradbury, p. 124.

6. Edward Sackville-West, ed., *Confessions of an English Opium Eater* (New York: Chanticleer Press, 1950), p. 337.

7. Ibid., p. 333.

8. Ibid., p. 339.

9. Ibid., p. 340. Italics added.

3 *The Adventures of Augie March*

The uneven, uncertain structure of *Augie March* reveals itself in its texture, the language fabric with which Bellow made it. The first two paragraphs of chapter 11 convey the feel of the prose, its pace, its rhythms, its recklessness.

The first paragraph comments on the darkness in which all mankind has to live:

> Now there's a dark Westminster of a time when a multitude of objects cannot be clear; they're too dense and there's an island rain, North Sea lightlessness, the vein of the Thames. That darkness in which resolutions have to be made—it isn't merely local; it's the same darkness that exists in the fiercest clearnesses of torrid Messina. And what about the coldness of the rain? That doesn't defeat foolishness in its residence of the human face, nor take away deception nor change defects, but this rain is an emblem of the shared condition of all. It maybe means that what is needed to mitigate the foolishness or dissolve the deception is always superabundantly about and insistently offered to us—a black offer in Charing Cross; a gray in Place Pereires where you see so many kinds and varieties of beings go to and fro in the liquid and fog; a brown in the straight unity of Wabash Avenue. With the dark, the solvent is in this way offered until the time when one thing is determined and the offers, mercies, and opportunities are finished.[1]

The second paragraph goes on to describe a student house near the University of Chicago and Augie tells us how he came to know almost everyone living there:

> The house where I was living on the South Side was a student house within range of the university chimes and chapel bell when the evenings were still, and it had a crowded medieval fullness, besides, of hosts inside the narrow walls, faces in every window, every inch occupied. I had some student book customers and even several

57

friends here. In fact I really knew everybody through the
circumstance that Owens, the old Welshman who operated the place,
had me answering telephone calls and distributing the mail in the
little varnished hole called the lobby. This I did in exchange for my
rent. And as I sorted the letters I unavoidably read return addresses
and postcards, and, signaling by bell to call people to the telephone, I
had to hear their conversations since there was no booth. Owens too
listened in, he and his spinster sister who was housekeeper, the door
of their stale parlor was always open—the smell of the kitchen
governed over all the other smells in the house—where I at my post in
the wicker rocker two hours every evening could see their after-supper
state, their square pillars of walnut, the madnesses of starched lace,
the insects, eye inspiration of cutglass, the screwy detail of fern both
fiddle-necked and expanded, the paintings of fruit, which were full of
hardness against liberty, plus the wheels of blue dishes around the
wainscotting. With such equipment making an arsenal of their
views—I musn't forget the big fixtures of buffalo glass hanging on
three chains—they demonstrated how they were there to stay and
endure. Their tenants were transient, hence the Owenses probably
needed something like this to establish home for themselves, and it
was made very heavy. [211–12]

What hits one instantly about these paragraphs is that they aim
themselves not so much at the eye as at the ear. It is their lively tempo,
their erratic rhythms, that insist on attention. The sentences whether
presenting a thought process as in the first paragraph, or description as
in the second, speed breathlessly along. There is no abating of pace. The
movement is continuous, brisk. There is no time for the reader to think,
even in the speculative first paragraph, or to pause in order to make
connections and establish definite meaning. No time here for the
self-conscious slow meditations of Joseph, or for the heavy, deliberate
broodings of Leventhal. No time at all to ponder the significance of a
detail, or a reflection, or even a word. For the words do not call attention
to themselves, their semantic pressure being light and momentary.

The first paragraph endeavors to hurry the reader along to an
awareness of a darkness that is everywhere together with a sense of the
accompanying rain that somehow acts as a solvent. The vague, abstract
words, the uncertain grammar and the loose sentence rhythms conspire
to produce a blur of meaning. The place names supply a range of
reference but lack associative force; the reader is expected to link
Westminster with the Abbey and necessarily with death, or to think of
Conrad's *Heart of Darkness* when he hears the Thames mentioned. The
torridness of Messina is no surprise. "Dark" is repeated in its various

forms but does not acquire amplified meaning. The rain can be accepted, by way of the American naturalists, as an emblem of the shared condition of all mankind, but it is not clear how the varieties of rain, black, gray, and brown, act as solvents for this condition. Also, the use of the indefinite "it" and the linguistic relations offered by terms such as "that," "but," "of" (the human face) are, to say the least, unclear. The total impression is that of listening to someone who is not quite sure of his feelings and ideas—he uses the term "maybe" and utters an occasional doubt in the form of a rhetorical question—but is in a hurry to state whatever he thinks about the human condition.

The uncertainty and blurring of the first paragraph contrast strongly with the narrative impetus and detailed clutter of the second, with which it has no real connection. The words in the second paragraph lack semantic thickness as in the first, but are concrete instead of abstract, piled one on top of the other so that the meaning is accumulative. The sentences are quick with nervous life and allow the reader immediate intimacy with the place the narrator lives in and the people he lives among: we get to know the sounds, sights, even the smells of the place. The crowded "medieval" fullness of scene is boldly realized: the after-supper state of the Owenses comes to graphic life not because of the narrator's photographic skill, but because of the strange associations he makes, starched lace with madness, ferns with fiddle necks. The whole paragraph is not an interwoven complex unit, but a length of sentences, knotted together one to the next on the associative, assimilative principle.

Three-fourths of *Augie March* consists of paragraphs and chapters that teem with description and thick detail. The words jostle and rattle against each other freight-train-wise and fill the air with clatter and rumble. Here is a subway descent into the ethnic mix at the University of Chicago:

> And the students were children of immigrants from all parts, coming up from Hell's Kitchen, Little Sicily, the Black Belt, the mass of Polonia, the Jewish streets of Humboldt Park, put through the coarse sifters of curriculum, and also bringing wisdom of their own. They filled the factory-length corridors and giant classrooms with every human character and germ, to undergo consolidation and become, the idea was, American. In the mixture there was beauty—a good proportion—and pimple-insolence, and parricide faces, gum-chew innocence, labor fodder and secretarial forces, Danish stability, Dago inspiration, catarrh-hampered mathematical genius; there were waxed-eared shovelers' children, sex-promising businessmen's

daughters—an immense sampling of a tremendous host, the
multitudes of holy writ, begotten by West-moving, factor-shoved
parents. Or me, the by-blow of a traveling man. [132]

The crude energy of this paragraph which seeks to dramatize both the
melting pot theory and the drive westwards comes in part from the
naturalistic catalogue of the different ethnic sections of Chicago, partly
from the surrealist image of the curriculum as a giant sifter, partly from
the submerged metaphor of a factory where people are processed, and
also from the double-barreled words (pimple-insolence, gum-chew
innocence) that mix the abstract with the concrete. The reader cannot
pause to enquire why the children of shovelers should be wax-eared for
the din and hurry of the language will not allow him to. The strange,
dangling, slangy, abrupt phrase at the end cunningly allows the narrator
to reenter his story as protagonist.

The final section of the novel, after Augie March's Mexican
adventures, is scattered with numerous paragraphs of the speculative
kind. The narrator is full of theories about life and its meaning and lets
loose his ideas amidst his narrative. After the hunting accident Augie
treats us to certain reflections:

> It takes some of us a long time to find out what the price is of being
> in nature, and what the facts are about your tenure. How long it takes
> depends on how swiftly the social sugars dissolve. But when at last
> they do dissolve there's a different taste in your mouth, bringing
> different news which registers with dark astonishment and fills your
> eyes. And this different news is that from vast existence in some way
> you rise up and at any moment you may go back. Any moment; the
> very next, maybe. [377]

The language that Augie uses here is vague and abstract (dark
astonishment, vast existence); the images implied in terms such as
"tenure," "social sugars," "news," do not produce a sense of assurance.
The whole passage lacks the power and appeal of the earlier paragraph.

To recognize the two kinds of linguistic units, the narrative-descrip-
tive paragraphs and the speculative ones, that compose the novel is to
see that structurally *Augie March* is a lumpy amalgam of the picaresque
and the *Bildungsroman*. Augie writes out his memoirs presenting a
chronological account of his adventures from childhood to manhood.
This recall of his past is not a form of nostalgic self indulgence. The act
of writing is for Augie an enactment of the process of self discovery. The
digging up of the past demands a frantic excavation into the self, for
therein is one's history buried. It involves hard work:

Hard, hard work, excavation and digging, mining, moling through tunnels, heaving, pushing, moving rock, working, working, working, working, working, panting, hauling, hoisting. And none of this work is seen from the outside. It's internally done. [542]

The first thirteen chapters, which make up half the novel, record the "influences" (46) on Augie's life, the varieties of people and places he is involved with, the picaresque adventures he is flung into. The reader's experience of Augie March the protagonist is not disturbed by the occasional intrusion of Augie March the commentator. In the second half, the reader gradually gets accustomed to the two Augie Marches, the protagonist/experiencer whose adventures become less compelling and more fantastic, and the narrator/brooder who takes command and indulges in long bouts of introspection and analysis. The two Augies overlap in the last chapter: "I have written out these memoirs of mine since, as a traveling man, traveling by myself, I have lots of time on my hands" (538).

Augie March has to be viewed and appreciated in its totality. To respond joyously to the teeming variety of character, incident, and situation in the first thirteen chapters, to the daring gusto of its prose and to the fertility of Bellow's comic invention, and then to dismiss as weak and abstract and of little consequence the account of Augie's education would be to misread the novel. The discerning reader needs to be aware of the structural strategies that Bellow the artist has deployed in his desperate effort to impose some kind of order on his seemingly uncontrolled, bewildering, sprawling panoramic novel.

Augie March, as narrator, is not a dispassionate, cold-eyed artist but a human being, profoundly involved in and a product of the story he tells. Augie's perspective on his past is not coldly orthogonal; his is not a mind's eye that reduces experiences to order by using distancing, foreshortening, and scale and by making all relations logical and intelligible. Instead, Augie's sensibility modifies the contours of the past because that is how it perceives them now; certain areas of experience are heightened, certain periods of time become stained with meaning. To use the distinctions of James J. Gibson in *The Perception of the Visual World*, *Augie March* projects for us the visual field of Augie, not his visual world.[2]

Augie's retrospection is set forth in twenty-six chapters. Certain contours of time and experience appear meaningful to the narrator. The first four chapters, which constitute a block by themselves, concentrate on Augie's childhood. The next three tell of Augie's involvement with the Einhorns. Chapter 8 deals with the Renling phase in Augie's life. The next four chapters find Augie involved in a number of adventures and jobs, running immigrants across the Canadian border, acting as assistant in a luxurious dog service, stealing books. He gets entangled with the Magnus family and with Mimi Villars; he also becomes involved in union activities with Grammich, a professional labor organizer. Chapters 14 to 20 relate Augie's adventures with Thea and the eagle, Caligula, in Mexico. The next four chapters, relatively short, deal chiefly with Augie's talks with his friends in Chicago. Chapter 25 focuses on Augie's experiences during the war and the novel ends with a chapter about Augie's travels in postwar Europe.

The significant contours of Augie's past can now clearly be seen. Augie highlights certain time-periods, while slurring over others. Despite his claim in the opening paragraph of the novel, his story is not a completely free-style composition, "first to knock, first admitted" (5). The marriage to Stella and the wartime experiences of Augie form a single chapter, whereas the Einhorn experiences take up three long chapters. The Mexican adventure with Thea is obviously important because Augie devotes seven chapters to it. Augie's awareness of his progress through time is erratic. Unlike Joseph, who is continuously aware of days drifting slowly by, Augie is so immersed in his experiences that he is uncertain about chronology: his growth into manhood and maturity is never fixed in terms of years. The reader is not provided with dates but dimly, not insistently, is made aware of historical time against which Augie's adventures are set. Robert Shulman maintains that Bellow organized his novel partly around a parallel between "the stages in Augie's life and that of the nation—the twenties, the Crash, the politics of the thirties, World War II, post-War prosperity and problems—such that Augie's history becomes a representative history."[3]

The erratic contouring of the past and the sense of historical time are both not powerful enough to contain the geographical and temporal sprawl of the novel. The Mexican adventures, for example, do not really communicate a sense of the 1930s, though Augie does see Trotsky at Acatla and there's the possibility of his acting as one of Trotsky's bodyguards. Postwar prosperity is barely mentioned in the last chapter. It is only if we regard Augie's adventures as a quest that the novel reluctantly assumes an uncertain coherence. Joseph wanted to know his real business as a man; Leventhal had to travel toward the craters of the spirit; Augie gradually, belatedly, realizes that he is a pilgrim on his way to the human. *Augie March* begins as a picaresque novel and slowly becomes an account of the drama, the discoveries and vicissitudes of one man's "pilgrimage" (440), an account sprawling and hospitable enough to include the travels and findings of a multitude of other travelers whom Augie meets on his life's journey.

Augie's restless search for a worthwhile, higher, and independent fate gradually becomes the dominant concern of the novel. In his search he is aided, abetted, hampered, pushed, taught, badgered, compelled, and harangued by a wide variety of characters themselves involved in the human struggle. Almost all the major characters in *Augie March* and almost all the major incidents, significant though they are in themselves, are even more important as "influences" on Augie. Their impact on Augie the picaro is strange: "All the influences were lined up waiting for me. I was born, and there they were to form me, which is why I tell you more of them than of myself" (46). They do not really "form" Augie. Machiavellians and theoreticians want to impose their views on him. Teacher figures offer him advice and illumination. Stimulated by all these people, guided later by his own observations, reflections, and intuitions, erratically, by fits and starts, Augie arrives at a number of truths, the most crucial one being that one should be a person, a human being, that one should have a fate and not a mere function. Like *Dangling Man* and *The Victim, Augie March* is yet another, if confused story of an education in humanness.

As in *Dangling Man,* despite the change in tone and in language, Bellow makes use of the technique of parallelism and contrast, on a magnified scale here, to dramatize the quest of his protagonist. The Machiavellians (the novel was originally titled *Life among the Machiavellians*) with their constructions form an absolute contrast to Augie and his search for a worthwhile fate. They loom large and menacing in the first eight chapters of the novel, offering Augie the lessons of power as the ultimate and only response to the human condition. The three dominant Machiavellians are Grandma Lausch, with her tough tactics for survival in this cruel world; William Einhorn, who preaches and practices lessons and theories of power; and Mrs. Renling, who wants to save him from the rat race and construct a different Augie in order "to consolidate what she affirmed she was" (159). The philosophy of naked, aggressive power and domination over other human beings is forcefully stated by that modern Machiavelli, Einhorn, who insists that

> one should choose or seize with force; one should make strength from disadvantage and make progress by having enemies, being wrathful or terrible; should hammer on the state of being a brother, not be oppressed by it; should have the strength of voice to make other voices fall silent—the same principle for persons as for peoples, parties, states. [192]

Einhorn is contemptuous of the antheap, the mass of mankind: " 'Look here, because they were born you think they have to turn out to be men?' " he asks Augie (307).

Bellow, like Augie, is fascinated and also horrified by the immense energy these Machiavellian grotesques generate. Augie realizes that Mrs. Renling's pale-fire concentration, her wrath-ruled mind, her damnation chats issue from the tremendous energy bottled within her. Grandma Lausch and William Einhorn, perhaps the most vivid characters in the novel, exude power and are linked with the cruel animal world. Like Joseph, Augie has an anthropologist's sensibility. Grandma Lausch is a "pouncy old hawk of a Bolshevik" (9). Einhorn's appetite is that of a hungry animal: "His appetite was sharp and he crowded his food. A stranger with a head on him, unaware that Einhorn was paralyzed, would have guessed he was not a well man from seeing him suck a pierced egg, for it was something humanly foxy, paw-handled, hungry above average need" (72). Augie is compelled to celebrate the animal spirits of Einhorn: "The spirit I found in him was the Chanticleer spirit, by which I refer to male piercingness, sharpness, knotted hard muscle and blood in the comb, jerky, flaunty, haughty and bright, with luxurious slither of feathers" (162). But he can also see the ravages that such an exercise of power imprints on Einhorn's harrowed face.

In contrast to the Machiavellians who would impose their own constructions and controls on people are those whose lives have been fixed for them and those obsessed by and lost in a theory or project of their own. They are object lessons warning Augie not to imprison himself in any construction. On the simplest level is Jimmy Klein, Augie's boyhood friend, who becomes a store detective and has surrendered himself to the will of others: " 'I go where they put me and do what they tell me' " (280). Two of Augie's friends, Hooker Frazer and Sylvester, surrender themselves to communist ideology. Frazer becomes one of exiled Trotsky's secretaries, while Sylvester believes in the communist dream: "That humiliated, bandy-legged, weak-haired, and injured-in-the-eyes Sylvester, however, the subterranean draftsman and comedy commissar of a Soviet-America-to-be, teaching himself the manner and even the winner's smile and confidence, why, he was going to blast off the old travertine and let the gold and marble shine for a fresh humanity (224)." He becomes one of Trotsky's bodyguards. Augie sees the ravages written on Sylvester's face: it is "severe, melancholy, duty-charged, and baffled." (390). Augie can now understand Mimi Villars' vivid image of Sylvester leaking misery all over, and respond to her metaphor of Sylvester's spirit as a bad kiln that has distorted his flesh (223). Before leaving Mexico for Chicago, Augie comes to realize the deadly pressure ideology and ideologists exert on a human being: "My next idea was how nothing was more dreadful than to be forced by another to feel his persuasion as to how horrible it is to exist, how deathly to hope, and taste the same despair. How of all the impositions this was the worst imposition. Not just to be as they make you but to feel as they dictate. If you didn't have the strongest alliance you surely would despair at last and your mouth would drink blood" (434).

Augie, who refuses to allow any theory to rule his life, runs into two theoreticians caught in the grip of their own obsessions. Robey, the eccentric millionaire, crazy about Great Books, is busy putting together a guide and a program for mankind. Basteshaw, brilliant, crazy, a genius, offers Augie a theory of human boredom and a vision of the new brotherhood of man which his experiments will achieve. Augie can respond to the fervent desires of both men (both are modern parody versions of visionaries such as Campanella and Thomas More), but can see the damage that their utopian dreams inflict on them. With his blood-streaked eyes, his sullen lips and his belly-heavy walk, his five marriages and his stinginess, Robey is a warped idealist. Augie finds him one day "standing on a kitchen chair, wrapped in his bathrobe, pumping Flit into a cupboard while hundreds of roaches rushed out practically clutching their heads and falling from the walls. What a moment that was! He wildly raised hell as he worked the spray gun, full of lust" (461). And the cold inhumanity of a Basteshaw, who wanted to rescue all mankind from endless suffering, both shocks and enlightens Augie: "I realized how much he was barren of, or trying to be barren of in order to become the man of his ideas" (532). Both theoreticians open Augie's eyes to the comic horror of being a mere function, the slave of an idea.

In his journey toward a worthwhile fate, Augie is educated by his encounters with a number of people. Together these encounters spell out the truth that society today does not encourage anyone to have a fate of one's own. Instead, society demands an expert. Augie tells Clem Tambow after his Mexican experiences: "In the world of today your individual has to be willing to illustrate a more and more narrow and restricted point of existence. And I am not a specialist" (453). Aware of the dangers of being a specialist, Augie takes a quick, ironic look at himself, but cannot determine who he is. He sees a figure that is ever restless, always circling around in an elliptical orbit, never stopping to be defined: "Lord, what a runner after good things, servant of love, embarker on schemes, recruit of sublime ideas, and good-time Charlie!" (449).

Augie pursues his fate in this exuberant, persistent, bouncy fashion. Along his crowded way he encounters three who, like him, are also in search of a fate of their own. The most assured of these is Arthur,

Einhorn's only son, who considers himself lucky in simply being a poet. He is to Augie what John Pearl in *Dangling Man* was to Joseph. The most interesting human being around Augie is Padilla, who befriends Augie and who refuses to accept crookdom as his fate: he seeks freedom in knowledge. Padilla is a type of what he himself admires, "the little individual who tries to have a charge counter to the central magnetic one and dance his own dance on the periphery" (200). The most ardent seeker of the three is Mimi Villars, always described as "push-faced," the term proclaiming her bullying vitality, the energy she devotes to love. Like Augie, she has "opposition" in her; unlike Augie, however, Mimi does not accept the human condition, but attacks it with outspoken vigor, denouncing its abominations, its swindles, its horrors. Like Allbee, she is convinced about the reality of evil, suffering, and injustice in this world. When Augie feebly suggests that one should feel grateful for the miracle of life, she directs him to the Fulton egg market to discover gratitude there! Augie is fascinated by the paradox that Mimi presents: the power that issues from her, manifest in her clinging will, her hard reason and her obstinate voice and, in contradictory contrast, her irrational faith in love and her tenderness. Augie helps her when she has an abortion (it is the married Hooker Frazer who gets her pregnant) and his innocent involvement with Mimi changes the course of his life at a time when he is drifting toward marriage with Lucy and an alliance with the prosperous Magnuses. Augie admires the brave front that Mimi puts up during her severe hemorrhaging: life cannot "be decided for you by any old thing that comes up," she maintains (286). Augie leaves the hospital intrigued by the sad, cryptic question Mimi asks him, as to "whether she had outwitted a fate or met it" by having an abortion (295).

Augie's quest appears in clearer relief if it is set against the career and progress of his brother, Simon. Simon marches slowly and determinedly to success. His steady rise to prosperity, like that of Amos, contrasts markedly with Augie's erratic circling movements which parallel Joseph's dangling. Simon's business adventures are a deliberate foil to Augie's more human ones: "My brother Simon wasn't much my senior, and he and others at our age already had got the idea there was a life to lead and had chosen their directions, while I was circling yet" (89).

Even as boys they are different, Augie enjoying the strategy of lying, Simon handicapped by a notion of honor picked up from *Tom Brown's Schooldays*. But Simon discards this notion and becomes practical soon, a doer, not a dreamer: witness his immediate recognition of the need to send George away to a home, his success in handling both jobs and people. Significantly, when both work in a clothing shop, Simon is upstairs in men's suits, while Augie works in the bargain basement under the sidewalk selling women's shoes. Their love affairs and marriages also offer a pattern of contrast. Simon chooses his woman: Augie drifts in and out of love. Soon after he is turned down by Cissy Flexner, who marries a moneyed grotesque, Five Properties, Simon rejects all nonsense about love and marriage and opts for marriage and money. From then on it is a steady climb to wealth and prosperity. Unlike Augie, who never finds out what he really wants to do, Simon is sure of what he wants and gets it: "Not only did Simon make what he had to do, but he went the limit. It astonished me how he took his objectives and did exactly what he had projected" (225). Driven by the great energy that all business people possess (a fact that impresses Augie), Simon becomes a millionaire. Our final glimpse of him is through the angry, hostile eyes of Charlotte, his wife: we see a man bald, with a fat belly and a face that proclaims a wasted life. It is Augie who realizes with love and tenderness that all Simon could really be accused of was "his mismanaged effort to live" (553). The novel does not insist on a pattern provided by their contrasting fates: to recognize the pattern, however, is to be aware of yet another attempt by Bellow to pull his novel together.

By using juxtaposition, parallelism, and contrast (techniques that had a measure of success in *Dangling Man* because of its limited range and time-span), Bellow sought to impose a semblance of order on the countless picaresque adventures of Augie. The faint skeletal unity that holds the first thirteen chapters of *Augie March* together is apparent not to a reader who immerses himself in the story but to one who rises above the incidents narrated and the characters described, rises indeed above the narrator himself, to see Augie and his quest for a worthwhile fate highlighted by other characters who also journey to the craters of the spirit. The range of Augie's experiences up to the time of the Mexican adventures with Thea is tremendously wide and various. Refusing to be a specialist, refusing to be imprisoned in any single job or to be trapped by a construction of any one else's devising, Augie is open to all varieties of people and places. As union organizer, book thief, saddle-shop salesman, dog valet, student-house helper, he is at home anywhere and everywhere in Chicago: "I touched all sides, and nobody knew where I belonged. I had no good idea of that myself" (119).

The Chicago adventures do not tell Augie where he belongs, but they condition and prepare him for the visions, insights, and intuitions that will descend on him toward the end of his pilgrimage. But before he can tread the way to grace, he has to learn how to avoid pitfalls, traps, and constructions. The attribute that Einhorn made Augie aware of, his opposition, his ability to hurl a secret "No!" at people's ideas while appearing to agree with them allows him to resist his persuaders: "I never had accepted determination and wouldn't become what other people wanted to make of me" (124). Again and again Augie's spirit of resistance manifests itself. Just when Mrs. Renling is about to entrap him, Augie bounces away, asking: "Why should I turn into one of these people who didn't know who they themselves were?" (159). He bounces from job to job, discovering that he has no particular vocation. After his experiences as union organizer come to a disastrous end, he abandons the job without a qualm: "No, I just didn't have the calling to be a union man or in politics, or any notion of my particle of will coming before the ranks of a mass that was about to march forward from misery. How would this will of mine have got there to lead the way? I couldn't just order myself to become one of these people who do go out before the rest, who stand and intercept the big social ray, or collect and concentrate it like burning glass, who glow and dazzle and make bursts of fire. It wasn't what I was meant to be" (324).

Augie does not have a calling, but a secret dream which all his friends are aware of. Padilla tells Augie that it is a dream too ambitious to be realized. Clem Tambow pokes good-natured fun at Augie's "campaign for a worthwhile fate" (449). Augie himself does not define his dream, but he senses its propulsive power within him all through his adventures. Augie dreams of "a good enough fate" (31); he has a restless desire "to be taken up into something greater than myself" (213). But he refuses to be goaded on by others; sensing the needs of his own being, he insists on setting his own pace, "I never tried to exceed my constitution. In any case, when someone like Clem urged me and praised me, I didn't listen closely. I had my own counseling system. It wasn't infallible, but it made mistakes such as I could bear" (214).

The involvement with Thea Fenchel and his adventures with Caligula in Mexico (chapters 14–20) drive Augie for the first time to a crucial investigation of his own character and destiny. The seven chapters form a transitional section in the novel: what all along had been largely a racy, exciting, Chicagoan picaresque, punctuated by moments of occasional insight, now transforms itself into an accelerated *Bildungsroman* that bundles together the wisdom that Augie acquires in the "consummation and final form" (465) of his life.

Augie, who has always refused commitment, who has never entangled himself with another human being, falls powerfully and absolutely in love. It is a strange state for this searcher for an independent fate to be in: "The great astonishment of this state was that the unit of humanity should maybe be not one but two" (338). "I was never before so taken up with another human being," he confesses. For the first time he surrenders his self to another: "I went where and as she said and did whatever she wanted because I was threaded to her as if through the skin" (330).

For a while Augie almost abandons his quest for an independent fate to help Thea realize her dreams of greatness. Appropriately named, Thea is Augie's goddess. He is forced to accept her views of everything, especially the idea that one should hunt for a better, nobler version of reality, refusing to accept the common, gray one offered to mankind. With her careless disregard for money (she keeps it in the refrigerator in company with rotting salad leaves and saucers of bacon grease), her love of shopping in dime stores, her fierce, possessive love, her snake-catching equipment, her passionate love of animals (she would never travel anywhere without an animal), her jealousy, defiance, crudity, generosity, her capacity for self-abandonment, Thea is a fascinating compound of strange contradictions. Her latest craze was to hunt and capture iguanas in the mountains of Mexico with a trained bald eagle. She wanted to make history, for very few people since the Middle Ages had hunted with manned eagles. She recruited Augie to help her achieve this nobler reality.

By plunging Augie into the exotic world of Thea and Mexico instead of allowing him to drift along in familiar Chicago, Bellow sought to dramatize and accelerate Augie's moral growth. Translated from the city to the country, involved now in a primitive world of animals and wild nature, Augie becomes aware of the blue Mexican sky holding back "an element too strong for life" (353). This menacing element, a sense of power and energy, also issues from Caligula. When Augie first sees the fierce eagle in its cage, he feels as if he is struck by darkness, a darkness like the one he had encountered in Chicago. Like Joseph and Leventhal, Augie discovers that animal and human natures are inextricably linked together. Influenced by Augie, Caligula slowly becomes humanized. The riotous, ferocious behavior of the international set in Acatla was such that, according to Augie, "wolves or wild swine or the giant iguanas themselves or stags wouldn't have been noticeable if they had slipped in from the mountains" (388).

Augie is not only given some insights into human nature in Mexico, he also experiences intense suffering for the first time in his life. The love affair with Thea gradually comes to a bitter end. Augie cannot share Thea's enthusiasms, her world of birds, snakes, horses, guns, and photography. Caligula abandons his animal ferocity and refuses to hunt the giant iguanas. The inglorious incident, when Augie is kicked on the head by his own horse, puts an end to the hunt for a "nobler reality." Intensely disillusioned, Thea seeks relief by collecting rare snakes. Augie is also disillusioned and disappointed. After the accident, the terrifying suddenness and the utter finality of death horrify Augie as they horrified Joseph. When Thea, outraged because Augie had helped Stella Chesney escape from her current love, outraged further when Augie reveals what he really thinks about her hunting, runs away, Augie feels utter desolation and despair. His friend Iggy suggests that Augie had to experience suffering before he could get anywhere: " 'You got to be knocked over and crushed like this. If you don't you'll never understand how much you hurt her. You've got to find out about this and not be so larky' " (416).

Augie begins a "terrible investigation" into his own nature. He cannot harmonize his desire to be simple and free, unencumbered by money or profession or duties, with his genuine desire to please people and be a sincere follower of love: "An independent fate and love too—what confusion!" (417) he exclaims painfully. Thea was right when she told him that love would always appear strange to him no matter what form it took. He discovers that he is a child-man. His desire to please people, he now realizes, did not spring from a real love for them, but from his need for protection: "While as for me, whoever would give me cover from this mighty free-running terror and wild cold of chaos I went to, and therefore to temporary embraces" (419).

Augie returns to Chicago a sadder, if wiser, man. He has lost some of his larkiness. In spite of his deeper awareness of the darkness that surrounds man, he still retains like other Bellow protagonists his faith in human existence. Before leaving Mexico he arms himself with the important insight that it is impossible to live "without something infinitely mighty and great" (429).

Back in Chicago Augie has an overview of the exploding metropolis, and sees it as if for the first time. He senses the immense power lodged within the city's confines and recognizes its kinship with the Mexican mesas, with the darkness and the wild animals he found there: "Well, here it was again, westward from this window, the gray snarled city with the hard black straps of rails, enormous industry cooking and its vapor shuddering to the air, the climb and fall of its stages in construction or demolition like mesas, and on these the different powers and sub-powers crouched and watched like sphinxes. Terrible dumbness covered it, like a judgment that would never find its word" (441). Chicago is no longer a city for adventure, but a place in which Augie can bethink himself and examine the human condition. Augie has changed, but the change is not apparent to Simon and to Augie's friends.

Simon cannot understand Augie's reluctance to settle down to a profession. Augie's friends, aware of his desire for a higher, independent fate, badger him good-humoredly. Padilla, Clem Tambow, and Mimi

Villars urge Augie to accept reality. Mimi insists that Augie accept the weaknesses of human nature and the fact that people "dug for unreality more than for treasure" (453). Padilla and Clem warn him that he has too ambitious a dream about human greatness. Padilla says that "the big investigation today is into how *bad* a guy can be, not how good he can be" (448). Clem Tambow, who has been reading psychology, suggests that Augie cure himself of his nobility syndrome, his belief in Man, by taking some of Freud's medicine.

Augie is still the listener he was, but the "opposition" in him now asserts itself. He insists on remaining an amateur and refuses to be an expert, a specialist with a function. He offers a firm, if simple, challenge to the reality principle advocated by his friends: "It can never be right to offer to die, and if that's what the data of experience tell you, then you must get along without them" (453). Augie meditates upon his experience before he is launched into the postwar, wider, European world. He arrives at two conclusions not in logical fashion but in his own intuitive way. One idea is out of Thoreau, that the reason for solitude can only be reunion; the other, that it is tiresome "to have your own opinions on everything" (464). Later, fortified by Kayo Obermark's insight that love is the only protection against the overwhelming conditioning forces of life, provoked by Sophie Geratis into proclaiming his need for the mystical, great things of life, Augie offers Clem Tambow a grand summary of all the wisdom he has gained.

The wisdom is Emersonian. Man has to base his existence on the axial lines of truth, love, peace, bounty, usefulness, and harmony. These thrilling lines had passed through the center of Augie's being as a child. Like the nineteenth-century romantics, like Wordsworth in particular, Augie believes that these lines demand to be rediscovered in later years and are miraculously bestowed upon anyone who stops hunting furiously for them: "At any time life can come together again and man be regenerated" (472). Like an older Joseph, taught by suffering, Augie believes in the marvelousness of human existence and offers a mystical vision of human possibility. Man "will be brought into true focus. He will live with true joy. Even his pains will be joy if they are true, even his helplessness will not take away his power, even wandering will not take him away from himself, even the big social jokes and hoaxes need not make him ridiculous, even disappointment after disappointment need not take away his love. Death will not be terrible to him if life is not. The embraces of other true people will take away his dread of fast change and short life" (472).

This act of faith marks the climactic moment of Augie's search for humanness. It reveals Augie's (and Bellow's) sacramental reverence for the gift of life. It implies that everyone vibrates with intimations of immortality in the lost world of one's childhood, intimations that can be recovered again. Augie acknowledges the presence of disappointment, pain, absurdity in human life but refuses to accept the clichés of alienation, anxiety, doom, and despair as inevitable to the human condition. He ends with a dream of a vast colony of the spirit wherein man can truly be himself, redeemed from his fear of death by the warmth of human brotherhood.

Augie March does not end on this final note of hope and affirmation. Augie pursues his visionary dream but Bellow's artistic sense and fictional tact could not allow Augie to achieve it. Clem Tambow warns Augie that it cannot even happen. The incidents, adventures, encounters that follow are neither remarkable in themselves nor coherent. The marriage to Stella, the teachings of Mintouchian, the wartime adventures with Basteshaw, the postwar experiences in Europe, and the strange ride with Jacqueline to the Normandy coast show us an Augie who knows that his dream can never be translated into reality.

His reactions when World War II breaks out are uncharacteristically loud and boisterous (he is carried away, makes long speeches, and wants to volunteer immediately), but in many ways they parallel those of Joseph. Augie abandons his dream for a while, telling himself that he will pursue it after the war. The war is a "hell-making project" (475), but he cannot bear the idea of the Dostoevskian universal antheap that would be established if the enemy won. He undergoes a painful operation for inguinal hernia before he gets into the merchant marine. Bellow deliberately does not elaborate on Augie's war experiences: he concentrates on Augie's efforts to get to war and on the long conversations with Basteshaw. Basteshaw's desire to have a better fate, to be a *stupor mundi*, to create a world without injustice and cruelty, a world full of love and a new brotherhood of man is a monstrous parody of Augie's own dream.

The encounter with Mintouchian, a week before Augie's marriage to Stella, forces Augie to temper his dream and accept a reasonable measure of human greatness. Mintouchian, like *Tu As Raison Aussi* and Schlossberg, is yet another of "those persons who persistently arise before me with life counsels and illumination throughout my entire earthly pilgrimage" (497). He teaches Augie to accept human limits, to submit to the law that love is adultery and expresses change, and to recognize also that man is an actor always adopting disguises to protect himself. Above all, Mintouchian teaches Augie Pindarian wisdom, the need to accept and become what one is: "It is better to die what you are than to live a stranger for ever" (504). One has to stake everything on what one is, Mintouchian tells Augie. Paradoxically one must move, but aim at being still, for there's a double poser, that "if you make a move you may lose but if you sit still you will decay" (504). The lesson is completed by Mintouchian's wife who pays this tribute to her husband: " 'He is great, even if he's all too human.' " (506).

Mintouchian's ideas about love, adultery, and change allow Augie to accept Stella's lies and the news about her former lover, Cumberland, without much despair. Augie abandons his bubble-headed dream of a foster-home academy, recognizing it for what it was, not a construction or an overpowering obsession, but a feather-light millenarian notion, unacceptable to Stella, with whom his fate is linked and who takes up the career of a film actress in Europe. Augie now involved in black-market deals in Europe as Mintouchian's agent, still hopes to settle down with Stella and their future children. But he can never sit still or settle down. Our last view of Augie is as a Chaplinesque figure, not walking, but traveling in a Citroën along the very edge of Europe, larky, bouncing, laughing at Jacqueline's lifelong dream of going to Mexico, laughing at the idea of himself as a kind of Columbus, discoverer of a newfound land, laughing above all at the enigma and the paradox that is man. Laughing, happy, he disappears into the blue distance.

Bellow's achievement in *Augie March* becomes clear if one is aware of the circumstances in which it was composed, the literary excitement that it generated before and after publication, the interviews Bellow gave soon after it was published, and his recent strictures on the novel.

Bellow started *Augie March* in 1948, after junking 100,000 words of a serious, grim novel he had been working on.[4] He was in Europe on a Guggenheim fellowship and wrote the novel in Paris, Salzburg, Rome, in trains and cafes, in hotels and eating places, in New York, Portland, Seattle. The last two paragraphs, according to Bellow, were "completed on a Viking Press typewriter. Not a single word of the book was composed in Chicago."[5] He took five long years to complete the novel. According to Laura Z. Hobson, who wrote the literary gossip column "Trade Winds" for *The Saturday Review of Literature*, Bellow watched with dismay his book grow longer and longer. At one moment he was ready to have the first half published as part 1. "But Viking Press," wrote Laura Hobson, "with whose financial connivance Bellow was operating anyway, persuaded him to hold off publication until his giant was really completed.[6]

The New York literary world eagerly awaited Bellow's new novel. Samples and excerpts, published in *Partisan Review, Sewanee Review,*

The New Yorker, Harper's Bazaar and *Hudson Review,* had created a stir
of anticipatory excitement. Robert Penn Warren, Lionel Trilling, and
Clifton Fadiman had read parts of the manuscript and were full of
enthusiasm. When *Augie March* was published in the fall of 1953, it was
greeted with tremendous praise; all the reviewers, with the exception of
Norman Podheretz, hailed it as an epic, a classic. It won the National
Book Award and was considered "the most distinguished work of fiction
published in 1953."[7]

As a literary celebrity, Bellow gave a number of interviews in which
he talked about the making of his novel, about how and where he wrote
it. In an article in *The New York Times Book Review* Bellow said that the
novel wrote itself.[8] To Harvey Breit he confessed that the writing of
Augie March had been a spontaneous act: "It just came to me. . . . The
great pleasure of the book was that it came easily. All I had to do was be
there with buckets to catch it. That's why the form is loose."[9] Bellow
went on to comment on the kind of form he had used: "I kicked over the
traces, wrote catch-as-catch-can, picaresque. I took my chance."[10] To
Bernard Kalb, Bellow revealed the sense of freedom he experienced: "In
'Augie' one of my great pleasures was in having the ideas taken away
from me, as it were, by the characters. They demanded to have their own
existence. It was a liberation for me."[11]

A decade later, after *Henderson* and after *Herzog,* Bellow looked back
at *Augie March* with critical severity. No longer was he drawn to the
novel and to Augie as a character: he found Augie "so ingenuous—the
ingenue."[12] In a 1964 interview Bellow said: "I am grateful to the book
because it was so liberating to write it. But I do not consider it a success
because I only just discovered a new possibility. I was incapable at the
time of controlling it and it ran away with me. I feel that Augie was too
effusive and uncritical."[13] The *Paris Review* interview tells us of the
uncertain handling of the novel: "I took off many of these restraints. I
think I took off too many and went too far but I was feeling the
excitement of discovery. I had just increased my freedom, and like any
emancipated plebian I abused it at once."[14] A recent interview tells that
"there was something delirious about the writing of *Augie March.* It
over-ran its borders."[15] In a tribute to his friend, John Berryman, who
admired the exuberance of the novel's language and its devotion to the
Chicago streets, Bellow refers to *Augie March* as "naive, undisciplined,
unpruned."[16]

Augie March is clearly not the fictional classic many considered it to
be, but it is a novel that had to issue out of Bellow's creative being before
he could write supreme fiction. Writing *Augie March* was, for Bellow, a
freeing of his energies, an act of liberation from certain artistic

inhibitions and repressions, a discovery of the true country of his fiction, its shape and substance.

Dangling Man and *The Victim*, had been sober, well-knit, well-ordered pieces of fiction. Highly conscious of the sophisticated, European tradition of Sartre, Dostoevski, Kafka, E. M. Forster, writers strongly endorsed by *Partisan Review* in the articles it published all through the 1940s, Bellow practiced the craft of fiction, using devices the older writers had used, and wrote neat, black parables about the diminishment of modern man, seen as dangler and as victim. In *Augie March*, to use the language of gambling, Bellow let himself go for broke. Having absorbed all he could from the European practitioners of fiction, he now turned for nourishment to the American tradition of the novel.

Rejecting the mode of his immediate predecessors such as Hemingway, Bellow reached back to the ampler, more hospitable and open-ended forms of American fiction used by Melville and Mark Twain. The title of the novel, which originally had been *Life among the Machiavellians*, was changed to deliberately echo *The Adventures of Huckleberry Finn*. The opening line, "I am an American, Chicago-born," summons up the opening of *Moby-Dick* confidently announcing the reappearance of another Ishmael who has been saved from urban shipwreck to tell his tale. In the last paragraph, Augie refers to himself as a sort of Columbus and, like Huckleberry, lights out for his territory ahead, the *terra incognita* that spreads out in every gaze. Bellow endows Augie with an assured Emersonian joy and belief in human existence. Augie has also been given the Whitmanesque temperament, large, open, free eluding definitions, able to contain multitudes. The novel is Augie's song of the open road, a song of himself, a celebration of America with its protean variety. Augie proclaims his kinship with Whitman, "being democratic in temperament, available to everybody and assuming about others what I assumed about myself" (155).

The writing of *Augie March* also compelled Bellow to accept the fictional challenge of capturing the dark forces, the savage tensions, the tumults and bewilderments of the big city in which modern man finds and has to find himself. Joseph's Chicago oppresses his spirit: as a passive witness, he casts a cold eye on the streets and the scenes of Chicago, but cannot respond to them and therefore cannot describe them or make them come alive. In *The Victim* Bellow succeeds in evoking a New York as seen through the dark, resentful, limited eyes of a Leventhal who can only respond to its hot, yellow, gloomy, crowded, bleak streets, its towering buildings and the grinding noises of its traffic. The Chicago of *Augie March* is magnificently alive in its multitudinous variety. It is not seen, but experienced. Augie is not a mere witness; as one Chicago-born, one who has roamed its crowded, colorful streets, the city is part of his being. And because he is thickly involved with Chicago, he can make it spring to vivid life. "I grew up there and consider myself a Chicagoan, out and out," Bellow has said in an autobiographical note.[17] The vigor, authority, excitement, and completeness of Augie's Chicago springs in part from Bellow's passionate involvement with and love for the city he grew up in.

The power of Augie's Chicago derives also from Bellow's adoption of the practices and techniques of the Chicago naturalists, Farrell, Dreiser, and Norris, who had written about Chicago. Bellow, in a review essay, has referred to the "lifting power" of Dreiser, his ability to convey forcefully the "facts of our American modern reality."[18] Bellow uses the method of heaping raw, accumulative detail to stamp the city upon the reader's consciousness. The details offered are not single, separate, static, but mobile, dynamic units, charged with energetic life. Here is a description of the County Hospital in Chicago after the declaration of the war:

> The hospital was mobbed and was like Lent and Carnival battling. This was Harrison Street, where Mama and I used to come for her specs, and nof far from where I had to go once to identify that dead coal heaver, the thundery gloom, bare stone brown, while the red cars lumbered and clanged. Every bed, window, separate frame of accommodation, every corner was filled, like the walls of Troy or the streets of Clermont when Peter the Hermit was preaching. Shruggers, hobblers, truss and harness wearers, crutch-dancers, wall inspectors, wheelchair people in bandage helmets, wound smells and drug flowers blossoming from gauze, from colorful horrors and out of the deep sinks.

Augie goes up to the roof of the hospital and has an overview of Chicago:

> Around was Chicago. In its repetition it exhausted your imagination of details and units, more units than the cells of the brain and bricks of Babel. The Ezekiel caldron of wrath, stoked with bones. In time the caldron too would melt. A mysterious tremor, dust, vapor, emanation of stupendous effort traveled with the air, over me on top of the great establishment, so full as it was, and over the clinics, clinks, factories, flophouses, morgue, skid row. As before the work of Egypt and Assyria, as before a sea, you're nothing here. Nothing. [476]

The prose has a distinct power. Here is the language not of a mere spectator, but of a participant. Not only is the eye involved, all the senses are. The historical sense manifests itself in the reference to Troy, Egypt, Assyria. The biblical references—Babel, Ezekiel—suggest yet another dimension. The catalog cluster, presenting the patients in the hospital, is a riot of facts, smell, abstraction, and surreal image—as if the technique of the catalog used by Dreiser were combined with that used by Melville and Whitman. Above all, Chicago is not viewed as an object, but as an organism with an electric vitality of its own, a gigantic living crucible in which man can experience the terror of the contemporary human condition and the insignificance of the shriveled self.

By writing *Augie March*, Bellow was also able to release a hitherto untapped source of his creative energy. In *Dangling Man* and *The Victim* Bellow's Jewish sensibility lay dormant. It manifested itself briefly in the humanistic wisdom proferred to Asa Leventhal by old Schlossberg, a Judeo-Christian belief in man and an acceptance of the human condition. In *Augie March*, for the first time, Bellow deliberately permitted his Jewish heritage to assert itself and ignite his imagination. This heritage, a vital ingredient of his creative sensibility, had been carefully nurtured in his childhood. He grew up in an orthodox Jewish household, brought up by a mother who wanted him to become a Talmudic scholar. In the *Show* interview he says: "My childhood was in ancient times which was true of all orthodox Jews. Every child was immersed in the Old Testament as soon as he could understand anything, so that you began life by knowing Genesis in Hebrew by heart at the age of four. You never got to distinguish between that and the outer world. I grew up with four languages, English, Hebrew, Yiddish and French."[19] In the *Paris Review* interview, Bellow tells us about how the pressure exerted by the WASP world inhibited him as a writer and an artist: "I had to touch a great many bases, demonstrate my abilities, pay my respects to formal requirements. In short, I was afraid to let myself go."[20] *Dangling Man* and *The Victim* were written, in part, with what may be termed a borrowed sensibility. According to Bellow, "a writer should be able to express himself easily, naturally, copiously in a form which frees his mind, his energies."[21]

The novelist who wrote *Augie March* is one who has flung away his repressions and, proud and aware of his own past, writes as the son of immigrant Russian Jews, trying to repair the damage done to his self. Bellow's Jewishness is now no longer a hoarded jewel, but a valuable and inexhaustible birthright. It manifests itself in fundamentals, not in the use of minor detail, the references to Old Granum, the Psalm reciter and deathbed watcher, and to the razor slits in the vests of Einhorn and Dingbat after their father, the Commissioner, dies. It refuses to idealize, and so to sentimentalize the oppressions and difficulties of Jewish life in the New World: "for sadness the Kaddish, for amusement the schnorrer, for admiration the bearded scholar."[22]

In his introduction to *Great Jewish Short Stories* Bellow isolates two fundamental qualities of the Jewish imagination. One quality is the tendency to overhumanize everything, to invest all things in the universe with intense human meaning. The other is perhaps more essentially Jewish, the ability to respond to the human condition in a manner that teeters on the knife edge between laughter and trembling. The Jewish imagination accepts the predicament in which all mankind (and Jews, specially) finds itself in and yet it opposes to this terrible fact a comic sense of life. According to Bellow, the Jewish protagonist uses laughter as an antidote to achieve sanity and at times appears "to invite or encourage trembling with the secret aim of overcoming it by means of laughter."[23]

Thea accuses Augie of overhumanizing everything: "Oh, you screwball! You get human affection mixed up with everything, like a savage. Keep your silly feelings to yourself" (362). Augie acknowledges the way in which most people accept the terrible human condition. Like Allbee, like Alf Steidler, they do not act but instead become actors: "External life being so mighty, the instruments so huge and terrible, the performances so great, the thoughts so great and threatening, you produce a someone who can exist before it. You invent a man who can stand before the terrible appearances. This way he can't get justice and he can't give justice, but he can live. And this is what mere humanity always does" (418). At the end of his adventures, Augie does not learn how to act, but he does have a faint inkling of why Jacqueline with her dream of Mexico refuses to lead a disappointed life and why he himself travels all through Europe. It is the *animal ridens* in him, the Jewish comic sense of life that is mysterious and inexplicable for he cannot understand its secret origins: "Or is the laugh at nature—including eternity—that it thinks it can win over us and the power of hope? Nah! Nah! I think. It never will. But that probably is the joke, on one or the other, and laughing is an enigma that includes both" (556–57).

It is this bounteous humor that loudly and emphatically asserts the difference between Bellow's first two novels and *Augie March*. The laughter proceeds from a joyous acceptance of the human condition. Augie is aware of the darkness in which mankind exists; he knows about human disappointment and deformation, and yet he bounces merrily along, choosing to laugh at life's inconsequentialities rather than to rage or weep at its wickednesses. His laughter and his hope and his joy issue from a sweeping comic vision of life which embraces and reconciles the tragic sense and then transcends it.

That is why Augie is friends with the world. Nothing human is alien to him and he enjoys and participates in the human scene as it sprawls before him. *Augie March* foams with an immense cast of characters. The minor characters have pungently comic, ethnic names: "Five Properties," Nails Nagel, Nosey Mutchnik, Dingbat Einhorn. The millionaire Robey and Basteshaw, the biochemist, are grotesques, realized in vivid detail. Augie accepts human variety and is never bitter or harsh about human behavior. It is as if he had the temperament of a creative writer and the ability to set down graphically every detail and nuance, every secret drive and desire, in an effort to penetrate the mystery completely.

For Augie is perhaps a novelist manqué. He does not have a genuine self because Bellow does not endow him with one. Augie is a medium, a container for the ideas, problems, questions that troubled Bellow as artist at the time, but which he could not adequately dramatize. Into Augie Bellow poured his sense of Jewishness, his love for Chicago, his desire to belong to America. He bestows on his protagonist his own faith in human existence and makes him wrestle with questions to which there are as yet no answers. *Augie March* is a Great Books book. The torrent of learned allusions, historical references, biblical echoes that sweeps through the memoir has its source not in Augie (despite the frequent references to the encyclopaedias and the books Augie read) but in Bellow's mind, a mind educated at the University of Chicago in the 1930s, the mind of one who had worked on the Index *(Syntopicon)* of the Great Books series.

Above all, the language of the memoir is not really that of Augie. Lacking a true self, Augie lacks a true language with which to talk about himself. His language doesn't well out of his being; it pours out of him as from a faucet. He is a mouthpiece through which the voice of the author issues. The language of *Augie March* is that of a writer who is trying to discover, form, and possess a "language" that will enable him to realize his deep fictional needs. Bellow needed a language that would have both range and flexibility. Augie's voice tries to be like that of Montaigne who, according to Bellow, was able to pass with ease from kitchen matters to metaphysics. Like Huckleberry Finn, Augie speaks a vernacular, stained by the slang of the Chicago streets. Unlike Huck, he can also use the idiom of an educated mind that meditates on and at times waxes lyrical about existence. The two voices of Augie do not merge into one authentic voice.

Like the structure, the language of *Augie March* is uneven and uncertain. It doesn't show achievement but reveals promise. *Augie March*, like *Dangling Man*, was another pioneering work for Bellow, one that allowed him to solve the problem of language later. No longer is his language cool and proficient, a language detached from his true artistic self. It is a rich and powerful mixture, alive with elements of Yiddish, Chicago slang, literary allusion. It is above all thickly and distinctly American, a language that has the capacity to respond to and capture an American reality that is "new, promising, changing, dangerous, universal."[24] The language of *Augie March* is not a success, but Bellow needed to learn how to play that instrument before he could produce the magnificent rhythms and harmonies of *Henderson the Rain King*, *Herzog*, and *Humboldt's Gift*.

NOTES

1. Saul Bellow, *The Adventures of Augie March* (Greenwich, Conn.: Fawcett Publications, Inc., 1965), p. 211. Hereafter page references will be cited in the text.

2. See chapter 3 of James J. Gibson, *The Perception of the Visual World* (Cambridge: The Riverside Press, 1950). Wylie Sypher in *Literature and Technology* (New York: Random House, 1968, pp. 106–107) explains the distinctions clearly: "The visual world, the world of things 'out there' in Newtonian space, is an abstraction that can only be thought but cannot be seen. We actually see in a visual field, which is quite unlike the visual world we 'know.' The visual field shifts with the movement of the eye, and it has a single sharp focus at the center of the (roughly speaking) oval area of perception. We know that we live in a visual world, yet it is a three-dimensional construct of things arranged stably and logically in a space that is alien to our sensations."

3. Robert Shulman. "The Style of Bellow's Comedy." *Publications of the Modern Language Association* (March 1968), p. 113.

4. Bernard Kalb, "Biographical Sketch," *Saturday Review of Literature* 36 (September 19, 1953): 13.

5. Saul Bellow, "How I Wrote Augie March's Story," *New York Times Book Review*, 59 (January 31, 1954): 17.

6. Laura Z. Hobson, "Trade Winds," *Saturday Review of Literature* 36 (August 22, 1953): 6.

7. *Current Biography* (New York: The H. W. Wilson Company, 1965), p. 24.

8. "How I Wrote Augie March's Story," p. 3.

9. Harvey Breit, *The Writer Observed* (New York: The World Publishing Company, 1956), p. 273.

10. Ibid.

11. Bernard Kalb, p. 13.

12. Nina A. Steers, " 'Successor' to Faulkner?" *Show* 4 (September 1964): 38.

13. Ibid.

14. *Writers at Work*, Third Series, p. 182.

15. Chirantan Kulshrestha, "A Conversation with Saul Bellow," *Chicago Review* 23, no. 4, and 24, no. 1: 13.

16. Saul Bellow, "John Berryman, Friend," *New York Times Book Review*, May 27, 1973, p. 1.

17. Stanley J. Kunitz, *Twentieth Century Authors*, First Supplement (New York: The H. W. Wilson Company, 1955), p. 72.

18. Saul Bellow, "Dreiser and the Triumph of Art," *Commentary* 11 (May 1951): 502.

19. Nina A. Steers, pp. 36–37.

20. *Writers at Work*, Third Series, p. 182.

21. Ibid., p. 183.

22. Saul Bellow, ed., *Great Jewish Short Stories* (New York: Dell Publishing Company, 1963), p. 13.

23. Ibid., p. 12.

24. Saul Bellow, "In No Man's Land," *Commentary* 11 (February 1951): 204.

4 *Seize the Day*

A lmost all of Bellow's secret creative energies converge for the making of *Seize the Day*, a richly textured, intricately patterned novella packed with a number of vibrant themes and images. *Seize the Day* marks an important stage in his development as artist. By 1956 Bellow had absorbed all the literary and intellectual nutrients he needed to realize his own creative strength. *Seize the Day*, with its tone of assurance, is the work of a novelist who has just begun to discover his true artistic self.

Seize the Day is yet another parable about the quest for the human. Like his earlier fellow protagonists, Tommy Wilhelm is driven to the craters of the spirit to discover his fate. Bellow presents him as "a visionary sort of animal. Who has to believe that he can know why he exists. Though he has never seriously tried to find out why."[1] The novella enacts the process by which Tommy Wilhelm arrives at the true meaning of his existence.

This process is presented not from a single perspective, as in *Dangling Man* and *Augie March*, but from a number of viewpoints. The narrative tactics of *Seize the Day* are an improvement over those of *The Victim*. Most of the events are routed through Wilhelm's point of view which, at times, slides into the first person. Behind Wilhelm stands the narrator, who is aware of the predicament of the protagonist. At other moments Wilhelm is seen through the eyes of the minor characters in the novella. This at times abrupt shifting of narrative angles creates problems for the reader, who has to maintain the ironic distance necessary to smile wryly at a comic slob, and then adopt the stance of one who has to look with sympathy at a passive sufferer living through a terrible day. Like Asa Leventhal, but unlike Joseph, Tommy Wilhelm is not an intellectual and is unable to interpret the experiences he undergoes and the vision vouchsafed to him at the end. He has the experience; the reader must supply the necessary meaning.

The title is a good starting point for the unraveling of the dense, radiant web of intertwined images and themes in *Seize the Day*. Unlike the titles of the first two novels, this one does not denote a condition. Tommy Wilhelm, who appears to be both dangler and victim, is urged to

open his eyes, stretch forth his hands and partake of a mysterious glory
that is his birthright:

> Seek ye then that which art not there
> In thine own glory let thyself rest.
> Witness. Thy power is not bare.
> Thou art King. Thou art at thy best.

[75]

Seize the day, an insistent voice proclaims, speaking not the language of
Horace, but that of Blake and the Talmud. The imperative is an
exhortation to action. It urges Wilhelm to seize and understand his own
tragic condition; he has to know who he is, acknowledge the sins and
mistakes of his past; more, he has to seize the magic moment of truth that
will be offered to him on this day.

For the day itself, which Wilhelm has metaphorically to seize, is a
dark night which he has to go through before day can dawn. It is a day
when his routine will break up, a day when a lifetime's accumulation of
troubles will avalanche down upon his being, when his physical and
psychical woes will reach a climax. All through the day he feels choked
and strangled because of a tremendous pressure in his chest. His wife,
who will not grant him a divorce, tortures him with excessive financial
demands. His father rebuffs him denying Wilhelm the love and help the
son demands. And it is a day of utter financial disaster, the day he pays
for his tenth and final mistake when he loses all his savings at the stock
market. On this day, too, hidden antibodies in Wilhelm's damaged
psyche are summoned to attack the cancer within and restore him to
health. For it is a day of memory, a day of truth and discovery. Wilhelm
himself has intimations that it is a day of reckoning: what he does not
realize is that is is a personal day of atonement, when the deep needs of
his Jewish self will be met. And it is also the final day of a secret course
of therapy that Wilhelm has been undergoing, unbeknown to himself.

The story of Tommy Wilhelm's day, a morning through an afternoon,
is presented in seven short chapters. The first four slowly summon up
Wilhelm's past. The action is confined to the Hotel Gloriana, and
Wilhelm spends the morning brooding about his mistakes, having
breakfast with his father, Dr. Adler, and talking to Dr. Tamkin. The
remaining three chapters, which concentrate largely on the present,
narrate a sequence of simple events—he is wiped out at the stock
market, his friend, Dr. Tamkin disappears, his father rejects him, his
wife brutally insists that he send her money—that culminates in
Wilhelm's complete breakdown in a Jewish funeral chapel. With

marvelous economy Bellow makes every moment of Wilhelm's brief day vibrate with rich resonance. Every character he meets, every conversation he has, almost everything he sees, does, or remembers, serve simultaneously to resurrect the past, unfold the present, and propel him toward the final moment of truth.

The opening paragraph, deceptively simple in its use of casual detail, begins:

> When it came to concealing his troubles, Tommy Wilhelm was not less capable than the next fellow. So at least he thought, and there was a certain moment of evidence to back him up. He had once been an actor—no, not quite, an extra—and he knew what acting should be. Also, he was smoking a cigar, and when a man is smoking a cigar, wearing a hat, he has an advantage; it is harder to find out how he feels. [3]

Wilhelm is worried about his appearance chiefly for the sake of his father, whom he expects to meet on the way to breakfast. But, the paragraph continues,

> there was no stop on the fourteenth, and the elevator sank and sank. Then the smooth door opened and the great dark red uneven carpet that covered the lobby billowed toward Wilhelm's feet. In the foreground the lobby was dark, sleepy. French drapes like sails kept out the sun, but three high narrow windows were open, and in the blue air Wilhelm saw a pigeon about to light on the great chain that supported the marquee of the movie house directly underneath the lobby. For one moment he heard the wings beating strongly. [3–4]

The paragraph is more than a mere account of Tommy Wilhelm's descent in an elevator to the lobby of the mezzanine of the Hotel Gloriana. The end of the paragraph prepares us for the consummation that will occur in the final paragraph. Bellow's use of realistic detail—the chain, the marquee, the movie house—successfully disguises but does not entirely mute the religious vibrations released by the three high narrow windows, the blue air, and the hesitant dove. Wilhelm's anxiety about his father's opinion of him points to an important motif, the conflict between fathers and sons. Significant also is the introduction of two dominant images that run through the novella. The water imagery, here a mere trick of style—the elevator sinks, the carpet billows, the drapes are like sails—will gradually amplify to project Tommy Wilhelm's tragic condition and his final salvation. The images of theater and acting—Wilhelm has been an actor, the hotel lobby is above a movie house—introduce us immediately to the world Wilhelm inhabits and to the kind of person he is.

Tommy Wilhelm's tragicomic drama is enacted, appropriately, on Broadway, specifically along the upper stretch of the Seventies, Eighties, and Nineties, a highly artificial microcosm. Here is a glamorous, empty world of hotels and supermodern cafeterias, dental laboratories, reducing parlors, beauty parlors, funeral homes, all dedicated to the business of pampering the body and putting up a show. At one end are the hotels: Hotel Ansonia looks as if it were a baroque palace from Prague or Munich, enlarged a hundred times; the lobby of the Hotel Gloriana (a name with ironic overtones) has dusky, indirect lighting and its mirrors are deliberately dark-tinted to conceal the defects of its aged inhabitants. Opposite Hotel Gloriana is a supermodern cafeteria with a fake exterior of gold and purple mosaic columns where Tamkin and Wilhelm go for lunch. The inside is as false as the outside: "The food looked sumptuous. Whole fishes were framed like pictures with carrots, and the salads were like terraced landscapes or like Mexican pyramids; slices of lemon and onion and radishes were like sun and moon and stars; the cream pies were about a foot thick and the cakes swollen as if sleepers had baked them in their dreams" (90–91). Broadway itself, though it is bright afternoon, appears to be artificially lighted, the sunshine throbbing with the dust and fumes and the gas spurting from the buses. At the other end of Wilhelm's world, a few hundred yards away, is the "narrow crowded theater of the brokerage office" (78).

Bellow focuses on New York as the unreal city. Its inhabitants, too, are unreal, the elderly and the retired, undone by their fear of death, whose nearness they refuse to acknowledge. The old ladies wait out the day wearing rouge and mascara and costume jewelery. Actresses all, they use blue hair rinse and eye shadow to disguise their age. Wilhelm has a terrifying impression of a swirling, tumultuous, carnival crowd, each determined to act out his own particular fantasy role, each one babbling a language of his own: "And the great crowd, the inexhaustible current of millions of every race and kind pouring out, pressing round, of every age, of every genius, possessors of every human secret, antique and future, in every face the refinement of one particular motive or essence—*I labor, I spend, I strive, I design, I love, I cling, I uphold, I give away, I envy, I long, I scorn, I die, I hide, I want*" (115).

The frenzied fury of this crowd of egos (no colony of the spirit, this) is a result of the money fever that has seized them, the American dream of success, their inordinate desire for the material world of things. Money has become their god: "They adore money! Holy money! Beautiful money! It was getting so that people were feebleminded about everything except money" (36). The temple, where they go to propitiate this god, is Wall Street, of which the brokerage office is an uptown branch. The image of the brokerage office as a theater, where actors congregate, modulates and shifts into a religious image, for it is also a place where the false god is worshipped. The board on which the shining market quotations tumble and whir reminds Wilhelm of a Chinese theater. The golden board is also the fickle, fluctuating god of fortune. Bellow shifts to yet another image, that of sight and vision. The eyes of the worshippers are riveted to this board. The German manager reads it continually with a pair of opera glasses that he wears around his neck. Wilhelm cannot decipher the tiny figures on the board, but Dr. Tamkin with his sharp eyes can. Old Mr. Rappaport, who has smoky and faded eyes, needs to be continually informed about the figures on the board, which he jots down on a pad that he hides from view.

Bellow makes brilliant use of these four images—water, acting, sight, religion—that dissolve and merge into one another to highlight ironically the false, hollow world that surrounds Wilhelm. The same images blend together to characterize Dr. Adler, the perfect incarnation of the world that has created and conditioned Tommy Wilhelm.

Dr. Adler is a clean, dapper, handsome, bland old man. Going on eighty, he is still concerned about his appearance and loves looking fine in the eyes of the world. His white vest and the red-and-black striped shirt he wears defy the approach of death. A master of social behavior, he carries himself with great style and poise. With all his might, the narrator states with unmistakable irony, he was a healthy and fine small old man. Dr. Adler is a success in every way, financially as well as socially. Idolized by everyone in the Hotel Gloriana, he talks affably to all people—except to his own son. He hoards his money, spending it only on the needs of his ancient flesh, just as he hoards his tight, withered, insulated self, refusing to share it with anyone else. Money and self are his twin gods. Dr. Adler has no religion, no ancient one, that is, with values, sanctions, pieties. Wilhelm mistakenly considers him the right kind of Jew, one who has abandoned his heritage and has accepted the modern, secular way of urban life with its materialism, its gospel of money and success.

Dr. Adler so loves himself that he is blind to his son's wants. "He doesn't see what I want," his son complains bitterly (50). Dr. Adler is also deaf (he carries a hearing aid in his pocket) to his son's cries for help and love. A retired doctor, he reserves his sympathy for what he terms "real ailments," those of the body, not ones of the spirit. That is why he prescribes hydrotherapy and exercises for his son's troubles.

Wilhelm cannot stand the odor of the wall-locked and chlorinated water of the baths underneath the Hotel Gloriana to which Dr. Adler descends in order to have his aged body toned up by massage and steam. When Wilhelm goes there to plead for help, he looks at this father's body, fresh from the steambath, laid out on the table, and he sees his father's true condition: "His ribs were narrow and small, his belly round, white, and high. It had its own being, like something separate. His thighs were weak, the muscles of his arms had fallen, his throat was creased" (108). This actor's mask and trappings have fallen away. The eyes are shut. The water treatment has proved ineffectual, for the signs of approaching death and decay are written all over Dr. Adler's body. The body itself is a mere husk: it is like something separate because it does not contain the vital spirit of life. Here lies no human being, but a living corpse.

In complete contrast to Dr. Adler is Wilhelm, who is both son and product of the world his father incarnates. Almost half his father's age, Wilhelm is untidily dressed; he has a stooped back, stump teeth, red-rimmed eyes and his gut is fat. Obviously a mere extra, he does not know how to act in the glittering world of money and success. His troubles are clearly written out upon his face.

Wilhelm's troubles are complex: they are physical and psychical, financial and emotional, all intertwined to form a gigantic burden that he has to bear. A clue to Wilhelm's plight is provided in a 1955 story which reads like a fragment of *Seize the Day*. Rogin, in "A Father-to-Be," becomes suddenly aware that to think of money was to think according to the way of the world. He also realizes that money and love are polar opposites: "When people said they wouldn't do something for love or money, they mean that love and money were opposite passions and one the enemy of the other."[2] Money and love battle together for the possession of Wilhelm's soul. In order to measure the true dimensions of this psychic conflict, to unearth its root, to understand the strange physical symptoms of Wilhelm's illness, and finally, to appreciate the singular manner by which Wilhelm is treated and shown the way to life, one has to keep in mind the ideas and concepts of Wilhelm Reich that influenced Bellow deeply at the time of the composition of *Seize the Day*.

Bellow has casually referred to his fascination with Reichianism in a 1962 tribute to his friend, Isaac Rosenfeld, where he mentions the fact that Reichianism absorbed them both for a time.[3] Rosenfeld (who died in 1956) was apparently a charmingly eccentric Reichian: he would ask people about their sexual habits and calculate how much character armor they wore; he even constructed a homemade orgone box which he used to produce better tomatoes and to treat the headaches of his friends. Bellow did not immerse himself in Reichianism the way his friend did.

He borrowed what he needed from Reich for his own creative purposes, disguising, dissolving and adapting Reichian elements so that they are not immediately apparent. *Seize the Day* is powerfully charged with Reichianism, but the deliberate restriction of fictional space and time, the need to pack other thematic concerns into this complex novella, and the continuous shifting of narrative perspectives did not allow Bellow to maneuver its Reichian elements with ease.

The central premise in Reichian theory is the existence of an energy that pervades and permeates all of nature and is the active vital force in every human being. "The cosmic orgone energy," wrote Reich, "functions in the living organism as specific biological energy."[4] This energy, a principle both of life and love, should freely circulate in the body. Unfortunately, this living, pulsing energy in man, disturbed at first by strict parental frustrations and repressions, is dammed up and distorted because of the brutal pressures exerted by man's social, economic, and political institutions. Human character structure, molded by a society that is patriarchal, authoritarian, death-dealing and barren, consists of three layers: the outer one with a mask of politeness and artificial sociality; the second layer, which consists of all the inhibited impulses of greed, lust, envy, and sadism; and finally, the deepest layer, where the natural orgone energy vibrates. Most human beings, according to Reich, are armored in this fashion with hard, rigid, and polished exteriors that effectively trap the life energy within.

The denizens of the Hotel Gloriana and the gamblers at the stock exchange, all consummate actors, wear perfect masks that hide the second layer. The German manager of the brokerage office, a model of correctness, is "silvery, cool, level, long-profiled, experienced, indifferent, observant" (6). Dr. Adler, that master of social style, wears an expression of "healthy, handsome, good-humored old age" (11). The core layer has either been stifled in most cases or else manifests itself in a distorted form, as in the ancient Mr. Rappaport's strange love for Teddy Roosevelt.

The three layers of Tommy Wilhelm are apparent as he lives through his tragic day. He tries to assume the mask of success, but is a failure as an actor, being merely an extra. He tries to sound gentlemanly and tasteful like his father, but his gestures are awkward and his behavior, according to his father, is that of a slob. Wilhelm tries hard to be sociable, polite, and charming. But his second layer, suggested by the gruff voice within him, expresses the anger and resentment concealed behind his social mask. His outer layer greets Mr. Perls politely, but his second layer asks: "Who is this damn frazzle-faced herring with his dyed hair and his fish teeth and this drippy mustache?' " (31)

What differentiates Tommy Wilhelm from the other inhabitants of the glamorous world that is upper Broadway is the fact that his core layer has not been completely stifled. It is still alive, though it has been greatly damaged. It is from this layer that he receives mysterious promptings. It is from these depths that he gets an obscure message which suggests that the real, the highest business of his life is "to carry his peculiar burden, to feel shape and impotence, to taste these quelled tears" (56). This feeble voice, which whimpers, weeps, and complains, issues from the very center of his soul and signals the presence of the orgone energy within him. This vital force does not circulate freely within Wilhelm; trapped within, it manifests itself at strange moments and in distorted forms. On this day the energy, which Wilhelm mistakenly believes "had done him the greatest harm" (7), will assert its imperatives. But he suffers from the masochistic fear of bursting: he will not and cannot allow his pent-up energy to discharge itself.

Tommy Wilhelm embodies a form of armoring that constitutes the masochistic character. In 1932 Reich published an essay that set forth his preliminary clinical investigations of masochism.[5] It signaled Reich's break with Freud and refuted the Freudian explanation of masochism as the expression of a hypothetical death instinct. Reich demonstrated that the masochistic drive toward suffering was not an inevitable result of the biological will to suffer, but a product of the disastrous impact of social conditions on the biopsychic apparatus.

According to Reich, masochism is the result and the expression of an inner tension that cannot be discharged. To illustrate the masochistic dilemma Reich made use of a vivid image, the biopsychic apparatus seen as an armored bladder:

> *How would a bladder behave if it were blown up with air from the inside, and could not burst?* Let us assume that its membrane would be tensile, but could not be torn. This picture of the human character as an armor around the living nucleus was highly relevant. The bladder, if it could express itself in its state of insoluble tension, would complain. In its helplessness, it would look for the causes of its suffering on *the outside*, and would be reproachful. It would ask to be pricked open. It would provoke its surroundings until it had achieved its aim as it conceives this. *What it could not bring about spontaneously from the inside, it would passively, helplessly, expect from the outside*. [DO, 213]

Typical masochistic character traits, according to Reich, are:

> Subjectively, a chronic sensation of *suffering* which appears objectively as a *tendency to complain;* chronic tendencies to

self-damage and *self-destruction* ("moral masochism") and a compulsion to *torture others* which makes the patient suffer no less than the
object. All masochistic characters show specifically *awkward, atactic
behavior* in their manners and in their intercourse with others, often so
marked as to give the impression of mental deficiency. [CA, 219]

Bellow translates these masochistic character traits and forms of
behavior into vivid, concrete, and at times oddly comic detail. Wilhelm
is a gigantic human bladder, a Rouault tragic clown at times, at other
times, a pathetic buffoon. He has a nodding Buddha head, and an
obscenely huge belly. He walks, observes the narrator, "like a tower in
motion" (74). Dr. Adler sees with disgust that his son is "either hoisting
his pants up and down by the pockets or jittering with his feet. A regular
mountain of tics, he's getting to be" (28). Wilhelm's laments and
complaints assume grotesque forms. In the restaurant he eats the
remains of his father's breakfast (signifying that he needs some form of
sustenance from his father) and then sits "gigantically in a state of
arrest" (42). This clown victim then grasps his own broad throat and
proceeds to choke himself to demonstrate by an act of self-sabotage how
his wife strangles him at long distance. He is sloppy in his personal
habits, and his car and apartment are greasy and filthy. He hurls names
at himself in self-depreciation. He calls himself an ass, an idiot, a wild
boar, a dumb mule, a hippopotamus. Like a hippopotamus, Tommy
Wilhelm wallows in his own sufferings.

The person to whom Wilhelm has returned for relief from his
sufferings is his father who psychically stands for the frustrating reality
Wilhelm identifies with. It was Dr. Adler, the immediate and forceful
representative of the tyrannical world of money and success, who
initially damaged his son's psyche. Reich regarded the patriarchal
family as a fortress of modern social order and as a factory for tyrannical
ideologies and conservative structures. Tamkin terms Dr. Adler "a fine
old patriarch of a father" (62) and refers to the parent-child relationship
as "the eternal same story" (61). More than an Oedipal battle-ground,
the family was the domestic arena where the masochistic damage began
and where the anchoring of the social order within the individual took
place.

Bellow does not dramatize (again, perhaps, because of lack of time
and space) the psychodynamics of Wilhelm's masochism, but he does
provide the reader with some hints. Tommy Wilhelm deliberately returns
after twenty long years to the source of his conflicts. " 'I expect *help!*' "
he cries out loudly and frantically at the breakfast table (53). " 'When I
suffer—you aren't even sorry. That's because you have no affection for

me, and you don't want any part of me,' " he complains bitterly (54). *"Dear Dad, Please carry me this month, Yours, W."* is his childish plea on the note he slips into an envelope together with his unpaid hotel bill (74). And yet, with his pill taking, his dirty habits, his whining pleas for help, he invariably irritates his father and provokes him to fury.

These provocative pleas offer a clue to the genesis of Wilhelm's masochism. Reich focuses on deep disappointment in love during childhood as the root origin of masochism. The provocative tactics of a masochist are directed against those persons who were loved intensely and who either actually disappointed or did not gratify the child's love:

> "You must love me, I shall force you to; or else, I'm going to annoy you." The masochistic torturing, the masochistic complaint, provocation and suffering, all explain themselves on the basis of the frustration, fantasied or actual, of a demand for love which is excessive and cannot be gratified. This mechanism is *specific* for the masochistic character and no other form of neurosis. [CA, 225]

There is no dramatic Freudian moment when the rejection that damaged Wilhelm's psyche occurred. Instead, Bellow suggests that there had been a series of critical conflicts during Wilhelm's childhood and adolescence. Wilhelm's dissatisfaction always reaches its intensest when he discusses family matters with his father. He is nostalgic about a "warm family life" (26), but is unsure about the reality of his father's kindliness to him as a child. He complains that his father had starved him of affection. Dr. Adler was at the office, or at the hospital, or out lecturing. "He expected me to look out for myself and never gave me much thought," broods Wilhelm (14). Bellow focuses on the period when Wilhelm commits his first mistake by going to Hollywood. Wilhelm is vaguely aware of the masochistic nature of this mistake: "Like, he sometimes thought, I was going to pick up a weapon and strike myself a blow with it" (17). His father's attitude had been one of cold indifference. Wilhelm had quarreled with his mother who had tried to stop him. Four years later she died and, as Wilhelm reminds his father, their family life came to an end. Dr. Adler freed himself from the shackles of his family, but his son has not been able to break away. An umbilical cord of memories still binds him to his mother. And now, at forty-four, Wilhelm demands from his father the love and help he was denied as a child. He is aware of his own childish demands: "It's time I stopped feeling like a kid toward him, a small son." (11).

The sufferings of Wilhelm spring from the continuous tension within him. But the methods he uses to insist on his father's love are doomed to fail. For these demands, in the form of provocation and spite, increase both his fears of losing love and his feelings of guilt, for it is the beloved father who is being tortured. Wilhelm suffers from the peculiar masochistic dilemma: the more he tries to get out of his situation of suffering, the more he gets involved in it. Tamkin diagnoses Wilhelm's condition correctly when he tells him there is lots of guilt in him and warns him not to be dedicated to suffering.

The details that Bellow provides about Wilhelm's psychophysical condition at forty-four assume a clear Reichian pattern. When he was a young man, before his first mistake, Wilhelm's body bespoke his health: "Wilhelm had the color of a Golden Grimes apple when he was well, and then his thick blond hair had been vigorous and his wide shoulders unwarped; he was leaner in the jaws, his eyes fresher and wider; his legs were then still awkward but he was impressively handsome" (17). His present disfigured and armored condition needs to be treated and dissolved. Reich divides the human into seven armored segments— ocular, oral, neck, chest, diaphragmatic, abdominal, and pelvic. In *Seize the Day* Bellow refers to the four upper armor rings of Wilhelm's bodily system.

Wilhelm's problems are directly visible and emotionally expressed in these four regions. Bellow disguises the Reichian symptoms in unobtrusive modes of behavior which appear to be quite natural to Wilhelm. The symptoms to look for in the head and neck are: a slight indication of the facial expression of a suckling infant, a wrinkling of the forehead, a hasty, jerky way of talking, a certain way of holding the head to one side, of shaking it, etc. After recalling how he had disappointed his mother, Wilhelm drinks his Coca-Cola as if he were a baby at a bottle: "He swallowed hard at the Coke bottle and coughed over it, but he ignored the coughing, for he was still thinking, his eyes upcast and his lips closed behind his hand" (15). On his forehead there is "a wide wrinkle like a comprehensive bracket sign" (6). His movements are jerky; he continually keeps nodding his large head, and he stammers and talks in staccato bursts and in exclamation marks. His troubles are indeed inscribed on his anxious face.

It is in the region of the chest, the central part of the muscular armor, according to Reich, that Wilhelm experiences severe pains. His breathing is highly irregular: he either pants like a dog, or else draws and holds a long breath in an effort to control his feelings. He retracts his heavy shoulders (biophysical extensions of the chest segment) and draws his hands up into his sleeves, gestures that denote the attitude of holding back. More significant, he suffers from a continuous feeling of strangulation, choking, and congestion all through the day.[6] When his problems assert themselves, and when he thinks about his father, the energy within kicks at his armor and his body proclaims its pain: "He pressed his lips together, and his tongue went soft; it pained him far at the back, in the cords and the throat, and a knot of ill formed in his chest" (14). After the angry exchange with his father at the breakfast table, Wilhelm suppresses his rage and feels the tightening pressures of his armor: "He was horribly worked up; his neck and shoulders, his entire chest ached as though they had been tightly tied with ropes" (55–56). Any inhibited aggressive impulse, according to Reich, directs the energy toward the musculature of the peripheral extremities, where it becomes manifest. With sly humor, Bellow suggests that even Wilhelm's hair registers the expansion of this energy: it "twists in flaming shapes upward" (50) and rises "dense and tall" (53) when he is angry. The energy manifests itself clearly in the warm panting laugh (the oral segment) that issues from him throughout the day,[7] and is also seen in his wide, gray, circular eyes that are so oddly expressive (the ocular segment).[8] It displays itself at moments when Wilhelm controls the rage that boils furiously within him: "His face flamed and paled and swelled and his breath was laborious" (48). That is why Wilhelm is not a good actor.

Nor does he worship in the way of the world, for his troubles are not purely psychosomatic. Bellow heightens the significance of Wilhelm's tragic day by giving it a religious dimension. For the day is a secular Yom Kippur, the most solemn holy day in the Jewish calendar, THE DAY according to the tractate of the Talmud. It is not, as some critics have suggested, literally the eve of Yom Kippur (which always occurs in early fall). Tommy Wilhelm's day, which takes place in early summer, is a metaphorical Yom Kippur.

Unlike his father, who has completely renounced his Jewish faith, Tommy Wilhelm still retains a faint vestige of his Jewish essence despite discarding the outer forms of orthodox ritual and worship. He does not go to the synagogue, but he does pray in his own manner. He does perform certain devotions—he visits the grave of his mother every year—according to his feelings. On this day, Tommy Wilhelm will symbolically participate in the liturgical services of the Day of Atonement, and begin a new year and a new life.

Yom Kippur is a day of complex significance. It occurs at the end of a ten-day period that begins with Rosh Hashanah and marks the beginning of the Jewish new year. It is a day of self-scrutiny and remembrance, when every Jew has solemnly to contemplate his past conduct, repent, and resolve to improve himself in the future. It is a day of inner cleansing and self-purification, a day of confession, prayer and atonement. The twenty-four-hour service of the day begins in the evening with the *Kol Nidre*, resumes early at dawn, continues throughout the day, and culminates at dusk. The whole day is spent by orthodox Jews at the synagogue, where penitential prayers are said, confession is made, and memorial prayers recited for the dead. It is a day of the affliction of the soul, but not a day of mourning. For at the end of the day one turns away from evil to the path of righteousness.[9]

Wilhelm's secular synagogue is the upper Broadway triangle where he enacts symbolic rituals and performs the rites of the day. Bellow provides a clue to the religious dimension of the day when old Mr. Rappaport abruptly asks whether Wilhelm has reserved his seat at the synagogue for Yom Kippur to say *Yiskor* for his parents.[10] Unlike his father, who cannot remember the year of his wife's death, Tommy Wilhelm says his *Yiskor*—the service to remember and pray for the dead—throughout the day, continually recalling his dead mother, remembering how he had disappointed her, remembering her warning that he would destroy himself in Hollywood, feeling guilty that he cannot afford to repair the broken bench next to her grave. All through the day, he summons into memory the ten critical mistakes of his past, among them the decision to go to Hollywood (his first mistake), the changing of his name, his elopement and marriage, the investing of his savings with Tamkin (his final mistake). It is his day of reckoning and truth. He confesses his sins and is aware of the need for forgiveness: "You had to forgive. First, to forgive yourself, and then general forgiveness" (30). And Wilhelm prays. He prays that he may find a way out of the world's business. He even addresses a prayer to God for help:

> "Oh, God," Wilhelm prayed. "Let me out of my trouble. Let me out of my thoughts, and let me do something better with myself. For all the time I have wasted I am very sorry. Let me out of this clutch and into a different life. For I am all balled up. Have mercy." [26]

Wilhelm's cries of sorrow, his prayer for forgiveness and mercy, his fervent plea that this "clutch" of vexatious problems be untangled, and that he be led into a different way of life will be heard at the end of his day. The different levels of his greatly damaged being—the physical, the psychological, and the spiritual—will be treated and the healing process will begin. It will be a day of release, when Wilhelm will suffer a breakdown, a complete dissolution of his armored condition. Reich states that a breakdown of personality is inevitable and necessary before a new personality can develop: "There is no other way to get to health than through the complete revelation and experience of the ill smelling, blocked off, sequestered realm of the self. And to do so, to have to face this humiliation, one gets worse instead of better on the approach to health" (SW, 465). The structural thrust of *Seize the Day* is toward the moment of dissolution. All through this terrible day—"This has been one of those days, Margaret. May I never live to go through another like it" (111)—Tommy Wilhelm experiences the surge of the energy within him as it hurls itself repeatedly against his armor. On this day, too, the cumulative assaults of the world outside become so overpowering and insistent that Wilhelm is on the verge of utter collapse. This day will also mark the end of Yom Kippur and the ushering in of a new year and a new life. Finally, this day of truth and discovery will see the end of Dr. Tamkin's therapeutic treatment. Tamkin says: " 'As a matter of fact you're a profound personality with very profound creative capacities but also disturbances. I've been concerned with you, and for some time I've been treating you' " (72–73).

The mysterious Dr. Tamkin is a fascinating creation, a protean figure who assumes a variety of roles that shift and dissolve as he swindles Wilhelm, educates him about the real business of life, propels him to the last of the Yom Kippur rituals, and finally vanishes just before the moment of Wilhelm's rebirth. Tamkin's literary progenitor is surely Melville's confidence man, who also plays a number of shifting roles and teaches a bitter wisdom about the human condition. Tamkin owes part of his fictional existence to Yellow Kid Weil, a real con man of Chicago, one of the many who haunted Bughouse Square in front of the Newberry Library. Fascinated by these self-appointed pundits and pseudo philosophers, Bellow has written two short stories about them, and also published an interview, laced with irony and admiration, with the Yellow Kid, "one of the greatest confidence men of his day."[11] Dr. Tamkin also springs from the tradition of the zaddik, the Hasidic leader and teacher who helps man in times of need, and then suddenly disappears.[12] Tamkin is also a kind of Reichian who utters Reichian truths and hastens the release of the pent-up energy within Wilhelm. According to Bellow, Tamkin is the most interesting character in *Seize the Day*, with whom he wishes he had done more.[13]

Tamkin continues the line of teacher figures that help the Bellow protagonist discover his true self and his humanness. Joseph, who finally realizes that he had not done well alone, had the help of that vague abstraction, *Tu As Raison Aussi*. Augie March tells us about all his reality instructors, including his most important teacher, Mintouchian. Dr. Tamkin is a more complex version of the enigmatic Allbee, who propels Asa Leventhal to a kind of truth and then abruptly disappears.

None of the other characters can quite understand Dr. Tamkin. Dr. Adler, who immediately senses that he is a threat to his world, warns his son that Dr. Tamkin is a con man, a cunning operator whom he shouldn't trust. A charming talker, Dr. Tamkin knows and talks to everyone in the hotel and at the brokerage office. But Wilhelm cannot figure the guy out: "Funny but unfunny. True but false. Casual but laborious, Tamkin was" (66).

Our first view of Dr. Tamkin is in the dark lobby of the Hotel Gloriana under the dusky, yellow indirect lights. He is an amazing apparition:

> The indirect light showed the many complexities of his bald skull, his gull's nose, his rather handsome eyebrows, his vain mustache, his deceiver's brown eyes. His figure was stocky, rigid, short in the neck, so that the large ball of the occiput touched his collar. His bones were peculiarly formed, as though twisted twice where the ordinary human bone was turned only once, and his shoulders rose in two pagoda-like points. At mid-body he was thick. He stood pigeon-toed, a sign perhaps that he was devious or had much to hide. The skin of his hands was aging, and his nails were moonless, concave, clawlike, and they appeared loose. His eyes were as brown as beaver fur and full of strange lines. [62]

The physical details about Dr. Tamkin are significant. The skull and hands betray his age, but we are never told how old he really is. His body and his bones convey an impression of deformed strength. The nose, eyebrows, and mustache give him an air of deceptive distinction. The eyes, brown as beaver fur, and his clawlike nails, tell of his kinship with the fierce animal world. Wilhelm is disturbingly aware of Dr. Tamkin as a bird of prey: "What a rare, peculiar bird he was, with those pointed shoulders, that bare head, his loose nails, almost claws, and those brown, soft, deadly, heavy eyes" (89–90).

What Wilhelm does not realize is that the fantastic Dr. Tamkin does not belong to the Broadway world of money and success. The hypnotic eyes fail Dr. Tamkin at times, and the face takes on a look of foolishness. He appears to be at home at the stock exchange, but is not really part of it. Like Wilhelm, he is a failure not a success. He, too, suffers. He is a better actor, but his mask slips occasionally. Wilhelm sees nervous fear and humility, at times the look of a dog, written upon Dr. Tamkin's face. Tamkin sweats blood when he signs the check for three hundred dollars. Bellow provides many clues to suggest that Wilhelm and Tamkin are kin. Both are pigeon-toed and related to animals, Wilhelm to the domesticated variety, Tamkin to the predatory. Both dislike water and neglect to wash themselves. Above all, their names proclaim their kinship, for both names, Tommy and Tamkin, are diminutives of Thomas, a name that means "the twin."

At moments when he is not a con man and a teller of impossible tales, Tamkin confesses to being a teacher and healer. His special mission, he tells the uncomprehending Wilhelm during breakfast, is to introduce people to the real universe and show them how to seize the day: "Bringing people into the here-and-now. The real universe. That's the present moment. The past is no good to us. The future is full of anxiety. Only the present is real—the here-and-now. Seize the day" (66). Tamkin's message is partly derived from Blake, who bewailed the fact that man is so obsessed by the past and preoccupied with the future that he fails to surrender to the magic, living, present moment. Later, during lunch, Tamkin daringly announces that his real calling is to be a healer: " 'I get wounded. I suffer from it. I would like to escape from the sicknesses of others, but I can't. I am only on loan to myself, so to speak. I belong to humanity' " (95).

Tamkin flaunts himself as a psychological poet, one who has studied the "ultimates of human and animal behavior, the deep chemical, organismic, and spiritual secrets of life" (69). His hotel room is full of various kinds of books, among them the volumes of Korzybski, Aristotle, Freud, and W. H. Sheldon. Carol M. Sicherman has pointed to the ironic juxtaposition of Aristotle and the non-Aristotelian, Korzybski, and of Freud with the violently anti-Freudian, Sheldon.[11] This juxtaposition of the trivial and the profound in Tamkin's collection parallels the mishmash of jargon and wisdom that pours out of him. Mr. Perls is right when he characterizes Tamkin as both sane and crazy. Bellow deliberately does not allow the narrative angle to shift to Dr. Tamkin's point of view in order to create an aura of mystery about him.

Tamkin, "the confuser of the imagination" (93), both attracts and repels Tommy Wilhelm. Irritated by the pretender, the "puffed-up little bogus and humbug" (95), Wilhelm is drawn to the Tamkin who talks about the deeper things of life. The psychological jargon that Tamkin uses about spontaneous emotion, open receptors, and free impulses makes no impact on Wilhelm, who is also highly suspicious of the fantastic stories Tamkin spins out about his adventures and about the patients he has treated. The here-and-now exercises (Bellow parodies here the techniques of Gestalt thereapy[15]) that Tamkin uses in order to demonstrate how Wilhelm should calm himself, have no effect for Wilhelm is back in the past brooding about his wife.

Wilhelm feels profoundly moved only when Tamkin tosses out bits of advice and wisdom that touch his inner being. They happen to be fragments of Reichian insights which Tamkin has made part of his vocabulary and repertoire as a conman-psychologist, despite the fact that no books by Wilhelm Reich can be seen in his collection. Wilhelm is unmoved when Tamkin twice uses the word "background" (66), a significant term in Gestalt theory, but is impressed when Tamkin uses the Reichian term, "plague" (63, 64), defined as "the neurotic character in destructive action on the social scene" (DO, 360).

Wilhelm's Reichian education into the human condition begins at the breakfast table with Tamkin's cryptic analysis of the two souls that reside in the human breast, the real soul one is endowed with, and the pretender soul that the societal mechanism produces: "The interest of the pretender soul is the same as the interest of the social life, the society mechanism," says Tamkin (70). The two souls, the one that merely needs love, and the false one, that loves money and success, are in incessant conflict, each trying to destroy the other. The real soul has to eradicate the pretender that has taken root within. But it is the pretender soul, that actor, that is usually the killer: "Biologically, the pretender soul takes away the energy of the true soul and makes it feeble, like a parasite. It happens unconsciously, unawaringly, in the depths of the organism" (71). Tamkin forces Wilhelm to realize that this world is, if not a kind of hell, at least a purgatory, where a strange drama takes place, "the human tragedy-comedy" (72).

Wilhelm immediately responds to Tamkin's analysis of the human condition. In Tommy, the name he shifted to after his decision to become an actor, he sees the pretender that longs for fame, money, and success. His real self, uncontaminated by the pretender, was present when he was Wilky, the name his father used for him as a child. And, Wilhelm suspects, it existed in a purer state at the time when his grandfather called him Velvel, a name which in Hebrew means "wolf."

Tamkin's insight into the human condition, which Wilhelm instinctively feels is right, springs from the sociological concerns of Reich, who thought that the vast majority of human beings suffer from a character neurosis because of the "*sharp conflict between natural demands* and certain *social institutions*" (SW, 103). The world of business and money makes brutal demands on the individual and is the cause of the "social tragedy which has befallen the human animal for thousands of years" (SW, 309). "Money-making is aggression," explains Tamkin (69). Wilhelm is horrified at the idea that money is the world's business, and he wants to find a way out. His true self wants to know the real business of life, not the world's business. Reich elaborates in some detail about how money destroys the true soul:

Money-making as the content and goal of life contradicts every

natural feeling. The world required it and molded humans
accordingly, by bringing them up in certain ways and by placing them
in certain life situations. The chasm . . . between the demands of
nature and culture was present, in a different form, *within* people. In
order to be able to exist in this world, they had to fight and destroy in
themselves that which was most true, most beautiful, most their own;
they had to surround it with the thick walls of their character armor.
[DO, 160]

Tamkin's Reichianism is surreally clear in the strange poem he offers
Wilhelm. The title, "Mechanism vs. Functionalism/Ism vs. Hism,"
springs straight out of the pages of Reich. The introduction (which is
really an essay by Reich himself) to *Selected Writings* announces that
orgonomic functionalism is a way of exploring and dealing with the
living, a method of bringing "the human animal again into harmony with
his natural biology and with surrounding nature" (SW, 23). In opposition
to functionalism is mechanist thinking which cannot understand the
processes of nature.

The poem itself is a wonderful parody of romantic poetry in general
and of Blake and Emerson in particular, a mixture of claptrap (as
Wilhelm immediately realises) and wisdom. Beneath its absurd surface
(the outrageous rhymes, the archaisms, the pseudo-Blakean rhythms) is
the truth that man is part of nature and essentially great, if he would only
open his eyes and discover his own nobility:

> Look then right before thee.
> Open thine eyes and see.
> At the foot of Mt. Serenity
> Is thy cradle to eternity.

[75]

Tamkin explicates the poem insisting that it applies both to Wilhelm
himself and to the sick humanity that makes up this world. For Tamkin
sees Wilhelm as a representative of sick humanity. Wilhelm is one of
those poor human beasts who cry *de profundis* and make up the human
tragedy-comedy.

The poem is both a warning and a plea. The world of money and
mechanism destroys the real self: "The main idea of the poem is
construct or destruct." There is no ground between. Mechanism is *destruct.*
Money of course is *destruct.*" Instead, suggests Tamkin, one should not
tarry but seize the day, and surrender oneself to the processes of nature:
"Creative is nature. Rapid. Lavish. Inspirational. It shapes leaves. It
rolls the waters of the earth. Man is chief of this. All creations are his

just inheritance. You don't know what you've got within you. A man either creates or he destroys" (77).

The poem also allows yet another theme in *Seize the Day* to emerge, the need for man to return to the natural state. It prepares us for the vision that Wilhelm will "see" at the end. And it marks the climax of a course Tamkin has been giving Wilhelm on the great English poets, perhaps a kind of poetry therapy.

All through the day, Wilhelm, under the influence of Tamkin, recalls poems that moved him profoundly when he was an adolescent. He remembers lines from four poems—Shakespeare's seventy-third sonnet, Milton's *Lycidas*, Keats's *Endymion*, and Shelley's *Ode to the West Wind*—that voice the needs of his self and speak of natural, human experiences, suffering, love, death, and the healing influences of nature. Wilhelm has been preparing himself for the Blakean message that Tamkin's poem sends forth. The poem reminds one of the following lines from *The Everlasting Gospel* (d: 73–77):

> "If thou humblest thyself, thou humblest me;
> "Thou also dwell'st in Eternity.
> "Thou art a Man, God is no more,
> "Thy own humanity learn to adore,
> "For that is my spirit of life."

It urges Wilhelm to see his real self, its regal glory and greatness. In *Milton* (Plate 32: 30–31) Blake insists that man should explore his true self:

> Judge then of thy Own Self: thy Eternal
>   Lineaments explore,
> What is Eternal and what Changeable, and
>   what Annihilable.

Like the other Romantics, Blake recognized the intimate interconnectedness of man and nature.

The poem urges Wilhelm and sick humanity to return to nature and to accept its processes in order to be restored to health. Urban existence with its artificiality and its taboos, its fear of real life and its reluctance to accept death, its complete dependence upon technology, has cut man off from nature and from his own human self. Wilhelm feels that he doesn't belong to New York which he apocalyptically sees as "the end of the world, with its complexity and machinery, bricks and tubes, wires and stones, holes and heights" (83). He longs for the peace he enjoyed in the garden at Roxbury, where he had listened to the long, morning phrases of the birds. In New York, the only bird heard is an occasional pigeon. A helicopter flies over the city in a long leap, "light as a locust"

(74). The shining numbers that hum, tumble, and whir on the board in the brokerage office remind Wilhelm of a huge cage of artificial, mechanical birds and of a swarm of electrical bees. Unlike the other characters, however, unlike the tight-lipped Rubin, unlike the office manager who conceals his opinions of others, Wilhelm manages to cling to his human self. His unwillingness to hurt any man's feelings and his own vulnerable emotions suggest that he can turn back to the natural world that Tamkin sketches for him in bright, rhythmic images: " 'Nature only knows one thing, and that's the present. Present, present, eternal present, like a big, huge, giant wave—colossal, bright and beautiful, full of life and death, climbing into the sky, standing in the seas' " (89).

The last stage of Wilhelm's education, which began at the breakfast table, takes place during lunch in the cafeteria. Dr. Tamkin casually, subtly lets fall the idea that the symptoms of Wilhelm's neurosis (Wilhelm had earlier violently rejected the implication that his was a neurotic character) manifest themselves especially in his anxiety about what Margaret and his father think about him. Wilhelm begins to brood about his intense love for his parents, about his mother's death, and about the terrible possibility of losing his father. The father and father-surrogate react to Wilhelm's account of his emotional problems (Olive, whom he adores, is tired of waiting for a divorce; Margaret has turned the children against him; she demands money and refuses to give him a divorce) in different ways. Dr. Adler coldly warns his son that his behavior is not normal and advises him to get a lawyer to institute divorce proceedings. " 'Carry nobody on your back,' " he tells his son (55).

Dr. Tamkin, on the other hand, tosses out fantastic stories about how his own father, how his own wife, and how Mr. Rappaport tackled their emotional problems. Tamkin's father abandoned his five motherless children without a qualm to marry an opera singer. Tamkin's wife was an alcoholic suicide. Old Mr. Rappaport maintains two wives and two families. What Tamkin so cryptically suggests is that Wilhelm obey the life principle and follow his instincts: only then will he be able to rid himself of morbid guilt feelings. Wilhelm had complained to his father that he was completely in the dark about women and money. His emotional problems, especially with Margaret, arise out of his exaggerated masochistic feelings of guilt and his dedication to suffering. Tamkin warns Wilhelm that these feelings will lead to his destruction.

Wilhelm's education is now almost complete. Profoundly moved by some of the words of Tamkin, he has learned certain truths about guilt, suffering, nature and man's natural state, money, the societal mechanism, and the real and the pretender souls in man. The Bellow protagonist cannot accept such abstract truths unless they are inscribed on his being by sorrow and genuine suffering. Before Wilhelm can discover his true self and enact the real business of life, he has to undergo three ordeals that will purge and redeem his soul. At what point should I start over? he asks himself. He would like to postpone the moment of decision, and rushes across the street to discover his financial fate, ignoring the warning of an ancient fiddler who ominously says, "You!" Tamkin intervenes, deflecting Wilhelm from the brokerage office, directing him to seize the day and perform a pure deed by helping the blind Mr. Rappaport across the street. " 'Don't think of the market. It won't run away," says Dr. Tamkin (100). It is after this moment that Wilhelm's ordeals begin.

The lard and rye figures drop;[16] the electronic bookkeeping machinery closes him out; and Wilhelm realizes he is wiped out financially. The second ordeal ends when Wilhelm is finally and completely rejected by his father. His masochistic self now has no prop for its woes. The climactic and most excruciating ordeal occurs during the telephone call to Margaret. Her hard, merciless voice, which insists on money and refuses to yield even an inch, makes Wilhelm feel as if his very life were strangled within him. This ordeal marks the very limit of his capacity for endurance.

Crushed by these cumulative ordeals, Wilhelm rushes madly along Broadway, stupefied with pain and anger. He sees the apparition of Tamkin, as zaddik, under the canopy of a Jewish funeral parlor, calls wildly to him, and then finds himself moved forward by the pressure of the crowd into the chapel. It is here, in this dark and cool chapel with the blue star of David above, that Wilhelm finally seizes the day.

Bellow carefully prepares for Wilhelm's vision at the end. The different levels of meaning—Reichian, Blakean, Jewish—are no longer separable, but dissolve and coalesce into a brilliant finale. To achieve economy, Bellow makes use of the same four pungent, ironic images he had used earlier, but he now transforms and transfigures them.

On the Reichian level Wilhelm's cumulative ordeals lead to the dissolution of his character armor. The talk therapy provided by Dr. Tamkin did not have sufficient power to cause such a breakdown. Bellow had, therefore, to invent a dramatic process of therapy that would lead to the cure of his protagonist. He put together a strange process, one involving self-therapy and self-awareness (as his own therapist, Wilhelm is given Wilhelm Reich's first name), variations and parodies of Reichian therapy, and ordeals that lead to genuine suffering.

The dissolution of Wilhelm's armor begins in the lobby of the Hotel

Gloriana when he senses the first stirrings of the energy within him, and becomes aware that his routine is about to break up and that "a huge trouble long presaged but till now formless was due" (4). He feels a "knot of ill" form in his chest. All day long tears from deep within approach his eyes, but he does not let them flow. Bellow allows his protagonist to indulge in a comicoserious form of self-therapy at the breakfast table. Wilhelm's choking of himself is comically grotesque, but it is also the Reichian "gag-reflex"[17] which induces the vomiting of emotions that are held back by neck armoring. The armor begins to loosen as Wilhelm's energy mounts steadily to its climax. After the lard figures drop and he knows he is wiped out financially, Wilhelm realizes that his pretender soul no longer has any sustenance to feed itself. He senses his unshed tears rising, wavelike, and, the narrator tells us, he looked like a man about to drown. He is in a state of panic, but he steels himself lest he break down and cry. This effort "made a violent vertical pain go through his chest, like that caused by a pocket of air under the collar bones" (104). After Wilhelm is rejected by his father he tries desperately to suppress the murderous anger and fury within him and experiences these emotions in physical terms: " 'Dad, I just can't breathe. My chest is all up—I feel choked. I just simply can't catch my breath' " (109).

Lacking a human agent who could act as a Reichian therapist, Bellow had to resort to a parody of a Reichian therapeutic device to stage the breakdown of Wilhelm's armored condition. Invented by Reich in 1940, the Orgone Energy Accumulator was a six-sided box that consisted of several layers of alternating organic and metallic material in which the patient sat and absorbed concentrated orgone energy. According to detractors of Reich, like Robinson and Rycroft,[18] it was shaped like a narrow telephone booth. It is in a telephone booth that Wilhelm's final ordeal takes place. With deliberate care Bellow sets down the details that indicate the furious upheaval within Wilhelm.

During the conversation with the hard and unyielding Margaret, Wilhelm at first breaks into a heavy sweat. As he reels under her verbal assaults, his voice (without his realizing it) begins to grow louder. It rises, the narrator tells us, and then, as Margaret notes, Wilhelm begins to rave and yell. His face expands and he feels suffocated as if he is about to burst. What he experiences in the booth is what he had demonstrated to his father, a form of strangulation that once again results in the "gag-reflex," which impels him this time to action: "He struck a blow upon the tin and wood and nails of the wall of the booth" (114). By focusing on such unusual detail about the makeup of an ordinary telephone booth, Bellow forcefully suggests that the combination of metallic and organic material (the tin and the wood) transforms it into an orgone box, while the pointed reference to the wood and the nails makes it into a kind of cross. Bellow's "orgone-box" is a parodic device, which has also to be regarded as an enclosure where Wilhelm, whose armor is in the process of breaking down and who is therefore porous, can be charged by the energy the box radiates. It is also a place where Wilhelm experiences genuine pain and suffering.

The energy now storms within Wilhelm so that he is driven to forceful action: "He struck the wall again, this time with his knuckles, and he had scarcely enough air in his lungs to speak in a whisper because his heart pushed upward with a frightful pressure. He got up and stamped his feet in the narrow enclosure" (114). The breathless condition, the upward thrust of the heart, and the violent stamping of his feet indicate that a tremendous churning is taking place within Wilhelm. So enraged is he that he yells loudly, grinds his teeth, and tries to tear the telephone apparatus from the wall "with insane digging fingers" (114) like an animal; an elderly woman is appalled by the distorted look on his face. The chest armor cannot be dissolved, according to Reich, without "liberating the emotions of raving rage, of intolerable longing and genuine crying" (CA, 379). Chest armoring usually occurs at the time of critical conflicts in a child's life. When this armor segment is dissolved, says Reich, traumatic memories of parental mistreatments and frustrations are summoned up.

Bellow offers a dramatic clue to the genesis of Wilhelm's chest armor by having Margaret refer to her husband's ravings as the howls of a wolf. " 'I won't stand to be howled at,' " says Margaret (114). Wilhelm now senses the truth of what Tamkin had told him, that the lonely person feels impelled to howl from his city window like a wolf when he cannot bear his loneliness any longer, especially when night comes. Reich links the child's excessive demands for love with the fear of being left alone which the masochist experiences intensely in very early childhood. The name Velvel (meaning "wolf"), which had grandfather called him, pointedly suggests the utter loneliness and lack of paternal love which Wilhelm now experiences and must have experienced as a child.

As he rushes out on to Broadway, significantly abandoning all his change in the booth, Wilhelm makes a number of resolutions: to divorce Margaret, to sell the car and get money for his needs, to return to Olive and her love. He will change his relationship with his father, though he is not sure how: " 'As for Dad—As for Dad' " (115). These resolutions continue the Yom Kippur level of the novella. For, on the Day of Atonement, one resolves to change one's ways and walk along the path of righteousness.

All the rhythms, themes, and images that Bellow has been working with converge in the last scene of *Seize the Day*. Wilhelm steps out of the moving line of visitors and stands next to the coffin amidst the lilies, the lilacs, and the roses. He gazes hypnotized at the dead man: "On the surface, the dead man with his formal shirt and his tie and silk lapels and his powdered skin looked so proper; only a little beneath so—black, Wilhelm thought, so fallen in the eyes" (117). What Wilhelm sees in the coffin is not a mere corpse, but his lifeless pretender soul, that actor, decked out for burial. Wilhelm begins to weep, softly at first, and then loudly and compulsively.

Wilhelm's weeping is the last and most complex of the Yom Kippur rituals he performs. He weeps for the dead man before him, another human creature. He weeps his *Yiskor* for his father, whose "corpse" he had seen laid out on the table a little while earlier. His grief amplifies, for this is a "huge funeral" (115) and here lies one of the "murderers" that Tamkin had talked about, one of the poor human beasts that cry *de profundis* and wring their hands, one of his brothers. He recalls his mistakes, his agonies, his children, Olive, Margaret, and in crying out, "Take, take it, take it from me" (117), he recites the last of his prayers. For he performs his *Teshuvah* (the post-biblical Hebrew term for repentance, derived from the verb *shuv*, "to turn" or "to return"). Wilhelm turns away from his sins and will return to the ways of righteousness.

The final ritual of the day of atonement is also the last stage of Wilhelm's Reichian therapy. For the sight of the dead man triggers a huge explosion within Tommy Wilhelm. An eruption takes place, the armor cracks completely, and tears, like lava, flow from the depths within: "The source of all tears had suddenly sprung open within him, black, deep, and hot, and they were pouring out and convulsed his body. . . . The great knot of ill and grief in his throat swelled upward and he gave in utterly and held his face and wept. He cried with all his heart" (117–18). What Wilhelm experiences is the Reichian throat spasm, the final stage in the dissolution of his armor. The tears and the cries and the sobs that well out of Wilhelm are the form the energy within him takes as it struggles painfully out of its black prison.

The last paragraph, a miracle of compression, flashes before us Wilhelm's moment of illumination and ecstasy:

> The flowers and lights fused ecstatically in Wilhelm's blind, wet eyes; the heavy sea-like music came up to his ears. It poured into him where he had hidden himself in the center of a crowd by the great and happy oblivion of tears. He heard it and sank deeper than sorrow,

through torn sobs and cries toward the consummation of his heart's ultimate need. [118]

Almost all the words and images in this paragraph, freighted with accumulated meaning, flow in unison to produce a feeling of transcendence. The *flowers* speak of the world of nature to which Wilhelm has to return. The *lights* are not those of the illuminated screen in the brokerage office, but the light of true knowledge. The *sea-like music* that pours into Wilhelm signifies his acceptance of the natural processes of life and death, which Tamkin had likened to a giant wave. The word *ecstatically* amplifies the ecstasy that Tamkin's poem promised Wilhelm would feel when he became aware of man's essential greatness. The *crowd* within which Wilhelm hides himself is the larger body of disfigured and lurid-looking egos that Wilhelm saw milling along Broadway and whom he had blessed as his brothers and sisters.

The image of sight, purged of its earlier ironic bitterness, suggests that Wilhelm, now no longer clown or victim, has become the "visionary animal" who knows why he exists. Unlike the lid-blinded, smoky-eyed worshippers of the false god, he can now see with his blind eyes, full of cleansing tears. Bellow shifts from the image of sight to the combined archetypal and Reichian image of water that is both a purifying agent and the abode of orgone energy. Money has contaminated and inflamed Wilhelm's inner self: "When I had it, I flowed money. They bled it away from me. I hemorrhaged money" (40). The chemically treated water of the swimming pool could not cleanse Wilhelm's being. What he needs are the healing waters of life and energy that spring from deep within him when the source of all tears opens.

The tears that flow are a form of the orgone energy that has been liberated. And this energy fuses with the primordial cosmic energy suggested by the sea-like music that pours into him to produce the vast oceanic feeling of submergence and drowning. All day long Wilhelm has had the sensations of a man about to drown. Reich tells us that masochists "cling to the rigid armoring of their movements and attitudes as a drowning person clings to a board" (*CO*, 229). Wilhelm finally lets go and experiences the Reichian vision of man emerging from the ocean of being and eternally returning to it. The waters of the earth roll over Wilhelm as he becomes aware of the fundamental unity between man and nature. The reader can now appreciate the unerring rightness of Bellow's allusion to Lycidas, who sinks beneath the watery floor, but who, at the end, mounts high through "the dear might of him that walk'd the waves." As he sinks beyond sorrow,[19] his experience becomes both religious and mystical. Words such as *consummation, ecstatically, lights,* and *oblivion* conspire with each other and, aided by the slow, deliberate, majestic rhythms of the whole paragraph, compel the reader to participate in Wilhelm's moment of *samadhi* and transcendence. A Reichian parable of hope for sick humanity, *Seize the Day* ends at the moment when the doors of perception fling open, and Wilhelm realizes his heart's ultimate need, a feeling of brotherhood and a love for all mankind.

NOTES

1. Saul Bellow, *Seize the Day* (New York: Viking Press, Viking Compass Edition, 1961), p. 39. Further page references to this edition are incorporated in the text.

2. Saul Bellow, *Mosby's Memoirs* (New York: Viking Press, 1968), p. 148.

3. Isaac Rosenfeld, *An Age of Enormity,* edited by Theodore Solotaroff, Foreword by Saul Bellow (Cleveland: World Publishing Co., 1962), p. 14.

4. Wilhelm Reich, *Selected Writings: An Introduction to Orgonomy* (New York: Farrar, Straus and Giroux, 1970), p. 145, hereafter cited as SW. Other works of Reich mentioned in the text are *Character Analysis* (third, enlarged edition; New York: Farrar Straus and Giroux, 1971), cited as CA; *The Discovery of the Orgone: The Function of the Orgasm* (New York: Noonday Press, 1970), cited as DO.

5. Originally published as an article in the *Internat. Zeitschr. f. Psychoanalyse* 18 (1932), "The Masochistic Character" is chapter 11 of CA. References to masochism can be found in almost every book by Reich.

6. References to Wilhelm's chest pains and congestion can be found on pp. 14, 36, 43, 46, 56, 76, 89, 91, 104, 109, 114, 118.

7. The references to Wilhelm's panting laugh are on pp. 9, 18, 20, 41, 65, 87.

8. Wilhelm's eyes are mentioned on pp. 12, 15, 17, 25, 31, 37, 81.

9. For the significance of Yom Kippur, see S. Y. Agnon, *Days of Awe* (Schocken Books, New York, 1948).

10. Mr. Rappaport is an odd figure whose character and function Bellow does not have the fictional space to develop. Older than Churchill, older than Dr. Adler, with sunken knees, shriveled pelvis, spotted face, and blind eyes, Mr. Rappaport is on the brink of death. He cannot "act" at all, but is still a persistent and an inveterate worshipper of the false god. Unlike Dr. Adler, he has a human dimension, his strange affection for Roosevelt, who had once yelled at him during the war. It is rather ironical that Mr. Rappaport, the Rockefeller of the chicken business, one who has amassed his wealth by the murder of millions of chickens, should be an orthodox Jew. He reminds Wilhelm, who has a strong aversion to the chicken industry, about Yom Kippur.

11. Saul Bellow, "A Talk with the Yellow Kid," *The Reporter* 15 (September 6, 1956): 42. See also my article, "Bellow's Confidence Man," *Notes on Contemporary Literature* 3, no. 1 (January 1973): 6–8.

12. Ralph Ciancio has explored the dimension of Tamkin as zaddik in his interesting article, "The Achievement of Saul Bellow's *Seize the Day,*" The University of Tulsa Department of English Monograph Series, no. 7, 1969, pp. 49–80.

13. Joseph Epstein, "Saul Bellow of Chicago," *New York Times Book Review,* May 9, 1971, p. 12.

14. Carol M. Sicherman, "Bellow's *Seize the Day:* Reverberations and Hollow Sounds," *Studies in the Twentieth Century* 15 (1975): 18.

15. See Sarah B. Cohen, *Saul Bellow's Enigmatic Laughter* (University of Illinois Press, 1974), p. 112.

16. It is significant that the lard figures drop before Wilhelm's Jewish essence can be renewed.

17. The gag-reflex is described on p. 375 of CA: "The armoring of the *third* segment is found

mainly in the deep neck musculature. . . . One has only to imitate the attitude of holding back anger or crying to understand the emotional function of the armoring of the neck. . . . The movements of the Adam's apple show clearly how an anger or crying impulse, without the patient's being aware of it, is literally 'swallowed down.' This mechanism of suppressing emotions is very difficult to handle therapeutically. *One cannot get with one's hands at the larynx muscles as one can with the superficial neck muscles*. The best means of interrupting this 'swallowing' of emotions is the elicitation of the *gag-reflex*. With this reflex, the wave of excitation in the esophagus runs counter to that occurring in the 'swallowing' of rage or crying. If the gag reflex develops fully or the patient even reaches the point of actually vomiting, the emotions which are held back by neck armoring are liberated" (italics mine).

18. That the orgone accumulator looked like a telephone booth is mentioned in Charles Rycroft, *Wilhelm Reich* (New York: Viking Press, 1972), p. 84, and in Paul A. Robinson, *The Freudian Left* (New York: Harper Colophon Books, 1969), p. 73.

19. In the original version of *Seize the Day* (*Partisan Review*, 23, Summer 1956) the final sentence of the novella is significantly different: "He heard it and sank deeper than sorrow, *and by the way that can only be found through the midst of sorrow*, through torn sobs and cries, he found the secret consummation of his heart's ultimate need" (italics mine). The words italicized, omitted in the final version, suggest that Bellow had in mind the need for Wilhelm to undergo genuine suffering before he could be redeemed.

Bellow considers 1959, when *Henderson the Rain King* was published, as the year when he achieved the fullest command of his powers.[1] *Henderson the Rain King* issues from a writer who has not only discovered a creative self authentically his own, but has also developed the technical ability to translate his unique vision into artistic form.

In dramatizing, once again, the quest for the human, Bellow does not hoard his creative valuables as he had done in *Seize the Day*, but spends them with lavish abandon. Unlike *Augie March*, *Henderson the Rain King* is under Bellow's perfect control. He can now tame the turbulent intellectual and literary forces within him so that they are obedient to the commands of his imagination. The quest is magnified into an odyssey. No longer confined to New York or Chicago, it takes place in the jungles of America and Africa. The protagonist descends into the heart of darkness and returns not with an awareness of horror, but with a radiant confidence in man and in human possibility.

Henderson seeks answers to the same questions about the significance of human existence and action that had tormented his brother protagonists. But his approach to them is strikingly different. Joseph, Leventhal, and Tommy Wilhelm were timid, passive questers, full of querulous complaint about the human condition. Augie, seeking his true fate, had bounced larkily through his adventures and obtained at the end an unearned awareness of the axial lines of life. Henderson is a huge, passionate, and vociferous seeker after wisdom. By creating a gargantuan clown as his protagonist, Bellow extends and enriches the quest for humanness. No longer is the search simple and straight-forward. No longer is it serious and solemn. Farce, wit, and humor combine to transform it into a tempestuous, rollicking, and glorious safari into the fundamentals of human life.

Henderson the Rain King insists on being hugely enjoyed before it surrenders its multitude of meanings. The reader needs to respond to the comic vitality of every incident and event. Farcical situations abound in the book. "DO NOT DISTURB" is the note that Henderson pins to the skirt of Miss Lenox, who has just died of a heart attack. Henderson wrestles with his Guarnerius and produces weird sounds: "And after all, I am a commando, you know. And with these hands I've pushed around the pigs; I've thrown down boars and pinned them and gelded them. So now these same fingers are courting the music of the violin and gripping its neck and toiling up and down on the Sevcik. The noise is like smashing egg crates".[2] Bellow uses comic juxtaposition to produce hilarious comedy. The African beauty, Mtalba, built like Mount Everest and clad in transparent violet trousers, dances and woos her bridegroom, Henderson, stronger than many bulls, who ignores her because he is busy, his huge head between his knees, concocting a bomb. The Wariri rain festival is a comic riot revolving around Henderson, the mad clown. He grips his chest and roars loudly, acknowledging the wild greetings of the crowd—very much like Khrushchev playing up to the gallery at the U.N.[3] After he lifts Mummah, he is stripped naked, dressed up in vines and leaves, and hurled into the mud of a huge cattle pond. At the end of the festival he is left standing in his earth costume "like a giant turnip" (171).

The wild humor of *Henderson the Rain King* erupts largely from Henderson's startling use of language, which has a comic range that stretches from sudden inflation to witty diminution. Some images are blown-up cartoons and huge caricatures. Henderson describes his face as "an unfinished church" (67). In another description it is a monstrous gargoyle: "My face is like some sort of terminal; it's like Grand Central, I mean—the big horse nose and the wide mouth that opens into the nostrils, and eyes like tunnels" (47). Henderson uses daring similes, strange metaphors, farfetched analogies. He looks down at the Nile from an airplane and describes the view thus: "The cataracts resembled seltzer" (236). On the lion hunt Henderson suddenly realizes that the king and he "didn't have so much as a diaper-pin" (247) with which to defend themselves. In a meaningful pun, he tells King Dahfu that Lily, his wife, is "the altar of my ego" (133).

This use of comic exaggeration and fantastic farce enabled Bellow to extend the dimensions of his fictional world. "Obliged to choose between complaint and comedy," Bellow said in an interview, "I choose comedy as more energetic, wiser and manlier."[4] By working in the hospitable and expansive mode of comic fiction, a mode used by Rabelais, Cervantes, Sterne, Swift, and Joyce, Bellow was able to give free rein to the powers of his imagination. He could now project the questions, problems, ideas, and concerns that haunted him. He could dissolve his tremendous learning into his fiction. In writing *Henderson the Rain King*, Bellow discovered the fictional form that could both accommodate and allow him to exploit his creative genius. Here, for the first time, he fulfilled his sense of destiny as an artist, and arrived at the "power in the novel" Kazin (in 1942) had sensed Bellow was heading toward.

Bellow's confidence in his fictional powers and in his creative vision reveals itself in the challenge he throws out to his fellow writers. No longer is Bellow timid as in *Dangling Man*, where he dismissed the style and stance of Hemingway. In *Henderson the Rain King* Bellow launches an attack against Hemingway with the missile of laughter. The Hemingway attitude to life is unmercifully pilloried and parodied. Bellow boldly tacks on the Hemingway initials, E. H., to the name of his protagonist. Henderson puts bourbon in his morning coffee from a big flask—and then spends the day on the beach smashing bottles with a plywood slingshot. He goes to the wilds of Africa armed with a powerful .375 H & H magnum rifle, but tamely surrenders it to the Wariri. Bellow pours ridicule upon the Hemingway mystique that hunting is a way of achieving grace: "Myself, I used to have a certain interest in hunting, but as I grew older it seemed a strange way to relate to nature. What I mean is, a man goes into the external world, and all he can do with it is to shoot it? It doesn't make sense" (82).

Not so comic or so barbed are the casual sideswipes at Salinger, Dreiser, and Henry Adams. Like Holden Caulfield, the protagonist of Salinger's *The Catcher in the Rye*, a novel immensely popular during the 1950s, Henderson affects a red wool hunting cap which he wears at all times and on all occasions. Holden wears his cap to proclaim his eccentric defiance of the hypocritical world he lives in; for Henderson, however, the cap merely keeps his head in one piece. Holden dreams of saving all the children in the world; Henderson merely pulls down the bill of his cap to hide his embarrassment when he hears the cries of the foundling his daughter, Ricey, brought home. Bellow also dismisses Henry Adams's nostalgia for a lost unity that can never be recaptured. Henderson visits the cathedral towns of France, where the religion and beauty of the churches enthrall him. But they do not satisfy the huge demands of his soul. He gets drunk in every one of the great cathedrals and at Chartres, home of Adams's Virgin, the symbol of medieval unity, Henderson threatens Lily with suicide. Bellow also rejects Dreiser's theory of social determinism. Henderson's visit to the aquarium at Banyules, where he stares at an octopus, deliberately echoes the opening of *The Financier*, where Frank Cowperwood fascinatedly watches a lobster gradually eat up a squid and learns the Darwinian law of human survival in this hostile world. The Brownian motion of the speckles of the octopus relays the same message of icy determinism to Henderson, who experiences a feeling of "cosmic coldness" (20) and flees the place in horror.

More basic is Bellow's total rejection of Eliot, whom he regards as the chieftain of the contemporary prophets of doom and despair. *Henderson the Rain King* is a massive counterblast against the fears of the apocalypse generated by *The Waste Land*. Against the mythic figure of the impotent, paralytic Fisher King, Bellow opposes the Rain King, an embodiment of power and motion. Before sending him to Africa, Bellow has Henderson parody an incident in Eliot's poem. On his way back from Providence, Rhode Island, Henderson plays solitaire not with a Tarot pack but with an ordinary deck of cards, which keep falling on the floor. Drunk and in despair, he keeps muttering helplessly: " 'There is a curse on this land. There is something bad going on. Something is wrong. There is a curse on this land' " (36). Bellow discards Eliot's explanation of the human predicament and also the solution that the later Eliot put forward. Henderson pokes fun at Eliot's Christian nightingale, whose message is that mankind cannot bear too much reality. But how much unreality can humankind stand? asks Henderson. " 'So what if reality may be terrible. It's better than what we've got' " (91). *Henderson the Rain King* gives us, among other things, Bellow's view of true reality.

Henderson the Rain King presents Bellow's intense dissatisfaction with the wasteland outlook of his generation. He vigorously opposes their bitter and jaundiced conception of human life by offering an independent interpretation of contemporary facts in the light of his own deep intuitions. The self is not dead, suggests Bellow, it can be redeemed. Man is not nothing, he can be something. Existence is not absurd, but marvelous. Civilization is not doomed, it can be transformed. Bellow does not present these truths in the mode of pontifical affirmations, nor does he couch them in the form of strained, abstract argument as he did in *Dangling Man*. Transformed in the magic crucible of Bellow's imagination, these truths shed their solemnity, don fantastic comic masks, assume weird disguises and clown postures, and pop up unexpectedly all through the novel.

Structurally, *Henderson the Rain King* can be divided into three parts. The first four chapters, which make up section 1, provide a chaotic summary of Henderson's life and set down the reasons that drive him to Africa. Section 2, chapters 5 to 9, narrates Henderson's adventures in Arnewiland, where he meets Queen Willatale and destroys the Arnewi water cistern. In the third section, chapters 10 to 22, which takes up two-thirds of the novel, Henderson becomes Sungo, the Rain King of the Wariri, is educated and treated by King Dahfu, after whose death he returns to America.

Section 1 initiates the major themes of *Henderson the Rain King* but skilfully camouflages their presence. What made me take this trip to Africa? is Henderson's opening question. The first four chapters supply the answer, which is a disorderly rush of nonchronological facts, strange incidents such as the death of Miss Lenox, bewildering pieces of information (Henderson and Lily both suffer with their teeth), and seemingly irrelevant detail (a thunderstorm begins at the exact moment when Lily and Henderson make love the first time). There is method behind this madness, however. The narrative madness is Henderson's; the fictional strategy is Bellow's. By making Henderson pour out his reasons for going to Africa in this crazy, tumultuous manner, Bellow achieves compression of and control over time. His technique is parallel in many ways to Faulkner's in the Benjy section of *The Sound and the Fury*. Benjy's monologue projects almost all the significant events in the Compson past. The first four chapters present the crucial moments that are needed to understand Henderson's past. What compels Henderson to go to Africa is not a mere whim, but the imperatives of a lifetime.

Section 1 plunges the reader into Henderson's predicament before the journey to Africa. Henderson is a giant of a man in a gigantic state of confusion. Six feet four inches tall, he weights 230 pounds (he weighed fourteen pounds at birth). His neck size is a formidable twenty-two. His face is enormous: it is almost as big as the entire body of a child (we are told later) and is half the length of another person's body. This gargantuan figure is also a millionaire, fifty-five, a successful breeder of pigs, intensely dissatisfied both with himself and with the world he lives in. He is always quarreling: he provokes fights with everyone he meets. He brawls and curses his way through life, weighed down with suffering and inexplicable misery. He knows that he "is considered crazy, and with good reason—moody, rough, tyrannical, and probably mad" (8).

Henderson is aware that he behaves like a bum and he senses, vaguely, what precipitates his mad antics. He has a contempt for the way he lives: that is why he, the sole heir of a famous name and estate, becomes a pig farmer. He bewails the fact that despite his famous ancestors and his name, Eugene, he is not really an aristocrat but a displaced person, occupying a position not rightfully his. He feels out of touch with nature whose beauty only intensifies his misery, and leads him to ask himself: so what am I doing here? Through Henderson's comic complaints about his plight, Bellow satirizes, on one level, the contemporary grievances about the loss of the self and of identity, and the fashionable clichés about alienation and inauthenticity. On another level, however, Henderson's despair is serious and genuine. Bellow presents this dimension of Henderson's suffering psyche in the form of a clamorous, insistent voice that arises from the turmoil in Henderson's heart. Every afternoon the voice tortures him with its savage, nagging, repetitious demand, I want, I want, I want. Everywhere he goes, through brawls, drunkenness, furious labor, this voice persecutes him but never reveals what exactly it wants. It is this ceaseless voice that drives Henderson to despair and makes him behave like a bum.

This voice, Bellow's central metaphor, unifies the major themes in *Henderson the Rain King*. The words that the voice speaks have been taken from *The Gates of Paradise*, the emblem book that Blake created in order to lead man to true vision. Plate 9 of this guide to Paradise shows us a man crying out at the foot of a long ladder that reaches up to the moon: "I want! I want!"[5] Henderson, Bellow suggests, is a Blakean pilgrim, mankind itself, caught in the grip of a boundless desire for a new and vital life. The voice is also a cry from the depths of Henderson's true being, a desperate plea for self fulfillment. "I have often thought," wrote William James, "that the best way to define a man's character would be to seek out the particular mental or moral attitude in which, when it came upon him, he felt himself most active and alive. At such moments there is a voice inside which speaks and says: '*This* is the real me!' "[6] Henderson's voice is also a seriocomic dramatization of the central premise in Reichian theory, a manifestation of the orgone energy which has been dammed up in Henderson and which now clamors for release. Finally, it is the voice of America itself, a Jeffersonian cry for the renewal and resurrection of the true spirit that had animated America in the past.

The amplitude of fictional space allowed Bellow to develop all these themes in copious detail. The lubricants of comedy and farce permitted him to shift with skillful ease from one thematic plane to another. The themes flow and dissolve into one another as one section leads to the next. Announced in section 1, they are developed in section 2, and they gather speed and momentum in the Wariri section, where they coalesce into a dazzling finale.

To sustain the simultaneous pressure of these interwoven, developing themes, Bellow had to create a protagonist whose outlines were fluid, not fixed. He had to invent a being who, at one moment is unmistakably real and at another, assumes a mythic dimension. Henderson is a twentieth century individual who, at certain moments, looms into Man himself. He is a human being who is magnified into a country.

Bellow establishes Henderson's factual reality by providing an abundance of detail that roots Henderson in twentieth-century America. Henderson is a Purple Heart veteran of World War II; he tramps about the streets of New York, a city he knows and loves; he is fifty-five; he divorced his first wife, Frances, in 1948; he has remarried and now has five children. Bellow even introduces topical allusions to reinforce the fact that Henderson is of this time and of this place. Henderson refers to Jimmy Walker, mayor of New York City, to Typhoid Mary, to the abdication of the Duke of Windsor. He has obviously seen *Some Like It Hot*, for when Lily asks him if he is studying music, he makes a joking reference to the opening sequence in that movie: " 'Well, if it isn't music then I'm in a gang war, . . . Because this case holds either a fiddle or a tommy gun' " (26–27). When making a bomb to rid the Arnewi cistern of the frogs, Henderson mentions an actual bomb-scare man who terrified New York in 1956–57 with his pipe bombs.

By using such wealth of factual detail, Bellow fixes the fictional thereness of Henderson but does not bind him to the realistic plane. He offers us a number of hints in the first section to suggest that *Henderson the Rain King* is a parable for the enlightenment of mankind. Henderson addresses his tale to "you people" (7), and insists that he has brought back living proof of something of the highest importance for all mankind. When Miss Lenox dies, Henderson tells himself to get out to Africa not merely for his own sake, but "for the sake of all" (37). At one moment, bewailing the sterile comforts of modern existence, Henderson makes a biblical allusion to the unclean spirits ready to attack both him and mankind: "All is swept and garnished. And who is in the midst of this? Who is sitting there? Man! That's who it is, man!" (24). Henderson is Man himself; his tale is a tale for all mankind.

That Henderson is also America is indicated first by his huge physical dimensions and his monumental appearance. He is indeed continentally large; more significantly, he contains multitudes. He is acutely conscious of the swirl of ancestral forces inside him that drives him to bursts of furious action: "Now, I come from a stock that has been damned and derided for more than a hundred years, and when I sat smashing bottles beside the eternal sea it wasn't only my great ancestors, the ambassadors and statesmen, that people were recalling, but the loony ones as well" (75). Proud of the martial blood that flows through him and of the service ideal that exists in the family, Henderson seems to have leaped straight out of the melting pot of American history. The founder of the family was a Dutch sausage maker who became "the most unscrupulous capitalist in America" (72); one ancestor fought in the Civil War under General Grant; Henderson's great-grandfather was Secretary of State, and his father was a famous scholar, a friend of William James and Henry Adams. Through Henderson flow the currents of American history including the very beginning of it all. "My ancestors," he confesses sadly, "stole land from the Indians" (22). Henderson, the millionaire, is truly a strange heir to a great estate, America.

Like America, he is an amalgam of contradictory forces. Violent, impetuous, a buffoon at times, restless—"From earliest times I have struggled without rest" (61)—he is also an idealist, childlike in many ways, a romantic who clamors for instant salvation. Henderson has to be seen as the embodiment of mid-twentieth-century America, bursting with vital energy, at the very peak of its prosperity. And yet, out of the depths of this America, comes a cry of intense yearning, I want, I want.

It is at the narrative moment when the voice that tortures Henderson and will not let him rest is introduced that the correlation between Henderson and America becomes unmistakably clear. The voice that springs from his harried American soul is the secret promise of hope and rejuvenation that was made when the Old World came to the New. But modern America with its technological routine, its nine-to-five business day, its dreams of material success has forgotten its original dream and has lost sight of the fresh, green breast of the new world that beckoned the Dutch sailors. The voice within torments Henderson and drives him to despair: "By three o'clock I was in despair. Only towards sunset the voice would let up. And sometimes I thought maybe this was my occupation because it would knock off at five o'clock of itself. America is so big, and everybody is working, making, digging, bulldozing, trucking, loading, and so on, and I guess the sufferers suffer at the same rate" (25).

The mythical motifs, the use of shifting planes, the blend of fantasy and farce, all make it abundantly clear that *Henderson the Rain King* is not so much a novel as an orbic romance (the phrase is Whitman's) in the American tradition, which Bellow continues and carries forward. It has obvious affinities with Mark Twain's *A Connecticut Yankee in King Arthur's Court*, with Melville's *The Confidence Man*, and with Mailer's *An American Dream*. Unlike *A Connecticut Yankee* and *An American Dream*, whose fictional surfaces are rough and highly uneven, *Henderson the Rain King* is a smooth fusion of realism and fantasy, like *The Confidence Man*. Bellow adopts the fictional strategy of having his narrator remind his readers, at various moments, that all travel is mental travel (a Blakean echo), and that his adventures happened as in a dream. *Henderson the Rain King* is the fictional version of a dream, a deliquescent medium in which disparate elements can be reconciled. To create an atmosphere of dreamlike consistency, Bellow had to invent a special language for his narrator.

Henderson the Rain King is a triumph of language. Augie March had spoken with a voice that sounded loud and confident, but was patently artificial; he was a mere mouthpiece for Bellow. Henderson's voice is authentically his very own. To produce this voice Bellow had to pierce through the outer layers of his protagonist, enter and take complete possession of Henderson's being. "When I was working on *Henderson the*

Rain King, I imitated Henderson around the farm. I went roaring at people, making scenes. It was one of the more trying periods," Bellow said in an interview.[7] Not only had Bellow to *be* Henderson, he had to discover a "language" for him, one that could capture the rhythms of Henderson's very soul. "The limits of my language mark the limits of my world," wrote Wittgenstein in the *Tractatus*. Bellow had to endow his narrator with a language commensurate with the immense sweep of Henderson's "world." Its vocabulary had to be far-ranging so that Henderson could speak of laughter and lions, of tears and madness, of trivia such as teeth and fundamentals such as love, suffering, reality, and nobility, of realistic details in America and of fantastic events in Africa. Bellow had also to achieve the right narrative pitch, one that would be in perfect tune with Henderson's inner being.

Bellow found it extremely difficult initially to create an exact voice for Henderson, with tones and inflections that would be unmistakably Henderson's own. Early drafts of *Henderson the Rain King*, published as late as in 1958, tell of Bellow's problems with his narrator. Here is a paragraph from the version published in *Botteghe Oscure*:

> We were conducted to a hut and left there alone without fire or meat or fruit. This was a strange sort of hospitality. We had been held since nightfall. It must now be nearly midnight. The village was in darkness, and all seemed asleep except for strange little stirrings of restlessness of, perhaps, savage customs of the night. Our armed escort went away and left us by this hovel of foul and old grass. And I am very sensitive about lodgings. But I wanted some supper. I had an anxious stomach, and with the annoyance of a broken bridge I rebelled at the thought of dry rations. I said to Romilayu, "We'll build a fire." He did not applaud the suggestion but I told him, "A little fuel, and get busy, too."[8]

Bellow rewrote this paragraph for the final version:

> We were then conducted to a hut and left alone. They set no guard over us, but neither did they give us anything to eat. There was neither meat nor milk nor fruit nor fire. This was a strange sort of hospitality. We had been held since nightfall and I figured the time now would be half-past ten or eleven. Although what did this velvet night have to do with clocks? You understand me? But my stomach was growling, and the armed fellow, having brought us to our hut, went away and left us. The village was asleep. There were only small stirrings of the kind made by creatures in the night. We were left beside this foul hovel of stale, hairy-seeming old grass, and I am very

sensitive about where I sleep, and I wanted supper. My stomach was not so much empty, perhaps, as it was anxious. I touched the shank of the broken bridge with my tongue and resolved that I wouldn't eat dry rations. I rebelled at the thought. So I said to Romilayu, "We'll build a little fire." He did not take to this suggestion but, dark as it was, he saw or sensed what a mood was growing on me and tried to caution me against making any disturbance. But I told him, "Rustle up some kindling, I tell you, and make it snappy." [114]

The difference between these two paragraphs is striking. The 1958 paragraph plods steadily along, its rhythms determined by sentences that are short and jerky. The words appear restrained and ill at ease. There is an abstract air about the details presented, especially the reference to the "savage customs of the night," a phrase that sounds as if it had strayed out of *Heart of Darkness*. The "I" lacks a distinct character for the words he uses are flat and colorless; even the command to Romilayu sounds unconvincing.

In complete contrast, the revised 1959 paragraph proceeds from one who is very much his own man. "Rustle up some kindling," "make it snappy," Henderson tells Romilayu not hesitating to use colloquialisms. "You understand me?" he rhetorically asks the reader, after referring daringly to the "velvet" night. The words, no longer held in check, flow easily along, freighted with abundant detail. Henderson's stomach, which had earlier merely been "anxious," is now both growling and anxious. The abstract "lodgings" is abandoned for the more specific "where I sleep." The sentences are no longer steady and regular, but vary their rhythms to convey the tensions and the excitement of the narrator.

The revisions that Bellow made in the process of composing *Henderson the Rain King* reveal his increasing involvement with his protagonist-narrator. Here are two versions of a paragraph describing Henderson's reactions when King Dahfu tells him about the rain festival. The 1958 paragraph runs thus:

Mischief! What a person to meet at this distance. Believe me, that the world is mind and all travelers mental travelers. I always had suspected so. What we call reality is our own pedantry. As we tread carefully our over-anxious ways, we see no blue silk, no purple velvet. The extraordinariousness of all experience, because our eyes are made sick by prudence, is withdrawn from us. But

That ocean where each kind
Doth straight its own resemblance find.[9]

Bellow rewrote this paragraph:

> I put my fist to my face and looked at the sky, giving a short laugh
> and thinking, Christ! What a person to meet at this distance from
> home. Yes, travel is advisable. And believe me, the world is a mind.
> Travel is mental travel. I had always suspected this. What we call
> reality is nothing but pedantry. I need not have had that quarrel with
> Lily, standing over her in our matrimonial bed and shouting until
> Ricey took fright and escaped with the child. I proclaimed I was on
> better terms with the real than she. Yes, yes, yes. The world of facts is
> real, all right, and not to be altered. The physical is all there, and it
> belongs to science. But then there is the noumenal department, and
> there we create and create and create. As we tread our overanxious
> ways, we think we know what is real. And I was telling the truth to
> Lily after a fashion. I knew it better, all right, but I knew it because it
> was mine—filled, flowing, and floating with my own resemblances; as
> hers was with *her* resemblances. Oh, what a revelation! Truth had
> spoken to me. To *me*. Henderson! [142]

The timidity of the 1958 paragraph, its hesitation and uncertainty, its
abstract solemnity, give way to the extraordinary vitality of the final
version. The reactions of Henderson remain more or less the same. But
the changes introduced—the exclamations with their ironic overtones,
the repetitions of "yes" and "create" to convey the nervous excitement of
the narrator, the introduction of American memories to maintain the
continuity of Henderson's past in the African present, the deliberate
avoidance of the abstract and the insistence on the concrete, the comic
mode of utterance that does not interfere with but reinforces the serious
slant of the passage, above all, the surgical excision of the two lines from
Marvell's *The Garden* (which sound raw and affected in Henderson's
mouth) while retaining the allusion to the poem by the use of the word
"resemblance"—all proclaim a novelist who is in complete control of his
narrator and the story he narrates.

Bellow makes Henderson speak a tongue that derives its supple
strength from a number of sources. The colloquialisms, which contribute
a comic pungency and an ironic raciness to the narrative, spring from
Henderson's roots in twentieth-century urban America. Attuned to the
idiom of city streets, especially the streets of New York, Henderson can
incorporate it into his speech. "I think after lunch my man and I had
better blow," says Henderson to King Dahfu (140). It is as if Henderson
had dropped in at a Connecticut neighbor's for a casual visit. The
colloquial "blow" sounds incongruous addressed to the royal Dahfu, who
uses highly formal speech; while the loosely specific "after lunch" is

comic in its context, the wilds of Africa. Terms such as "razz," "muff," "smooch," "cocksy-wursy," "snuckered" indicate that Henderson is in touch with the common man. But he is also a New England aristocrat, sensitive to beauty, educated, a soldier by temperament, a potential doctor. All these leanings of Henderson insinuate themselves into his language.

Henderson's language, like Henderson himself, is, to use the words of King Dahfu, "an exceptional amalgam of vehement forces" (228). Military and medical terms abound in his vocabulary. He quotes French, is thoroughly familiar with the Bible, knows Handel's *Messiah*, has read Homer and Darwin, can quote from obscure poems by Shelley and Clare, has done an enormous amount of reading in anthropology. "I am a nervous and emotional reader," says Henderson (205). His reading has been unsystematic. "As a matter of fact, I didn't know enough to read one single book" (206). Henderson is unlike Augie March, who parades his knowledge at every opportunity. His eclectic reading is precipitated into his language in the form of allusion. Bellow could thus introduce his own encyclopedic learning into the language he invented for Henderson. The language of *Henderson the Rain King* is rich with literary, mythical, and biblical allusions, all dissolved into the narrative flow. During the burning-bush episode, when the Arnewi children stand looking at him in silence, Henderson refers to himself as "reality's dark dream," a phrase out of Coleridge's *Dejection Ode*. Henderson immediately grasps and elaborates on Romilayu's biblical allusion to the Wariri as the children of darkness. "God does not shoot dice with our souls," proclaims Henderson, putting Einstein's saying, "God does not play dice with the world," to seriocomic use.

The range and resilience of the language of *Henderson the Rain King* cleverly disguise the ideas and therapeutic methods of Wilhelm Reich which pervade the novel and supply it with a structure. Henderson's condition, which is also the human condition, demands an exotic form of therapy. *Henderson the Rain King* is a detailed account of Henderson's peculiar illness, his frantic running around all through America and Africa seeking a cure, and his complete therapeutic transformation after he has been treated by the Reichian King Dahfu of the Wariri. Bellow adopts the fictional strategy of having the patient himself (who insists that the world's wrath has been somehow removed from him; who knows he suffers but doesn't know why; who realizes he has been cured but doesn't really know how) narrate the highlights of his journey to spiritual and physical health.

Henderson, like Tommy Wilhelm, is one within whose monumental self the orgone energy is dammed up and imprisoned. Henderson's energy, more furious and passionate than that of the passive Tommy Wilhelm, tries to blast itself out of the armor blocks that prevent its natural, spontaneous streaming forth. Clamoring for release, it manifests itself most strikingly in the form of the insistent voice that comically and tragically plagues Henderson with its irrational and reiterative demand, I want, I want, I want. It is the armored plight of Henderson that drives him to act in strange fashion. That is the secret of his tremendous but misguided strength. That explains his bursts of uncontrollable rage. That is why he suffers from a pressure in his chest.

Significant also are the hidden symptoms of his condition that spring from the same source. Death, even the idea of death, fills him with intense horror: the octopus at Banyules threatens him with death; the death of Miss Lenox terrifies him into thinking of the grave and of the annihilation that awaits him. Nature, instead of filling him with peace and joy, intensifies his misery: "The crimson begonias, and the dark green and the radiant green and the spice that pierces and the sweet gold and the dead transformed, the brushing of the flowers on my undersurface are just misery to me" (29). Strangely, he suffers from his teeth. Also, all through the first section, Henderson keeps referring to and recalling his father; the violin playing is his desperate attempt to reach out to his dead father; when he goes to France, he lives at Albi, where his father had done some research for a book on the Albigensians; he got his M.A. and he married his first wife, Frances, merely to please his father. Obviously, the relation to his father has something to do with his restless condition.

Henderson tries several remedies: violin playing, pig breeding, violent cursing and yelling, furious labor. None of these work. The only person who tames the demanding voice for a short while is his second wife, Lily. Bellow carefully and subtly establishes the importance of Lily, using her as an anchoring reference all through the novel. Henderson goes away from her to Africa, but it is to her that he returns finally. She is in his thoughts all through his experiences in Africa. Lily is the one who intuitively understands him, who knows he is the only man for her. " 'You ought to divorce your wife' " (12), she tells him at their very first meeting. Lily, unlike his first wife, is not surprised when he tells her he wants to enter medical school. With her painful teeth, her face with its pure white color that darkens toward the eyes, and the baking odor that arises from her during their lovemaking, Lily is the first person who can assuage the turmoil in Henderson's heart for a while. She is a Reichian without knowing it: " 'Maybe I'm not at all there and I don't understand,' she said. 'But when we're together, I *know*' " (20). Hers is a knowledge that proceeds from her love. But she cannot help

Henderson to wisdom, for she is neither a teacher nor a therapist. She tends to moralize: " 'One can't live for this but has to live for that; not evil but good; not death but life; not illusion but reality' " (18). All these truths Henderson will arrive at in Africa and perhaps that is why Lily does not object to his going there: " 'Maybe you ought to go,' she said" (38).

Bellow thrusts Henderson into the African experiences without wasting narrative time. Henderson accompanies Charlie, his childhood friend (both wear short pants), and his bride on their honeymoon to Africa. After three weeks of peace, he finds that the voice begins to torment him again. So he takes off with Romilayu, his African guide, who leads him to the Arnewi. The Arnewi and the Wariri, the second tribe that Henderson encounters, together with the landscapes that surround their villages, constitute the Africa wherein Henderson hopes to discover the fundamentals of human life.

Bellow's Africa is an esemplastic creation, a magic world spun into existence out of bits and pieces of his anthropological reading. Bellow had not visited Africa by 1959, and his imagination was at liberty to invent a special Africa, just as it had to produce a special language, for his protagonist. Henderson travels to the original place, as he puts it. Romilayu takes him beyond time, beyond history, beyond geography, to "the real past, no history or junk like that. The prehuman past" (42). The terrain they have to traverse just before they come to the Hinchagara plateau has a strange geological character: "The mountains were naked, and often snakelike in their forms, without trees, and you could see the clouds being born on the slopes. From this rock came vapor, but it was not like ordinary vapor, it cast a brilliant shadow" (42–43). Henderson senses that this village is of great antiquity, "older than the city of Ur" (44).

Here live a cattle tribe, the Arnewi, gentle and innocent as the cattle they raise and love. They are very like children: the men pipe on their fingers and the women play cat's cradle with a piece of string.[10] Their eyes have a circular frame of darkness (very like those of Lily), while the palms of their hands look like freshly washed granite. "As if," reports Henderson, "they had played catch with the light and some of it had come off" (47). The Arnewi are the children of light. They form a nonrepressive society in which neuroticisms are strikingly absent. The emotions are always freely released. When Henderson appears, a naked young woman leading a party of naked people bursts into tears and makes a public confession of their troubles. Love is openly declared. Violence is unknown. The wrestling match between Prince Itelo and

Henderson is merely the customary ceremony of acquaintance; when Itelo loses, he does not begrudge Henderson his victory but becomes his friend.

All these details about the Arnewi suggest that Henderson has reached the childhood of mankind. Arnewiland is beautiful and strange, the home of the original form of human society, before the first step toward culture and civilization. Bellow, who studied African ethnography with Professor Herskovits at Northwestern University, was aware of the quarrel among ethnological scholars about the historical development of primitive society. His creation of the Arnewi suggests that Bellow leans toward the ideas of Bachofen, Morgan, Engels, and Malinowski, who maintained that earliest society was characterized by the maternal line of succession, and that there was a gradual transition from general matriarchy to patriarchy. The mores of Bellow's Arnewi parallel in many ways those of the Trobriand Islanders of northwestern Melanesia studied by Malinowski, who discovered that the matriarchal organization of society among the Trobriands made for a free, natural, and healthy life.[11] The Arnewi are ruled by Queen Willatale, who is "not only a woman but a man at the same time" (66), a Bittah. Bellow comicalizes the matriarchal system as a form of Bittahness: Queen Willatale is both husband and wife to her people; the children call her both father and mother.

Bellow's treatment of anthropology in *Henderson the Rain King*, like his handling of Reichianism, is that of an artist, not a scholar. Professor Herskovits scolded him for writing *Henderson the Rain King*, saying that the subject was too serious for such fooling. Bellow countered by stating that his fooling was fairly serious.[12] He made creative use of what he needed from his anthropological studies discarding what he found irrelevant. He does not emphasize the sexual freedom of the Arnewi, but does show us that Mtalba, Queen Willatale's sister, is free to choose Henderson as her lover and husband. Prince Itelo defers to his aunts, the two Bittah sisters, but the fact that he has a number of wives suggests that the Arnewi form of social organization is in the process of being slowly transformed into the patriarchal system, which will include polygamy. Bellow drew upon *The Cattle Complex in East Africa* by Professor Herskovits and John Roscoe's *The Soul of Central Africa* for details about the Arnewi love of their cattle. The extreme reluctance of the cow-tribe to kill their beloved cattle for food, the extraordinary vocabulary range of cattle terms generated by the complete involvement with their cattle, the extreme grief displayed when a cow falls ill or is on the point of death: Bellow translates all these cold anthropological facts, borrowed from Herskovits and Roscoe, into vivid descriptive detail.[13]

Henderson's adventures in Arnewiland, a prelude to his more shattering experiences among the Wariri, are important for Bellow's strategy as novelist. They introduce and accustom the reader to Bellow's Africa and establish its fictional reality. The journeys of Prince Itelo and King Dahfu to Malindi and Beirut provide a plausible explanation for their knowledge of English and solve Bellow's problem of effecting communication between primitive and twentieth-century man. Romilayu develops in this section from a mere sidekick and travel guide into a foil to Henderson and his impulsive rashness. The Arnewi section also allows Bellow to elaborate on significant symptoms of Henderson's illness and to indicate the armor blocks that prevent the free flow of the orgone energy within him.

The Arnewi section reinforces the fact that Henderson has the build of a gnarled giant. He presents a strange appearance to Queen Willatale. Itelo interprets her reactions thus: " 'You weigh maybe a hundred-fifty kilogram; your face have many colors. You are built like a old locomotif. Very strong, yes, I know. Sir, I concede. But so much flesh as a big monument . . .' " (73). Henderson bewails his physical condition: "But the condition! Oh, my condition! First and last that condition!" (58) The sadness that weighs down upon him has made him physically tough and ponderous, so that his movements are sluggish and awkward. He refers to the different areas of the body and tells us how they react in times of stress and trouble. His pendulous belly is hard and tough. He butts the muscular Itelo with it during their wrestling match and knocks him down. When he is profoundly moved by Queen Willatale's words of wisdom, he feels the hardness of his belly melting and a strange pleasure resulting therefrom. Also, when he broods about his condition, he suffers from a recurring pressure in his chest: "This again smote me straight on the spirit, and I had all the old difficulty, thinking of my condition. A crowd of facts came upon me with accompanying pressure in the chest" (67).

Perhaps the most striking of Henderson's anatomical features in his huge, cartoon face, which he compares to Grand Central. Henderson's troubles, like those of Tommy Wilhelm, are written upon his face. His emotions proclaim themselves there: "Whole crowds of them, especially the bad ones, wave to the world from the galleries of my face" (49). In moments of stress and tension his face gets overheated and inflamed, his great nose (a Jewish joke, this) puffs out and reddens, and his jaws begin to swell.

In Reichian terms, Henderson is clearly an armored individual in dire need of orgone therapy. The basic task of such therapy is to destroy muscular armor, to reestablish plasma mobility, and to dissolve the attitude of holding back. In order to grasp the full force of this therapy, one needs to know the emotionally significant organs of the body. Reichian muscular blocks are not the same as individual muscles or nerves. Reichian therapy involves an understanding of the segmental structure of the muscular armor. The human body, as has been noted in the chapter on *Seize the Day*, can be divided into seven segments (ocular, oral, neck, chest, diaphragmatic, abdominal, and pelvic) separated by armor rings at right angles to the spine. The orgone energy streams longitudinally from the center of the organism along the body axis, but is inhibited by the armor rings that block the orgonotic stream. The orgonotic current flows from the tail end over the back to the head, and then runs backward over the chest and abdomen toward the genitals.

The therapeutic process starts with the progressive dissolution of the upper four armor rings (beginning with the ocular/oral rings) apparent to any observer and even to the patient himself. The lower three armor segments, the diaphragm, the abdomen, and the pelvis, are not readily accessible or obvious and are difficult to dissolve. Therefore, according to Reich, "since the body of the patient is held back and since the goal of orgone therapy is that of reestablishing the plasmatic currents in the pelvis, it is necessary to start the dissolution of the armor in the regions farthest away from the pelvis. Thus, the work begins with the facial expressions" (SW, 158).

Henderson's predicament and his pathologic symptoms now become a little clearer in the light of Reichian physiology. The life force within him has been trapped by segmental armor rings which have transformed his body into "a gross old human trunk" (61), into a "great pine whose roots have crossed and choked one another" (93). The abdominal ring is the cause of the hardness of his belly. His chest armor produces a pressure within him. "In certain patients," Reich writes, "we meet a syndrome stemming from the armoring of the chest which produces a particularly complicated system of difficulties. These patients complain, typically, of a 'knot' in the chest" (SW, 165–66). The face of Henderson, with its various colors, its mobility, its expressiveness, and its distortions, is the biological region where the energy, especially in the form of aggressive rage, manifests itself clearly.

Perhaps the easiest way to grasp the armored plight of Henderson is to contrast his character structure with that of Queen Willatale. According to Itelo, the queen has risen above ordinary human limitations. In Reichian terms, she has no pathological armor. With her smile, the happy light in her eye, the supple movement of her forehead, the stable harmony of her body, she breathes forth orgone energy: "Good nature emanated from her; it seemed to puff out on her breath as she sat smiling with many small tremors of benevolence and congratulation and welcome" (63). There is no ocular ring segment in her for she can furrow up "her brow in that flexible way peculiar to the Arnewi as a whole, which let the hemisphere of the eye be seen, purely, glistening with human intention" (72). Her heart is not in turmoil: when Henderson's hand is placed between her breasts as a form of greeting, he feels "on the top of everything else, I mean the radiant heat and the monumental weight which my hand received, there was the calm pulsation of her heart participating in the introduction. This was as regular as the rotation of the earth, and it was a surprise to me; my mouth came open and my eyes grew fixed as if I were touching the secrets of life" (63). Not only is she in harmony with her being, as a Bittah she is also in tune with the universe.

More mysterious and forceful in their impact on Henderson are the heat and power that radiate from Queen Willatale's middle. Henderson gives her a ceremonial kiss on her yielding belly:

> Then I kissed, giving a shiver at the heat I encountered. The knot of the lion's skin was pushed aside by my face which sank inward. I was aware of the old lady's navel and her internal organs as they made sounds of submergence. I felt as though I were riding in a balloon above the Spice Islands, soaring in hot clouds while exotic odors arose from below. My own whiskers pierced me inward, in the lip. . . . I drew back from the significant experience (having made contact with a certain power—unmistakable!—which emanated from the woman's middle). [65–66]

Twice Henderson experiences this strange power: "A second time my face sank in her belly, that great saffron swelling with the knot of lion skin sinking also, and I felt the power emanating again. I was not mistaken" (68). The power is, of course, orgone energy streaming through the genitals. According to Reich, "*genital excitation* is orgone energy pressing forward at the tail end" (SW, 349). In Henderson the flow of this energy is reversed when he is about to hurl the bomb into the Arnewi water cistern: "And meanwhile all the chemistry of anxious fear, which I know so well and hate so much, was taking place in me—the light wavering before my eyes, the saliva drying, *my parts retracting* [my italics], and the cables of my neck hardening" (93). Queen Willatale's orgone energy pours onto Henderson's armored condition and bestows temporary peace upon his soul: " 'Now please tell the queen for me, friend, that it does wonderful things for me simply to see her. I don't know whether it's her general appearance or the lion skin or what I feel emanating from her—anyway, it puts my soul at rest,' " he tells Itelo (71).

Queen Willatale is a Reichian who intuitively possesses the secrets of life but can offer Henderson only a few grains of wisdom. Bellow deliberately underplays her significance. Poised between Lily and King Dahfu, with the skin of a maned lion (the sworn enemy of her cattle tribe) on her back, with her two eyes, one live and brightly human, the other with a cataract, bluish white, communicating both humor and a sense of inwardness to Henderson, Queen Willatale is an embodiment of stability. "She was sustained," says Henderson (69). The queen calmly accepts the human condition, reconciled to its terror (the lion skin) and its beauty, to good and evil, to death and suffering and love, and to the plague of frogs. That is why, when Henderson speaks of troubles, she smiles "as steady as the moonlight at the bottom of a stream" (64). That is why she never moves, unlike Henderson who is always restless and in perpetual motion. Queen Willatale is, as Henderson states in the Wariri section, a Be-er, content merely to be.

Profoundly affected by the orgone energy of the queen, Henderson is confident that she will impart the wisdom he has been seeking. Bellow uses the strategy of repeating some of the problems that stung Henderson to comic fury in the first section. Henderson amplifies the Socratic demand of Joseph:

> Who—who was I? A millionaire wanderer and wayfarer. A brutal and violent man driven into the world. A man who fled his own country, settled by his forefathers. A fellow whose heart said, *I want, I want*. Who played the violin in despair, seeking the voice of angels. Who had to burst the spirit's sleep, or else. So what could I tell this old queen in a lion skin and raincoat (for she had buttoned herself up in it)? That I had ruined the original piece of goods issued to me and was traveling to find a remedy? Or what I had read somewhere that the forgiveness of sin was perpetual but with typical carelessness had lost the book? [67]

The paragraph illustrates Bellow's newly attained skill in the handling of ideas. The odd notation (the old queen buttoned up in a raincoat in the sweltering heat) and the comic extravagance of language disguise the urgent sincerity of the questions posed, whose seriousness is reinforced by the buried allusions to Shelley ("burst the spirit's sleep"), to Blake ("the forgiveness of sin was perpetual"), and to Peer Gynt ("that I had ruined the original piece of goods issued to me"). Henderson would like instant solutions to the problems of duty, happiness, solitude, and to the enigmas of death, brotherhood, and crime. He tells the queen that he undertook the journey to Africa for his health, but does not elaborate on the truth that he is searching for physical, psychological, and spiritual health. He complains that it is miserable to be human and to suffer all the ailments human beings are heir to. Man is a regular bargain basement of deformities. All Henderson's questions coalesce into one commanding question that he seeks to hurl forth: "So, in short, what's the best way to live?" (71)

Queen Willatale offers Henderson three significant truths: she gives him an insight into his own condition; she presents him with a cryptic message to decipher; and she reinforces his faith in mankind.

She tells him first, that he is a man who loves sensations: " 'You heart is barking' " (72). Sensation is a highly significant term in Reichian vocabulary. It is a human antenna, according to Reich, a tester of reality, a tool of natural research. This sensory apparatus has to be kept clean by continuous self-criticism and self-control. Only then can we "feel out, investigate, arrange, and understand ourselves and nature around us" (SW, 292). Henderson is a man of intense sensations; hence his quest for, among other things, reality. But his tool has become irrationally blurred. That is why he is not really in touch with reality even though he proudly announces to Lily that he is: " 'I know more about reality than you'll ever know. I am on damned good terms with reality, and don't you forget it' " (34).

Queen Willatale announces the second truth—"world is strange to a child" (73)—while clutching at her lion knot and simultaneously gazing at the peaceful palm leaves of her hut to prepare Henderson and to warn him about the profound ambiguity of her statement. Henderson begins with a true interpretation of this romantic truth, that all his decay had dated from his childhood. But he then takes off at a tangent equating the strangeness of life with the remoteness of death. "I was pretty proud of myself" (74), he tells us, as the Arnewi queen shakes her head softly. Perhaps admiringly, says Henderson, misreading the import of her gesture which suggests she disagrees with his interpretation.

The third truth, *grun tu molani*, "man want to live," is the Reichian "life function": the purpose of all life, animal and human, is just to live, to be. Henderson, like his brother protagonists, has always had this life principle within him. It is, in the Latin phrase, *aviditas vitae*. Comically raising his pith helmet to the queen and all her court, Henderson rejoices because the queen has reminded him of his great mission: " 'Not only I molani for myself, but for everybody. I could not bear how sad things have become in the world and so I set out because of this molani' " (74). Later, after putting together his bomb, Henderson, identifying himself as all mankind, proclaims his faith that man with his intense desire to live can never become an extinct species: " 'I am Man—I myself, singular as it may look. Man. And man has many times tricked life when life thought it had him taped' " (91).

It is not merely the Arnewi queen and the three truths she offers but the cumulative experiences in Arnewiland that affect Henderson: the wrestling match with Prince Itelo that supplies him with the romantic and Shelleyan desire to burst his spirit's sleep;[14] the golden radiance that the Arnewi village emits; Princess Mtalba with her demonstrations of love, her dancing in the bluish moonlight, and the poetry and enchantment of her wooing. All these experiences lead Henderson back into the world of his own childhood and remind him of a time of innocence when his spirit was alive and in touch with the sources of life. The soft, pink color that he sees on the wall of his hut is the same color that he had seen when he was five years old in the Adirondacks: "I *knew* that this place was of old" (88), exclaims Henderson, acknowledging the link between the Arnewi as the childhood of mankind and the glory of his own, forgotten childhood. He has a fleeting feeling of transcendence as he wakes up and sees the light at daybreak in Arnewiland: "Some powerful magnificence not human, in other words, seemed under me" (87).

The Arnewi experiences touch Henderson's being to the quick, but are not lasting enough to purchase him real wisdom. The Arnewi are good and generous, and Queen Willatale does have Vedantic serenity, but they are not capable of translating their wisdom into effective action. The incapacity to deal with the plague of frogs suggests certain limitations of the Arnewi approach to existence. Henderson, too, despite his recall of a moment of glory in his own childhood, has not changed enough to know how to act effectively.

The blowing up of the Arnewi cistern to rid it of the frogs is not a pure deed. Henderson does not see the frogs as harmless, little semi-fishes but regards them as vermin, buggers, bastards on whom he wants "to let fall the ultimate violence" (77). He would like to be hailed as a benefactor of the Arnewi. And therefore he lavishes all his blind will and ambition on the poor creatures. Also, Henderson labors under a sense of guilt in regard to his relation with animals. On the eve of his demolition of the Arnewi cistern, he recalls an episode that occurred just before he set forth for Africa when he tried to shoot a cat. Fortunately he missed, but he felt as if he had almost committed a deadly sin. Henderson finds himself "fatally embroiled with animals" (78) because he refuses to accept the bitter truth that Allbee compelled Asa to acknowledge, that the animal lodges deep within man.

Using Western technology and his own technical ingenuity, not the power within him, Henderson manufactures a bomb to blast out the frogs. The bomb destroys the Arnewi cistern and Henderson's hopes of learning wisdom from the Arnewi.

More than a geographical region, Waririland, like Arnewiland, is a real unreal world that Bellow created in order to stage the spectacular cure of his protagonist. The landscape changes its geological character as Henderson travels towards the Wariri. No longer golden and edenic, it is harsh and fiercely real: "Mesas and hot granites and towers and acropolises held onto the earth; I mean they gripped it and refused to depart with the clouds which seemed trying to absorb them" (97). In Waririland they see jumbled, white limestone rocks that must have, Henderson guesses, originated in a body of water. The landscapes of Arnewiland and Waririland spring from an obsolete geological theory that Bellow puts to fantastic use. According to the Neptunists, all rocks were precipitated from the water of the primordial universal ocean which held in solution great quantities of mineral matter. The first precipitate consisted of granite and hard rocks. Limestone, according to this theory, was a transitional rock formed by later crystallization. One can now understand why the Arnewi mountains were "naked" and why clouds are born on their slopes. The clouds in Waririland are separate from the earth and the limestone speaks of a later geological time.

Henderson sees diabolo-bodied ants and huge spiders with their nets like radar stations. The Wariri men are of smaller build than the Arnewi; their buildings are larger; their children, distinctly unfriendly. Waririland is not the "original place"; it represents an onward stage in the development of human civilization, a transition from the state of nature from which man emerged into that of culture. Bellow hints at this shift in societal forms by having King Dahfu refer to the legend that the two tribes were once one but had separated over the "luck" question. The matriarchal form of society has developed into a patriarchate with its stress on action, authority, and repressive control. Women are not dominant in Wariri society: even the Amazons are completely under the control of men. Polygamy is common: the Bunam, Horko, and King Dahfu have many wives. The queen mother of the Wariri, unlike Queen Willatale, is a mere figurehead. The natural and healthy state of the Arnewi has been replaced by a civilization full of discontents.

Henderson the Rain King is not, however, an ethnographical treatise. Having established the anthropological reality of the Wariri, Bellow was free to add further dimensions of meaning. Romilayu's biblical reference to them as "dem chillen dahkness" (99) compels the acknowledgement that these people are wise in the ways of the world. Shrewd and pragmatic like the unjust steward, they take advantage of every situation. They do not accept the myth of a curse or take upon themselves the responsibility for the lack of rain; they will compel the gods whom they take for granted to accede to their demands. They do not accept the processes of nature, but will harness nature and force it to do their bidding.

The Wariri, it is evident, are not merely a primitive tribe, but a paradigm of modern society. The towers and the acropolises and the radar stations prepare us for this dimension of meaning. The military character of their society, their use of cunning ambush and force, their crudeness and lack of hospitality impress Henderson forcibly. This is not the world of his childhood, but a world familiar to him as an adult, a cruel, chaotic world, full of suffering, violence, and injustice. Henderson discovers that Waririland is very much like a modern police state: he is kept waiting for hours before he is grilled by the Bunam, who is both police chief and high priest. Trials, hangings, and executions are commonplace in Waririland as the swinging corpses and the many skulls testify.

Composed of the elements of violence, mystery, terror, hostility, and suffering, the barbaric Wariri universe is the modern world in miniature, reduced to its essentials and then viewed through a distorting, fantastic, and comic lens. Henderson has not really escaped from modern civilization. He confronts its terrors and chaos in their purer form, unhampered and undeflected by the crushing demands for money that Tommy Wilhelm had to succumb to. His experiences with the Arnewi and the Wariri parallel those of Asa Leventhal, who is removed from his insulated, cocoon-like Arnewi existence and plunged into the Wariri realities of life by Allbee and the death of Mickey. The Wariri world is also the Hobbesian world where existence is "nasty, brutish and short," one that Joseph does not know how to account for. It is also the dark world which Augie is aware of but larkily refuses to succumb to.

The world of the Wariri is an alchemic fusion of Bellow's anthropological reading, his inventive skill and imaginative daring as novelist. For most of the physical details about the Wariri Bellow relied heavily on Sir Richard Burton's *A Mission to Gelele the King of Dahomey*.[15] He took over from Burton's travel-book details about King Gelele to create King Dahfu. Dahfu's garments (the knee-length purple silk drawers), the extraordinary devotion of his many wives, the Amazon guards, the colorful umbrellas, the ceremonial obeisances—all are based on Burton's portrayal of King Gelele and the royal levees he held. Bellow also transferred into Waririland many of the sights that Burton saw in the capital of Dahomey—the ubiquitous skulls, the corpses strung up by their feet, the gagged prisoner at the center of the town. All these cold Dahomean facts are ignited into vivid Wariri detail and event. Certain items taken from the travel book—the three brass-mounted skulls always set in front of King Gelele and the description of the king dancing with two leopard wives by his side—undergo a remarkable metamorphosis when translated into the novel. King Dahfu and a beautiful, tall woman do not dance but play a ballet-like game, tossing into the air skulls which have their brass fittings removed and purple and blue ribbons tied through the eye sockets.

To the details borrowed from Burton Bellow added other anthropological items that do not belong to the Dahomean scheme of things and yet blend together in fictional harmony. The practice of having the king strangled when he cannot meet the sexual demands of his many wives is one of the customs of the Shilluk tribe. Yet another anthropological item that is non-Dahomean is the *Fanany* myth, the notion that in the worm that emerges from a king's dead body the king's soul dwells. Bellow took this item from Roscoe's description of the royal burial customs of the Bahima, a cow tribe of Enkole. After the death of a Bahima king the body, wrapped in cowhide, is taken to Enzanzi, the royal burial place, a forest inhabited by lions. Here it lies in state for several days until the body decomposes and grubs form. The high priest then selects a large grub, which he takes into the forest and returns with a lion cub into which he affirms the grub has turned. The king lives in the cub, which is set free in the forest.

Despite the elements borrowed from Burton and Roscoe, Waririland has to be considered an original creation, a fictional universe summoned into existence by Bellow. He had to bring together the Dahomean and the Bahima worlds, and had also to elaborate on and improvise certain details that would all blend together. He extended the *Fanany* myth by introducing the custom of requiring the Wariri successor king to capture his lion father during a hopo hunt. He reduced the five-day barbaric festivities of the Dahomeans into a one-day spectacular rain festival. He also invented a political setup for Waririland. Instead of Gmilo, his lion father, King Dahfu has captured the lioness, Atti, who is regarded as a sorceress in disguise and an evildoer. The Wariri are split into two factions—the king's faction and that of the Bunam, who is high priest, police chief, and executioner. Bellow's Waririland is an imaginary world that is as fully realized in all its thick detail as Augie's Chicago and Tommy Wilhelm's upper Broadway triangle.

This far-ranging, chiaroscuric, and multileveled world is the fictional setting for the complete cure of Henderson's being, his body, mind, and soul. The cure is a continuous process but certain stages need to be distinguished. The first stage ends with Henderson's becoming the Sungo. His talks with King Dahfu and the imitations of Atti make up the second stage. The third, which begins with the hopo hunt for Gmilo, completes the cure of Henderson's mind and body, initiates the cleansing of his soul, and deposits him on the threshold of America, Newfoundland.

The Wariri exploit Henderson for their own purposes as soon as he enters their territory. They thrust him and Romilayu into a hut that houses the corpse of the ex-Sungo, strangled because he was no longer able to lift Mummah. Henderson's encounter with the corpse may appear remarkably similar to the initiation ordeal that the medieval hero had to undergo in the Perilous Chapel. But Bellow does not tack on such a dimension to this episode. He uses the event to further his plot, for Henderson can now assume the role of the Sungo. Also, the nocturnal adventures of Henderson with the corpse supply important clues to understand his psychological condition.

The powerful orgone energy within Henderson is apparently highly erratic in its working and in its manifestations, but a pattern is now evident. One begins to recognize the signals on Henderson's face when he controls the rage that boils within him. His face begins to contort and glower:

> This face, which sometimes appears to me to be as big as the entire body of a child, is always undergoing transformations making it as busy, as strange and changeful, as a creature of the tropical sea lying under a reef, now the color of carnations and now the color of a sweet potato, challenging, acting, harkening, pondering, with all the human passions at the point of doubt. . . . A great variety of expressions was thus hurdling my nose from eye to eye and twisting my brows. I had good cause to hold my temper and try to behave moderately. [112]

Any inhibited aggressive impulse, according to Reich, directs the energy toward the musculature of the peripheral extremities, where it becomes manifest. The suppressed wrath when Lily, against Henderson's wishes, goes for her portrait sittings, takes the form of a ferocious desire to "seize the whole building in my mouth and bite it in two, as Moby Dick had done to the boats" (105). Furious with anger when the Bunam keeps him waiting, he breaks one of the bridges of his teeth, and suffers pangs of anguish and despair. One can now understand the enigmatic references to teeth in the first section. The cold and aloof Frances has had all her teeth removed and porcelain teeth installed in her mouth. In contrast, Henderson and Lily both wear bridges and suffer intensely with their teeth. Teeth constitute the oral segment of the muscular armor. The breakdown of this segment marks the first stage of the dissolution of Henderson's armored condition.

Besides rage, Henderson also displays symptoms of anxiety and fear during the adventures with the corpse. These impulses, according to Reich, reverse the flow of the energy excitation so that the direction is toward the center of the organism. Under the stress of terror, Henderson's fever increases; there is a strain at the back of his neck and in his eyes, and he feels as if his nose will burst: "Dread and some of the related emotions will often approach me by way of the nose." When he sees the black corpse in the hut the orgonotic flow in Henderson beats back in wild fashion: "The entire right side of me grew stiff as if paralyzed, and I could not even bring my lips together. As if the strange medicine of fear had been poured down my nose crookedly and I began to cough and choke" (115).

On the day of the Wariri rain festival Henderson's energy gains momentum. He feels "a scratchy sensation in my bosom, a little like eagerness or longing. In the nerves between my ribs this was especially noticeable" (123). Profoundly stirred by his first meeting with Dahfu, Henderson accompanies the king to the rain-making festivities. The tingling eagerness in his bosom is aggravated as he acknowledges the greetings of the crowd with a magnificent roar. He sheds the role of a spectator as his fervor grows intense and intenser. He identifies with Turombo's efforts to lift Hummat. After Turombo's failure to raise Mummah, the fierce energy within Henderson asserts its imperatives in bodily signs. It is a burning, a craving, "a flowing estuary" (160): "I was excited to the bursting point. I swelled. I was sick, and my blood circulated peculiarly through my body—it was turbid and ecstatic both. It prickled within my face, especially in the nose, as if it might begin to discharge itself there. And as though a crown of gas were burning from my head, so I was tormented" (158).

It is at this moment of overwhelming desire that Henderson is propelled also by another force, the inexorable message of the Bunam. Bellow transposes the Bunam to another plane of fictional existence. No longer merely a witch-doctor, the Bunam with his "grim, exalted, vein-full, knotted, silent face" (159) and his "stare of wrinkled and everlasting experience" (159) transmits a message of practical wisdom to Henderson.

Intensify . . . what you are. This is the one and only ticket—inten-sify. Should you be overcome, you slob, should you lie in your own fat blood senseless, unconscious of nature whose gift you have betrayed,

the world will soon take back what the world unsuccessfully sent forth.
Each peculiarity is only one impulse of a series from the very heart of
things—that old heart of things. The purpose will appear at last
though maybe not to you. [159]

Here is rational advice relayed by one wise in the ways of the world. This
"silent speech of the world" (159) demands that Henderson intensify his
sense of individuality and perform the task assigned to him by nature. It
insists that he accept his inevitable fate as a human unit, as a mere part
of the blind evolutionary process, whose meaning and purpose he cannot
know.

Impelled by these powerful stirrings within his body and his mind,
Henderson lifts Mummah, the female power, a wooden Queen Willatale,
an abode of orgone energy, an alive old woman who "was a living
personality, not an idol" (163). After he lifts her an explosion bursts
through Henderson's armor blocks:

> I stood still. There beside Mummah in her new situation I myself
> was filled with happiness. I was so gladdened by what I had done that
> my whole body was filled with soft heat, with soft and sacred light.
> The sensations of illness I had experienced since morning were all
> converted into their opposites. These same unhappy feelings were
> changed into warmth and personal luxury. . . . I have also known a
> stomach complaint to melt from my belly and turn into a delightful
> heat and go down into the genitals. This is the way I am. And so my
> fever was transformed into jubilation. My spirit was awake, and it
> welcomed life anew. Damn the whole thing! Life anew! I was still alive
> and kicking and I had the old grun-tu-molani. [163–64]

Henderson's feat of lifting and carrying Mummah causes clouds to
form in the windless sky. Here is no African mumbo-jumbo but a direct
consequence of cosmic orgone engineering. Bellow's creative magic is in
evidence here. The rain-making ceremonies seem to belong to a
primitive Africa and may appear to have been derived from Bellow's
anthropological reading, but they are in fact a vivid and comic
dramatization of the Reichian method of "cloud-busting" and rain
making.

"One may create clouds in the cloud-free sky," writes Reich, "in a
certain manner, by disturbing the evenness in the distribution of the
atmospheric OR energy; thus clouds appear upon drawing energy
from the air" (SW, 444). Cosmic orgone potential always flows from a
weak or low system to a strong or high one. At Orgonon, Reich's home
and research laboratory in Rangeley, Maine, he caused long hollow

pipes to be aimed at the cloud-free sky in order to draw off OR energy: "The OR charges are drawn (not into the ground but) into WATER, preferably into *flowing* water of brooks, flowing lakes and rivers. We draw into water since the attraction is greater between water and OR energy than between other elements and OR energy. Water not only attracts OR speedily but it also holds it, especially in clouds" (SW, 442).

The Reichian principles behind some of the Wariri rain-making rituals, behind priming the pumps of the firmament, as Dahfu puts it, now become clear. It is obvious why Henderson is flung into the cattle pond. He has increased the OR potential of the Wariri region and therefore clouds are drawn toward Waririland. Bellow indicates that Henderson is a Reichian "hollow pipe" by making Henderson describe the peculiar shape the rain clouds assume, those "colossal tuberous forms" (170). "And meanwhile the sky was filling with hot, gray, long shadows, rain clouds, but to my eyes of an abnormal form, pressed together like organ pipes or like the ocean ammonites of Paleozoic times" (169). Even more clear now is the magnetic interaction, almost sexual in character, (there had been thunder, lightning and rain when Henderson and Lily made love the first time) between the cosmic and the individual orgone energies:

> Under the thickened rain clouds, a heated, darkened breeze sprang up. It had a smoky odor. This was something oppressive, insinuating, choky, sultry, icky. Desirous, the air was, and it felt tumescent, heavy. It was very heavy. It yearned for discharge, like a living thing. . . . I felt like Vesuvius, all the upper part flame and the blood banging upward like the pitch or magma. [169]

Bellow carefully disguises the Reichian dimensions of the rain-making rituals by dissolving them into the fast pace of the narrative. Henderson's voice takes on a rising urgency, a frenzy, a wild comic dismay, after the lifting of Mummah. He thinks he has done the Wariri a favor, but discovers that he is now trapped and an integral element in the barbaric Wariri universe, the rain king with the title of the Sungo. The Wariri gaze at him with "all the darkness, all the expectancy, all the wildness, all the power, of their eyes" (165). They strip him of the meagre trappings of civilization (his helmet, his Bermuda shorts, the travel-stained jockey underpants) and dress him up in vines and leaves before making him run with them through the lanes of their town. The rhythms of the language with its pauses, its many commas, its syllabic shrieks, its short, staccato beat, enact the hectic hurry of their movements:

Everybody began to yell, "Sungo, Sungo, Sungolay." Yes, that was me, Henderson, the Sungo. We ran. We left the Bunam and the king behind, and the arena too, and entered the crooked lanes of the town. My feet lacerated by the stones, dazed, running with terror in my bowels, a priest of the rain. No, the king, the rain king. The amazons were crying and chanting in short, loud, bold syllables. The big, bald, sensitive heads and the open mouths and the force and power of those words—these women with the tightly buttoned short leather garments and swelling figures! They ran. And I amidst those naked companions, naked myself, bare fore and aft in the streamers of grass and vine, I was dancing on burnt and cut feet over the hot stones. I had to yell, too. Instructed by the generaless, Tatu, who brought her face near mine with open mouth, shrieking, I too cried, "Ya—na—bu—ni—ho—no—mum—mah!" [167–68]

Henderson's mind too is in a state of frenzy as he makes a desperate attempt to summarize his achievements, past and present, his terrible condition, and then hurls a deliriously comic prayer to the gods above:

Yes, here he is, the mover of Mummah, the champion, the Sungo. Here comes Henderson of the U.S.A.—Captain Henderson, Purple Heart, veteran of North Africa, Sicily, Monte Cassino, etc., a giant shadow, a man of flesh and blood, a restless seeker, pitiful and rude, a stubborn old lush with broken bridgework, threatening death and suicide. Oh, you rulers of heaven! Oh, you dooming powers! Oh, I will black out! I will crash into death, and they will throw me on the dung heap, and the vultures will play house in my paunch. And with all my heart I yelled, "Mercy, have mercy!" And after that I yelled, "No, justice!" And after that I changed my mind and cried, "No, no, truth, truth!" And then, "Thy will be done! Not my will, but Thy will!" This pitiful rude man, this poor stumbling bully, lifting up his call to heaven for truth. Do you hear that? [168–69]

That is why the final act of the ritual, the savage whipping of the Wariri gods, the general scourging inflicted on everyone, including himself, so horrifies Henderson. Unlike the Arnewi, who accept what the gods send, the Wariri compel their "gods" to do their bidding. The gods know us, King Dahfu tells Henderson (171). For it is only after the gods are "beaten" that there is a thunderclap, a blast of wind, and the deluge. Modern man, to use the words of Joseph, has "assassinated the Gods" in himself and equipped himself with a strange power.

The explosion of Henderson's orgone energy does wonders for the Wariri, but is only the first step for Henderson. His spirit is awake, he tells the king, he has recovered his old *grun-tu-molani*. But he has not yet reached his depth and requires elaborate therapy that only King Dahfu can provide. Bellow blends together the physical appearance and trappings of King Gelele of Dahomey, the passionate convictions of William Blake, and the strange, daring theories of Wilhelm Reich to produce a magnificent creation, a powerful figure who threatens to run away with the novel's meaning.

What Henderson says about King Dahfu is surely what Bellow thinks of Wilhelm Reich: "And it is possible that he lost his head, and that he was carried away by his ideas. This was because he was no more dreamer but one of those dreamer-doers, a guy with a program. And when I say that he lost his head, what I mean is not that his judgment abandoned him but that his enthusiasms and visions swept him far out" (198). Reich was a revolutionary thinker and psychoanalyst whose ideas are now being taken seriously. A brilliant eccentric, he tossed around original concepts and insights almost in the way King Dahfu played, quite seriously, with the skulls of his ancestors during the rainmaking ceremonies.

Reich began as a disciple of Freud but modified and later abandoned Freudian theory to announce new and daring discoveries derived from his psychotherapeutic practice, clinical observation, and scientific explorations. In the 1920's he developed his method of character analysis and set down his technique and his findings in *Character Analysis* (1933), which contains rich psychological material: it defines character as "essentially a narcissistic protection machine" (CA, 158); it sets forth the technique of analysis; it describes the formation of character and the process by which the character armor can be loosened and dissolved; it presents different clinical character types (the hysterical, the compulsive, the phallic-narcissistic, the masochistic character forms); it distinguishes between the genital character and the inhibited neurotic character; and it establishes the therapeutic goal as the liberation of psychic energy and the attainment of orgastic potency.

In the 1930s Reich moved swiftly away from depth psychology and character analysis. Convinced of the inseparability of the psyche and the soma in man, he developed the technique of "vegetotherapy," a method of working simultaneously on the psychic and the somatic apparatus in order to liberate the vegetative energy trapped within the organism by muscular rigidity. But he was not happy with the term "vegetative": it was a correct term in German, he wrote, but made one think of vegetables in English.[16] His difficulties were solved with the discovery in 1939 of orgone energy, the specific life energy that is a physical reality and that flows through both man and nature.

It was the aim of orgone therapy, a term which after 1939 subsumed both character analysis and vegetotherapy, to free this bioenergy from the muscular blocks within man. To achieve this goal words and language were completely abandoned during the therapeutic process: action was substituted for talking, and there was often dramatic interplay between the patient and his biotherapist. Reich advocated a slow dissolving of the biophysical armor. Massage was frequently used, rigid muscles were stimulated, and breathing exercises, especially expiration, were insisted on. At times Reich would indulge in violent mimicry of a patient's behavior in order to force a response and a breakthrough: "I would imitate his attitude. I began to use his infantile language. I lay on the floor and kicked and yelled as he did. At first he was surprised, but one day he began to laugh, in an absolutely adult and unneurotic way; a breakthrough, although only temporary, had succeeded" (CA, 225).

Reich's discovery of orgone energy propelled him to Dahfu-like enthusiasms and far-reaching visions. He was fired with the dream of transforming man and human society and even the very universe in which man lived. He advocated experimental orgone therapy for the treatment of cancer. In 1940 he invented the orgone-energy accumulator. In the early 1950s he wrote about orgone physics and about cosmic orgone engineering. He performed experiments to show how the inorganic could be transformed into the organic: the forms of transition were known as bions or energy vesicles blue in color. In 1952 he demonstrated that it was possible both to create clouds and to destroy them to produce rain. Perhaps the most sweepingly ambitious of his ideas was one parallel to the concept of Atman equals Brahman of the Upanishadic thinkers: "THE SAME ENERGY WHICH GOVERNS THE MOVEMENTS OF ANIMALS AND THE GROWTH OF ALL LIVING SUBSTANCE ALSO ACTUALLY MOVES THE HEAVENLY BODIES" (SW, 289).

It was a stroke of genius that led Bellow to create King Dahfu as the very embodiment of the ideas of Wilhelm Reich. He had to put together a fabulous (Henderson's word) figure that could minister to the gigantic needs, desires, and questions and to the terrible ailments of his equally fabulous protagonist. For Henderson, even more than Tommy Wilhelm, is sick humanity that demands a doctor even more fantastic than the fantastic Tamkin.

Bellow endows King Dahfu with a great deal of charm, nobility, and vigor. To give him a human dimension and to hint at a slightly eccentric Reich, Bellow gives the king a name that has suggestions of "daftness." Unlike Henderson, King Dahfu has orgone energy that flows naturally and easily through his body. He is the greatest of the Reichians in the novel and Bellow, in a suggestive paragraph, brings in the other two to highlight the fact that only Dahfu could be Henderson's doctor as well as his teacher:

> Like all people who have a strong gift of life, he gave off almost an extra shadow—I swear. It was a smoky something, a charge. I used to notice it sometimes with Lily and was aware of it particularly that day of the storm in Danbury when she misdirected me to the water-filled quarry and then telephoned her mother from bed. She had it noticeably then. It is something brilliant and yet overcast; it is smoky, bluish, trembling, shining like jewel water. It was similar to what I had felt also arising from Willatale on the occasion of kissing her belly. But this King Dahfu was more strongly supplied with it than any person I ever met. [176–77]

King Dahfu is Bellow's translation into the living, the human, and the concrete of Wilhelm Reich's abstract statement about the genital character: "Purely from the point of view of appearance, sexual charm goes with a relaxed musculature and free-flowing psychic activity. The rhythm of the motions, the *alternation* of muscular tension and relaxation, combines with modulation in speech and general musicality; in such people one also has the feeling of immediate psychic contact" (CA, 348).

The numerous details about King Dahfu now gain added significance. His figure is elegant; he is always sumptuously at rest; he breathes deeply and watches events with impervious calm; he moves with powerful grace during the skull-tossing game as he "ran and jumped like a lion, full of power, and he looked magnificent" (148); his voice is hypnotic and reminds Henderson of the hum of a New York power station; above all, Dahfu gives Henderson the impression that they could "approach ultimates together" (132). His face proclaims that he is not an armored individual: it slopes forward, it isn't held back; his eyes are "huge, soft, eccentric" (143), unlike Henderson's tunnel-like eyes, and they gleam with a soft light; there is a continuous smile on his lips which are large, red and tumid; and on his head, says Henderson, hair did not grow, it lived. Henderson immediately senses the difference between his own condition and that of the king: "He seemed all ease, and I all limitation. He was extended, floating; I was contracted and cramped. The undersides of my knees were sweating. Yes, he was soaring like a spirit while I sank like a stone" (136). It is this regal creature who will transform Henderson into a new man.

The therapeutic process by which Henderson is treated is the climactic core of the novel, the section in which Bellow's creative energy asserts itself triumphantly. The therapy sessions are totally farcical and uproariously funny: Henderson being investigated by the lioness—"I felt her muzzle touch upward first at my armpits, and then between my legs, which naturally made the member there shrink into the shelter of my paunch" (188); Henderson, whose vocal cords "seemed stuck together like strands of over-cooked spaghetti" (224), trying to roar like a lion; Henderson clumping and pounding along trying to imitate Atti's graceful leaps but sinking flat on his hard belly. Bellow allows his imagination to go for broke and indulge in comic horseplay. Reichian technique is turned topsy-turvy. Character analysis, vegetotherapy, and orgone therapy jostle against each other as they are put to strange use. Reich's fantastic action therapy is made even more fantastic by having a lioness as therapeutic agent. And the effects of this therapy are wonderfully strange. Beneath the riotous surface of the narrative, however, is Bellow's subtle control over the stages of Henderson's transformation.

Henderson's transformation is also mental, a change of perspective. The talk sessions with King Dahfu propel him towards illumination. Bellow can now handle ideas with perfect ease. Having conjured up an entire world, he places therein two characters both intensely real and substantial. King Dahfu and Henderson do not exchange ideas: they talk passionately about the essentials of life. Not mere mental posturings, their views spring from the deep recesses of their being. They think what they think because they are what they are.

Bellow carefully establishes the underlying similarities between King Dahfu and Henderson who immediately become friends. They make a pact of understanding and mutual trust. The king is thoughtful but, unlike Frances, does not make thinker's faces. Henderson realizes that the king is a "genius of my own mental type" (183). That is why they can "approach ultimates together" (132). Both have asked the same fundamental questions about human existence. Henderson used to have great confidence in understanding, but he now realizes: " 'Figuring will get me nowhere, it's only illumination that I have to wait for' " (172). The king has arrived at some answers, not by way of the mind but by way of intuition: he had a "hunch about the lions; about the human mind; about the imagination, the intelligence, and the future of the human race" (198).

Henderson comes to King Dahfu with a swarm of problems that torment him. Bellow cleverly allows Henderson to release these questions in piecemeal fashion. Henderson asks some of them in America; he would like Queen Willatale to answer others; more questions spring to his mind when he is examined by the Bunam. They all add up to the major questions that Western civilized man from Socrates to Sartre has asked in the course of his history.

So what am I doing here? Why is it miserable to be human? Do human beings have to live by the laws of suffering and decay? What is reality? Since existence is odious, is life absurd? Are we nothing but instruments of the world's processes, parts of the evolutionary mechanism? Why is man always in a frenzy of motion, always in a state of Becoming? Why can he not achieve Being? Should man be terrified of death? And finally, what's the best way to live? Joseph, Asa Leventhal, Augie March, and Tommy Wilhelm had asked some of these questions but had arrived at timid and tentative solutions.

King Dahfu cannot and does not provide Henderson with the answers to all these questions, but does put him on the track to wisdom. Henderson himself, like Joseph with his belief that it is marvelous to be alive, is equipped with beliefs that allow him to respond to the insights that King Dahfu offers. Henderson believes in Lazarus and like Allbee, in the possibility of resurrection and regeneration for man. He believes that "chaos does not run the whole show" (149). Human life is definitely not "a sick and hasty ride, helpless, through a dream into oblivion" (149). Like John Pearl in *Dangling Man*, Henderson holds that art is one way of meeting chaos.

King Dahfu lays down two important conditions that Henderson has to accept. First, one has not to make terms with life, but accept its conditions and the terrible fact that the world is not consistent and that no man can make it consistent. In fictional terms, the scientific and medical education of King Dahfu has to be accepted along with the Bunam and the skulls and the amazons. Henderson has to accept what Leventhal was finally reconciled to, that in many ways human life is "a shuffle, all, all accidental and haphazard" (TV, 248). Secondly, Henderson has to be prepared for truth to arrive unexpectedly in a form he does not anticipate.

The king begins Henderson's education by asking him to accept a basic law of human nature—that man is a creature of revenges. Man, according to King Dahfu, unlike animals, cannot stand still under blows; he always insists on vengeance and transfers the blows to others. Dahfu pounces on a truth that Bellow picked up from his studies in anthropology, a truth that vaguely brushes Leventhal's mind as he responds to the harsh sunlight on his way to Staten Island, that the inhuman is implanted in every human being. "In many respects," says William James in *Psychology*, a book King Dahfu refers to, "man is the most ruthlessly ferocious of beasts."[17] According to Dahfu, everybody feels those "prime-eval" blows. For James, ferocity is the primitive attribute of human nature, one that is blind and can only be explained from *below*.

Henderson counters this reading of human nature by urging that there are people who can rid themselves of this burden of wrath and return good for evil. The king agrees making a daring prediction that the human species as a whole will slowly, but ultimately evolve toward goodness. The noble will have its turn in this world, says King Dahfu. To achieve nobility, however, more is required than *grun-tu-molani*, the mere will to live which Henderson has accepted.

Dahfu's prediction thrills the core of Henderson's being. Spell-prone and mediumistic as he is, he responds instinctively and extravagantly to the king's faith in mankind. According to ancient Hindu tradition, the guru is found only when the pupil, the *shishya*, is ready for him. The first talk session with King Dahfu casts a magic spell on Henderson: "I was blazing with fever and mental excitement because of the loftiness of our conversation and I saw things not double or triple merely, but in countless outlines of wavering color, gold, red, green, umber, and so on, all flowing concentrically around each object. Sometimes Dahfu seemed to be three times his size, with the spectrum around him. Larger than life, he loomed over me and spoke with more than one voice" (182). The poetical extravagance of Henderson's language, not undercut by any irony, the halo of flowing colors, the shifting voices and shapes of King Dahfu, all suggest that Bellow had in mind the striking manifestation of the Lord of the Universe that is vouchsafed to Arjuna in the *Bhagavad Gita:* "Wearing the crown and bearing the mace and the discus, a mass of splendor radiating on all sides, I see you—hard to gaze at—all around me, possessing the radiance of a blazing fire and sun, incomprehensible"[18] The divine Krishna, in guise of a charioteer, teaches Arjuna, the human soul, philosophical wisdom and arouses him from deep spiritual despondency just before the great battle of Kurukshetra.

King Dahfu is not divine, but there is, Bellow implies, a divine element in truly great men, like Plato and Einstein, that can lead their fellow human beings onward. As teacher, King Dahfu is not rational or systematic. His daring theories hit Henderson below the belt, so to speak, of his intellect. According to Reich, word language and concepts cannot penetrate the pathological depth forms of expression. To understand one's condition intellectually is not enough. What Henderson needs is a savage and dynamic form of therapy.

King Dahfu's lion therapy proceeds from his belief that human material now groaning under the burden of fear and wrath can be transformed. Man, that prince of organisms, that artist of suggestions, can, like Vishnu, churn the elements of wrath within him and become a new man. He can be taught, nourished and enriched by the animal heritage he has abandoned.

Bellow combines the ideas of Wilhelm Reich with those of William

James for the process of psycho-somatic conversion that King Dahfu so passionately believes in. Wilhelm Reich's clinical character forms are obviously the basis for King Dahfu's comic catalogue of deformed character types that now prevail on earth: " 'The agony. The appetite. The obstinate. The immune elephant. The shrewd pig. The fateful hysterical. The death-accepting. The phallic-proud or hollow genital. The fast asleep. The narcissus intoxicated. The mad laughers. The pedantics. The fighting Lazaruses' " (184). Reichian concepts are scrubbed clean of jargon and presented in lay terms: "Disease is a speech of the psyche" (200). "The spirit of the person in a sense is the author of his body," is an idea that springs out of James's *Psychology* (200). King Dahfu's statement about " 'the flesh influencing the mind, the mind influencing the flesh, back again to mind, once more to the flesh,' " (199) is a free and easy rendering of the Reichian idea of the indissoluble organic unity of the psyche and the soma. It is also a Jamesian concept. Dahfu, of course, takes the idea to a comic, impossible extreme by maintaining that a " 'pimple on a lady's nose may be her own idea, accomplished by a conversion at the solemn command of her psyche' " (200).

The strange theories of King Dahfu, like the fantastic therapy sessions, confuse Henderson. He reads some of the literature that the king offers him in his own erratic fashion and presents a rough summary of the king's views. Bellow deliberately does not allow the king to explain and clarify his ideas about the mechanism of conversion. Ideas, according to Bellow, do not provide the way to health. And the ideas of King Dahfu appear to be eccentric and blurred. "It is possible," says Henderson, "that he lost his head, and that he was carried away by his ideas" (198).

What Bellow stresses are the passionate convictions of King Dahfu, his glorious belief in human possibility. The therapeutic transformation of Henderson, in whose constitution Dahfu sees the world (184), betokens the possibility of the general regeneration of mankind. It is the human imagination that can perform this miracle and create types of goodness and beauty instead of monstrous forms and deformed types. " 'What Homo Sapiens imagines, he may slowly convert himself to' " (229), claims King Dahfu. Led on by the ideals of nobility and high conduct, mankind can evolve to the very summits.

Bellow also endows King Dahfu with the visionary daring of William Blake, who had an absolute belief in the regnerative power of the human imagination. Blake rebelled against the rationalistic and materialistic England of his time, a land cursed by the unholy trinity of Bacon, Locke, and Newton. Bellow sets King Dahfu's dreams of human greatness as realized by the imagination against the Bunam's cold and rational plans for Henderson. The Bunam and his assistant, whom Henderson calls a "a leather-winged bat" (210), constitute the Spectre, which was the reasoning power in man for Blake. The visual images for the Spectre include bat-winged hovering forms. One can now understand why the Bunam ignored the little knickknacks that Henderson offered him during their first encounter, why he used an atlas to ask Henderson where he came from, and why he made Henderson sign his name. The antagonism between the King and the Bunam is more than a tribal quarrel: it represents the conflict between the reasoning power in man and the human imagination.

The Bunam is the leader of the anti-lion forces: "I thought his wrinkled stare, the stern vein of his forehead, and those complex fields of skin about his eyes must signify . . . what they would have signified back in New York, namely, deep thought" (211). The Bunam is on the side of death, not life. For Henderson he is a "sexton-beetle," that rejoices among graves and corpses. His assistant is a "soul-eater" (211). Blake has written about the destructive forces of reason when, cut off from other human qualities, it assumes an authoritarian attitude:

> The Spectre is the Reasoning Power in Man; and when separated
> From Imagination, and closing itself as in steel, in a Ratio
> Of the Things of Memory. It thence frames Laws and Moralities
> To destroy Imagination! the Divine Body, by Martyrdoms and Wars
>   [74: 10–13, E 227 *Jerusalem*]

King Dahfu, on the other hand, celebrates life and the triumphs of the human imagination: " 'Imagination, imagination, imagination! It converts to actual. It sustains, it alters, it redeems!' " (229) It is the imagination, source of all human accomplishment and mankind's most valuable possession, that allows man to translate his dreams and desires into reality. The human imagination has to cooperate with the divine in order to generate new and vital forms of life.

"The tigers of wrath are wiser than the horses of instruction" (219): Dahfu, who knows his Blake, quotes from *The Marriage of Heaven and Hell*. " 'Let us embrace lions also in the same view,' " he goes on. He could have quoted another saying from the same source: "The wrath of the lion is the wisdom of God." The lioness, Atti, is more than an agent of Reichian therapy; she is Blake's tiger, burning bright in the forests of intellectual night. Bellow makes Henderson repeatedly refer to her eyes as clear circles of wrath, with which she stares at him. Unlike the wrinkled, everlasting stare of human experience on the face of the Bunam, Atti's stare is impersonal, lacking any direct threat. Her eyes project the wrath of this world: they are "clear circles of inhuman wrath, convex, brown, and pure, rings of black light within them" (200). They tell Henderson to be absolute for death; they compel him to accept the terrifying reality of existence. Only after the fear of Atti has subsided, suggests King Dahfu, will Henderson be able to appreciate her beauty. Only when man is no longer terrified of the world, only when he realizes that its terrors are not directed toward his individual self will that self be free and man will come to realize the utter beauty of nature and of human life.

The lion therapy is at once Reichian and homeopathic. Fear is treated by fear as Henderson faces for the first time the stern impersonal countenance of wrath, of death, that he has always avoided. The terror Atti produces in him hurls itself against his armor. An explosion occurs in his chest and he begins to cough. An electric shock passes through him when he is made to touch Atti: "The bones of the hand became incandescent. After this a frightful shock passed right up the arm into the chest" (192).

The loosening of Henderson's armor has begun. According to Reich, resistances exert their pressure as soon as therapy begins. Henderson's whole system resists the dissolution of his protection machine and all the orifices begin to shut: "I stood there half deaf, half blind, with my throat closing and all the sphincters shut" (189). King Dahfu describes in comic detail the anxiety reactions of Henderson: " 'I love when your brows move. They are really ex-traordnary. And your chin gets like a peach stone, and you have a very strangulation color and facial swelling, and your mouth spread very wide. And when you cried! I adored when you began to cry' " (193).

King Dahfu urges Henderson to imitate the rhythmic behavior of Atti, the fluid movements of her supple body: " 'Moreover, observe Atti. Contemplate her. How does she stride, how does she saunter, how does she lie or gaze or rest or breathe? I stress the respiratory part,' he said. 'She do not breathe shallow. This freedom of the intercostal muscles and her abdominal flexibility . . . gives the vital continuity between her parts' " (219). This neo-Stanislavski method will establish vital continuity in Henderson's own system, will make him in tune with the universe:

"Now, sir, will you assume a little more limberness? You appear cast in one piece. The midriff dominates. Can you move the different portions? Minus yourself of some of your heavy reluctance of attitude. Why so sad and so earthen? Now you are a lion. Mentally, conceive of the environment. The sky, the sun, and creatures of the bush. You are related to all. The very gnats are your cousins. The sky is your thoughts. The leaves are your insurance, and you need no other. There is no interruption all night to the speech of the stars." [224]

Only then, suggests King Dahfu, will the change that Henderson desires occur: " 'You could be noble. Some parts may be so long-buried as to be classed dead. Is there any resurrectibility in them? There is where the change comes in' " (219).

The impact of Dahfuian therapy on Henderson assumes strange manifestations. The king consoles him by telling him that " 'sometimes a condition must worsen before bettering' " (232). Reich states that a breakdown of personality "is inevitable before a new, rational personality structure can develop" (SW, 98). Bellow's strategy, whereby the "shot in the arm from animal nature" (212) uncovers and releases pig elements in Henderson instead of transforming him into a lion, is a stroke of comic genius. Bellow evokes the very last note of farcical laughter from every situation: Henderson emitting suspicious noises that sound more like grunts than roars; Henderson touching his eyelashes surreptitiously wondering whether they have turned into bristles; Henderson stretched out "from the trotters to the helmet," lying on the ground, heaving and groaning and grunting. Perhaps Bellow did pick up a suggestion of this comic transformation from Reich who hints at such a possibility: "The total bodily expression can usually be put into a formula which sooner or later in the course of the character-analytic work appears spontaneously. Peculiarly enough, such a formula is usually derived from the animal kingdom, like 'fox,' 'pig,' 'snake,' 'worm,' " etc. (DO, 269).

The impact of Atti causes a profound upheaval within Henderson. The roaring loosens him up and releases a lifetime accumulation of grievances. These express themselves in the form of a "cry which summarized my entire course on this earth, from birth to Africa" (231). He discovers strange changes taking place. Black curls begin to sprout on his head; he becomes strangely sensitive to the clamoring color of flowers; his beard grows like a broom; he begins involuntarily to spout forth the French he knew as a child. The letter to Lily, with Henderson's interspersed thoughts and comments, makes it clear that here is a changed man. Even his language and its narrative tone change. From this moment on, comic boisterousness and witty turns of phrase are subdued. Literary references and biblical allusions are more frequent as Henderson communicates "something of the highest importance" (22) that has been presented to him.

The letter to Lily has its comic moments. Henderson describes the tumult within him as "a whole troop of pygmies jumping up and down inside me, yelling and carrying on" (241). But it also has elements of poetry and daring insight. Henderson has been called "*from nonexistence to existence*" (239); he has matured "twenty years in twenty days" (237). He quotes from *Hamlet* to characterize his body as a "great instrument." He suggests that humankind should sway itself more intentionally toward beauty. The stars are now endless fire to him, as they were to Blake. The world is strange, as Queen Willatale told him it would be to a child. Henderson senses a childlike oneness with nature, which formerly was sheer misery to him. A Marvellian peace descends upon him: "*It is very early in life, and I am out in the grass. The sun flames and swells; the heat it emits is its love, too. I have this self-same vividness in my heart. There are dandelions. I try to gather up this green. I put my love-swollen cheek to the yellow of the dandelions. I try to enter into the green*" (238). And the service ideal of his ancestors bubbles up within him. He asks Lily to enroll him as Leo E. Henderson in medical school, for he would like to be a medical missionary, perhaps in India.

Henderson has indeed changed but neither the therapeutic process nor the process of enlightenment is complete. Both continue and are fused together in marvelous fashion on the day of the hopo hunt. Henderson thinks about his past mistakes and like Tommy Wilhelm, makes a number of resolutions: "I must change. I must not live in the past, it will ruin me . . . I must break Lily from blackmail and set love on a true course" (242). Like Allbee, who tells Asa that man has to live for ideals not nature, Henderson acknowledges man's kinship with the animal world but also realizes that man has to travel beyond mere animal existence: "We had our share of this creature-blessing until infancy ended. But now aren't we required to complete something else—project number two—the second blessing?" (242).

The king implants certain ideas in Henderson's mind as they travel to the hopo and as they sit on the platform waiting for Gmilo to appear. He repeats the idea that the universe has to be accepted as a mystery that cannot be replaced or resolved by man. He suggests that a noble individual will seek to break the wheel of fear and desire upon which mankind has been bound from generation to generation. Death then will no longer appear terrible. These ideas about death, suffering, the mystery of the universe, the wheel of fear and desire upon which mankind is bound, will affect Henderson later. What impresses him deeply on this lion day is the calm, noble and assured manner of the king, who ignores the ill omens and the Bunam, and sets out to complete Becoming. King Dahfu, eager to capture his lion father, climbs up to the hopo platform, all afire with orgone energy. Henderson sees "the smoky, bluish trembling of his extra shadow" (248); later, "the blue of the atmosphere seemed to condense" (256) about the king's head. Henderson himself is in a strange emotional state: horrified at the idea of facing a wild lion without a weapon, he is intensely afraid; he is also worried and anxious about the king, his friend. His face is in a state of turmoil: the king notes that Henderson's chin keeps moving up and down. As he starts to climb up the ladder of the platform, something bubbles out from deep within Henderson: "Illness, strangeness, and danger combined and ganged up on me. Instead of an answer, a sob came out of me. It must have been laid down early in my life, for it was stupendous and rose from me like a great sea bubble from the Atlantic floor" (250–51). Later, as the King begins to maneuver the net to capture the lion, Henderson feels a "globe" "about the size of a darning egg" (259) rising in his throat. This is a comical version of the Reichian throat spasm and indicates the dissolution of an important block, the chest segment. The armoring of the chest, according to Reich, "was developed at the time of critical conflicts in the life of the child, probably long before the pelvic armor" (SW, 167).

It is the fierce apparition of the lion, a beast more huge and more savage than Atti, that sends a shock through Henderson's being. The shock is electrifyingly physical for it shatters Henderson's chest armor. It is also a mental blow, a sudden truth that Dahfu warned him could come in a form for which he could be unprepared. Henderson stares at the lion's ferocious face full of the darkness of murder. He senses its breath, hot as oblivion, raw as blood. Its snarls proclaim death. For the first time Henderson confronts the naked wrath of this world (Atti's face merely prepared him for this savage encounter) and the terrifying reality of death. The combined shock and the death of his friend, the king, lead to Henderson's total collapse.

The collapse is the penultimate stage of Henderson's transformation which is presented in the last two chapters. Henderson has to work out his own salvation, with the help of the healing power of memory, some auspicious omens, and Romilayu.

Romilayu's role increases in significance as Henderson's adventures come to an end. Bellow develops him gradually from a "function" to a character. In the Arnewi section, he is merely a guide and an interpreter, an ear into which Henderson pours out his woes. Bellow tosses in a number of casual details about Romilayu. Romilayu's calm behavior, his dignity as an interpreter, his habit of praying, impress Henderson greatly. It is Romilayu who helps him to escape. It is Romilayu who restrains Henderson and prevents him from killing the Bunam's helper. It is he who helps Henderson survive in the mountains.

Henderson slowly recognizes the inner strengths of Romilayu. In Romilayu's soft, sympathetic eyes he sees a "light that didn't come from the air" (233). During his delirium at Baventai Romilayu's black face seems to be "like shatter-proof glass to which everything had been done that glass can endure" (276). It tells him that the human spirit will always endure in spite of suffering and disaster. Romilayu is an important ingredient in Henderson's education. When they part at Harar, they part as friends.

Henderson's education continues as he travels back to civilization. He is his own teacher now. The ideas implanted by the king, fertilized by Dahfu's noble example and high conduct in life and in death, take root in Henderson's soul. He voices certain truths about human existence in accents very like those of King Dahfu. Crouching on all fours in the stone hut, anointed by his friend's blood which signifies to Henderson that he should continue Dahfu's existence (264), sprinkled with the dust of the earth, Henderson announces his belief in the essential nobility and greatness of man: "But the universe itself being put into us, it calls out for scope. The eternal is bonded onto us. It calls out for its share. This is why guys can't bear to be so cheap. And I had to do something about it" (267). He waxes eloquent about the rhythm of the universe which man has to be in tune with. And when he sees the clouds on his way to Newfoundland, he speaks like the romantic he is, in Blakean accents, about the oneness of man and nature and the elements: "Only they aren't eternal, that's the whole thing; they are seen once and never seen again, being figures and not abiding realities; Dahfu will never be seen again, and presently I will never be seen again; but every one is given the components to see: the water, the sun, the air, the earth" (279).

Henderson has changed. He has burst his spirit's sleep and come to himself. He has leapt out of the prison of his ego and discovered true freedom. He is not what he thought he was, a bum. His beard, significantly, is a riot of color: "On one side it gushed out half white but with many streaks of blond, red, black and purple" (279). He now knows that he is royal material that can start life anew. He is no longer tormented by the voice. He knows now what it wanted, not unreality, but reality. He does not have philosophical answers to the question: what is reality? His intuition and his experiences have given him the answer: friendship, human kindness and noble conduct, all constitute reality.

Henderson has obtained some fundamental answers to fundamental questions. Unlike Augie March, he has earned his faith through pain and suffering. Henderson embodies Bellow's own faith in individual man, in mankind as a whole, and in America. Man is a noble savage, according to Bellow, capable of change. Henderson brings back Bellow's message of the highest importance to mankind. Mankind, like Henderson, is unkillable: "Nature has tried everything. It has thrown the book at me. And here I am" (277). That is what Lily meant when she called him unkillable. There is a vital current flowing through the generations, there is an evolution, as King Dahfu proclaims (200).

The message is also to America itself. The Wariri section pursues the parallels between Henderson's plight and that of America, established in the first four chapters but merely hinted at in the Arnewi section. What Henderson, like America, wants is to stop their suffering and achieve their true destinies. Like Whitman, that poet of the national consciousness, he wants to complete true being. He equates his own plight with that of America during his first meeting with King Dahfu: "Enough! Enough! Time to have Become. Time to Be! Burst the spirit's sleep. Wake up, America! Stump the experts" (136).

Henderson wants the dormant national consciousness to arouse itself and awaken to its true greatness of soul. He does not know how to arrive at this greatness, but he is convinced that the experts are wrong. The "experts" are those advocates of doom, wastelanders who predict the downfall of the West and the collapse of industrial America. Bellow does not accept such a vision of apocalyptic despair based on a facile rejection of technology. Bellow deliberately makes Henderson a New Yorker, modern urban man conditioned and affected by the new technology. Henderson loves New York, he has traveled on its subways, he knows the hock shops and army-navy stores on Third Avenue. His experiences in Africa are frequently measured by New York standards. The noises of the Wariri rain-festival are like "Coney Island or Atlantic City or Times Square on New Year's Eve" (144).

As a representative of modern technological America wanting desperately to burst its spirit's sleep, Henderson ventures into primitive Africa. In Arnewiland he makes "one of those mutual-aid deals" (76): he will help the Arnewi with his technology in exchange for the wisdom of life they have. However, the bomb he concocts destroys the cistern. The incident signifies that unless technological power is put to proper use in the right spirit, the result will be disaster and suffering. Henderson and America have to learn how to control this tremendous power, a lesson they learn in Waririland.

Henderson is fascinated by the magnificent, rhythmic power displayed by the Wariri King Dahfu in all his gestures and actions. The voice of the king reminds him "of the sound you sometimes hear from a power station when you pass one in New York on a summer night; the doors are open; all the brass and steel is going, lustrous under one little light, and some old character in dungarees and carpet slippers is smoking a pipe with all the greatness of the electricity behind him"

(178). The king, who is in control both of himself and of his people (he too smokes a pipe and wears slippers), is closely parallel to the old man who is in charge of the power station that lights up a city and has luster of its own. Henderson learns the lesson that technological power and the power of the human spirit, incarnate in King Dahfu, are vitally interconnected. He can now understand and respond to the great achievement of a dedicated American engineer like Slocum, who has such power and who built the great dams in the Punjab Valley. In the letter to Lily, Henderson celebrates the marriage of the human imagination with man's technical capability. The airplane flight to Africa testifies to mankind's capacity to realize its own marvelous dreams: "We are the first generation to see the clouds from both sides. What a privilege! First people dreamed upward. Now they dream both upward and downward. This is bound to change something, somewhere" (236).

King Dahfu, with the aid of Atti and her animal power, awakens Henderson to a new awareness of human possibilities, to the reality and need of love and human brotherhood, to the fact that human nobility can be realized even in our terrible technological day. The spirit's sleep has burst and Henderson now has a vision of what America can be. He knows that America can transform and renew itself as it had done in the past:

> Americans are supposed to be dumb but they are willing to go into this. It isn't just me. You have to think about white Protestantism and the Constitution and the Civil War and capitalism and winning the West. All the major tasks and the big conquests were done before my time. That left the biggest problem of all, which was to encounter death. [233]

What Henderson celebrates so emphatically here is the shaping spirit in the American past that propelled its peoples to magnificent achievement. In today's age of madness America faces the greatest challenge in its history—death, the death of the human spirit damaged by a technology it cannot control, valuing junk (like Miss Lenox, who dies after listening to Henderson's terrible rage), swollen with empty success and purposeless power. Henderson himself has come to realize that the tremendous power compressed within his own being has to be controlled and unselfishly directed toward the welfare of others. He is sure that America can, Whitman-like, go forth again and achieve true greatness:

> Millions of Americans have gone forth since the war to redeem the present and discover the future. I can swear to you, Romilayu, there are guys exactly like me in India and in China and South America

and all over the place. Just before I left home I saw an interview in the paper with a piano teacher from Muncie who became a Buddhist monk in Burma. You see, that's what I mean. I am a high-spirited kind of guy. And it's the destiny of my generation of Americans to go out in the world and try to find the wisdom of life. [233]

Armed with such healing, prophetic knowledge, Henderson has to return to America so that both their destinies may be fulfilled.

Bellow apparently wrote the last fifty or sixty pages of *Henderson the Rain King*, which dramatize the journey toward America, in a kind of creative frenzy.[19] His superb fictional skill proclaims itself in .the confident ease with which he controls and directs the fast momentum of the narrative while packing it with a multitude of meanings. For it is a symbolic return attended by auspicious omens and by intimations of a new America, a journey that ends with a highly significant, though strange, rite of celebration.

Henderson travels back to America in seemingly erratic fashion by way of Baventai, Bakhtale, Harar (Ethiopia), Khartoum (Sudan), Cairo, Athens (where he sees a strange, yellow, bonelike, rose-colored light on the heights of the Acropolis), Rome, Paris, London, and Newfoundland. The stops he makes are a strange reversal of the stages of his reading of the history of Western civilization: "When I started to read something about France, I realized I didn't know anything about Rome, which came first, and then Greece, and then Egypt, going backward all the time to the primitive abyss" (206). Henderson, the mental traveler who has visited the original home of mankind, now enacts in symbolic fashion the historical development of Western civilization as he returns from Africa to Europe to Newfoundland, the name suggesting (as in Donne's poem) an America- and a world-to-be.

Henderson travels also towards his childhood dream that had been inspired by a medical missionary, Sir Wilfred Grenfell of Labrador; at fifty-six he will enroll in medical school as Leo E. Henderson, the first name signifying the nobility he has recovered, the initial (for Eugene) revealing that he is truly well-born. After graduation, he will take up missionary work, perhaps in India. The lion cub, an enigmatic form of his dead friend, King Dahfu, travels with him in a wicker basket. On the plane Henderson meets a stewardess from the Midwest who reinforces his faith in his people and in their ability to resurrect and renew themselves:

She was from Rockford, Illinois. Every twenty years or so the earth renews itself in young maidens. You know what I mean? Her cheeks had the perfect form that belongs to the young, her hair was kinky gold. Her teeth were white and posted on every approach. She was all sweet corn and milk. [280]

Here is a marriage of soil and soul. The stewardess is the corn maiden, an emblem of fertility, the incarnation of the innate power of the American spirit to revitalize itself. Henderson feels a religious propulsion to pronounce a psalm-like blessing on her:

> Blessings on her hips. Blessings on her thighs. Blessings on her soft little fingers which were somewhat covered by the cuffs of her uniform. Blessings on that rough gold. A wonderful little thing; her attitude was that of a pal or playmate, as is common with Midwestern young women. [280]

Her natural friendliness and her gold hair signify that elements of the Arnewi (whose landscape is golden) and of Atti (that Blakean creature of gold) can still be found in America.

Henderson is also sustained by an idea out of Emerson, that "corporeal things are an image of the spiritual and visible objects are renderings of invisible ones" (284). Everything he sees and experiences on his journey toward America is a spiritual sign. He identifies himself with Ishmael, Melville's Ishmael surely, one who has unflinchingly faced the evil in the world and is saved at the end to tell his tale. And the stewardess introduces Henderson to the American-Persian orphan (Henderson's hair, in chapter 1, was like Persian lambs' fur) on the plane, one who "was still trailing his cloud of glory" (285). Henderson looks into the child's eyes and sees intimations of immortality there, his own past and man's future in them: "Two smoothly gray eyes moved at me, greatly expanded into the whites—new life altogether. They had that new luster. With it they had ancient power, too. You could never convince me that *this was for the first time*" (285). The luster and the power call to mind the radiant energy of King Dahfu and suggest that here is a "power station" in miniature. The eyes proclaim a victory over death and the continual renewal of the human spirit.

Holding this child in his lap, Henderson takes the final step toward health just before the plane lands at Newfoundland. He summons back fugitive memories of his boyhood years, shadowy Wordsworthian recollections that provide a "master light" for his seeing. They make a sizable difference to him, for they uncover the roots of his neurosis and set his true self free. Bellow does not hesitate to blend Wordsworthian intimations with an idea out of early Reich, that "a consistent dissolving of character resistances provides an infallible and immediate avenue of approach to the central infantile conflict." (CA, 48) A footnote, added in 1945, tells us: "In orgone therapy, the pathogenic memories appear *spontaneously* and *without effort* when the somatic emotions break through the muscular armor." (CA, 21)

Henderson is now able to recall directly the origins of his conflict. "Now I understand it," he writes (282). He can now accept and understand his father's disappointment and anger toward him after Dick died. He can now understand that he had violently suppressed his bitterness and his rage against his father (they come out in the form of a sob) on the day of Dick's funeral and expressed them by wrecking old cars and cutting them up with a torch even on the day of the funeral. The reader can now understand the buried logic of Henderson's attempts to please his father and reach out to him on the violin.

Linked up with Henderson's recall of Dick's death and funeral is the memory of Smolak the bear, their roller coaster rides together and their closeness to each other. The comic anxiety about the grunting and the bubbling forth of pig elements is now resolved for Henderson: "So before pigs ever came on my horizon, I received a deep impression from a bear" (284). Smolak the bear probably sprang from Bellow's imagination but the roller coaster has been imported from the pages of *Character Analysis*, where it is mentioned three times in connection with the fear of falling: "People with inhibited vegetative motility experience them [excitations] as unpleasurable sensations of anxiety or oppression in the solar plexus region. These sensations are very similar to those experienced in fright or with the sudden descent in an elevator or on a roller coaster" (CA, 352). One understands now the reason why Henderson is subject to fits of fainting and to blackouts in elevators (139).

Bellow invests Smolak the bear with yet another dimension of meaning besides the Reichian one. For it was to Smolak that Henderson turned for comfort and love after he ran away from home when his father rejected him. Smolak was Henderson's first teacher. This huge, old, tottering clown of the fairground, who had accepted his wretched condition, taught Henderson a truth that he had forgotten, the truth that one has to accept the conditions of life, the truth that "for creatures there is nothing that ever runs unmingled" (284).

The final truth that Henderson arrives at before the plane lands at Newfoundland is about love: "Whatever gains I ever made were always due to love and nothing else" (284). Henderson clarifies here what he had set down so cryptically in the letter of Lily: " 'And moreover it's love that makes reality reality. The opposite makes the opposite' " (241). One of Bellow's favorite quotations is from Simone Weil: "Those whom we love, exist."

All is now in readiness for the marvelous conclusion of *Henderson the Rain King*. The plane lands on the frozen airfield at Newfoundland for refueling (having lost temporarily its source of power) and Henderson feels impelled to rejoice and to express his joy in his own fashion. " 'Breathe in this air, kid, and get a little color,' " (286) says Henderson the Reichian to the orphan. Gathering him up in his huge arms and the lion-cub too, he begins a ritual dance, a reenactment in Newfoundland of the therapeutic dance in the African jungle. But now Henderson is full of flowing orgone energy. No longer does he lumber around in awkward fashion: he leaps and bounds exultantly like a very lion around the motionless plane:

> Laps and laps I galloped around the shining and riveted body of the plane, behind the fuel trucks. Dark faces were looking from within. The great beautiful propellers were still, all four of them. I guess I felt it was my turn to move, and so went running—leaping, leaping, pounding, and tingling over the pure white lining of the gray Arctic silence. [286]

Here is magic. Bellow the creative wizard has cast a spell to compel almost all the thematic elements into a triumphant finale. Every word is exactly right. Every detail is significant. There is no sense of strain, no disorderly rush of words, as when Henderson began his tale. Henderson has also achieved the perfect human voice in full command of itself. Its secret, vibrant power is unmistakable, for it is also the voice of Bellow the artist.

Henderson dances to celebrate the possibility of a new America, vitalized by the spirit of brotherhood and love. He dances in preparation for Thanksgiving which the stewardess tells him will be next week. Bellow is not afraid to be a prophet of hope. He discards as irrelevant earlier myths and metaphors that interpret America in terms of the American Adam, the lost Eden or the waste land. In the nineteenth century, Thoreau and Hawthorne had seized on the locomotive, that power of blackness, as a graphic image of the technological demon that was beginning to ravage their virgin land. Leo Marx has described how the sensibilities of their twentieth-century successors—Frost, Faulkner, Hemingway, and West—were thrown into turmoil as they faced the metaphysical horror of "the machine's sudden entrance into the garden."[20] The tensions thus generated did not allow these writers to design "satisfactory resolutions for their pastoral fables."[21] Bellow's resolution is both optimistic and Emersonian. In an 1843 journal entry Emerson had noted rather simply: "Machinery and Transcendentalism agree well."[22] *Henderson the Rain King* offers us what Leo Marx requires of the contemporary American artist, that he create new symbols of human possibility. One such symbol is the stewardess on the plane, a virgin who works in perfect accord with the dynamo, Henry Adams's other kingdom of force.

The last paragraph of *Henderson the Rain King* is an epiphany of awakening and hope. It presents a vision of a technological America that can be transfigured by the noble ideals of love, service and brotherhood when they are set in motion. The twin sources of America's strength are vividly presented. Her twentieth-century technological power is symbolized by the lustrous plane with the great, though now still, propellers that brought Henderson to Newfoundland. And the unquenchable and radiant power of the human spirit is now incarnate in Henderson, and will lead both him and America to true glory.

The dance also acknowledges the continuing vitality of mankind which death cannot destroy. King Dahfu lives on in the lion cub; he also lives on in Henderson who is his successor; and Henderson's own successor will be the little orphan whose eyes have both a new luster and an ancient power. Henderson's dance, then, is the dance of human life, past, present and future circling together in absolute harmony.

The harmony will be temporary. Being will yield to Becoming. The stretching silence amidst which Henderson performs his human dance suggests the mystery in which man moves. The dark faces that look from within and the gray of the Arctic, warnings that nothing in human life ever runs unmingled, are touches that only a writer of supreme fiction could introduce.

NOTES

1. Joseph Epstein, "Saul Bellow of Chicago," *New York Times Book Review*, May 9, 1971, p. 12.

2. Saul Bellow, *Henderson the Rain King* (Greenwich, Conn.: Fawcett Crest Book, 1959), p. 29. Hereafter page numbers will be cited in the text.

3. Saul Bellow in "Literary Notes on Khrushchev," *First Person Singular*, edited by Herbert Gold (New York: Dial Press, 1963), pp. 46–47, describes Khrushchev as a political actor: "He poured it on, holding press conferences in the street and trading insults from his balcony with the crowd, singing snatches of the *International*, giving a pantomine uppercut to an imaginary assassin. He played up to the crowd, and luxuriated in its attention, behaving like a comic artist in a show written and directed by himself."

4. *Writers at Work*, 3rd series, p. 188.

5. Michael Allen, "Idiomatic Language in Two Novels by Saul Bellow," *Journal of American Studies* 1, no. 2 (1967): 275–80, and Irving Stock, "The Novels of Saul Bellow," *Southern Review* 3 (Winter 1967): 13–22, both refer to this.

6. "Literary Notes on Khrushchev," pp. 49–50.

7. Nina A. Steers, " 'Successor' to Faulkner?" *Show* 4 (September 1964): 38.

8. Saul Bellow, "Henderson in Africa," *Botteghe Oscure* 21 (1958): 187.

9. Ibid., p. 207.

10. Bellow gently satirizes the use of the cat's cradle game for anthropological research. At one time it became a fashion in ethnographic investigation. See Robert H. Lowie, *The History of Ethnological Theory*, (New York: Holt, Rinehart and Winston, 1966), p. 131.

11. In *Sex and Repression in Savage Society* (London: Routledge & Kegan Paul, Ltd., 1953) Bronislaw Malinowski refers to a society of primitive people on the Amphett Islands who are very similar to the Trobrianders in everything but social organization. Though a matriarchal society, they have a strict sexual morality, a restricted family life, and a strong sense of patriarchal authority. Wilhelm Reich, in *The Invasion of Compulsory Sex-Morality* (New York: Farrar, Straus and Giroux, 1971), acknowledges his immense debt to the work of Malinowski.

12. *Writers at Work*, 3rd series, p. 189.

13. See my article, "Bellow's Africa," *American Literature* 43 (May 1971): 242–56.

14. Robert R. Dutton has pointed out that the bursting of the spirit's sleep has been taken from the third stanza of the introduction to "Revolt of Islam." See his *Saul Bellow* (New York: Twayne Publishers, 1971), pp. 111–12.

15. See "Bellow's Africa."

16. CA, p. 358. Bellow has Henderson refer to this term thus: "He [King Dahfu] kept talking about vegetal functions, some such term, and he lost me every other sentence" (201).

17. William James, *The Principles of Psychology* (Chicago: Encyclopaedia Brittanica, 1952), p. 717.

18. Wm. Theodore de Bary, ed., *Sources of Indian Tradition* (New York: Columbia University Press, 1969), 1: 288–89.

19. Nina A. Steers, p. 38.

20. Leo Marx, *The Machine in the Garden: Technology and the Pastoral in America* (Oxford University Press paperback, 1967), p. 365.

21. Ibid., p. 364.

22. Quoted by Marx, p. 232.

6 *Herzog*

Referring to his compulsion to rewrite heavily, Bellow has said that there are twenty drafts of *Herzog*.[1] Actually, there are twenty-one. For *Seize the Day* was the first "draft." A number of clues, thematic and linguistic, suggest that Bellow refashioned in *Herzog* some basic material he had used in the earlier work.

Tommy Wilhelm and Moses Herzog do not belong to the hard, treacherous, aggressive world of power, success, and money. Wilhelm complains of hemorrhaging money, while Herzog thinks of himself as a medium through which money flows in the shapes of taxes, mortgage, rent, and legal fees. Both use the word "mistake" to characterize their lives. Wilhelm sees his life as a series of ten fatal mistakes. Herzog complains that his life has taken form through several wrong decisions: the trip to Vineyard Haven is a "mistake"[2]; the buying of the Ludeyville house "was one of his biggest mistakes" (64); accepting Sandor Himmelstein's hospitality after leaving Madeleine was "still another characteristic mistake" (102). Even more significant, both protagonists arrive at their moments of fatal choice in an identical manner. Herzog tells his brother: "I think, I figure things out. I see exactly what I should avoid. Then, all of a sudden, I'm in bed with that very thing, and making love to it. As with Madeleine" (406). "After much thought and hesitation and debate he invariably took the course he had rejected innumerable times," broods Wilhelm (STD, 23).

Emotionally, they are akin. Led by their hearts, both are extremely vulnerable to suffering. And both sufferers are persecuted by their wives. Herzog enjoys the flavor of subjugation in his love for Madeleine, even though he accuses himself of "developing the psychology of a runaway slave" (233). "From the time I met her I've been a slave," says Wilhelm of Margaret (STD, 49), who lives to make him suffer. Both wives make extravagant financial demands on their husbands. Herzog's Madeleine is an amplified combination of the strong-willed Margaret and of Olive, who is a Catholic. Like Margaret, Madeleine is a tyrant and both wives want to get their doctorates. Even the language makes it clear that Margaret was the first sketch for what was to become the domineering, colorful Madeleine. Wilhelm pictures Margaret with "her graying *bangs* cut with strict *fixity* above her pretty, *decisive* face" (STD, 112; italics mine). Herzog watches Madeleine transform herself into an older woman before going to Fordham: "Then she picked up a pair of large tailor's shears and put them to her *bangs*. She seemed to have no need to measure; her image was *fixed* in her will. She cut as if discharging a gun, and Herzog felt an impulse of alarm, short-circuited. Her *decisiveness* fascinated him" (139; italics mine).

The relations between the protagonists and their parents are also deeply similar. Herzog's mother with her melancholy, her love of gentility, her early death and her submission to the fate of being human is kin to Wilhelm's mother from whom he has inherited his sensitive, soft heart and brooding nature. And the fathers are alike in their preoccupation with money, their anxiety about death, and in their treatment of their sons. The scene of Herzog's confrontation with his father a year before Papa Herzog's death telescopes the two scenes between Wilhelm and Dr. Adler.

Other clues, minor in character, also strongly suggest that both novels have sprung from the same matrix. Omens are introduced to warn the protagonists of coming disaster. The aged fiddler who points his bow at Wilhelm on the way to the stock market becomes the middle-aged woman who points threateningly to the cast on her foot when Herzog comes out of the courthouse. The fiddler admonishes Wilhelm, saying, "You!" (STD, 100). The woman fixes Herzog with a penetrating look that silently identifies him: *"Thou fool!"* (294). In both novels the protagonist encounters a strange woman with chihuahuas on a leash. The same significant phrase, a "day of reckoning," occurs in both novels. Finally both protagonists make use of a line from "Ode to the West Wind" to characterize their suffering. Tommy Wilhelm refers to his tendency to "fall upon the thorns of life" (STD, 56). Herzog also invokes the same line from Shelley to mock his own masochism: "I fall upon the thorns of life, I bleed. And then, I fall upon the thorns of life, I bleed. And what next? I get laid, I take a short holiday, but very soon I fall upon those same thorns with gratification in pain, or suffering in joy" (254).

Both novels clearly have a common nucleic root. From this root sprang forth in 1956 a tightly knit, ironic, sober, rich novella, a parable of a modern urban victim who is finally redeemed. From the same source erupted in 1964 a work of enormous range and textural density, teeming with people, bursting with ideas and social criticism, a comic novel that dramatizes the predicament of man in the twentieth century and ends on the trembling edge of transcendence. The leap from *Seize the Day* to *Herzog* is that of an artist in full possession now of his creative self and in powerful control of the exploding energies within his being.

Bellow had arrived at the peak of his fictional powers in 1959. *Henderson the Rain King* marks the culmination of his developing talent in handling the symbolic mode that was strongly evident in *The Victim* and in *Seize the Day*. A magnificent parable, perhaps the most finished of his fictions, *Henderson* did not allow Bellow to exploit the major skills he had developed in his earlier fiction, his genius for rendering the thick particulars and the magic actualities of contemporary experience. In *Herzog* Bellow returned to a mode of fiction that was predominantly, though not exclusively, realistic, a mode that could "accommodate the full tumult, the zaniness and crazed quality, of modern experience."[3] He arrived at a form into which he could pour almost every theme he had worked with, into which he could release all the questions that had tormented him. It was a form which allowed him to transform his limitations into fictional assets; above all, it was a form that could present his increasingly complex vision of what being human means in our time. Like *Henderson the Rain King, Herzog* also is a culmination (they form twin, though not identical peaks) and marks, according to Bellow, "the end of a literary sensibility."[4]

Herzog the man is a vectorial center into whose inner space converge all the various forces that had shaped Bellow's earlier protagonists. Emotionally akin to Tommy Wilhelm, Herzog is a blood relative of Asa Leventhal, who is led by the needs of his vulnerable heart. He is an intellectual like Joseph, deeply troubled by questions about human existence. He is equipped with the basic belief that Joseph and Augie March had about the marvelousness of life. Like all his fellow protagonists, Herzog is a good man. And like them, he too goes forth on a quest for the human.

It is a quest that subsumes all previous quests, a huge amplification of the journeys the other protagonists had set out on. Joseph had sought for answers to two interrelated questions: he wanted to know who he was and how a good man should live; the first, a Socratic question, the second, an existential one. Asa Leventhal, Tommy Wilhelm, and Augie March (despite his vast reading) do not ask any searching intellectual questions about human life and its meaning. Their experiences, thickly emotional, lead them to a faint uncertain awareness of what humanness is. The African ordeal teaches Henderson wisdom about brotherhood, suffering, death, and love. The major questions about human existence are however not "answered" but resolved by King Dahfu's deep faith in man and in the human imagination. Herzog hurls himself into a quixotic quest for complete wisdom. As a student of intellectual history, he wrestles with and can articulate (as Joseph and Henderson could not) the great ideas of the Western world (not of the Eastern) that twentieth-century man has inherited. As one who staggers under the combined emotional and psychic burdens of Asa Leventhal, Tommy Wilhelm and Henderson, he represents twentieth century man struggling to achieve modes of true being in a chaotic and outrageous universe.

Bellow brought all the fictional energies he had generated for the making of this enormous *Bildungsroman* of an adult. *Herzog* is the work of an artist who is driven to create a fictional universe, a cosmos. Such a creator cannot be a nail-paring god, like Flaubert and like Hemingway, who in search of a pure order set down neat, limited fictional constructs. Creators of macrocosms, novelists like Dostoevski in *The Brothers Karamazov* and Melville in *Moby-Dick,* incorporate, amalgamate, and naturalize heterogenous and alien elements into their novels. Passionately involved in their fictional material, they tear themselves away from it in order to control it. Within their creations and also without, they exercise a control magnanimous and imperial, with a lofty tolerance of impurities, loose ends, deliberate repetitions and tangential characters. The coherence of *Herzog* is an internal, invisible one, that of a whole world held together in a precarious state of dynamic equilibrium. Its outer structure is more apparent.

Herzog has a concentrated time-span of five days into which Bellow compresses the lifetime of his protagonist. It opens on a summer's day in Ludeyville in the Berkshires, and cuts immediately to a morning, five days back, with Herzog on the sofa of a kitchenette apartment in New York. He takes a train to Vineyard Haven, but flies immediately to New York. On the next day he has dinner with Ramona, his mistress, and spends the night with her. The following morning he goes to the municipal court and, on an impulse, takes the plane to Chicago. He spends two days there, is involved in a traffic accident after taking his daughter to the aquarium, and is arrested by the police for carrying a gun. By the afternoon of the fifth day, Herzog is back at Ludeyville and the story returns to the present: "He recognized that with his arms behind him and his legs extended any way, he was lying as he had lain less than a week ago and his dirty little sofa in New York. But was it only a week—five days? Unbelievable! How different he felt!" (397)

Herzog is an immense retrospective, an act of total recall. Herzog relives mentally the past five days when his life hits its crisis, five days that are themselves also a period of furious remembrance of things past. Bellow had to wrestle with the artistic perils of such a feat of memory. There was the danger of solipsism. There was the danger of the flashbacks becoming boring and stale. There was the problem of introducing ideas and the further problem of making them exciting, relevant, and alive. Bellow adopted a fictional strategy that he had announced but not used in *Augie March*. Augie had claimed that thinking about one's condition is hard work, internally done, and he explains why:

> It happens because you are powerless and unable to get anywhere, to obtain justice or have requital, and therefore in yourself you labor, you wage and combat, settle scores, remember insults, fight, reply, deny, blab, denounce, triumph, outwit, overcome, vindicate, cry, persist, absolve, die and rise again. All by yourself! Where is everybody? Inside your breast and skin, the entire cast. [AM, 542]

Bellow dramatizes Herzog's consciousness in this manner. More than a stage, Herzog's mind is a Kurukshetra, a huge battlefield upon which many skirmishes and combats, intellectual and emotional, comic and tragic, take place.

Herzog's throbbing mind, like Henderson's gigantic body, is in frenzied motion. The narrative tactics used to enact its feverish state and to reduce the distortions of solipsism, are a magnified and accelerated version of those used in *Seize the Day*. *Herzog* has a subjective narrator, wise, understanding, tolerant, whose voice is usually even and unhurried, and who reports the behavior of the protagonist sympatheti- cally. Often, however, and abruptly, he assumes the eyes, the sensibility, and the hectic accents of a tormented Herzog. Everything is then relayed through Herzog's point of view and Herzog's stream of consciousness, so that there are dramatic changes in pace and tempo. At other times Herzog takes over the narrative in his own right and uses a passionate form of the first person singular to tell his story. The narrative angle jumps around shifting wildly from one mode to another without warning and often within the same paragraph, creating an illusion of constant rapid nervous motion and a continuity of tempo that offsets the tortoise pace of the action and the cramping time schedule. The sensation of different kinds of speed, despite the fact that all action occurs in Herzog's consciousness, is heightened by the use of the mental letter.

The device of the mental letter that is at times jotted down but never sent was an inventive reworking of the eighteenth-century mode that gave Bellow freedom to range over space and time. As a shifting gear, it allowed him to regulate and vary the novel's ongoing rhythms. As a form of punctuation, it broke up what could have been long, monotonous stretches of brooding and meditation. It allowed Bellow to tunnel into the hidden recesses of Herzog's psyche. And it solved a major problem for Bellow, that of naturalizing ideas in his fiction.

All through the five days Herzog writes to everyone under the sun, "endlessly, fanatically, to the newspapers, to people in public life, to friends and relatives and at last to the dead, his own obscure dead, and finally the famous dead" (7). He writes letters that are long and letters that are short, letters that stretch through a chapter and letters that peter out in the middle of the first sentence. The letters are comic, tragic, bitter, furious, pungent, tender, witty, pathetic, prophetic, maudlin, savage, written in different moods, tones and modes. Herzog can adopt the pompous stance of an editorial writer or assume the serious tone of a reviewer. He addresses a letter to himself, another to God. He writes as a father, as a husband, as a Jew, as a lover, as a philosopher, as a friend—all manifestations of one who has not yet discovered his true human self.

What causes this lava to erupt out of Herzog is the incandescent state he is in. He has fallen under a spell from which he is desperately trying to exorcize himself. It is a condition of near delirium and chaotic turbulence lit up by brilliant flashes of self-knowledge. He feels "both visionary and muddy" (46).[5] In the train to Vineyard Haven he experiences "his eager, flying spirit streaming out, speaking, piercing, making clear judgements, uttering final explanations, necessary words only. He was in a whirling ecstasy" (88). His muddied spirit is also present: "He felt at the same time that his judgements exposed the boundless, baseless bossiness and willfulness, the nagging embedded in his mental constitution" (ibid.). The letters and the whirling thoughts they trigger are not completely within his control. When Joseph began dangling, he was compelled to keep a diary. Herzog is driven to write mental letters because, like Henderson, he is tormented by a voice within him: *"There is someone inside me. I am in his grip. When I speak of him I feel him in my head, pounding for order. He will ruin me"* (19). The demon that drives Herzog to his eccentricities is a recent possession. Though intensely aware of his own condition Herzog cannot account for or fully understand it. Bellow allows his protagonist to hurl out vast chunks of remembered facts and incidents from the craters of his spirit. But these clues are deliberately tossed out in haphazard, nonchronological fashion, and range from remote events in Herzog's childhood to the incident that precipitated his breakdown.

The incident occurred in March after his return from Europe when Herzog learned *"the whole funny, nasty, perverted truth about Madeleine"* (56) from his friend, Asphalter, that Madeleine has been cuckolding him with his dearest, his most trusted friend, Valentine Gersbach. The shock leads to the collapse of Herzog, for it is the last of a series of tremors, emotional and intellectual, that have gradually undermined his being. His emotional life is a complete failure; in Sandor

Himmelstein's obscene but picturesque phrase, Herzog's heart has been "shat upon." His intellectual life is in shambles as the bundles of notes for a book stuffed into an old valise abandoned in a closet signify. It is after the explosion in March that Herzog laboriously begins to put his being in order. "Late in spring," the narrator tells us, "Herzog had been overcome by the need to explain, to have it out, to justify, to put in perspective, to clarify, to make amends" (8).

The presentation of Herzog's clownish and lacerating self-excavation, his frantic attempts to discover where he went astray, was one of the tasks that Bellow set himself. It involved autopsiac forays into Herzog's past to lay bare a whole milieu for Herzog (an environment of parents, parents-in-law, teachers, lawyers, friends, doctors, wives, lovers) so that the reader can understand Herzog in the process of Herzog's trying to understand himself. At the same time, since this was to be a *Bildungsroman*, Bellow had to set in motion a forward movement that would culminate in Herzog's recovery. On the crisscrossing tensions formed by the two movements Bellow launched all the intricate questions and problems about what it means to be a human being in our time. In the process, Bellow had to give Herzog the dimensions of a real, twentieth-century human being without mythicizing him. *Herzog* demonstrates Bellow's power to channel these aims into a form both ample and structurally resilient.

Herzog has nine chapters, each one consisting of a number of sections, ranging from just two in chapter 8 to six in the first chapter. The nine chapters (deliberately not numbered in order to continue an illusion of disorder) have to be grouped according to the time pattern of the novel. The first three chapters deal with events on the first day, the next two with those on the second. Chapters 6 and 7 describe the third day's happenings, including the arrival at Chicago. Chapter 8 concentrates on the fourth climactic day. With chapter 9 on the fifth day we return to the scene of the introductory first section in chapter 1.

The first chapter dives into the troubled world of Herzog. In the very first section, however, a brief moment before the plunge, Bellow presents a strong impression of a recovered Herzog to indicate that the work will be a *Bildungsroman*. Herzog feels "confident, cheerful, clairvoyant, and strong" (7). His face with the radiant line that vertically bisects it suggests that he has arrived at a condition of peace. He looks "weirdly tranquil" (8). His state is remarkably like that of Henderson who after his ordeals with Atti sees the stars not as small gold objects but as endless fire. Lying in his hammock at night Herzog is aware that "the stars were near like spiritual bodies" (8). He has a feeling of transcendence, of being one with nature which he looks at piercingly though he feels half-blind, as if he were a Willatale.

Bellow cuts swiftly back to the first of the five critical days. Lying on a smelly sofa in his New York apartment, Herzog, who at this stage is both psychoanalyst and patient, begins his self-examination. He tries to review his life calmly, dispassionately, but cannot maintain this cool posture for long. Bellow uses this short spell (the second section) to present a skeleton sketch of Herzog's life as an adult. This strategy, used earlier in *The Victim*, suggests that though Herzog can outline his past, he has not yet understood its real meaning. The intellectual and emotional elements seem curiously linked. When Herzog was married to Daisy, he had lived a respected and stable life as an assistant professor with a reputation based firmly on his first book, *Romanticism and Christianity*. He divorced Daisy and made a fresh start as husband and as scholar with Madeleine. Herzog's detachment as he thinks about this change reveals itself in the calm, neutral prose of the subjective narrator:

> With Madeleine, several years ago, Herzog had made a fresh start in life. He had won her away from the Church—when they met, she had just been converted. With twenty thousand dollars inherited from his charming father, to please his new wife, he quit an academic position which was perfectly respectable and bought a big old house in Ludeyville, Massachusetts. In the peaceful Berkshires where he had friends (the Valentine Gersbachs) it should be easy to write his second volume on the social ideas of the Romantics. [12]

Unfortunately, Herzog could not write his ambitious work at Ludeyville. Madeleine changed her mind about living in the Berkshires, decided to do her graduate studies, and they left for Chicago with the Valentine Gersbachs. After a year in Chicago, Madeleine asked for a divorce in October. Herzog had to see Edvig, a psychiatrist, who suggested he get away from Chicago. Herzog went to Europe for a lecture tour and came back to Chicago in March.

Having established these guidelines—the time pattern, the fact that the work is a *Bildungsroman*, the outline of Herzog's life—Bellow now flings the reader into Herzog's seething consciousness. The reader has to establish his bearings there, accustom himself to the erratic rhythms of an intellectual whose thoughts grip his heart and, at the same time, stand aside to watch Bellow the novelist at work.

Bellow keeps the plane of the present in continuous view. The sofa on which Herzog lies and broods is constantly referred to in the opening sections so that the reader does not get lost in the mazes of Herzog's mind. Herzog decides to escape to Vineyard Haven. He goes shopping for clothes, returns to his apartment, packs his Gladstone bag and, when the chapter ends, is about to enter the elevator. A cab takes him to Grand Central, where he takes the train to Vineyard Haven. He goes to the Sisslers but steals away from their bungalow almost immediately and takes a plane to Boston and New York. It is eleven at night when he returns to his apartment and falls asleep rereading Geraldine Portnoy's letter, the one that confirmed the stabbing news Lucas Asphalter had given him about his wife and his friend. The three chapters give an illusion of onward movement that turns out to be merely circular. The third chapter ends without any significant action occurring on the plane of the present.

What the first three chapters establish is the language of the novel, actually a whirl of languages that spin around and melt into each other to convey the illusion of a single language. Herzog stops in the middle of a mental letter to Ramona to think about her idea of sexual pleasure:

> Then he realized suddenly that Ramona had made herself into a sort of sexual professional (or priestess). He was used to dealing with vile amateurs lately. *I didn't know that I could make out with a true sack artist*.
>
> But is that the secret goal of my vague pilgrimage? Do I see myself to be after long blundering an unrecognized son of Sodom and Dionysus—an Orphic type? (Ramona enjoyed speaking of Orphic types.) A petit-bourgeois Dionysian?
>
> He noted: *Foo to all those categories!*
>
> "Perhaps I will buy some summer clothes," he answered Ramona. [26]

Herzog's brisk transitions of thought are matched by the ease with which the language changes. The sober, kindly evaluation of Ramona is conducted in terms that are formal and serious (priestess, professional, vile amateurs); the switch back to the mental letter is conveyed not only by the use of italics but also by the colloquial "*sack artist*"; the colloquial mode is then heightened as Herzog asks himself a serious question about his "vague pilgrimage"; but the heightening is immediately undercut by the inflated language of cocktail party cliché (Sodom, Dionysus, Orphic, petit-bourgeois). The puncturing process is completed by the slangy "*foo*" in the mental note. And the language reverts to the serious mode when Herzog resumes recalling his conversation with Ramona. The reader has to accustom himself to these rapid shifts of language and adjust himself to what Herzog calls his "obscure system of idiosyncracies" (18).

One idiosyncrasy is Herzog's habit of jotting down mental notes. These notes, early symptoms of his disintegration and precursors of the mental letter, are cryptic signals in linguistic shorthand. The very first note, "*Death—die—live again—die again—live,*" tells of the opposing impulses within Herzog and suggests he will tilt toward life (9). The quotation from Dr. Johnson—"*Grief, Sir, is a species of idleness*" (10)—is a rebuke to his masochistic tendencies. The echo of Pope in "*Not that long disease, my life, but that long convalescence, my life*" (11) and the line from *King Lear*, "*We have thought too little on this*" (62) indicate that Herzog's reading strongly colors his language. He combines the halves of two proverbs to achieve an economy of psychic expenditure: "*A bitch in time breeds contempt*" (31). More often Herzog uses the language of wit and irony to distance his suffering and to make it serious without making it sentimental. Henderson had used this technique when he referred to Lily as the "altar of my ego." Herzog twists an Emersonian proverb into a comic exhortation to himself: "*Hitch your agony to a star*" (26). The wit work in "*Lead me not into Penn Station*" (30)—Freud would use the phrase "condensation with substitutive formation"— comicalizes the struggle between Herzog's wanting and not wanting to run away from the temptation that is Ramona. Herzog sets down a curious mental note during his reflections on Wanda, his Polish mistress who had introduced him to her sick husband who knew of their affair. The punch line of a witty Jewish anecdote, the note captures Herzog's condition at the time, his intense need for love, his sense of guilt and suffering, all discharged into "*In my grief did I know what I was doing?*" (36).[6]

In contrast to this tart, laconic language is the language of the subjective narrator, the linguistic staple of the novel. This language is clear and vivid, full of energy, packed with references to sights, sounds, and smells:

> They were demolishing and raising buildings. The Avenue was filled with concrete-mixing trucks, smells of wet sand and powdery gray cement. Crashing, stamping pile-driving below, and higher, structural steel, interminably and hungrily going up into the cooler, more delicate blue. Orange beams hung from the cranes like straws. But down in the street where the buses were spurting the poisonous exhaust of cheap fuel, and the cars were crammed together, it was stifling, grinding, the racket of machinery and the desperately purposeful crowds—horrible! [44]

The narrator knows a multitude of contemporary facts about New York. He has an eye for thick detail, for contrasts, for colors. His ear is attuned to the noises of the big city which the rhythms of his prose enact. His vocabulary has a wide range and can grapple with the realities of the contemporary condition.

In counterpoint are the languages of Herzog's thoughts, his point of view, his memories, his first person narration, his mental letters. Together they make up a vernacular whose tremendous range and flexibility allow Bellow to avoid the dull monotone of the conventional flashback. It can express witty malice as when Herzog writes about the "*white buttocky face*" (68) of Strawforth or when he thinks about the "cerebral palsy canisters" (52) that Zelda is so proud of. Or it can refer knowledgeably to the "mire of post-Renaissance, post-humanistic, post-Cartesian dissolution, next door to the Void" (118). Strange elements are yoked together: Yiddish, Hebrew, precipitations of Herzog's wide and varied reading, the accents of academe and the idiom of the streets. They all combine to form an idiolect, the distinctive utterance of a suffering joker who can look at himself with comic detachment: "Ah, poor fellow!—and Herzog momentarily joined the objective world in looking down on himself. He too could smile at Herzog and despise him. But there still remained the fact. *I* am Herzog. I have to *be* that man. There is no one else to do it. After smiling, he must return to his own Self and see the thing through" (86).

Bellow uses all these languages to achieve his fictional tasks. The first three chapters present, in the form of hot fragments of memory, a detailed account of Herzog's disastrous life with Madeleine after he had won her away from the Church and married her. The Madeleine phase of his life was the logical place where the process of self-examination and so, of self-therapy, had to begin. This strategy allowed Bellow to establish the strong reality of Herzog as a human being, before going on to fulfill his other fictional aims.

Bellow begins with a crucial scene that captures in intense focus the tensions between Herzog and Madeleine. It is the day when Madeleine demands a divorce. Bellow presents this scene, set in Chicago, through Herzog's thoughts which are helped by the subjective narrator. The narrator sets down the visual details that have an odd significance. It is a bright, keen fall day. Herzog, who wears a beret, as though he might be going on a trip, is in the backyard putting in the storm windows, as though preparing for a change of weather. Madeleine has dressed for the occasion:

> She wore black stockings, high heels, a lavender dress with Indian brocade from Central America. She had on her opal earrings, her bracelets, and she was perfumed; her hair was combed with a new, clean part and her large eyelids shone with a bluish cosmetic. [16]

A superb actress, she announces her decision triumphantly, dictatorially, telling Herzog she had never loved him and would never love him, stating that he should go and stay with Sandor Himmelstein. Herzog can only stammer that he loves her. He makes no protest and goes back to fixing the storm windows. As he relives the scene, Herzog gains some new insights about himself and about Madeleine. He realizes, unlike Tommy Wilhelm, who never does, that there was a flavor of subjugation in his love for his wife. He knows that he used his passivity to appeal to her. More important, he realizes that this had been one of the greatest moments in Madeleine's life, that it was a theatrical performance involving the exercise of power: "She had prepared a great moment, she was about to do what she longed most to do, strike a blow" (16). Bellow slips in here two important themes, one of acting, the other of power, which he will later amplify.

Almost all the important letters that Herzog writes on the first day are aimed at those who conspired with Madeleine against him. Deliberately, no letters are directed to Madeleine or to Valentine, for then Herzog could not be the suffering joker he is. The letters and the thoughts they generate recreate the whole tragicomic affair in a series of vivid flashes. The chronology of the events that took place after the marriage is fractured but the pieces can be put together. The letter to Tennie, Madeleine's mother reveals the bitter fact that she was used by her masterful daughter. Tennie would be sent to the zoo with little June while Valentine and Madeleine made love in Tennie's New York apartment. The Shapiro letter throws light on the growing tensions between Herzog and Madeleine at Ludeyville. Herzog is full of resentment against Shapiro because, among other things, it was he who encouraged Madeleine to do her graduate studies in Chicago. The letter to the psychiatrist, Edvig, tells of the year Herzog and Madeleine spent in Chicago. Edvig was the dupe of Madeleine, who used him to help her dump Herzog. Sandor Himmelstein merits a letter because it was to his place Herzog moved after Madeleine put him out of the house. Sandor made Herzog sign papers that could damage his divorce case and forced him to take out an unnecessary insurance policy for June. The letters to Zelda and to Lucas Asphalter present Herzog's state of mind in March. After he returns from Europe his condition is worse than it was in the fall. He visits Zelda, but she doesn't tell him the truth about Madeleine and Valentine, the truth which he gets from Lucas.

By the end of the first day Herzog learns some bitter truths about himself. His wife and Valentine have not only conned and cuckolded him, they coldly planned and manipulated his every move, abetted by Tennie, Zelda, Edvig, Shapiro, and Sandor Himmelstein. He sees himself as a fool, a Gimpel[7] whom everyone has taken advantage of. He realizes that he does not know how to conduct himself in the real, pragmatic world. In the harsh jargon of modern psychology, his character is masochistic, narcissistic, anachronistic (10). Like Joseph in *Dangling Man*, Herzog considers himself a good man and cannot understand as yet, why what happened happened. He has not yet penetrated to the inner darkness in his being. He has, however, through the letters given vent to the anger, malice, spite, frenzy, spleen he had always suppressed, concealing this Freudian layer under the mask of a thoughtful expression.

Herzog's world together with its inhabitants begins to emerge slowly into view. Bellow focuses attention on the crises with Madeleine, but permits occasional views of other areas of Herzog's life. Two brief memories of Herzog's childhood in Montreal afford a quick glimpse into the distant past (yet to be revealed) inhabited by Papa and Mama Herzog and their children. The letters to Wanda, Zinka, Professor Byzhkovski and the opening of the letter to Sandor Himmelstein tell us about the people he met in Europe and establish Herzog's state of mind at the time. His immediate past, his condition in early June, is conveyed by the visit to Dr. Emmerich who finds Herzog in good physical health. The present is, of course, kept in constant view. The dominant figure in the foreground is Ramona. Despite her loving, warm sexual assets, she is caught by the narrator in a stance that is sensationally comic: "She entered a room provocatively, swaggering slightly, one hand touching her thigh, as though she carried a knife in her garter belt" (25). Like Lily, Ramona intuitively knows she is the woman Herzog needs: "She recognized, she said, that Moses was in a peculiar state, but there was something about him so dear, so loving, so healthy, and basically so steady—as if, having survived so many horrors, he had been purged of neurotic nonsense—that perhaps it had been simply a question of the right woman, all along" (24). Ramona is right about Herzog as survivor, but perhaps wrong in her belief that she, as the right woman, can cure his condition.

The eye does not however rest on Ramona but travels beyond her to consider the curious assortment of figures around Madeleine, that magnificent actress. Bellow takes the trouble to realize them in detail, so that they are not sketches but caricatures, gargoyles, each one with its own intense contours.

At fifty-five Tennie has gaunt legs but her hair is dyed and has turned stiff and quill-like; she wears butterfly-shaped eyeglasses and abstract jewelry. The most striking feature of Zelda is her nose which moves and dilates with suspicion. Sandor Himmelstein sits "like a sultan, the small heels gathered under his bulging belly" (106). The narrator has a sharp eye for the telling detail, but Herzog's thoughts temper the cruelty with understanding. The curious contradictions in the character are noted but not explained away in psychological terms. Sandor Himmelstein, who is a dwarf and a hunchback, can be a brutal reality instructor, but he has lapses of tearful sentimentality and potato love. Seen through an anthropological lens, Simkin, Herzog's New York lawyer, is a peculiar physical mixture. He has a thick back and small thighs; his head is imposing, shaggy, and aggressive, but his hands are small and timid. His voice is meek when he talks to Herzog, but can suddenly boom with anger when he talks to his secretary. Shapiro, dressed in his stylish pin-striped suit and pointed shoes, behaves like a courtly gentleman, but his laugh betrays the animal within: "What a brute he was! That snarling, wild laugh of his, and the white froth forming on his lips as he attacked everyone" (90).

What all these grotesques have in common is their refusal to come to terms with their animal elements which they suppress. Also, in self-defense against the terrors of the human condition they have become actors. Augie March, toward the end of his adventures, had explained in detail why this change occurs:

> External life being so mighty, the instruments so huge and terrible, the performances so great, the thoughts so great and threatening, you produce a someone who can exist before it. You invent a man who can stand before the terrible appearances. This way he can't get justice and he can't give justice, but he can live. And this is what mere humanity always does. It's made up of these inventors or artists, millions and millions of them, each in his own way trying to recruit other people to play a supporting role and sustain him in his make-believe. The great chiefs and leaders recruit the greatest number, and that's what their power is. [AM, 418]

Madeleine has recruited all these grotesque actors to serve her needs.

Madeleine, the reader slowly begins to see, is more than a woman who has betrayed Herzog just as Valentine is more than a cuckolding friend. Some strange facts about Madeleine now have to be taken into account: her desire to be queen of the intellectuals, her abandonment of the Church and the taking up of ideas and cultural pursuits. Herzog makes up a list of the medley of topics, serious as well as ludicrous, that interested her in quick succession at Ludeyville: Soloviev, de Maistre, the French Revolution, Eleanor of Aquitaine, Schliemann's excavations at Troy, extrasensory perception, Tarot cards, Christian Science, Mirabeau. Another curious fact is that she read three or four murder mysteries a day. When Herzog complains to his best friend that

Madeleine had surrounded herself with a wall of crumbling Russian books in bed, Valentine scolds him with long lectures about Buber and the I-Thou relationship. Valentine, who was a disc jockey in Pittsfield, assumes a new personality when he gets to Chicago. He blossoms into a public figure, a poet, a television intellectual lecturing at the Hadassah on Martin Buber. The narrator comments ironically: "Herzog himself had introduced him to cultural Chicago" (76). Madeleine and Valentine, it is clear, have somehow divided up and appropriated some of Herzog's characteristic tendencies and qualities. The story of Herzog's involvement with the two is more than the common story of a mere cuckold.

At Ludeyville Herzog was not only cuckolded, he was, as he tells Edvig, stoned out of his skull (72). He had isolated himself there with his brilliant young wife to continue his studies in Romanticism and to work on a grand project. Full of intellectual pride Herzog wanted to write a book that would account for the chaos and the upheavals of the twentieth century and would go on to predict the triumphant progress of democracy. Instead of a book, however, he produces 800 pages of focusless argument. Someone plays a strange joke on him, leaving a used sanitary napkin in a dish on the desk where he kept the bundle of notes for his Romantic studies. Herzog cannot understand his failure as a scholar just as he cannot understand his failure as a husband.

In the process of his self-analysis on the first day, Herzog finds himself writing short letters of either appreciation or of sharp protest to public figures. Vinoba Bhave, the leader of the Bhoodan movement in India, and Martin Luther King, Jr., are praised for their courageous stand on public issues; Strawforth and President Eisenhower are scolded and scoffed at for their mistaken views. Herzog himself cannot understand why he writes in this fashion and therefore fires off a squib to himself:

> *Dear Moses E. Herzog, Since when have you taken such an interest in social questions, in the external world? Until lately, you led a life of innocent sloth. But suddenly a Faustian spirit of discontent and universal reform descends on you. Scolding. Invective.* [88]

Herzog's Faustian interest in social questions, comic in its impotence, is a sign that he is breaking out of his isolation and his concern with abstract questions. As he observes in the middle of his letter to Bhave, one has to start with injustices that are obvious to everybody, not with big historical perspectives. Like King Lear, whose tragic sufferings made him acutely aware of human injustice, Herzog travels from his own pain to injustices in the world around him.

By way of the mental letter Bellow was able to introduce ideas into the novel, for Herzog, as intellectual and scholar, is naturally interested in the social, political, and metaphysical problems of his day. Bellow's fictional problem was to ingrain these abstract ideas into the textural flesh of the novel. The fact that they issue from a single consciousness was not enough to make for any real coherence. Bellow achieved the fictional miracle of establishing order among all these elements by gradually heightening the sad and funny story of Herzog into the tragicomic saga of twentieth-century man. The problems that torment Herzog turn out to be the major problems that haunt and baffle the mind of modern man.

Herzog's thoughts just before he arrives at the Sisslers' bungalow revolve around the predicament of modern man: how to retain one's precious individuality in these terrible times, how to be human in the face of the powers and forces that threaten to annihilate the self. Herzog, at this stage, cannot articulate the bewildering complexities of this enormous problem. He interprets his recent disasters as "a collective project, himself participating, to destroy his vanity and his pretensions to a personal life" (117–18). He, who had tried to be a marvelous Herzog, had connived with Madeleine, Valentine and the others who had insisted that he sacrifice his individuality, that "poor squawking, niggardly" thing to the demands of historical necessity (118).

The letter to Shapiro (who had written a fat monograph that Herzog had to review), a letter written with a passionate intensity, now gains added dimensions of meaning. Shapiro, who fascinated and who is fascinated by Madeleine, propounded the modern theory of the decline and doom of Western civilization, a theory that Herzog rejects with angry contempt, scorning *"the canned sauerkraut of Spengler's 'Prussian Socialism,' the commonplaces of the Wasteland outlook, the cheap mental stimulants of Alienation, the cant and rant of pipsqueaks about Inauthenticity and Forlornness"* (96). As historian, Shapiro is a version of Burckhardt with his aesthetic critique of modern history. As prophet of doom and producer of apocalyptic clichés, he is a summation of Spengler, Sartre, Eliot, and Camus. He is the theorist of modern civilization while Madeleine translates his theories into practice. Herzog has no theory to counter Shapiro's, just as he lacks the power to oppose Madeleine. But he insists that two important facts be taken into account: one, that mankind has somehow survived the horrors, the revolutions and the holocausts of our time; second, that this is an age of technology and of technological success. Herzog's belief in science and technology will be developed later. The first fact, that we are all survivors, has to be linked with Ramona's remark that Herzog had survived many horrors including the tyrannic despotism of Madeleine.

The letter to Shapiro also suggests a vital connection between the behavior of Madeleine and that of political and social leaders. Both seek to exercise power and both suffer from paranoia. Herzog is fascinated by Banowitch's theories that all struggles for power have to be understood in terms of paranoid mentality and that madness rules the world. The significance of Herzog's letter to Edvig, "one of his most essential letters" (69), now becomes clear. The diagnosis of the paranoiac traits of Madeleine—"Pride, Anger, Excessive 'Rationality,' Homosexual Inclinations, Competitiveness, Mistrust of Emotion, Inability to Bear Criticism, Hostile Projections, Delusions" (99)—prepares the reader for a Madeleine who exists on two planes simultaneously. Bellow gradually widens her significance and her role in the novel without reducing her human dimension.

Herzog's immoderate resentment against Edvig is now more easily understood. Bellow gives Edvig the typical look of a psychoanalyst: Protestant, Nordic, Anglo-Celtic, Edvig has a neat little beard, his lenses glitter, and he wears a calm smile. More than a Chicago psychiatrist, Edvig is the representative of Freud and his various disciples and descendants. The list of the traits of paranoia is based in part on Freud's famous Schreber analysis which notes that homosexual wishes, projections, and delusions function in the mechanism of paranoia.[8] Herzog dismisses Edvig's analysis of Madeleine in fierce terms: *"You knew nothing. You know nothing"* (84). Bellow here attacks the theory and practice of psychoanalysis and modern psychology, its reduction of human life to mere analytic material, its use of jargon, its arrogant dismissal of all higher emotions and moral tendencies, above all, its conception of human nature as base and ignoble.

Chapter 4 deliberately moves slowly to allow the reader to see patterns and to discover further connections and correspondences. No action takes place on the plane of the present, for Herzog is rooted to his chair, writing letters. The letters themselves lack speed and variety, and the thought currents they induce are acts of recall. There are only two important letters that stretch out through the chapter. The first letter is to Monsignor Hilton, who had converted Madeleine to Catholicism; the second to Herzog's childhood friend, Nachman.

Herzog rehearses his past in order to come to terms with it. The acts of recall, which include moments of savage satire and comic irony, lead to acts of perception: "He was busy, busy, in pursuit of objects he was only now and dimly beginning to understand" (128). The letter to Monsignor Hilton lights up that area of Herzog's life that stretches from his breakup with Daisy to his marriage to Madeleine. It leads to a vivid recollection of his life at Ludeyville when Madeleine was pregnant, and goes on to a fleeting glimpse of his married life with Daisy. The causes of Herzog's failure as a human being and as a scholar become gradually visible.

Visible, because Herzog's self-scrutiny is conducted in brilliant scenes that reenact the past. Bellow does not hesitate to pile detail upon detail and to carry over revealing particulars about a character from one scene to another. The earlier details about Pontritter—his hair ("powerful, isolated threads of coarse white grew from his tanned scalp"), his alpargatas, his blue eyes—are repeated in chapter 4 (40). The additional touches—the seat-fallen trousers, his cold detachment, the witty sarcasm about his daughter ("She's got more faggots at her feet than Joan of Arc")—transform what was in chapter 2 a mere outline into vivid caricature (134). "Very good novels," according to Bellow, "give us a sense of pleasant harassment of the novelist."[9] Shapiro's visit to the Herzogs is rendered with an abundance of detail. Herzog records the particulars of the conversation between Shapiro and Madeleine, noting their facial expressions, the tones of their voices, Shapiro's striped shirt and starched collar, Madeleine's yellow Chinese blouse, which Shapiro cannot take his eyes away from as she bends to set things out on the lawn table. He relishes the irony of Madeleine's opening the jar of pickled herring (which causes Shapiro's mouth to water) just as they discuss Berdyaev's concept of *sobornost*. He also has time to listen to the cicadas: "Meanwhile the cicadas all vibrated a coil in their bodies, a horny posterior band in a special chamber. Those billions of red eyes from the enclosing woods looked out, stared down, and the steep waves of sound drowned the summer afternoon. Herzog had seldom heard anything so beautiful as this massed continual harshness." Herzog the brooder is not completely locked into himself; he has also an extraordinary capacity and need to respond to the exciting world around him: "But I am a prisoner of perception, a compulsory witness" (93).

Herzog's life with Daisy is not presented scenically. Their married life had been earlier summarized as stable and ordinary. A brief scene of their first meeting in Chicago is followed by a brief account of a freezing winter Herzog forced Daisy to endure in a cottage in the eastern Connecticut woods, where he was finishing his book, *Romanticism and Christianity*. The breakup of their marriage occurs after this winter, but it is never made clear why they break up. As a conventional Jewish wife and mother, Daisy would put up with the disagreeable behavior of Herzog, the cold fogs, the sad music he played on his oboe, his brooding over Rousseau. Herzog, aware of how badly he has treated Daisy, offers this simple explanation: "I gave up the shelter of an orderly, purposeful, lawful existence because it bored me, and I felt it was simply a slacker's life" (129).

More than the rupture of a marriage, Herzog's breakaway from Daisy marks the rebellion of the self against a whole way of existence. With her large, green eyes, her clear skin, her golden but lusterless hair, her file card to cover every situation, her need for system, stability, symmetry, order, and containment, Daisy stands for the Enlightenment. Bellow provides many clues that reinforce such a connection. Herzog's involvement with Daisy coincides with his writing of his Ph.D. thesis: *The State of Nature in 17th and 18th Century English and French Political Philosophy*. The marriage begins to crack up as he debates the pros and cons of Enthusiasm with himself in the seclusion of the cottage. He is strongly attracted to the vigor and spirit of Enthusiasm and refers to his furious attempts to reconcile Bacon and Locke with Methodism and William Blake as he writes the chapter on "Romantics and Enthusiasts," a chapter which has significant human consequences: it "nearly did him in—it almost ended them both" (158). Finally, he broods over the theories of Rousseau who has been called the spirit of Romanticism moving in the very bosom of the Enlightenment.

The emotional and intellectual lives of Herzog are not merely linked but intricately intertwined. Herzog's travels from Daisy to Madeleine parallel the travails of the self as it journeys from the eighteenth century to our day. Certain patterns now appear under the thick welter of detail that the four chapters present. Certain connections need to be made, certain corollaries established.

Madeleine, that bewitching, domineering, inexplicable beauty, now looms large and casts menacing shadows on the screen of history. She is the goddess Kali, an embodiment of the evil powers and asuric forces that would trample upon the human soul. She is also the totalitarian spirit made flesh. She drugs people, like her Svengali father and like the modern dictator who exerts a hypnotic power over his subjects. Her photograph at twelve is that of a future dictator: "In jodhpurs, boots, and bowler she had the hauteur of the female child who knows it won't be long before she is nubile and has the power to hurt. This is mental politics. The strength to do evil is sovereignty" (157). With her murderous rages, her intense craving for revenge, this devourer of murder mysteries is also the fanatic revolutionary: "You know how I learned my ABC's? From Lenin's *State and Revolution*," she screams at Herzog (145).

Bellow does not make the mistake of offering simple equations between Madeleine and the juggernauts of modern power. He controls the two planes on which she exists, the human and the historical, in skillful fashion. The realistic level is kept in frontal view while occasional brush strokes and bold touches (the reference to Lenin) make us aware of the other Madeleine as a backdrop. The scenes that center on Madeleine in chapter 4 are viewed by a sharp eye that seizes every visual detail and then zooms in on a feature that deepens the focus:

> First she spread a layer of cream on her cheeks, rubbing it into her straight nose, her childish chin and soft throat. It was gray, pearly bluish stuff. That was the base. She fanned it with a towel. Over this she laid the makeup. She worked with cotton swabs, under the hairline, about the eyes, up the cheeks and on the throat. Despite the soft rings of feminine flesh, there was already something discernibly dictatorial about that extended throat. [139]

The intrusion of the startling "dictatorial" into this simple account of a woman applying makeup makes us aware that here is not only an actress but also an embodiment of modern power phenomena. The reader has from now on to keep several Madeleines in mind when witnessing a scene.

There is yet another layer to the reality that is Madeleine. This actress-dictator is also an aristocrat. She has a Byzantine nose, a medallion profile, an imperial air. There are prints of Flemish altar pieces in her mirror-paneled apartment. Herzog, stung by the enormous bills she has run up, taunts her about giving birth to Louis Quatorze. The key to Madeleine's aristocratic ways is in the letter to Monsignor Hilton when Herzog refers to the theater as *"the art of upstarts, opportunists, would-be aristocrats"* (141). In the letter to Shapiro, Herzog put forth the idea that the spread of democracy in our time had led inevitably to people claiming the privileges of aristocracy but not its duties. *"Circumstances of bourgeois privacy in the modern age,"* the letter continues, *"deprived individuals of scope for Grand Passions, and it is here that one of the most fascinating but least amiable tendencies of the Romantics develops"* (98). Madeleine indulges in the Grand Passions, but this would-be aristocrat has strange lapses of dignity. At one time she attacks Herzog in bed with her knuckles like a street fighter. The tongue lashing she unleashes is not the mere scolding of an enraged, pregnant wife. The manic blue glare in her eyes and her foul language, "balls," "shit," reveal the vulgar bohemian base of this modern aristocrat.

All Madeleines come together in a vivid exchange at the end of the Ludeyville scene:

> "Maybe I married you to improve my mind!" said Herzog. "I'm learning."
> "Well, I'll teach you, don't worry!" said the beautiful, pregnant Madeleine between her teeth. [156]

If Daisy is the Enlightenment, Madeleine is the modern age, in which the darker and debased forms of romanticism (a modern phenomenon, according to Bellow)[10] flourish. Madeleine and the world which she flings him into will teach Herzog a number of lessons, cruel, sad and comic, about himself. Herzog, the scholar of Romanticism, needs Madeleine, that archromantic, to teach him the truth about his intellectual pretensions, just as Herzog, *zisse n'shamele*, that sweet little soul (as Tennie calls him) needs Madeleine, the one with the murderous bitch foot, to tell him the truth about his own nature.

The acts of recall allow Herzog a clearer vision of the Herzog that was. The fierce, bitter anger of the first day has subsided and is now only occasionally vented as in the description of Gersbach as "that loud, flamboyant, ass-clutching brute" (128). Instead, flashes of wit and comic irony are directed against Herzog himself. In *Seize the Day* Tommy Wilhelm was aware of himself as victim. In *Herzog* the reader is aware of the simultaneous presence of Herzog the sufferer and Herzog the joker. Herzog in his New York apartment considers Herzog in the train to Philadelphia painfully grappling with Kierkegaard: "Herzog, at his desk, smiled. He let his head fall into his hands, almost silently laughing. But on the train he was laboriously studying, totally serious" (132). Earlier he had called himself "patient Griselda Herzog" (83). Pontritter considers him a poor fish. Together with Herzog we see him desperately working on his grand project in Philadelphia and we cannot help but smile: "Moses wanted to do what he could to improve the human condition, at last taking a sleeping pill, to preserve himself" (134).

The most comic avatars of Herzog appear during the scenes with Madeleine—Herzog the victim, Herzog the would-be lover, Herzog the great scholar. Herzog, the wooer of a recent Radcliffe graduate, does not want to acknowledge the fact that he is "a fatherly, graying, patient seducer" (140). He now sees that he, too, was an actor who did not choose his role but had to play the part assigned to him by Madeleine: "But the parts had been distributed. She had her white convert's face and Herzog couldn't refuse to play opposite" (140). It is in the remote Berkshires at Ludeyville that Herzog, that intellectual and emotional clown, gives his best performance. His ambitions are grandiose and he has bought a vast, palatial ruin with great old trees and formal gardens in order to realize his twofold plan. What he wanted to do was to change history and influence the development of civilization. More, he thought that his life would have historic importance in that it would provide a marvelous model that the world so desperately needed: "The husband— a beautiful soul—the exceptional wife, the angelic child and the perfect friends all dwelt in the Berkshires together. The learned professor sat at his studies" (156). The comic pretensions of Herzog are revealed by the reference to Louis XIV and to Blake: "Herzog, mulling over these ideas as he all alone painted his walls in Ludeyville, building Versailles as well as Jerusalem in the green hot Berkshire summers" (154). Ludeyville was to be both an earthly mansion and the heavenly city.

Herzog had wanted to be an aristocrat too, the reference to Versailles ironically recalling his taunt to Madeleine about Louis Quatorze. He puts in hard work to save the house from collapse but it is still, in the words of Madeleine, a "crappy old house" (154). Herzog struggles with Hegel but cannot produce his guide for mankind. Looking back at his antics as the Graf Pototsky of the Berkshires, Herzog now sees how absurd he was: "The progress of civilization—indeed the survival of civilization—depended on the successes of Moses E. Herzog. And in treating him as she did, Madeleine injured a great project. This was, in the eyes of Moses E. Herzog, what was so grotesque and deplorable about the experience of Moses E. Herzog" (156–57).

The letter to Nachman provides welcome and needed relief from this harrowing and deflating self-scrutiny. This half of the fourth chapter, which consists of one long section, proceeds at an even more leisurely pace than the first half which had three sections. It begins with the pathetic story of Nachman and Laura, and then leads to a detailed reminiscence of the Herzog family life in Montreal.

The story of the sad sufferings of Nachman the poet and Laura who is touched in the head seems at first to have only a tangential connection with the story of Herzog. Bellow introduces the gaunt, furrowed Nachman, who weeps as he borrows money from Herzog in Paris and whose voice throbs and drones with pain after he visits Laura in the insane asylum, as a contrast to Herzog. Nachman, a romantic dreamer who lacks a sense of irony, cannot control his excessive emotions. He gives in to his feelings which blur his vision of reality. Nachman finds human existence and human beings loathsome. Nachman hates the world he lives in unlike Herzog who has accepted "a mixed condition of life" (166).

The Nachman episode is also functional in that it opens the door to Herzog's childhood days. Herzog, a prisoner of memories too, relives and recreates those ancient times, but they are too distant and yet too near his heart, so that satire is filtered out of his vision. Eye and heart work together: "Napoleon Street, rotten, toylike, crazy and filthy, riddled, flogged with harsh weather—the bootlegger's boys reciting ancient prayers. To this Moses' heart was attached with great power" (174). Herzog travels back to the very roots of his being, to a time of heartache, poverty, suffering, to a time when he had experienced a wide range of human feelings, a time, above all, when he loved intensely and was loved in return. It had moments of pathos and laughter as when Papa Herzog helped their drunken boarder to bed:

> It amused the boys to hear how their father coaxed drunken Ravitch to his feet. It was family theater. *"Nu, landtsman?* Can you walk? It's freezing. Now, get your crooked feet on the step—*schneller, schneller."* He laughed with his bare breath. "Well, I think we'll leave your *dreckische* pants out here. Phew!" The boys pressed together in the cold, smiling. [170]

Unlike the theater of contemporary life, this family theater is innocent, human, smelly, and compassionate. Herzog recalls some of the inhabitants of his childhood world—Reb Shika, who scolded his students even as he taught them Hebrew, Uncle Yaffe with whom he played checkers, shrewd Tante Zipporah, harshly but affectionately critical of the dreams of the Herzogs. The center of Herzog's world were his parents: Mama Herzog, who spoiled the children and, despite their poverty, had great ambitions for them; Papa Herzog, a perennial failure who wept as he narrated the tale of his misfortunes. Everyone participated in the family drama:

> We were like cave dwellers. "Sarah!" he said. "Children!" He showed his cut face. He spread his arms so we could see his tatters, and the white of his body under them. Then he turned his pockets inside out—empty. As he did this, he began to cry, and the children standing about him all cried. [183]

Herzog in the past had talked nostalgically about his sad childhood. Madeleine taunts him bitingly during their Ludeyville quarrel: "Okay—let's hear your sad old story. Tell me about your poor mother. And your father. And your boarder, the drunkard. And the old synagogue, and the bootlegging, and your Aunt Zipporah . . . Oh, what balls!" (155) Herzog's present act of recall is punctuated by moments when he fights the temptation to indulge in nostalgia. He recognizes the "hygiene" of the matter, but is powerless to control his memories: "These personal histories, old tales from old times that may not be worth remembering. I remember, I must" (184). Plato said that remembering is an act of love. Herzog does not understand the full meaning of his childhood (that will come later), but he does realize that his "great schooling in grief" (184) has affected him deeply.

Chapter 5 presents no problems to the reader who has, by now, established his bearings and is aware of Bellow's strategies. He has lived within Herzog's mind and heart and knows how these strange organs function. The major characters and the major themes of the novel have been introduced, and certain links between can be detected though the total design is not yet clear. Almost the whole of Herzog's past has been disinterred. The forward movement now begins.

Herzog is startled out of his isolation and his letter-writing by Ramona's phone call. He cleans up, shaves, puts on his new clothes—the poplin shirt, the madras jacket, the straw hat—takes the Broadway subway to Ramona's apartment, where they have dinner, make love and fall asleep. In between these minor activities (the major one is the act of love) he writes two important letters and engages in long bouts of introspection.

Herzog's thoughts revolve at first around the present, around Ramona. Her sexual assets are, once again, stressed but a new feature is introduced, that she has genuine family feeling. Herzog rehearses the evening he will spend with Ramona. He can anticipate every detail—the menu, the music, the conversation, the moves—because it will be a duplicate of the many evenings he has spent with her. Thoughts about Ramona who has an international background (Spanish, Argentinian, French, Russian, Polish and Jewish), international tastes in food and music, and who could be important in Herzog's future (he wonders what kind of a mother she would make) lead to the recall of the high school graduation address he had given and to the writing of two crucial letters, one to General Eisenhower, the other to Herzog's former tutor. The reader is now in a position to discern a vague pattern which Herzog's thoughts and ideas assume. Highly fragmented and often repeated, they have their source in a mind seething with vital, obsessive concerns.

A central concern dating from his school days is the idea that private life should be a glorious, noble affair. For the graduation address Herzog took his text from Emerson: *"The main enterprise of the world, for splendor . . . is the upbuilding of a man"* (198). Herzog has always believed in the importance of the private common life of the individual. That is why, turning Heidegger's belief into metaphor, he resents the idea of the second fall of Man into the quotidian or ordinary. Madeleine and her crew of reality-instructors try to destroy his pretensions to a personal life. The letter to Monsignor Hilton insists that the ordinary life of humankind is a matter of great historical significance: *"The question of ordinary human experience is the principal question of these modern centuries, as Montaigne and Pascal . . . both clearly saw"* (133).

Because private life is important and because it is so vulnerable today, a number of letters are addressed to people in positions of authority, social, economic, and political. The letter to Smithers, a minor organization man, suggests that bureaucracy does not provide the people with any forms of inner sustenance—good sense, clarity, truth—that they need. The letter to the Secretary of the Interior, Mr. Udall, questions the use of hydrogen bombs to get polar oil. Dr. Emmet Strawforth of the U.S. Public Health Service is taken to task because he compares the risk to human life to Risk Capital in business. McSiggins is scolded because he has not investigated the real ethics that operate in American business.

More damaging to human life than the world of bureaucracy and business are the leaders who wield social and political power. The letter to Adlai Stevenson, who lost to General Eisenhower in 1952, bewails the difference between "those who think a great deal and effect nothing, and those who think nothing evidently doing all" (85). The most dangerous people seek power, thinks Herzog. These people, foolish, arrogant, crazy (like Madeleine) could destroy mankind, and must be begged not to do it (67).

Herzog addresses an appeal to one who had been the most powerful leader of the Western world, General Eisenhower, whose Committee on National Aims turned in a collection of anti-Communist truisms. Instead, Herzog offers the general some ideas about Death and History, quoting from Pascal, Tolstoy, and Hegel. He realizes, comically, pathetically, that Ike would pay no attention to this "bugging," to this "Great Books course," but he wants desperately to communicate two significant truths. First, that people are not satisfied with modern superstitions like the Gross National Product; and second, that there's more private life and freedom today than was available to the common man a century ago. The letter ends with a restatement about the importance of the question of an inward existence for Americans: *"The whole matter is of the highest importance since it has to do with invasion of the private sphere (including the sexual) by techniques of exploitation and domination"* (202). Herzog himself has suffered from such an invasion, his private life, even his sexual life, having been exploited and dominated by Madeleine.

The fictional strategies Bellow uses to make ideas live and to reveal them in action involve a series of intricate cross-references, parallels, correspondences, and corollaries. The reader can travel from character to the idea the character embodies, and also make the transition from idea to character with ease. The world of Herzog with its torments, its battles, its comic and tragic moments, is a microcosm of the huge public world with its confusions, its comedies, its chaos, its despair and its hopes. The ruins of his life, which needed to be put together again to be understood, are analogous to the ruins of the book he could not put together. Instead of a book, we have his whirling and fragmented thoughts and insights about the major questions of our time. The reader cannot write Herzog's book for him but can sketch its main ideas.

The letter to Pulver about the inspired condition is Herzog's reply to Shapiro, his delayed defiance of the theory of decline and fall, his testament of faith that mankind will make it despite the madnesses and the mass convulsions of the twentieth century. Also, it is a further intimation that Herzog himself will make it finally. The basis for his faith had been worked out in his first book on the significance of Christianity to Romanticism. Shapiro's theory of decline has its roots in the Christian view of history (Nietzschean, too) which, according to Herzog, sees "the present moment always as some crisis, some fall from classical greatness, some corruption or evil to be saved from" (71). Mankind, according to Christianity, needs to be ransomed from this condition. One can now understand why Madeleine turned to Monsignor Hilton, that TV actor-representative of Christianity, and through him to Christ, who would redeem her from death and the grave.

Herzog has a different interpretation of history. He sees the present stage of mass civilization not as a period of decline, but as a time of harrowing self-awareness in the onward development of mankind. Having read Hegel's *The Phenomenology of Mind* (one of the source books of the Romantic spirit), he begins with the proposition that *"evolution is nature becoming self-aware"* (203). The upsurge of romanticism in the nineteenth century led to the liberation of the human spirit. Today, this liberation has extended to the masses for we have arrived at the plebian stage of evolutionary self-awareness. This romantic consciousness, emerging after centuries of repression (caused in part by the stifling restrictions of Calvinic Christianity) and in dark as to its future, hates the present conditions in which it finds itself. *"The drama of this stage of human development,"* writes Herzog, *"seems to be the drama of disease, or self-revenge. An age of special comedy."* It is a time when the dark forms of romanticism prevail but not a time of doom. Rebelling against the intolerable pressures and demands placed on him, terrified of the great outer chaos, the individual *"is provoked to take revenge upon himself, a revenge of derision, contempt, denial of transcendence"* (203).

This denial of transcendence springs from definitions of human nature (Hobbesian, Freudian) that are perhaps obsolete. This is the time, suggests Herzog, for a *"total reconsideration of human qualities,"* especially in the light of the new developments in technology. Civilization and even morality are implicit in technological transformation, provided mankind chooses wisely. It can destroy itself, for annihilation is no longer a metaphor. Or, it can rebuild itself and all mankind can live in an inspired condition:

> *Finally, Pulver, to live in an inspired condition, to know truth, to be free, to love another, to consummate existence, to abide with death in clarity of consciousness—without which, racing and conniving to evade death, the spirit holds its breath and hopes to be immortal because it does not live—is no longer a rarefied project.* [205]

Herzog, fervent and intense, convinced he is absolutely right, ends his letter with his prescription for mankind: *"Each to change his life. To change!"* (205)

Abruptly, characteristically, Herzog then jerks himself out of his intellectual trance, his dream of legislating for the human condition, and turns his ironic eye upon the paradoxes of his own condition:

> Thus I want you to see how I, Moses E. Herzog, am changing. I ask you to witness the miracle of his altered heart—how . . . he communicates with the mighty of this world, or speaks words of understanding and prophecy, having arranged at the same time a comfortable evening—food, music, wine, conversation, and sexual intercourse. [205[6]]

The clashing ironies are merrily comic. His heart has not changed at all despite the ringing words of analysis and prophecy. The mighty of the world are unmoved by his unsent letter. And it is not the inspired condition but a night of intense pleasure that awaits this throb-hearted scholar-prophet.

Before he goes to Ramona Herzog writes a letter to his Japanese friend, Sono, a letter that throws light on the two troubled years when he was being divorced from Daisy. Morose and depressed at the time, Herzog went to her West Side apartment, where Sono soothed him with her teas, her baths, her massages, the music of Brahms, the picture scrolls of lovemaking, and her love. Herzog recalls the visits with tender affection and gentle humor, not poking fun at Sono but seeing himself comically as her concubine. Sono marks the transition from Daisy to Madeleine. While convincing as a character because of the numerous details that Herzog offers about her, Sono suggests the literature of enthusiasm that attracted Herzog after he gave up his orderly life with Daisy. Her tender heart, her undemanding ways, the fact that she speaks in French, all imply that she is the pre-Romantic world faintly colored by the Orient into which Herzog moves away from the cold, clear

Enlightenment. Sono calls Herzog a *"philosophe,"* but adds, significantly: "O mon philosophe, mon professeur d'amour" (213).

"I need this outing like a hole in the head" (217): Herzog uses a Yiddish turn of phrase as he locks up his apartment. The journey uptown to Ramona is not a mere outing, but the progress of a pilgrim through the "City of Destruction," a phrase out of Bunyan he had used in connection wtih Madeleine (13). Seen through the deepening, nightmarish dusk, New York is unreally real. Herzog pauses to watch a demolition job:

> The great metal ball swung at the walls. . . . Everything it touched wavered and burst, spilled down. There rose a white tranquil cloud of plaster dust. The afternoon was ending, and in the widening area of demolition was a fire, fed by the wreckage. . . . The workmen, heaping the bonfire with wood, threw strips of molding like javelins. Paint and varnish smoked like incense. The old flooring burned gratefully—the funeral of exhausted objects. . . . Herzog observed that people were spattered with red stains, and that he himself was flecked on the arms and chest. [217–18]

The realistic details of this slum-clearance scene, at first humanized by notations such as "tranquil," "fed," and "gratefully," are heightened by linguistic touches—"incense," "dust," "funeral of exhausted objects," "javelins," "red stains"—so that it becomes a ritual act of death and destruction.

New York is seen as the amphitheater of Hell when Herzog emerges on to upper Broadway. The lights are garish. Broadway is heavy and blue, almost tropical. On the benches are the old men and women of *Seize the Day* strongly marked with decay. A strange sexual omen flits by: "An escaped balloon was fleeing like a sperm, black and quick into the orange dust of the west" (221). And Herzog now has a closeup of the inhabitants of this unreal city:

> Moses took a keen interest in the uptown public, its theatrical spirit, its performers—the transvestite homosexuals painted with great originality, the wigged women, the lesbians looking so male you had to wait for them to pass and see them from behind to determine their true sex, hair dyes of every shade. Signs in almost every passing face of a deeper comment or interpretation of destiny—eyes that held metaphysical statements. And even pious old women who trod the path of ancient duty, still, buying kosher meat. [221–22]

Here is a sudden expansion of the kingdom of Madeleine who is not only queen of the intellectuals, but also empress of Broadway. A carnival crowd of actors wherein the sexes melt into each other (with the anachronistic, orthodox women on its fringes), these people are frantically defiant, frustrated in their hunger for something real and genuine. They embody the idea that Herzog set down in his letter to Pulver, that ours is an age of self-revenge, defiance, and special comedy. The signs on their faces parallel the graffiti Herzog saw on the walls of the subway which were the crazy outpourings of the soul of the masses: "Filth, quarrelsome madness, the prayers and wit of the crowd. Minor works of Death" (219). These are people who are free but do not know how to employ their freedom, which has become a "howling emptiness" (53). Ramona suggests that Herzog wash when he enters her apartment, and Herzog remembers that one had to wash when one came back from *Beth Olam*, the dwelling of the Multitude, the cemetery. Herzog has come to Ramona from the necropolis.

The pattern of the evening with Ramona has already been established so that there are no surprises for the reader. Herzog's Jewish sensibility revolts against the whining music of Mohammad al Bakkar and he satirizes it savagely, noting the guttural pimping voice, the braying wind instruments, the sounds of wire coathangers moving back and forth. Ramona turns the conversation to Valentine and Madeleine and, despite his resolution not to surrender to temptation, Herzog retells the story of his sufferings. Bellow avoids boring repetition by having Herzog refer to incidents not mentioned earlier, ones that confirm Herzog's idiocy—the story of Madeleine's diaphragm which Herzog allows Valentine to take to her in Boston, and Madeleine's simple explanation (which Herzog, Gimpel-like, swallows) that Valentine was not her lover but the brother she never had!

The conversation with Ramona also suggests that Herzog has come to a better understanding of himself. He tells Ramona he is going through a change of outlook. He had been developing the psychology of a runaway slave and had deliberately indulged in the habit of suffering. He knows now that Madeleine, that powerful Reality Instructor, taught him a valuable lesson: "A good, steady, hopeful, rational, diligent, dignified, childish person like Herzog who thinks human life is a subject, like any other subject, has to be taught a lesson." Bellow also allows Herzog to utter a significant truth about the mental explosions that characterize modern consciousness: "Modern consciousness has this great need to explode its own postures. It teaches the truth of the creature. It throws shit on all pretensions and fictions" (239).

It is after the conversation with Ramona that Bellow equates, nakedly now and with passion, Herzog with modern man burdened by the modern condition. It is an equation that the reader can accept because it is the climax of all the connections that the previous chapters have established. Herzog, like Asa Leventhal, has felt the entire world press upon his seismographic soul. His wild internal disorder, also that of modern man, is a fugue in three movements. The first movement presents the causes of this confusion:

Well, for instance, what it means to be a man. In a city. In a century. In transition. In a mass. Transformed by science. Under organized power. Subject to tremendous controls. In a condition caused by mechanization. After the late failure of radical hopes. In a society that was no community and devalued the person. Owing to the multiplied power of numbers which made the self negligible. Which spent military billions against foreign enemies but would not pay for order at home. Which permitted savagery and barbarism in its own great cities. [247–48]

Here, in summary, is the plight of modern man. These tremendous onslaughts against the separate self make it impossible to state what it means to be really human today. Lacking guidelines and limits, deprived of ancient certainties and of social and moral sanctions, modern man throws himself into curious forms of private behavior. He may, like George Hoberly, continually attempt suicide to get Ramona's attention; or, like Lucas Asphalter, try to resuscitate his pet tubercular monkey; or, like Tennie, be a slave to an indifferent, divorced husband; or, like Ramona, play the role of a tough Spanish broad—*una navaja en liga*. Or he can brashly seize the day in the mode of the transvestite homosexuals and lesbians. Or else, he can be a Herzog who, despite his powerlessness to do anything about his condition, can laugh, complain, suffer, hate—and understand it.

For Herzog is modern man who has not accepted the "hollow man" theory of civilization, but has seen the possibility of a new life as the second movement states:

At the same time, the pressure of human millions who have discovered what concerted efforts and thoughts can do. As megatons of water shape organisms on the ocean floor. As tides polish stones. As winds hollow cliffs. The beautiful supermachinery opening a new life for innumerable mankind. [248]

Herzog elaborates on and continues Henderson's belief in the transforming power of technology, provided it is put to proper use. The many references to science and technology can now be put together. The letters to Shapiro and to Pulver celebrated the technical success of the

West. Man can choose not to be destroyed. The postwar rise of industrial Germany and France makes one suspect the theory of decline and fall. The reader can now understand the urgency of the letters to Strawforth and Udall who were ready to use technology for destructive purposes. Herzog resists the argument (in the letter to Monsignor Hilton) that scientific thought has made for confusion in the realm of values. Rejecting Spengler, Herzog would ally himself with Auguste Comte, who wanted to combine the scientific spirit with sociology in order to realize his dream of a religion of humanity.

The third movement allows this huge problem of mankind to descend to a personal level. How is this "new life" to be achieved?:

> Would you deny them the right to exist? Would you ask them to labor and go hungry while you enjoyed delicious old-fashioned Values? You—you yourself are a child of this mass and a brother to all the rest. Or else an ingrate, dilettante, idiot. There, Herzog, thought Herzog, since you ask for the instance, is the way it runs. [248]

Herzog cannot answer the question for mankind, but he knows the answer for himself: "Oh, for a change of heart, a change of heart—a true change of heart!" (248) This exhortation repeats the one he ended the letter to Pulver with and is an echo of the last line of Rilke's great sonnet on an "Archaic Torso of Apollo: *du musst dein Leben ändern*"—"you must change your life." Herzog had wanted the impossible, that every human being should change his life, and had poked fun at the idea and at himself. Now, as the addition of "true" indicates, he is content if only he, as an individual, can change.

Ramona offers him Sombartian luxury and sex, her way of inducing this change, of renewing the spirit through the flesh. Bellow does not make fun of Ramona, but it becomes clear that she is a comic, though lovable, incarnation of the theories of Herbert Marcuse and Norman O. Brown, who set out to rescue modern man from the dangers of sexual repression. She borrows words (such as "Orphic") and ideas (the body is an instrument of pleasure) from Marcuse. By catering to Herzog's senses—her shrimp Arnaud and Pouilly Fuissé, the music of al Bakkhar, the insistence that he wear fine clothes—she becomes, like Polish Wanda, an embodiment of Marcuse's theory of polymorphous eroticism and pleasure, and she echoes traditional Christian language (Easter, Resurrection, Mystical Body) used by Brown in *Life Against Death*. Herzog is very fond of Ramona, but cannot stand the lectures she, Lily-like, inflicts on him. Like Joseph, who had found a measure of peace by polishing shoes, Herzog calms himself by washing dishes.

After lovemaking, he falls asleep next to Ramona. Wakened by the scream of a jet, he wants to jot down a message to Hoberly, but doesn't. Instead, he strokes Ramona's thick hair (as Allbee did Leventhal's) and falls asleep.

Conscious of a surge of strength after the night with Ramona, Herzog decides to do something practical about June and calls Simkin. Their phone conversation serves three purposes. It allowed Bellow to complete the earlier sketch of Simkin. Little Napoleon, as he is called, displays a taste for Palestrina, Monteverdi, and modern painting. Simkin plays a cat-and-mouse game with his friend, mocking Herzog, putting him on, prodding him, but he also gives him good advice and offers to help him. Human beings, Herzog slowly discovers, and this is part of the process of recovery, cannot be pigeonholed. Simkin is more than a reality instructor. The conversation also reveals that Ramona's therapy was only temporarily effective for Herzog's fears and feelings are easily agitated by Simkin.

The talk between Simkin and Herzog makes the reader thoroughly aware of the historical significance of Valentine, on whom the conversation focuses. Bellow makes Herzog use the language of comic exaggeration to describe Valentine. Valentine is a poet in mass communications. He is "a ringmaster, popularizer, liaison for the elites. He grabs up celebrities and brings them before the public. And he makes all sorts of people feel that he was exactly what they've been looking for. Subtlety for the subtle. Warmth for the warm. For the crude, crudity. For the crooks, hypocrisy. Atrocity for the atrocious" (264). The ghastly pun in the last sentence betrays Herzog's hysterical state. Language is not really under his control as the desperate references to Ivan the Terrible, to Rasputin, to Cagliostro, to Siberian shamans tell us. The outburst is, however, a magnification and a distortion of the truth about Valentine: "Anyway, I see the mobs breaking into the palaces and churches and sacking Versailles, wallowing in cream desserts or pouring wine over their dicks and dressing in purple velvet, snatching crowns and miters and crosses" (265). Valentine, too, like Madeleine, represents the vulgar aristocratization of the democratic masses.

Simkin is right when he slyly says he never saw a man pouring wine over his dick in any movie. But the reader, adding together the earlier references to Valentine, can now see him in historical perspective as the faceless, classless, terrified mob that acted so fiercely and wantonly in 1789, 1914, 1917, and 1939. Valentine resembles Putzi Hanfstaengl, Hitler's own pianist (29). He has a butcher's, teamster's, commoner's accent (78). Herzog remembers the books he had read on the French and

Russian revolutions when he thinks of Valentine. Valentine is an incarnation of mass man, kin to the lesbians and homosexuals that flaunt themselves on Broadway. He is an embodiment of the masses that throng the subway. Herzog earlier (unlike Wilhelm) had rejected the feeling of brotherhood with these masses as false, as a sentimental yearning for collectivity, as the attraction of atomized and isolated individuals for mass organization. This feeling was not true love, but the same cowardly potato love that had exuded from Sandor Himmelstein, another mass man with the soul of a mob. It was this potato love that had enabled Eisenhower to win the elections in 1952.

The human and historical dimensions of Valentine and Madeleine mesh together at the moment when Herzog recognizes the mutual love of these two love-actors for each other: "They have a right to each other; they seem even to belong together" (270). Their "love," together with Madeleine's strong magnetism over her followers, parallels the magic spell that totalitarian leaders cast over the masses. In *The Origins of Totalitarianism* Hannah Arendt refers to Hitler's awareness of such an interdependence and quotes from his speech to the SA: "All that you are, you are through me; all that I am, I am through you alone."[11]

The reader can now perceive the vast historical significance of the human triangle. Madeleine, Valentine, and Herzog are more than a comedy team with Herzog playing straight man. On the plane of modern history, the straight man is the individual seeking desperately to guard his valuable selfhood which the dictator and his hordes want to extinguish totally. Totalitarianism, with its secret police and with its use of concentration and extermination camps, demands total domination of the individual and attempts to reduce the human personality to a mere thing. It seeks to destroy the human person and kill his unique identity. Herzog later becomes aware of the significant fact that Madeleine would have had him cremated (393). The reader can now grasp the human implications of the idea expressed in the letter to Shapiro: "The Dictator must have living crowds and also a crowd of corpses" (99).

Terrified, bewildered, this living corpse looks in the mirror and asks itself furious questions:

> *My God! Who is this creature? It considers itself human. But what is it? Not human of itself. But has the longing to be human. And like a troubling dream, a persistent vapor. A desire. Where does it all come from? And what is it? And what can it be? Not immortal longing. No, entirely mortal, but human.* [270]

At the courthouse, awaiting Simkin, Herzog enters an immense courtroom with broad mahogany seats and an ornate ceiling. In this theater-like chamber he witnesses three trials. Elegantly dressed, averting his face to one side like his mother, Herzog begins with a spectator view of human justice. He enjoys the first trial, a simple one of assault with intent to rob, as if he were at a play, calmly relishing the comic and cruel details, the lard-faced cop and the criminal with the "wolfish tension within his voluminous ridiculous pants" (278). The second trial, that of a young German interne decoyed by a plainclothes man into committing a homosexual offense, stirs Herzog's feelings. The magistrate, possibly a political appointee, one who puts on an act for the people in court, suddenly appears to have a heart and unexpectedly proves to be human by warning the interne that a guilty plea would ruin his medical career in the United States. Herzog is disturbed by the paradoxes of both human nature and of social justice.

The third trial shatters Herzog's former calm. Aleck/Alice, the bisexual prostitute, is a crystallization and a close-up of the Broadway world of Hollywood extras. With his lined face, his green shirt, his long, dyed hair, his empty smile, his tight pants, and, above all, his shrill, icy voice, Aleck/Alice defies the world he has been flung into, treating it with comic contempt. Bellow transforms Herzog from a mere voyeur to one who can absorb and project the full meaning of the trial he witnesses.

It is a moment of revelation. Herzog sees that everyone (except the intensely human Marie Poont) there—idlers, lawyers, policemen, the magistrate himself—are actors. Aleck/Alice is a "dream actor," who rebels against the outrageous reality he finds himself in by thumbing his nose at the world, by defying its horrendous comedy by being outrageously comic himself:

> "Well, which are you, a boy or a girl?"
> The cold voice said, "It depends what people want me for. Some want a boy, and others a girl."
> "Want what?"
> "Want sex, your honor."
> "Well, what's your boy's-name?"
> "Aleck, your honor. Otherwise I'm Alice." [279]

The power structure, Herzog further realizes, can make whores of us all, as Sandor Himmelstein had angrily declared. It must have led the magistrate to do all that was necessary for his appointment; and it led also to Aleck/Alice's degeneracy. Unlike the magistrate, Aleck/Alice does not resort to hypocrisy but proudly confesses the "truth" about himself. The sentence—four or five years—does not quench his vengeful merriment: "Now he was going back to the cell, and he called out, 'G'by all. Goodby.' Sugary and lingering. 'By-ee.' An icy voice. They pushed him out" (281).

Herzog has, for the first time, broken out of his abstract, intellectual world and entered the world of Allbee and the Wariri. He feels a burning poison entering his bloodstream and stinging his heart, a poison that he realizes has sprung up from within. He has to conduct a terrible investigation (the term is Augie's) in order to discover the secret and source of his interior darkness.

He reaches deep into his past to uncover two crucial moments he had banished from memory, moments when his mother had implanted in him the truth about death. He finger-rubs his palm the way his mother had when, at the age of six or seven, he had asked how Adam was created out of dust. A particle of earth and darkness appears on it. She had repeated the lesson in reverse nine years later when, just before dying, she showed him her fingers: "Under the nails they seemed to him to be turning already into the blue loam of graves. She had begun to change into earth!" (287)

Herzog had turned his face away from the terrible reality of death. Instead, hugging the laundry girls whenever he could, he had wrestled with *The Decline of the West*, refusing to accept Spengler's view that this was an age of spiritual exhaustion, and that he, Herzog, as a Jew who belonged to the obsolete Magian era, would never be able to understand the Christian and Faustian world idea. Herzog now sees that it was not only a time when he refused to "see" death, but also the moment when his grandiose intellectual ambitions had begun, driven by the bitter need for revenge. His heart had been "infected with ambition, and the bacteria of vengeance" (286).

The fourth case, a criminal one, tried by jury, is conducted in a small room where the people have to sit on polished wooden rows. The subjective narrator records the details. A young couple is tried for the murder of a three-year-old. The terrifying details are presented coldly. The lawyer tabulates the woman's case history: an abandoned cripple, sexually abused, with a damaged brain, given to epileptoid fits of rage. The medical report on the child is given in professional terms: the malnutrition and the rickets, the carious teeth, the broken ribs, the ruptured liver, the hemorrhage and the injury to the brain. Bellow deliberately uses the ironic mode to purge the scene of melodrama and to intensify the horror of its impact. The savage details come from the lips of "tolerant, comfortable people" (288). The witnesses are calm and unruffled, especially the hotel clerk, who sees the murder:

> Would he tell the court what he saw? He saw the woman with the boy in her arms. He thought she was hugging him, but to his

astonishment she threw him from her with both arms. He was hurled against the wall. This made the noise he had been hearing below. Was anyone else present? Yes, the other defendant was lying on the bed, smoking. And was the child now screaming? No, at this time he was lying silent on the floor. [292]

The trial scene is a triumph, the work of a novelist who has learned how to lift the realistic mode of Dreiser and the naturalists to a tremendous pitch of intensity. There is no need for symbolism. Irony, passion and compassion burnish the sordid facts and the cruel details so that they flash with a wealth of meaning. Here is a living translation of all the earlier abstract discussions and debates about society, power, suffering, cruelty, evil, and justice.

Herzog in a state of shock rushes out of the courtroom. His heart and his mind cannot make sense of the horrors he has just witnessed. Only his eyes function as his imagination recreates the unbearable scene of the murder:

> The child screamed, clung, but with both arms the girl hurled it against the wall. On her legs was ruddy hair. And her lover, too, with long jaws and zooty sideburns, watching on the bed. [294]

Herzog the scholar of Romanticism, Herzog the human being, Herzog the suffering joker—all three are stunned into silence. His humane studies have not prepared him to understand *these* human beings. His own disasters and sufferings disappear as unreal and petty before such monstrousness. His vulnerable heart cannot lurch in response to the scene because the murdered child is beyond sentimental pity. His usually keen mind can see no ironies here. For here are no actors. Here is no justice. No theories, psychological, philosophical, or sociological, can explain away this hideousness and account for the child's brutal murder.

Herzog experiences a blow that is intellectual, emotional, and devastating, because it has come on top of the one Herzog received in March. Bellow does not allow Herzog to analyze the impact of the trial scene. The impact is deep, subterranean, parallel to the impact of Atti on Henderson. Herzog can only stammer out a few, futile questions. The narrator tells us: "He was wrung, and wrung again, and wrung again, again" (294). Bellow uses a tiny incident to convey the lightning truth that penetrates deep into Herzog without his being aware of it. Rushing out of the courtroom, Herzog blunders against a woman wearing a cast with metal clogs on her foot: "Her eyes, prominent, severe, still kept him standing, identifying him thoroughly, fully, deeply, as a fool.

Again—silently—'*Thou fool!*' " (293–94). Herzog, as man and as
scholar, has been a "fool"—he will slowly understand how and why.

A change of pace is apparent in chapter 7. Herzog does not write any
mental letters, except for two short notes to himself. Almost all the
parallels and cross connections have been set up, so that the reader does
not have to pause in order to identify them. Herzog's past has been
almost totally exhumed. The novel now begins to accelerate on the plane
of the present as it enacts the quickening process of Herzog's recovery.
    Without pausing to analyze the associational process, but significantly
discarding the glad rags of a clown and wearing a dirty, wrinkled
seersucker suit, Herzog impulsively takes a jet to Chicago. In March he
had locked his anger and rancor within himself merely discharging an
acronymic telegram to Valentine—Death Enters at the Heart. Now, he is
driven to act, though he does not know what he will do. The very
decision is an indication of change. Herzog is no longer the old Herzog.
He senses the change in himself. Even his stepmother, Tante Taube,
becomes aware of it: "She sensed that he was strongly agitated, missed
his habitual vagueness, the proud air of abstraction in which M. E.
Herzog, Ph.D., had once been clothed. *Them days is gone forever*"
(301).
    Herzog's visit to Tante Taube allows Bellow to slow down the pace of
the narrative before accelerating it again in the next scene. It provides
the necessary touch of comedy after the intense murder trial. Herzog
remembers what Tante Taube had told him about her first husband: "The
doctor thought it would be bad for mine heart. And every time . . .
Kaplitzky-*alehoshalom* took care on everything. I didn't even looked"
(303). The visit also gives us a look at yet another "actress" whose
tactics for survival involve delay, slowness, and stasis. Above all, the
visit confirms the fact that Moses enjoyed being an actor and a victim.
For Herzog recalls an event that took place just before his father's death.
Broke, involved in his ambitious Romantic studies, wavering between
Sono and Madeleine, he had come to Chicago and begged Papa Herzog
for a loan with a face leaking pain, misery, and conceit. Outraged by his
son's abject appeal to be saved (Herzog wears a "Christianized smirk" on
his face and now thinks he might as well have been a convert, like
Madeleine), in agony because he could not bear to see the "half-made"
Moses in front of him, troubled by thoughts of his approaching death,
Papa Herzog brandished a pistol and threatened to shoot his son.
    Armed with this pistol, with two bullets in it, Herzog drives to Harper
Avenue, bent on righteous vengeance. As he fantasizes about the murder

he will commit, the evil in him surfaces as it did after the Aleck/Alice trial: "Into his mouth came a taste of copper, a metabolic poison, a flat but deadly flavor" (312).

Bellow does not comicalize the scene of Herzog's stalking his own house, peering through the kitchen window at Madeleine, watching Valentine give little Junie her bath. The details are presented by the sympathetic subjective narrator: Valentine treats the child with affection and gentle authority; Junie is playful and happy. Herzog's decision not to shoot, like his decision to fly to Chicago, is sudden, abrupt. His nonaction has the force of action. Herzog acts by deciding not to "act."

For he realizes, in a burst of cumulative truth, that he himself is an actor and that the role he has just assumed is that of a brokenhearted avenger come to mete out justice. The scales now drop from his eyes: "As soon as Herzog saw the actual person giving an actual bath, the reality of it, the tenderness of such a buffoon to a little child, his intended violence turned into *theater*, into something ludicrous" (316). Also, the monstrous egotism that compelled him to view events in self-regarding terms now yields to an awareness of others and to the truth that his daughter is closer to these grotesque love-actors than she is to him. [12]

It is another moment of insight, another turning point. Herzog is in the state Henderson was in immediately after the death of King Dahfu. Bellow had now to dramatize the rebirth of Herzog's heart, mind, and soul. He had to control the rhythmic pace of his narrative and avoid sudden deceleration after this climactic moment. In *Henderson the Rain King* Bellow had introduced omens and intimations that Henderson experiences as he travels back to America. Herzog's return to health posed more problems because Herzog is a more complex character and because the psychic process had to be enacted in the realistic mode.

Bellow uses the brilliant strategy of introducing structural balance by paralleling the healing process with that of Herzog's crackup. The moment of insight takes the form of an implosion that causes a second upheaval within Herzog. It is as if he had fallen back into his March state again, for immediately after he gets into his car he jots down notes and tosses out ideas seemingly disconnected and in fragments. Herzog is in an excited streaming state. [13] He feels that blood has burst into his psyche and finds himself in a state of "simple, free, intense realization" (325).

This streaming state that leads to the making of a new Moses Herzog is a continuous process that begins with the decision not to shoot and ends at Ludeyville with the decision not to write any more letters. It can be

divided into two stages: the first consists of Herzog's encounters with
several people in Chicago, the second presents Herzog's encounter with
his new self in Ludeyville.

By presenting a series of encounters instead of letters or introspec-
tions Bellow was able to maintain the narrative pace he had set up in
chapter 7. These encounters reveal a new Herzog, one who, no
longer an actor, now knows how to act. His reactions during these
meetings, encounters and confrontations reveal that he has changed
emotionally, intellectually and spiritually, and is on the right road to the
human.

His heart, that throbbing vulnerable organ by which, as his name
signifies, he is led, is purged of its sentimental dross. The meeting with
Lucas suggests that Herzog will now no longer yield to potato love. "All
that hysterical stuff is finished" (322), he informs Phoebe Gersbach. His
love for June, his daughter, is intense, but he does not allow her childish
babblings about Madeleine and Valentine to provoke him to bitterness or
sorrow. He holds his feelings in at the police station and does not appeal
for mercy as he had done with Papa Herzog: "No weakness, or sickness,
with which he had copped a plea all his life (alternating with arrogance),
his method of preserving equilibrium—the Herzog gyroscope—had no
further utility. He seemed to have come to the end of *that*" (347).

The confrontation between Madeleine and Herzog is a climactic
confirmation that Herzog has indeed changed. Bellow the craftsman had
to put in this scene in order to remind the reader of the complex reality of
Madeleine. Madeleine the mother (she does love June as Geraldine
Portnoy had said, and as the American worship of kids dictates),
Madeleine the actress (her entrance is dramatic), Madeleine the dictator
(the clatter of her heels is commanding), Madeleine the aristocrat (she
has a blue-eyed, straight, Byzantine profile), all combine for the last
time into the terrifying Kali. Her hatred and her insane violence
projected through her icy stare launch a barbaric final assault against the
atomic self that is Herzog: "They expressed a total will that he should
die. This was infinitely more than ordinary hatred. It was a vote for his
nonexistence" (367). The powers of this world symbolically converge on
Herzog, that tiny and ineffective being now charged with an electrified
consciousness.

It is this consciousness that allows Herzog to realize that Madeleine
has no real power over him. He is free, free from the spell of Madeleine
and of Valentine too. He rejects their tyrannic definition and reduction
of his self. He can now see their hollow selves and dismiss them: "Ah,
this Madeleine is a strange person, to be so proud but not well

wiped—so beautiful but distorted by rage—such a mixed mind of pure diamond and Woolworth glass. And Gersbach who sucked up to me. For the symbiosis of it. Symbiosis and trash" (364). Herzog can now, like Aleck/Alice, but with a thorough awareness of his predicament, dismiss the tyrannies he has been living under. Bellow makes Herzog echo the language of Aleck/Alice: "And so I'm out of this now. Count me out. Except in what concerns June. But for the rest, I withdraw from the whole scene as soon as I can. Good-by to all" (364–65).

Herzog's dismissal of all that sought to destroy him springs also from a deeper recognition of the limitations of his own vulnerable self. "My emotional type is archaic," he confesses after leaving Phoebe (324). Emotionally, Herzog had in him the weakest elements of the Old World (as his extravagant weeping at his father's funeral testifies) with the "emotional goodies" he had got in the New World, "truth, friendship, devotion to children (the regular American worship of kids), and potato love" (325).

A further excavation into his strange emotional make-up leads Herzog to uncover its hidden source. On the way to the police station he summons up a homosexual attack he had experienced when he was eight. Herzog relives the terrors of those crucial moments, beginning with the ghastly sights, sounds, and smells of the chicken slaughter-house on Roy Street, going on to the snarling shrieks of dogs, and leading to Herzog's first encounter with death: "Moses watched him recede in the mud of the lane, stooping and gaunt in the long coat, walking swiftly, with bad feet; bad feet, evil feet, Moses remembered; almost running" (352).[14] Then Moses went home to supper as if "nothing had happened. Nothing!" (352)

Here is the first searing experience with death which Herzog kept buried within himself. The trial scenes had made the two lessons about death which his mother had taught him surface. Herzog now realizes that this cancerous fear has "bent and buckled his life into these curious shapes" (325). He now can see the pattern of behavior which his childish response to the challenge and terror of death has established. He now discovers that he too, like Madeleine, Valentine, Simkin, and Sandor Himmelstein, has been a Reality Instructor. Whereas Madeleine and the others had turned themselves into fierce, snarling, brutal realists, Herzog, terrified of death like them, turned himself into a child-man, like Augie March, basing his creed on a nursery rhyme: "I love little pussy, her coat is so warm, and if I don't hurt her she'll do me no harm" (355). By reducing Henderson's Atti to a little pussy Herzog had avoided facing the stern reality of death.

The crackup within Herzog releases these new insights about himself and also causes blinding flashes that light up the world around him. Like Henderson before he left for Africa, Herzog had known these truths before. He knew earlier that he had made a deal with life and had offered meekness in exchange for preferential treatment (191). But like Henderson and his fellow-protagonists, he had to have this knowledge cauterized upon his being by terror and suffering. Earlier he had dismissed Kierkegaard's ideas about the sickness unto death and the cure that faith bestows. He had offered Eisenhower stray thoughts out of Tolstoy and Hegel about Death and History and the meaning of the struggle for power. But these thoughts had been "like mocking flowers grown in the soil of fever and unacted violence" (201). The thoughts that erupt out of him now are not the cool clear ideas of a professor or a scholar or a Lovejoy, but the perceptions, passionate if fragmentary, of a survivor who has faced the terrors of today and can offer his fellow survivors some valuable suggestions about human existence.

These suggestions are presented in a voice that is also new. Herzog remains Herzog, but his words and phrases, no longer overspiced with wit and irony, lose their bitter pungency. They are no longer the words of ringing prophecy he had directed at Pulver. Aware of his limited humanness, Herzog now speaks a mellower language of concern and understanding.

His concern for Lucas who performs the strange exercises with death in an imagined coffin leads Herzog to reject not only Tina Zokoly, but Heidegger and the other preachers of dread in modern times. With hesitant authority but with real intensity Herzog sweeps away the frightening prescriptions of the tribe of German existentialists who insist that man cultivate the awareness of death, guilt and dread to heighten his awareness of life and to achieve freedom and authenticity. Our generation, Herzog realizes at the police station, infected by this cancerous philosophy, has erected Death as its God.

The reader can accept the truth of Herzog's statements because, together with Herzog, he has been a witness of the behavior of this generation. He has heard the snarls of the teachers of Reality who believe that facts have to be nasty and brutal, that "truth is punishment and you must take it like a man" (332). He has seen the hedonistic postures of the Broadway crowd of isolates; he has observed the curious ways of Aleck/Alice, Lucas Asphalter (who loves a monkey), Phoebe Gersbach (whom death has found still unripe), Tante Taube (who fought the grave to a standstill, balking death itself by her slowness), and the Pontritters. Valentine speaks majestically about death (80)—and hypocritically; while Madeleine flits from one solution to another hunting in vain for a cure.

Herzog sweeps aside the philosophy of this generation. But he cannot as easily dismiss the deadly nightmare that is history, which roars at him:

> You think history is the history of loving hearts? You fool! Look at these millions of dead. Can you pity them, feel for them? You can nothing! There were too many. We burned them to ashes, we buried them with bulldozers. History is the history of cruelty, not love, as soft men think. We have experimented with every human capacity to see which is strong and admirable and have shown that none is. There is only practicality. If the old God exists he must be a murderer. But the one true god is Death. [353]

Here is 1789, 1914, 1917, 1939. Here is totalitarianism and here are the concentration and the extermination camps. Here is also an abstract rendition of the terrifying fourth trial, which shattered Herzog's inner being and hurled out questions he had no answers to: "And what was there in modern, post . . . post-Christian America to pray for? Justice—justice and mercy? And pray away the monstrousness of life, the wicked dream it was?" (294)

Herzog still has no answers to these terrible questions about history and human life, perhaps because no logical answers can be given. What he throws out during the encounters in Chicago are fragmented and tentative hints and suggestions towards an answer.

The recent developments in science and technology sound a note of hope and possibility. Bellow inserts Herzog's visit to the Museum of Science to drive in this suggestion. Herzog sees the promise of the world to come in June, its future good but also its evil. It is his daughter who will "inherit this world of great instruments, principles of physics and applied science (338)." Herzog realizes the imminence of nuclear horror but he is also aware that man is capable of controlling the magnificent technology he has brought into being. Significantly the first thought that leaps into Herzog's mind after his decision not to shoot is: "*What a moment for the human soul!*" (316)

Herzog now has the answer to the "most real question" (218) he had asked himself in the subway after rejecting the frenzied craving of the crowd of damaged isolates for collectivity.[15] Potato love, which has its source in terror,[16] is replaced by genuine love. "I really believe that brotherhood is what makes a man human" (333), he tells Lucas Asphalter. The sincerity in Herzog's voice rings true and clear, reinforced as it is by lines from *The Four Zoas* by William Blake, his constant pocket companion: "Man liveth not by Self alone but in his brother's face. . . . Each shall behold the Eternal Father and love and joy abound" (333). This feeling of love and brotherhood has to be translated into action, not in terms of exploitation of one's fellow man (all the Reality Instructors, including Herzog, did just that), but as a form of active involvement. Herzog doesn't yet know what he will become, but he knows that "the real and essential question is one of our employment by other human beings and their employment by us" (333).

He knows however that he need no longer be the intellectual scholar juggling with ideas that would present a new angle on the human condition (as he told Zelda). He knows too that he has to cast away his former sense of being a victim, just as modern man has to throw off his sense of doom, of being a victim of the human condition. Instead of using his imagination as Blake and King Dahfu did, modern man accuses God of murder. This easy servile disastrous attitude to life Herzog now abandons.

Having thrown off these burdensome ideas, Herzog senses a change in himself. He looks ready to cave in, according to Lucas Asphalter, but Herzog insists that he is fine. His brother, Will, does not find him upset despite the broken rib. Herzog considers a Freudian, physiological explanation (derived from *Mourning and Melancholia*) that the metabolic wastes of fatigue have left him free. But, as the last chapter will convey, this state merely heralds the purer and joyous freedom of the human spirit he will attain.

Hineni, here I am, Herzog breathes softly to himself when he gets to Ludeyville. The Hebrew utterance, which a Jewish child uses in *cheder*, is the word that Abraham repeated three times, to God, to Isaac, and to his guardian angel. It is also the word the biblical Moses uttered when God called unto him out of the midst of the burning bush. Here I am, says Herzog to his Jewish self, which he had polluted but which he has now purified. The acts of loving recall of his ancient times summoned up the Jewish heritage which he (unlike Valentine, who is not only a parody Herzog, but also a parody Jew; unlike Shapiro, that fake Jewish intellectual; unlike Sandor Himmelstein, that Jew who exudes potato love; but like Tommy Wilhelm) had renounced during his involvement with Sono and with Madeleine, but which he still retains. He has abandoned the Old World schooling in grief and, at the police station, knows that he should not indulge in the "Jewish art of tears" (337). During the Nachman reminiscence he utters a *Yiskor*, a prayer for the soul of his dead mother, whose grave he has not visited for a long time, about which he feels guilty.[17] In the police station, fragments from the *Amidah*, recited thrice daily by orthodox Jews, spring spontaneously to his lips: "*Dear God! Mercy! My God!* Rachaim olenu . . . melekh maimis. . . . *Thou King of Death and Life* . . . !" (370) Herzog will never return to the faith of his fathers. The letter to Mermelstein refers to the "*old suffocating churches and synagogues*" (385), which have now to be abandoned. Nor will he be the rabbi his mother wanted him to be. For Herzog now returns to "an ancient system, of greater antiquity than the Jews themselves" (32). Accepting his Jewish roots as a vital part of the human system, Herzog returns to Ludeyville, which he had bought as a foolish, Jewish, defiance of WASP America.

Here I am, says Herzog to Ludeyville, where he wanted to cultivate solitude and self-sufficiency, and where he dreamed of building a Versailles and a Jerusalem. Not an Eden, it is very much a part of the larger world he has to return to, sparklingly green and beautiful and dangerous. This garden is a "thick mass of thorny canes, roses and berries twisted together" (377). There are insects and rats and snakes. The water of the cistern looks pure, but one could always find "a chipmunk or two, a rat, dead at the bottom though it looked pure enough when you drew it up, pure, green water" (392). Bellow gently invests Ludeyville with a number of associations. The house which Herzog had tried to hammer, paint, and patch together is a faint analogue of the world of ideas which he had desperately tried to put together into a system. It is also, as Herzog recognizes, the nineteenth century quietly dying in this remote green hole, a place which Madeleine called crappy and could not live in for more than one year. Herzog does not feel he owns the place; he has come to this place which is not on the Esso map, to this "*mere border of grassy temporal light*" (389), as he tells Nietzsche, merely to look things over.

Herzog has come back to seek clarity and peace, and to quieten the clamors of his being. No longer a slave to Madeleine, he is now filled with joy. He still feels the need to write letters, but now they issue from a "tranquil fullness of heart" (382). He can, for the first time, write to Madeleine and to Valentine. He sends messages of affectionate concern and understanding to those he loves, Marco, Luke, Ramona, and through them to his fellowmen. The story of the sick man from Scott's Antarctic expedition who deliberately loses himself so that the others could survive is a tiny example of brotherhood in action. The brief message to Luke predicts he will recover from his depression. To Ramona, Herzog offers two significant insights: first, that all men are capable of seeing the light of truth; second, that despite death, man, just because he has been summoned into existence, needs to lead a human life and not destroy himself seeking a dubious "freedom."

Looking things over, Herzog ignores the books in his Ludeyville library. He looks unperturbed at his scholarly notes scattered all over his study for he knows he will never again be a scholar performing abstract work. But he cannot help for the last time baiting two intellectuals whose ideas he admires. Nietzsche too, like Herzog, had believed in the possibility of human recovery. Herzog accepts Nietzsche's insistence that one has to ask the most piercing questions *"into evil, through evil, past evil"* (389). But he rejects Nietzsche's belief in the power of the Dionysian spirit to recover after witnessing Decomposition, Hideousness, Evil, and Nietzsche's rejection of mankind as it is. Survival is absolutely necessary, Herzog tells Nietzsche, though he doesn't mention the fact that he, Herzog, is a survivor.

The letter to the fictitious Professor Mermelstein who has scooped Herzog is skillful fictional strategy. It allowed Bellow to restate one of the main ideas in his novel, the close link between modern power systems and paranoia, to dismiss Kierkegaard's idea that Hell is essential for the leap to truth, and once more to reject Shapiro's apocalyptic visions. Bellow pokes gentle fun by making Herzog reprimand Mermelstein for using the very modes of presentation that Herzog himself has been using: *"I was somewhat bothered by borrowings and references which I considered 'hit and run,' or the use of other writers' serious beliefs as mere metaphors* (385)*."* This note of comedy continues at the end when Herzog tells Mermelstein to go and sin no more. But the letter is also serious in its advice that all those loyal to civilization *"have to have the power to employ pain, to repent, to be illuminated, you must have the opportunity and even the time"* (386). Herzog disclaims moral superiority but maintains that his own suffering has been *"a more extended form of life, a striving for true wakefulness and an antidote to illusion"* (386).

Herzog's sufferings and pilgrimage lead to a strange state of being. Bellow deliberately makes Herzog repeat the opening sentence, "if I am out of my mind it's all right with me" (384), to delimit the temporal and structural area of his novel; and to indicate that Herzog's "madness" is really sanity. Herzog is like Yeats's Crazy Jane. He was a fool, but now has become a holy fool, like Henderson on the way to Baventai: "His state was too strange, this mixture of clairvoyance and spleen, *esprit de l'escalier*, noble inspirations, poetry and nonsense, ideas, hyperesthesia —wandering about like this, hearing forceful but indefinite music within, seeing things, violet fringes about the clearest objects" (396). Bellow had the difficult task of making the human reality of such a state credible. He turned to the writings of Rozanov for a solution.

V. V. Rozanov (1856–1919) was a Russian writer who invented a new literary medium to register the noises of his soul when, according to Poggioli, he became "the prophet of the only God who is the Self."[18] He would jot down aphoristic utterances, incoherent and absurd notes, recollections and meditations whenever and wherever the idea came to him—in a train, in a cab, or even in the toilet. The preface to *Solitaria*, the only book that Herzog picks up in Ludeyville, presents Rozanov's technique:

> The wind blows at midnight and carries away leaves. . . . So also life in fleeting time tears off from our soul exclamations, sighs, half-thoughts, half-feelings. . . . Which, being fragments of sound, have the significance that they "come" straight from the soul, without elaboration, without purpose, without premeditation—without any-thing external. Simply, "the soul is alive," that is, "has lived," "has breathed." . . . I have always somehow liked these "sudden exclamations."[19]

Herzog, in his new state, voices the exhalations that arise from his soul. He writes down "songs, psalms, and utterances" (398). He utters a string of random quotations from *Solitaria*. Even his language echoes that of Rozanov: his cry for peace has its echo in "I do not want truth, I want peace[20]"; "I am simply a human being, more or less," says Herzog, while Rozanov notes on the sole of one of his slippers while bathing, "I am simply a wonderful man."[21]

Bellow makes use of Rozanov's voice and technique to reinforce Herzog's trembling belief that man is a mysterious creature whose life is not mere facticity. Man, gilded by God, as Rozanov said, is surely not what the Freudians and the existentialists think he is. Herzog is not disturbed by the implications about human nature that the recent anthropological discoveries that man has descended from fierce carnivorous apes suggest. That is why his last letter is a diatribe directed against the Navy psychiatrist who had dismissed him as immature. Herzog cannot define himself, but he feels sustained by the silence of the woods. The notes to God are not modern accusations of grievance or murder but gentle utterances accepting the incomprehensible, feeling the sense of resting within "*the hollowness of God*" (396). Herzog retires into himself to prepare for the future. Involved essentially with himself, he is at the same time involved with the world. He puts his face out to catch the radiance of the sun as he ends the message of love he sends to his mother: "*I want to send you, and others, the most loving wish I have in my heart. This is the only way I have to reach out—out where it is incomprehensible. I can only pray toward it. So . . . Peace!*" (398).

Bellow does not end on this note, for Herzog has not yet attained the peace he prays for. Will's visit reconfirms the change in Herzog. Herzog accepts Will's advice about the piano for June and his statements about selling the house and about Madeleine and Ramona are both sensible and practical. The visit also reassures Herzog about his true self which he can now accept. For the visit generates in him an extraordinary state of excitement. Will's presence and his questions stir up Herzog's heart: *"Why must I be such a throb-hearted character . . . But I am. I am, and you can't teach old dogs. Myself is thus and so, and will continue thus and so. And why fight it? My balance comes from instability. Not organization, or courage, as with other people. It's tough, but that's how it is. On these terms I, too—even I!—apprehend certain things. Perhaps the only way I'm able to do it. Must play the instrument I've got"* (402).

As a trembling, throb-hearted character, not practical like his two brothers, able to grasp certain things, wanting (as he said earlier) to share with other human beings, Herzog is eager to *begin* (392). He has yearned for a moral, useful, and active life, as his letter to Bhave suggested. He knows the Aristotelian recommendation that man should be a political, that is, a useful and involved animal (119). In the note to Ramona, Herzog proclaims his desire to perform real, relevant work (383).

Henderson wanted to be a medical missionary. Bellow does not tell us what Herzog will be, but he plants numerous clues that suggest what Herzog will probably become. Equipped with sharp senses, a passion for reminiscence, and a powerful memory, armed with an immense quantity of factual knowledge (275), blessed with a figurative and associative habit of mind, capable of inventing and telling stories (he makes up stories for June and tries out an Insect Iliad for her), aware of his powerlessness and of his tendency to go after reality with language (333), Herzog can share with other human beings by having recourse to words, by becoming a novelist. He knows that "awareness was his work; extended consciousness was his line, his business" (340). Unlike Augie March, that novelist manqué, Herzog has all the makings, including a passionate interest in ideas and a tendency to create constructions, of a writer of supreme fiction.

At Ludeyville however Herzog has no such ambition. He decides to stay on for a while. He does not arrive at any decision about Ramona but it is clear that there will be a change in their relationship: for it is Herzog now who invites Ramona to a dinner that he will cook and he refuses her offer to bring a bottle of wine. At the Tuttles', while looking at the Berkshire landscape, Herzog has the strange feeling that "the model of natural creation seems to be the ocean" (413). Herzog does not experience Tommy Wilhelm's oceanic feeling of submergence, but he is faintly aware of the primordial ocean from which all life sprang.[22] The feeling is continued at Ludeyville when his heart reaches out to the incomprehensible. In Chicago, in the police car, Herzog had felt the need for "something great, something into which his being, and all beings, can go" (353). "He does not need meaning as long as such intensity has scope. Because then it is self-evident; it *is* meaning" (353). Now he experiences this intensity in his heart, a holy feeling, an idiot joy, which compels him to exclaim: *"Thou movest me"* (414). Perhaps it is a sign and a proof of eternity, but Herzog has no desire to explain the intensity he feels. He accepts it and with it the human condition: *"I am pretty well satisfied to be, to be just as it is willed, and for as long as I may remain in occupancy"* (414).

Bellow translates this acceptance into an epiphanic scene at the very end. Lying on his Récamier couch, miles away from the New York sofa, Herzog becomes aware of the dust raised by Mrs. Tuttle. Not the New York dust of death and destruction, this dust recalls the finger-produced speck of dark that had told the young Herzog what Adam was made of. Herzog doesn't want Mrs. Tuttle to damp it down with water yet (though he will tell her to, later) because the dust is a message to him about his own humanness. He, himself, has no more messages to send anyone.

NOTES

1. Robert Robinson, "Saul Bellow at 60—Talking to Robert Robinson," *The Listener*, February 13, 1975, p. 218.

2. Saul Bellow, *Herzog* (Greenwich, Conn.: Fawcett Crest Book, Fawcett Publications, 1964), p. 117. Hereafter page references will be cited in the text.

3. Joseph Epstein, "Saul Bellow of Chicago," *New York Times Book Review*, May 9, 1971, p. 14.

4. David Boroff, "The Author," *Saturday Review of Literature* 47 (September 19, 1964): 39.

5. Tommy Wilhelm in *Seize the Day* was termed "a visionary animal."

6. Theodore Reik in his book, *Jewish Wit* (New York: Gamut Press, 1962), p. 177, relates the following Jewish anecdote: "The husband of a woman whose funeral is about to take place is nowhere to be found. His brother-in-law at last finds him in the room of the maid, with whom he had just had sexual intercourse. Full of indignation and rage, the brother-in-law abuses him for such conduct. The husband defends himself, saying: " 'Do I know what I do in my mourning?' "

7. Saul Bellow's translation of Isaac Bashevis Singer's story, "Gimpel the Fool," appeared in *Partisan Review* 20 (May–June 1953): 300–313.

8. Sigmund Freud, *The Standard Edition of the Works* (London: Hogarth Press, 1958), 12: 9–82.

9. Saul Bellow, "A Personal Record," *New Republic* 130 (February 22, 1954): 21. (Review of Joyce Cary's novel, *Except the Lord*.)

10. Saul Bellow, "Literature," *The Great Ideas Today* (Chicago: Encyclopaedia Britannica, 1963), p. 325.

11. Hannah Arendt, *The Origins of Totalitarianism* (New York: World Publishing Company, 1972), p. 325.

12. Bellow perhaps had in mind Reich's analysis of the fight for the child that typically occurs in divorce cases. According to Reich, it is not love for the child but destructive revenge on the partner that is the dominant motive. The plague-ridden individual, says Reich, "may demand the custody of his child because he hates his wife who, say, was unfaithful to him; in doing so, he honestly believes to be acting 'solely for the good of the child' when he keeps the child from the mother; he *cannot* be convinced that the real motive is that of a sadistic punishment for the mother" (CA, 258).

13. By 1964 Bellow had shed Reichianism from his creative system, though not completely. Occasional precipitations manifest themselves in *Herzog*. In the scene with Zelda, where she indirectly refers to his impotence, the narrator states: "A thick, hot, sick pressure filled his chest" (52). Herzog also suffers from this pressure when he rushes out of the court room after the fourth trial. The third trial causes the evil poison within him, the polluted orgone energy, to surface. It surfaces again when he approaches the house bent on righteous murder. After he decides not to shoot, he finds himself in a "streaming state" (324), an indication (the Reichian term is "orgonotic streaming") that his armor is cracking up. Finally, the Reichian belief that there should be "*biological joy in work*" (CA, 261) is echoed in Herzog's sincere cry for "*relevant work*" in the final chapter.

14. This homosexual attack is an expanded and more specific version of the attack that Joseph (DM, 81) experienced when he was a child. Joseph equates his attacker with the ancient figure of Death.

15. Bellow makes Herzog reject the yearning for collectivity which Tommy Wilhelm had blindly accepted as brotherhood. He probably took up Hannah Arendt's idea that social atomization and extreme individualization precede mass movements. That Madeleine is an incarnation of the totalitarian spirit is clear when we read Hannah Arendt's account of totalitarianism: "Totalitarian movements are mass organizations of atomized, isolated individuals. Compared with all other parties and movements, their most conspicuous external characteristic is their demand for total, unrestricted, unconditional, and unalterable loyalty of the individual member. This demand is made by the leaders of totalitarian movements even before they seize power" (p. 323).

16. Saul Bellow defines potato love thus: "Potato love is a weak emotion that people often have of friendliness and a melting heart toward other people, the real source of which is terror. It's a low-grade emotion, like potato sap." See Sanford Pinsker, "Saul Bellow in the Classroom," *College English* 34, no. 7 (April 1973): 977.

17. Tommy Wilhelm, too, utters a *Yiskor* for his mother.

18. Renato Poggioli, *Rozanov* (New York: Hilary House Publishers, Ltd., 1962), p. 24.

19. V. V. Rozanov, *Solitaria*, translated by S. S. Koteliansky (New York: Boni and Liveright, 1927), p. 47.

20. Ibid., p. 22.

21. Ibid., p. 116.

22. In "Thalassa," published in *The Psychoanalytical Quarterly* 3, no. 1 (January 1934), Sandor Ferenczi refers to the aquatic mode of existence abandoned in primeval times. The water references in *Herzog* are not symbolic, unlike those in *Seize the Day*, but perhaps mythic. "To the sea! To the sea!" thinks Herzog before his trip to Vineyard Haven. And, at one point, he refers to the human soul as amphibian.

7 *Mr. Sammler's Planet*

Bellow likens his next novel, *Mr. Sammler's Planet* (1970), to *Augie March* in that it deals with a new state of mind.[1] *Henderson the Rain King* projected Bellow's radiant faith in the human imagination and his belief in the possibility of a technological America redeemed by the ideals of love, service, and brotherhood. *Herzog* conveyed the assurance that mankind was capable of controling the magnificent technology it had brought into being, an assurance presented by a protagonist who has arrived at a precarious balance within himself. *Mr. Sammler's Planet* communicates a sense of crisis and apocalypse. The moon shot is a technical miracle, the greatest technological achievement of modern man. And yet, mankind now finds itself, to use a Wellsian title, at the end of its tether, its sole visible future being death and annihilation. The earlier solutions to the problem of being human no longer seem adequate. Dahfu's prediction that mankind will evolve towards goodness appears to be naïve at a time when there is a strong smell of universal decay and when "the suicidal impulses of civilization"[2] keep pushing strongly. Herzog, that survivor who claims to be a human being, more or less, did not directly confront the terrible questions about history and human life that totalitarianism and the concentration and extermination camps had raised. The protagonist of *Mr. Sammler's Planet*, who has personally experienced such horrors, is thrown into riotous New York, a city that "makes one think about the collapse of civilization, about Sodom and Gomorrah, the end of the world" (277). The novel records with a naked and fierce intensity the terrors and brutal challenges that contemporary man has to face, and in the process, hurls out angry and bitter questions about what it means to be human at such a time. These questions torment Mr. Sammler who, unlike his fellow protagonists, does not go forth bravely in search of the human. Instead, he labors painfully to come to terms with it, to define it, and to know its range.

At seventy-plus, Mr. Sammler is not a quester, but a dry and detached observer of the human scene in New York. A burnt-out case, he feels cut off from the rest of the species and therefore considers himself better able to comment on its crazy antics. He is a visiting consciousness (as he terms himself), who does not involve himself in the process of living, but surveys the madnesses of mankind with a kind of clinical coldness. His favorite pastime (he has no real occupation) is to take a philosophical stroll along Broadway inspecting the phenomenon that presents itself there.

He conducts this inspection with a pair of strange eyes, one of which has, as it were, usurped a central position in his impaired bodily system. According to Wallace, the world looks different, quite literally, to Mr. Sammler because of his eyes. The two eyes are different looking. The left, a filmed, sightless bubble, allows Mr. Sammler to distinguish only light and shade. It looks inward, as though examining the interior being of its owner. The undamaged, dark-bright right eye, despite the overhanging hairs of the brow, allows Mr. Sammler at certain moments to see objects and phenomena with heightened clarity. It is after he experiences moments of shock—after the disastrous lecture at Columbia, after he suspects that the pickpocket is aware of being observed, after he realizes that Elya Gruner is going to die—that there is an intensification of vision, and the eye sees "the world wickedly lighted up" (15). Mr. Sammler wears smoked glasses both to protect his vision and to conceal his strange eyes from the rest of the world.

He was not born with these odd binocular powers. They came into existence on a day in 1940 when his whole being suffered a traumatic shock in Poland. On that perfectly clear day he had been struck in the left eye with a gun butt. Then, stripped naked, he had, together with his wife, helped dig a mass grave and, after the gun blasts, choked with blood, had crept his way out, alone, from the corpses piled above him. Dropped out of existence almost into nonexistence, he had climbed out into existence again. Unlike his fellow protagonists, who emerge into a kind of humanness almost immediately after experiencing suffering or death in symbolic form, Mr. Sammler has literally faced death in the shape of blood, guns, graves, and famine, and has then lived on for nearly thirty long years. Bellow creates a different kind of protagonist with a special sensibility to achieve his fictional aims in *Mr. Sammler's Planet*.

To understand this sensibility the reader has to distinguish (as in the case of Joseph the dangler) the Mr. Sammler that was from the Mr. Sammler he has become. Before 1940 he had been an aristocratic Polish gentleman, Jewish in origin, studious and bookish, one who had spent the 1920s and the 1930s in London as correspondent for the Warsaw papers. He had lived in Woburn Square and was acquainted with the nearby Bloomsbury Group. His wife and he took snobbish delight in the fact that they were connected with the cultural best of England. Above all, Mr. Sammler was proud of the fact that H. G. Wells had acknowledged him, and that he had participated with Olaf Stapleton and Gerald Heard in the *Cosmopolis* project to build a planned, orderly, and beautiful world society based on tolerance and a rational and scientific attitude toward life.

His experiences in 1940 shatter both his simple, happy, innocent, personal world and that beautiful, kindhearted, ingenuous, fragile dream scheme. For a long time, indifferent both to other human beings and to his own self, Mr. Sammler felt he was not necessarily human. Ten or twelve years after the war, however, he began to be drawn back to the human condition: "It was a second encounter of the disinterested spirit with fated biological necessities, a return match with the persistent creature" (109). This second encounter, as Mr. Sammler becomes aware, turns out to be a complicated and strange resurrection of disagreeable and weak portions of his earlier self.

When the novel opens, Mr. Sammler is not sure at what point of life he stands. He is not a sitting sage, or the guru his daughter Shula-Slawa claims he is. Neither is he the fixed point that Feffer considers him to be, nor the judge and priest-confessor his family has made him. By his own high standards he is not the ideal commentator on contemporary chaos. To be such a one, according to Mr. Sammler, "you had to be strong enough not to be terrified by the local effects of metamorphosis. . . . You had to be able to bear the tangles of the soul, the sight of cruel dissolution" (70–71). Above all, he is not a mere mouthpiece (as many critics have claimed) for Bellow's attitudes and opinions. At this stage of his career, Bellow was too canny a writer to make such a mistake.

Mr. Sammler does voice some of Bellow's ideas and convictions (as expressed in interviews and essays), but they are deliberately heightened and intensified because they are channeled through an inflamed sensibility. Bellow has stated that *Mr. Sammler's Planet* would have been a better novel if he had dealt openly with some of his feelings instead of filtering them through Mr. Sammler.[3] He could have solved this problem if he had maintained the right fictional distance between his narrator and his protagonist. Oftentimes, the distance between the two is minimal so that the narrator-author appears to be endorsing the opinions of the protagonist. At other times it is clear that the narrator views Mr. Sammler in an ironic light. Finished in record time, as Bellow tells us a trifle proudly in a 1970 interview,[4] and written in a high degree of excitement,[5] *Mr. Sammler's Planet* (as Bellow acknowledged sadly in 1977) was not under his complete artistic control.[6]

The reader has to be alert at all times to the ironic and non-Sammlerian points of view and not allow Mr. Sammler's monologues, self-communings, and mental rushes to overwhelm him. The

narrative voice, which occasionally lapses into a quaint editorial "we,"
is inconsistent, but at certain moments is clearly ironic, as when it refers
to "Mr. Minutely-Observant Artur Sammler" (15) and when it remarks
that though Mr. Sammler knew about the danger and disgrace of
explanations, "he was himself no mean explainer" (21–22).

One needs to understand the physical condition and probe deep into
the psyche of this explainer. In an interview Bellow has maintained that
"the internal processes of Mr. Sammler require the very narrowest
attention."[7] Mr. Sammler realizes that there are gaps within his being
"as if he had been cast by Henry Moore. With holes, lacunae" (43), as
he wryly puts it. He is subject to explosive moods and to intense
migraines. His Polish nerves (as he calls them) rage and panic at
moments of stress and shock, and it is then, as if in self-defense, that his
right eye manifests its strange powers, making everything blindingly
clear. This superclarity (which Madeleine suffered from) is of the
rational variety, analytical, ruthless, piercing and, because it lacks the
dimension of human involvement and genuine sympathy, highly limited.

On the way to the hospital to visit his nephew, Elya Gruner, Mr.
Sammler walks along Broadway and, like Herzog, sees the histrionic
madnesses displayed everywhere:

> Just look (Sammler looked) at this imitative anarchy of the
> streets—these Chinese revolutionary tunics, these babes in unisex
> toyland, these surrealist warchiefs, Western stagecoach drivers—
> Ph.D.'s in philosophy, some of them (Sammler had met such, talked
> matters over with them). They sought originality. They were obviously
> derivative. And of what—of Paiutes, of Fidel Castro? No, of
> Hollywood extras. Acting mythic. Casting themselves into chaos,
> hoping to adhere to higher consciousness, to be washed up on the
> shores of truth. [137]

Mr. Sammler, like Herzog, is aware of the frantic search for individuality
and originality by these dark, modern-day romantics, these Hollywood
extras. Both protagonists make use of the same image, that of actors and
of acting, but there is a difference of tone and mood. Rage and
intolerance manifest themselves in Mr. Sammler's language. The
contempt betrays itself in a phrase like "these babes in unisex toyland."
Unlike Herzog's eye, which could take in the special comedy of
Broadway and even glimpse the presence of old women buying kosher
meat, Mr. Sammler's eye is pitiless in its seizure of every detail—the
Chinese tunics, the stagecoach drivers. The voice has an edge of despair
and exasperation, despite the fact that the paragraph ends with "Mr.
Sammler, sorry for all and sore at heart." The protagonist is a voyeur, not

given to any significant purpose but enjoying his "aesthetic consumption of the environment." Unlike other human beings, he transforms any shock to his system not into emotions and feelings, but into "delicate, even piercing observation" (44).

The events that occur during three crucial days in early spring will teach this voyeur a number of lessons about himself, about human beings and about the human condition. Like all Bellow's fiction, *Mr. Sammler's Planet* is a *Bildungsroman*. "All my books," says Bellow, "are about education and have therefore a somewhat boyish spirit. Bring characters to the conclusions of their errors and leave them prepared to take the first step."[8] The process of Mr. Sammler's education is not, however, clearly visible and is difficult to chart. The lack of distance between the narrator and the protagonist accounts for some of the confusion. Also, the change in Mr. Sammler, a highly self-conscious individual, is a subtle, internal one, a change he is not aware of till the very end. Further, the narrative currents in the novel, though connected, do not flow together into one compelling stream. The novel consists of three major narrative sequences (with the lecture at Columbia University as a prelude)—the story of the gorgeously dressed black pickpocket who rides the Riverside bus, the story of what happens after Shula steals Dr. Lal's manuscript, *The Future of the Moon*, and the account of Elya Gruner's death—interspersed with numerous memories, reflections, and moments of brooding, all of which Bellow pulls together into a loose unity.

Lionel Feffer, one of the university students Shula had hired to read to her father, provides the context in which Mr. Sammler receives his initial lesson and his first shock. For the last four or five years Mr. Sammler had been fascinated by the historians of civilization, those great systematizers, Toynbee, Freud, Burckhardt, Spengler, Karl Marx, Max Weber, Max Scheler, Franz Oppenheimer, Ortega y Gasset, and Valéry. When the novel opens he is in a very uncertain state of mind: he knows that the diet proffered by these world explainers has not provided him with any sustenance and he is now interested only in certain religious writers of the thirteenth century—Suso, Tauler, and especially Meister Eckhart. Mr. Sammler has also steadily withdrawn himself from human contact, isolating himself, like Joseph the dangler, in his room. It is Feffer who gets him involved by conning him into addressing a seminar at Columbia University. Later, Mr. Sammler complains that Feffer is very noisy and turbulent, and has brought confusion into his life.

The afternoon lecture at Columbia has a twofold significance. It establishes the innocent Utopian world which Mr. Sammler had inhabited and believed in—the British scene in the 1930s with its Wellsian dream. And it forces Mr. Sammler out of his isolation, so that he becomes a performer, an actor. The thick-bearded, foul-mouthed radical breaks up the self-indulgent reminiscences of this speaker (it was not really a lecture) by flinging certain truths that Mr. Sammler's consciousness resists accepting: " 'Why do you listen to this effete old shit? What has he got to tell you? His balls are dry. He's dead. He can't come' " (42).[9] Mr. Sammler refuses to confront or even to consider such a charge. Instead, he translates the shock to his sensibility into a number of brilliant perceptions. He first gives vent to his anger by indulging in anthropological parallels, comparing the students to Barbary apes and to defecating spider monkeys. On Broadway he uses his eye power to escape from his own sensations of pain and dismay: "A delivery man with a floral cross filling both arms, a bald head dented, seemed to be drunk, fighting the wind, tacking. His dull boots small, and his short wide pants blowing like a woman's skirts. Gardenias, camellias, calla lillies, sailing above him under light transparent plastic" (43). Mr. Sammler can view the scene with cold, aesthetic clarity, but he does not perceive its human and religious significance. Finally, he discharges his bitterness into witty irony: "But what was it to be arrested in the stage of toilet training! . . . Who had raised the diaper flag? Who had made shit a sacrament?" (45).

Immediately after this prelude occurs the encounter with the pickpocket. Bellow deliberately has one shock follow another in order to reveal the defensive strategies Mr. Sammler uses and to illustrate how vulnerable his protagonist is. Mr. Sammler is totally unprepared for this second shock. Earlier that morning he had recalled the details of the pickpocket's crime with vivid relish. Driven by a craving for repetition, he had gone a dozen times to Columbus Circle to look for the thief and, on four fascinating occasions, had witnessed the crime being committed in the uptown bus. He had been powerfully affected, despite himself, by the majesty of the black and thought of him as an African prince, a great black beast. His hair had bristled when this "puma" had looked at him (as Henderson's had done in the presence of Atti) and his Polish nerves had awoken into painful life.

This time, as he boards the downtown bus, Mr. Sammler is in no condition to be a voyeur. When, despite strong internal resistance, he again witnesses the act, his heart beats strongly, and his throat and bad eye ache. The black sees him "seeing" the crime. The punishment for Mr. Sammler's "crime" is strange. The thief corners him in the lobby of the apartment building, removes the smoked glasses from Mr. Sammler's eyes, and compels him with silent power to gaze downward:

> The black man had opened his fly and taken out his penis. It was displayed to Sammler with great oval testicles, a large tan-and-purple uncircumcised thing—a tube, a snake; metallic hairs bristled at the thick base and the tip curled beyond the supporting, demonstrating hand, suggesting the fleshly mobility of an elephant's trunk, though the skin was somewhat iridescent rather than thick or rough. Over the forearm and fist that held him Sammler was required to gaze at this organ. [48–49]

He then replaces Mr. Sammler's glasses on his nose and departs.

The narrator notes every detail carefully. The black acts in a lordly, serene, assured manner. There is a light of supercandor in his eyes, as he concludes the "session, the lesson, the warning, the encounter, the transmission" (49). Mr. Sammler does not know what lesson he has just been taught, nor what has been transmitted. The narrator registers the physical condition of his protagonist after this session: "smarting feet, thin respiration, pain at the heart, stunned mind and—oh!—a temporary blankness of spirit" (ibid.). The interior of Mr. Sammler has been profoundly disturbed. The last two symptoms are significant: his spirit experiences a thinness, a kind of nullity: and his mind, that hyperactive organ, cannot function when faced by such an unanswerable mystery.

It is only after he has gained the safety of his own room that Mr. Sammler attempts to understand and explain the mystery. But he merely reduces it to an example of sex ideology and, by linking the incident with the sexual behavior of Walter Bruch and of his niece, Angela Gruner, expounds on the idea that a sexual madness is overwhelming the Western world. This act of reduction makes Mr. Sammler no different from Margotte, who is full of theories about the thief, or from Wallace, who is interested only in statistics about the black's organ, or from Feffer, who wants to profit from the situation.

It is the reader who has to ponder the mystery. The crimes of the black thief project his majestic defiance (like that of Aleck/Alice) of the sick world he lives in whose slackness and cowardice he takes for granted (46). On two separate occasions (13, 46) his movements during his crime are compared to those of a doctor toward a patient. The display of the organ transmits the same message (but in a masterful, elegant, and effective manner) that the Columbia University radical had assaulted Mr. Sammler with. Both proclaim that the life force does not flow through him and warn him that he is somehow not really human.

Shula, too, warns her father by stealing Dr. Lal's manuscript, which he finds on his pillow almost immediately after the confrontation with the pickpocket. With her peculiarities—her odd wigs, her shopping bags, her scavenging in trash cans, her lapses into Catholicism—she wishes to keep her father on the human level, wanting to "implicate him and bring him back, to bind him and keep him in the world beside her" (181). Like the black pickpocket, she generates strange and disturbing currents within her father by involving him with the sensitive, intelligent visiting scientist, Dr. Lal, whose manuscript opens with a challenging question: " 'How long will this earth remain the only home of Man?' " (50)

The conversation between Mr. Sammler and Dr. Lal, which takes up thirty-three pages (184–216), is perhaps the portion that Bellow had in mind when he confessed that *Mr. Sammler's Planet* "was his first thoroughly unapologetic venture into ideas."[10] Cast in the form of a dialogue, this venture is not so successful as the talk sessions between King Dahfu and Henderson. Bellow tries his best to make Dr. Lal a convincing character and a person intelligent enough for Mr. Sammler to talk to. Dr. Lal reminds Mr. Sammler of the late Ussher Arkin, husband of Margotte (there are strong hints that Dr. Lal and Margotte fall in love), whom he had liked every much. Dr. Lal has experienced disaster: he has lived through the Hindu-Muslim riots in Calcutta. Both are foreigners to the American scene and relish each other's dry wit. Above all, Mr. Sammler experiences a spontaneous feeling of friendship toward Dr. Lal.

Their conversation is not really a dialogue but an exchange of positions and views. Both begin with the premise that this is a fearful moment in human history. For Dr. Lal the human species is devouring itself and the earth has become a spatial-temporal prison. A biophysicist, he considers the imagination as a biological power seeking to overcome impossible conditions (100). Propelled by this power, man can now escape from the confinement of earth and soar into a new world. The moon expedition heralds a new future for mankind. It will introduce a new sobriety and result in a renewed nobility. He considers earth departure and the venture into space a rational necessity especially because of the teeming millions that crowd this earth. Much better the moon, states Dr. Lal, than to continue to live on our doomed planet. With his outer space perspective, this scientist becomes a poet urging mankind to plunge bravely into the sidereal archipelagoes of a dayless, nightless universe.

Coaxed, charmed, and drawn out by Dr. Lal, Mr. Sammler gives in to the temptation to "speak his full mind" (206). He has been meaning to speak out for some time now, but has never had the occasion or the opportunity to do so. Keenly aware of the present suicidal madnesses of civilization despite the technological miracle of the leap to the moon, believing that he has been spared in order to condense (as he told Feffer) the contemporary situation into a short statement, sensing that there is not much time left (both for himself and for mankind), Mr. Sammler boldly launches his views of the human situation today.

Mr. Sammler's explanation follows the same lines as the one put forward by Herzog in the letter to Pulver. The modern individuality boom, after centuries of repression and rejection, has produced monsters and grotesques, deformed human beings who are not interested in being human, do not want to be human, and perhaps do not know what it means to be human. Instead of choosing as examples the human actor-types found on the Broadway streets, Mr. Sammler focuses on the mad antics of Rumkowski, the Jewish dictator-king of the Lodz ghetto. An undistinguished man, suddenly elevated by the Nazis to a position of authority, he began to indulge in an orgy of theatricality and mad acting, and was transformed by the pressures of disaster and doom into a parody of a human being. Rumkowski was, first of all, a striking proof that the Nazi forms of evil were far from banal, as Hannah Arendt had suggested. Secondly, he illustrated "the weakness of the outer forms which are available for our humanity, and the pitiable lack of confidence in them." What is the true stature of a human being? asks Mr. Sammler, and is at a loss for an answer.

As a modern-day Job, Mr. Sammler registers a lament that "the great demand upon human consciousness and human capacities has overtaxed human endurance" (212). Bellow tries to account for Mr. Sammler's despair by having him confess to being a deformed person, one obsessed by "play-acting, originality, dramatic individuality, theatricality in people, the forms taken by spiritual striving" (210). The novel records a diminishment of Bellow's faith in mankind's ability to resurrect itself by using the human imagination alone. Mr. Sammler does not fall into total despair only because he believes that the sense of God is implanted deep in man. It is this knowledge that allows Mr. Sammler to receive almost daily "strong impressions of eternity" (216). His God adumbrations, which imply that mankind will never commit an act of universal self-destruction, are a reply to Dr. Lal's scientific justification for earth departure. The colonization of the moon will not lead to the growth of the human spirit and will therefore not be metaphysically advantageous for mankind.

Water, released by Wallace's tampering with the pipes in the attic during his search for his father's Mafia dollars, interrupts the flow of Mr. Sammler's ideas, and he has to hurry about and hold buckets under the splashing pipe. He has to perform what he had termed "Dutch drudgery" (7); he has to dam up "the invading sea" and deal with "the facts and sensations or ordinary life" (8). This sequence establishes a fictional zigzag pattern, one that allowed Bellow to pack in the odd musings and mental preoccupations of his protagonist, all of which slow down the novel's pace. Mr. Sammler seeks continually to isolate himself in the dry world of the intellect, but a conspiracy of people and events always brings him back to the ordinary flow of human existence.

Mr. Sammler wants to consider basic questions only, disliking any involvement with what he calls civilian matters, "wrangles, lawsuits, hysterias, all such hole-and-corner pettiness" (225). The long conversations he has with Walter Bruch, Angela, Wallace, and Feffer about their human problems are one-sided. With old-fashioned courtesy he listens to all they say, but his mind is busy with its own private thoughts. He categorizes people instead of responding to them with warmth and affection. He comforts Walter Bruch, but finds it more stimulating to regard his friend as an interesting case of sexual neurosis: "It was easier with a man like Bruch to transfer to broad reflections, to make comparisons, to think of history and themes of general interest" (59). Mr. Sammler is fond of Feffer, but can see him as a "combined oddity," (38) who leads a "high-energy American life to the point of anarchy and breakdown" (39). Angela Gruner is "sensual womanhood without remission" (31). Even his own daughter, Shula, whom he loves, illustrates modern limitless demand, and Wallace is easily placed in the Shula category (83).

The only person whom Mr. Sammler cannot categorize is Elya Gruner, who had rescued him and Shula from a DP camp and had taken care of them for twenty-two years "with kindness . . . without a day of neglect, without a single irascible word" (196). Elya is the only human being whom Mr. Sammler both loves and admires: "He was very full of his nephew, a man quite different from himself. He admired him, loved him. He could not cope with the full sum of facts about him" (98). When he learns that Elya will die in a day or two of the aneurysm in his head, Mr. Sammler suffers a shock, almost as profound as the one he had received in Poland when his faith in human goodness and in human rationality had collapsed: "A confusing, frowning moment, and, getting into the breast, the head, and even down into the bowels and about the heart, and behind the eyes—something gripping, aching, smarting" (80). Mr. Sammler's analytic mind is unable to come to terms with such a shock.

Mr. Sammler also knows that Elya knows about his imminent death. But Elya behaves with calm dignity and with his customary kindness and generosity. He tells Mr. Sammler not to worry about the future, hinting that he has provided for father and daughter. Mr. Sammler realizes that the moment of honor has come when Elya would have to summon up his best qualities. Mr. Sammler also knows that when death turns its full gaze on a human being, human help is needed. Elya's children, Angela and Wallace, are not capable of supplying such help. Instead, they molest their dying father with their demands. Mr. Sammler takes upon himself the task of offering his nephew a sign, a gesture, a word of comfort that will reassure Elya about the human bond. He wants to make this declaration: " 'However actual I may seem to you and you to me, *we are not as actual as all that*. We will die. Nevertheless there is a bond. There is a bond' " (238).

Odd circumstances keep Mr. Sammler from the bedside of Elya. On the climactic third day, having delivered his testament and having arranged for the return of Dr. Lal's manuscript, he hurries to his dying nephew. On the way to the hospital he is beset by further delays deliberately introduced to make him confront certain truths about himself. Bellow was not able to dramatize the first truth which comes to Mr. Sammler in the form of an insight. The enormous pressure of the feeling of apocalypse has led almost everyone, Wallace, Shula, Angela, Eisen, the black pickpocket, and Mr. Sammler himself, into heightening his own subjective style. Mr. Sammler's own particular concern has been to "get a handle upon the situation" (71), to explain life as the historians of civilization had done. He now realizes that he suffers from "the disease of the single self explaining what was what and who was who" (256).

In the lobby of his apartment building, to which he goes to get some clippings for Elya, the TV monitor (which has at last been repaired) allows Mr. Sammler to see himself as if for the first time, "the shuddering image of an aged man" (257). Near Lincoln Center he witnesses the brutal struggle between the black pickpocket and Feffer, who has photographed the crime with his Minox. Mr. Sammler turns to the crowd for help, but what he sees on their faces leads him to a terrible truth about himself. He realizes that they are voyeurs, neutral witnesses enjoying the spectacle but refusing to get involved. Bellow halts the action at this stage in order to present the feeling of horror that overwhelms his protagonist. For Mr. Sammler knows now that he too had been a voyeur, an old man without the power to act. He sees himself, perhaps with the inward looking eye, as one "poor in spirit. Someone between the human and non-human states, between content and emptiness, between full and void, meaning and not-meaning, between this world and no world" (264).

Nevertheless he summons all the feeble powers he still has within him and acts by calling upon Eisen, who proceeds to smash his baize bag containing the heavy metal medallions (with "comfort ye" and "strengthen thyself" inscribed on them) on the side of the black's face.

Horrified by the murderous fury of Eisen, Mr. Sammler is even more horrified by his own inability to counter Eisen's argument: " 'You can't hit a man like this just once. When you hit him you must really hit him. Otherwise he'll kill you. You know. We both fought in the war. You were a Partisan. You had a gun.' " Mr. Sammler has no analytical views, no philosophical wisdom to offer at this moment. "Here," he discovers, "there is nothing to say" (266). The arrival of the police saves the situation and Mr. Sammler hurries to Elya, to whom he *has* something to say.

Instead of Elya, it is Angela whom he finds in the hospital room. The encounter between them reveals how much Mr. Sammler has changed. When he confronts her bitter anger and her supersensuality, his right eye begins to function as usual, and he sees everything "with heightened clarity." Again he realizes that "to see was delicious" (271). He knows now what he has been: a philosophical voyeur, a "registrar of madness" (109), a "receiver of sordid goods" (148). He does not spell out this knowledge, but now understands that his attitude toward everything and particularly toward other human beings has been one of metaphysical detachment, "seeing" Wallace, Feffer, Bruch, as types of behavior instead of responding to them as real human beings with human problems.

It is this sense of detachment, abetted by his right eye, that he now rebels against as he confronts Angela. Instead of being merely an ear into which Angela can pour her woes, he treats her as a human being. Instead of seeing her as a sex symbol, he provokes her by making her aware that her Baby Doll costume is not appropriate at her father's deathbed. He begs her to come to terms with her dying father and to make some gesture of love and reconciliation toward him. Mr. Sammler acts instead of philosophizing despite knowing that Angela will never forgive him. Feeling highly insulted, Angela flings the same kind of charge that the Columbia University radical and the black pickpocket had hurled: " 'What do you mean about fellatio? What do *you* know about it?' " (280)

But Mr. Sammler has changed. In order to reveal how much his protagonist has changed, Bellow had to smuggle into the conversation with Angela Mr. Sammler's changed views on the human condition. Mr. Sammler is fully aware that signs of the apocalypse are in the air and that things are falling apart. He had thought that his experience of the grave had qualified him to make the pronouncements he had made. He knows now that he "was flat, dead wrong" (278). What he offers now is not an explanation but a testament of faith in mankind: " 'There is still such a thing as a man—or there was. There are still human qualities. Our weak species fought its fear, our crazy species fought its criminality. We are an animal of genius' " (ibid.). Here is his delayed response to the moral dilemma posed by Eisen, who believed that a blow had to be exchanged for a blow. For Mr. Sammler affirms, like King Dahfu, that though man is a creature of revenges, human qualities will ultimately prevail.

The phone conversation with Shula solves the problem of the missing Mafia money and it shows that Mr. Sammler no longer regards his daughter as an example of modern limitless demand, but appreciates her as a human, if fallible, being. His final words to her are: " 'You're a good daughter. The best of any. No better daughter' " (283).

Purged of his intellectual pretensions, aware now of how limited a human being he is, the reborn Mr. Sammler is ready at last to affirm the human bond to Elya. Bellow's fictional instincts led him to reject such a scene in order to present a more powerful declaration. Mr. Sammler is not given the opportunity to talk to Elya. On hearing of Elya's death, he first removes his smoked glasses and then insists on viewing the body before it is prepared for the funeral service. In the P.M. room he looks with his sightless eye at Elya's uncovered face and sees bitterness and obedience written on the lips. The combination points to the pain of duty which, according to Mr. Sammler, makes the human creature upright. It is only after he has gazed on Elya's face that Mr. Sammler breathes a mental whisper:

> Remember, God, the soul of Elya Gruner, who, as willingly as possible and as well as he was able, and even to an intolerable point, and even in suffocation and even as death was coming was eager, even childishly perhaps (may I be forgiven for this), even with a certain servility, to do what was required of him. At his best this man was much kinder than at my very best I have ever been or could ever be. He was aware that he must meet, and he did meet—through all the confusion and degraded clowning of this life through which we are speeding—he did meet the terms of his contract. [285–86]

Mr. Sammler's prayer is a tribute and a testament to the humanness of Elya Gruner. It takes in and understands his nephew's faults, his pride and vanity, and the illegal abortions he performed, out of real pity, for the Mafia. And yet, Elya Gruner was a warm person, full of family feeling, one who lived by the old system, based on human things like "feeling, outgoingness, expressiveness, kindness, heart."

He embodies Bellow's version of how difficult it is to be human in our day. The novel does not dramatize Elya Gruner's journey to the human. Mr. Sammler tells Angela that her father has a human look and has made something of himself (276). Elya Gruner *is* human, he does not *become* human. In these apocalyptic times one has to accept basic human qualities. The romantic affirmations of Augie March and of Henderson are no longer viable. It is the teacher figure (who himself has to be taught) who realizes how tremendously difficult it is in our time to achieve genuine humanness. So difficult, that to be human today is to be a saint, as Mr. Sammler knows: "A few may comprehend that it is the strength to do one's duty daily and promptly that makes saints and heroes" (87). Elya Gruner is naturally human. He meets the terms of his contract because of the natural knowledge his soul has.

It is Mr. Sammler who goes through a number of ordeals before the submerged knowledge of his soul can emerge. These ordeals constitute Bellow's attempt to dramatize the manner in which his protagonist is pushed (like an earlier fellow protagonist, Asa Leventhal) to the very edge of humanness and begins, according to Bellow, to "acknowledge the first stirrings of religion."[11] Mr. Sammler arrives at the threshold of the state of *askesis* and of the denial of the Will that Schopenhauer set forth in the fourth section of *The World as Will and Idea*, "The Assertion and Denial of the Will."

Marcus Klein has noted that *Mr. Sammler's Planet* "alludes to the system of the great Schopenhauer with some frequency though not systematically."[12] Bellow does not impose the Schopenhauerian system in gridlike fashion. Nevertheless, *Mr. Sammler's Planet* is an artistic projection of Schopenhauer's dramatic vision of the world and of human life. Bellow's protagonist has studied the system embodied in *The World as Will and Idea*, which his mother had given him on his sixteenth birthday. He tells Dr. Lal that he still remembers it:

"I learned that only Ideas are not overpowered by the Will—the cosmic force, the Will, which drives all things. A blinding power. The inner creative fury of the world. What we see are only its manifestations. Like Hindu philosophy—Maya, the veil of appearances that hangs over all human experience. Yes, and come to think of it, according to Schopenhauer, the seat of the Will in human beings is . . ."
"Where is it?"
"The organs of sex are the seat of the Will."
The thief in the lobby agreed. He took out the instrument of the Will. He drew aside not the veil of Maya itself but one of its forehangings and showed Sammler his metaphysical warrant. [191]

Here, in marvelous summary, is Schopenhauer's metaphysical Will, the Will to live, with its constant striving without aim or end. The phenomenal world of individuality and multiplicity is merely the veil of

Maya and not the unitary Will, the thing-in-itself. Mr. Sammler can now understand and interpret the real meaning of the lesson transmitted by the black pickpocket in the lobby. The thief's display of his organ, which strongly suggests to Mr. Sammler the infant it was there to beget (63), is an atavistic gesture of power which also dramatizes Schopenhauer's belief that it is in the sexual impulse that the most decided assertion of the Will is expressed. As the life-stimulating principle ensuring endless life to time, the genital organs are subject to and symbolic of the Will. The genitals are, according to Schopenhauer, "the *focus* of will, and consequently the opposite pole of the brain, the representative of knowledge, i.e., the other side of the world, the world as idea."[13]

The confrontation between the black pickpocket and Mr. Sammler is an encounter between a man in a state of nature, driven to assert life, and one who embodies, because of his knowledge, the possibility of the suppression and the denial of the Will. Mr. Sammler is fascinated by the beauty and the regal majesty of this beast who, at first provides for itself (by stealing) and then cares only for the preservation of the species. The display of the organ warns Mr. Sammler not to interfere with the process of the assertion of life.

Many of the other characters in the novel represent various human grades of the manifestation of the Will. The mad crowds on Broadway, hungrily searching for pleasure, desperately trying to escape from ennui, Wallace and Shula Slawa with their limitless demands, Angela with her sexual cravings, the restless Feffer, all are forms of egoism, striving to assert their own individual existence at the expense of other human beings. The most monstrous of egoists are the Nazis, a modern-day phenomenon of pure cruelty and bloodthirstiness which, according to Schopenhauer, "history exhibits so often in the Neros and Domitians, in the African Deis, in Robespierre, and the like."[14]

In contrast to these egoists are those who have seen through the web of Maya. The just man, like Dr. Lal, who has penetrated the veil of Maya, sets other human beings on the same level as himself and does them no injury. On a higher level is the man who has intuitively pierced the illusion of individuality to such an extent that he sees all human beings are really one. He has reached the ethical level of goodness and love (*agape* or *caritas*). Elya Gruner is Schopenhauer's good man, one who "lives in a world of friendly individuals, the well-being of any of whom he regards as his own."[15]

Beyond the good man is the one who knows the whole, comprehends its nature, and finds that it consists "in a constant passing away, vain striving, inward conflict, and continual suffering."[16] Such knowledge leads to a quietening of all volition which, according to Schopenhauer, "turns away from life; it now shudders at the pleasures in which it recognizes the assertion of life. Man now attains to the state of voluntary renunciation, resignation, true indifference, and perfect will-less-ness."[17]

It is Mr. Sammler who is gradually brought to such a state. In Poland he had been reduced to a condition wherein he was not entirely human. It is after the act of murder when he ambushed and shot a man who had pleaded for his life that, paradoxically and strangely, he reenters the human state: "When he fired his gun, Sammler, himself nearly a corpse, burst into life" (129–30). Mr. Sammler could not understand why his heart felt lined with brilliant, rapturous satin, as he puts it. In the Schopenhaurian system, self-maintenance is the first effort of man in a state of nature, the first assertion of the Will to live. The feeling of intense pleasure and ecstasy is a temporary state of "negative" happiness when one asserts one's own existence at the expense of another. *Homo homini lupus,* states Schopenhauer.

The visit to the Middle East during the Aqaba crisis reveals a Mr. Sammler who has seen through the veil of Maya. He cannot formulate clearly what he is, but he knows he is "human, in some altered way. The human being at the point where he attempted to obtain his release from being human" (229). The imperatives of his soul compel him to witness scenes of death and destruction: "The odor was like damp cardboard. The clothes of the dead, greenish-brown sweaters, tunics, shirts were strained by the swelling; the gases, the fluids. Swollen gigantic arms, legs, roasted in the sun. The dogs ate human roast. In the trenches the bodies leaned on the parapets" (228). Mr. Sammler had, the narrator states, his own need for these sights. Immediately after his return to New York, Mr. Sammler turns to Meister Eckhart, not to the world systematizers, for consolation and comfort:

> "Blessed are the poor in spirit. Poor is he who has nothing. He who is poor in spirit is receptive to all spirit. Now God is the Spirit of spirits. The fruit of the spirit is love, joy, and peace. See to it that you are stripped of all creatures, of all consolation from creatures. For certainly as long as creatures comfort and are able to comfort you, you will never find true comfort. But if nothing can comfort you save God, truly God will console you [230–31]

Schopenhauer states that the works of Meister Eckhart, especially his "Die Deutsche Theologie," are the most perfect exposition of the denial of the Will. Meister Eckhart is one of those who "preach, besides the purest love, complete resignation, voluntary and absolute poverty, genuine calmness, perfect indifference to all worldly things, dying to our own will and being born again in God, entire forgetting of our own person, and sinking ourselves in the contemplation of God."[18]

The ordeals suffered by Mr. Sammler instil in him a deep religious sense. One by one his wants and desires are torn out of his being. During the fight between the pickpocket and Feffer, before he gets Eisen to intervene, Mr. Sammler becomes aware of being quite literally "poor in spirit" (264). It is after he learns that Elya is dead that he becomes "poor in spirit" in the biblical (Matthew 5:3) and Eckhartian meaning of the phrase. On the way to the P.M. room he senses a breakup within his being: "He was deprived of one more thing, stripped of one more creature. One more reason to live trickled out" (285). What Mr. Sammler experiences here is the process of reaching a state of perfect disinterestedness. At this moment he is not the voyeur he was, nor is his state one of mere "detached and purified dryness" (31). According to Meister Eckhart, "God loved disinterested purity and unity. God Himself was drawn toward the disinterested soul" (109). It is this form of pure disinterestedness that allows Mr. Sammler to will as God wills (215) and to be aware of the profound need for human involvement.

More than an affirmation of the human bond to Elya, the mental whisper breathed by one who has reached down into the deepest layers of the soul and into the subtlest silences, where undiscovered knowledge is (70), modulates into a profound acknowledgement of the human contract, "the terms of which, in his inmost heart, each man knows. As I know mine. As all know. For that is the truth of it—that we all know, God, that we know, that we know, we know, we know" (286). The chantlike repetition of "know" insists on the natural knowledge of the human soul with which the novel opened. It affirms what Mr. Sammler had stated earlier, that growth is the real aim of the spirit's existence, and that there will always be human continuity. Above all, it calmly proclaims the psychic unity of mankind, the rich truth that all men are brothers because there is in the heart of every human being a splash of God's own spirit.

NOTES

1. Richard Stern, "Bellow's Gift," *New York Times Magazine*, November 21, 1978, p. 48.

2. Saul Bellow, *Mr. Sammler's Planet*, A Fawcett Crest Book, (Fawcett Publications, Inc, Greenwich, Conn.: 1970), p. 34. Future references will be cited in the text.

3. Jo Brans, "Common Needs, Common Preoccupations: An Interview with Saul Bellow," *Southwest Review* 62, no. 1 (Winter 1977): 14.

4. Jane Howard, "Mr. Bellow Considers His Planet," *Life* (3 April 1970), p. 59.

5. Ibid.

6. "Bellow's Gift," p. 48.

7. Chirantan Kulshreshtha, "A Conversation with Saul Bellow," *Chicago Review* 23, no. 4, and 24, no. 1 (1972): 8.

8. "Bellow's Gift," p. 46.

9. Apparently Bellow put to use an incident that occurred when he lectured at San Francisco State University. In a letter to Mark Harris ("Saul Bellow at Purdue," *The Georgia Review*, Winter 1978, p. 716) Bellow wrote: "The thing at S. F. State was very bad. . . . Being denounced by Salas as an old shit to an assembly which seemed to find the whole thing deliciously thrilling. Being told furthermore that 'this is an effete old man—he can't *come!*' "

10. "Mr. Bellow Considers His Planet," p. 59.

11. "Common Needs, Common Preoccupations: An Interview with Saul Bellow," p. 15.

12. Marcus Klein, "A Discipline of Nobility: Saul Bellow's Fiction," in *Saul Bellow: A Collection of Critical Essays*, edited by Earl Rovit (Englewood Cliffs, N.J.: Prentice-Hall, 1975), p. 159.

13. Arthur Schopenhauer, *The World As Will and Idea*, translated by R. B. Haldane and J. Kemp, (Garden City, N.Y.: Doubleday and Co., 1961), p. 341.

14. Ibid., pp. 374–75.

15. Ibid., p. 384.

16. Ibid., p. 389.

17. Ibid.

18. Ibid., pp. 396–97.

8 *Humboldt's Gift*

Humboldt's Gift, Bellow's Mount Everest, towers above those twin peaks, *Herzog* and *Henderson the Rain King*. From that magnificent height *Mr. Sammler's Planet* appears to be a crevasse filled with darkly luminous clouds. Down below rests that tiny, almost perfect plateau, *Seize the Day*, while immediately beneath it stretch the sprawling ridges of *The Adventures of Augie March*. In the far depths, glimpsed at through the swirling mists, lie those foothills, *The Victim* and *Dangling Man*.

By providing his protagonist with a Himalayan perspective Bellow was at last able to survey and solve almost all the basic questions that his earlier protagonists had agonized over before going on to offer ultimate and daring insights into the immortal longings of the human spirit. Like Henderson, Charles Citrine has come back with a message of the greatest importance to mankind. Henderson had got back from Africa with the prediction that mankind, helped by the human imagination, would ultimately make it despite these terrible technological times. Herzog, at the end, had gratefully accepted both the human and his own condition, stating softly: "*I am simply a human being, more or less*" (H, 387). In an act of faith over Elya Gruner's corpse, Mr. Sammler affirmed the brotherhood of all mankind because of the splash of the divine in every human heart. Charles Citrine comes back from his quest with the supreme discovery that we are not natural but supernatural beings. That nuclear term "human," around which all Bellow's fiction revolves, now acquires a radiance and a glory which Citrine's fellow protagonists had sensed and glimpsed, but lacked the confidence to proclaim.

Charles Citrine boldly announces his belief: "At this moment I must say, almost in the form of deposition, without argument, that I do not believe my birth began my first existence. Nor Humboldt's. Nor anyone's. On aesthetic grounds if on no others, I cannot accept the view of death taken by most of us, and taken by me during most of my life—on esthetic grounds therefore I am obliged to deny that so extraordinary a thing as a human soul can be wiped out forever. No, the dead are about us, shut out by our metaphysical denial of them."[1] Here is an extraordinary testament. Citrine is the first Bellow protagonist to take Plato's theory of immortality (which came to Greece from India) quite

225

literally and to take seriously the Hindu belief in reincarnation and in karma. He has solved the crucial problem of death which no longer holds any terrors for him. He refers directly and unapologetically to the "human soul" as the vital element in a human being. *Humboldt's Gift* is a torrential account of the process that led Citrine to such strange beliefs.

He is in a tremendous hurry to tell his tale to the whole world ("dear friends" he calls his readers) before he loses the "light-in-the-being" (177) he has experienced, something as vital as the breath of life itself. It is as if he has recovered his childhood soul and now wants to communicate the incredible discoveries he has made. It is as if Citrine's soul has, to use his odd idiom, flowed out into the universe and now records the human comedy he was involved in with the greatest vividness, naturalness, and gaiety. He has discovered certain truths about what it really means to be human. The core of the eternal, the God-deposited sound of truth, is in every human being. This deathless element indicates that human beings do not die, but continue to live on after death in a way that the rational mind cannot grasp. Citrine's experiences and intuitions compel him to believe that there is an invisible link between the *here* and the *there*, that the dead and the living form one community and mutually influence each other. More significant and daring is his belief that this mutual influence can occur here on earth. *Humboldt's Gift* offers proof positive that his beliefs are valid.

Bellow's vision of the human, now cosmic, at one point becomes cyclocosmic. Asked by Naomi Lutz to comment on the terrible question of death, which Walt Whitman knew was the main question for America, Citrine responds: " 'The whole thing is disintegrating and reintegrating all the time, and you have to guess whether it's always the same cast of characters or a lot of different characters' " (301). It is only in the Mahabharata that such a challenging vision of the human condition and process has ever been projected. In this epic of epics, human history is seen not as linear, sliced into significant periods of time, but as cyclical, with human beings and gods appearing and reappearing in different reincarnations and combinations as ages and aeons roll on.

Attempting a Mahabharata-like novel, Bellow had to direct all the creative energies he now possessed and use all the fictional strategies he commanded to demonstrate and dramatize such a cyclocosmic vision. He found it impossibly difficult to achieve his fictional aims because he had to work in the realistic mode and limit himself to a single lifetime, the human day, of his protagonist. He circumvents these limitations by flinging together a superabundance of facts and details. He casts aside symbolism as a mode inadequate to his fictional purposes and once again abandons structural neatness in order to create a universe in which the living and the dead continue to exist and interact, drawn together by the passionate bonds of love. Every character, even one tangential to the action, every incident, even one that appears to be irrelevant, is described in elaborate detail so that the reader can make cross connections between characters and between incidents. In order to grasp the structure of this enormous fictional universe the reader has to set aside the Cartesian approach to characters and to events, and allow both Bellow and Citrine their *données*. The temptation to equate Citrine the narrator with Bellow the novelist is almost overpowering, but has to be firmly resisted. For Bellow is in perfect control of his first person narrator, and challenges Henry James's pronouncement that the first person is a form foredoomed to failure.

Bellow endows his first-person narrator with a voice and a language that allow him to tell his cosmic tale. The narrative speed is under Bellow's confident control. Citrine does not plod along like Joseph, nor does he indulge in bursts of frantic and erratic movement as Augie March had done. The range of his language reveals the range of his world, one that encompasses and transcends the fictional universes of *Henderson the Rain King* and *Herzog*. Not only does Bellow provide his narrator with a magnificent human voice, he also dramatizes the process by which Citrine has developed such a voice.

The reader can understand Bellow's fictional strategies and respond to the voice, language and narrative speed of Charles Citrine only after he immerses himself in the world of *Humboldt's Gift*. A major problem is that of time. For Citrine's sense of time is chaotic: he is careless about time, a sympton, he says, of his "increasing absorption in larger questions" which demand a different time perspective (34). A successful biographer of political innocents (Harry Hopkins and Woodrow Wilson), Citrine does not know how to control an account that combines biography and autobiography. He makes forays into the past, writes about himself in the present, repeats accounts of the same incident, digresses, meditates on the past at regular intervals, interrupts an incident in order to work in another incident that he remembers, and creates a sumptuous sense of chaos that slowly, surely, turns into a cosmos. To establish his bearings in this cosmos, the reader gradually has to become aware of its time scheme.

Citrine begins his account some time after April 1974. He wants to understand what happened to him during an ordeal-filled five-month period that began in December 1973. Instinctively and intuitively realizing its vital significance, he summons forth not the immediate past but an event that occurred way back in May 1938, his first meeting with von Humboldt Fleisher:

> The book of ballads published by Von Humboldt Fleisher in the Thirties was an immediate hit. Humboldt was just what everyone had been waiting for. Out in the Midwest I had certainly been waiting eagerly, I can tell you that. An avant-garde writer, the first of a new generation, he was handsome, fair, large, serious, witty, he was learned. The guy had it all. All the papers reviewed his book. His picture appeared in *Time* without insult and in *Newsweek* with praise. I read *Harlequin Ballads* enthusiastically. I was a student at the University of Wisconsin and thought about nothing but literature day and night. Humboldt revealed to me new ways of doing things. I was ecstatic. I envied him his luck, his talent, and his fame, and I went east in May to have a look at him—perhaps to get next to him. The Greyhound bus, taking the Scranton route, made the trip in about fifty hours. That didn't matter. The bus windows were open. I had never seen real mountains before. Trees were budding. It was like Beethoven's *Pastorale*. I felt showered by the green within. Manhattan was fine, too. I took a room for three bucks a week and found a job selling Fuller Brushes door to door. And I was wildly excited about everything. Having written Humboldt a long fan letter, I was invited to Greenwich Village to discuss literature and ideas. He lived on Bedford Street, near Chumley's. First he gave me black coffee, and then poured gin in the same cup. "Well, you're a nice-looking enough fellow, Charlie," he said to me. "Aren't you a bit sly, maybe? I think you're headed for early baldness. And such large emotional handsome eyes. But you certainly do love literature and that's the main thing. You have sensibility," he said. He was a pioneer in the use of this word. Sensibility later made it big. Humboldt was very kind. He introduced me to people in the Village and got me books to review. I always loved him. [1–2]

Charles Citrine, fifty-six years old, evokes Charlie, his earlier self, the twenty-year-old graduate student at the University of Wisconsin, and they combine into an "I" to present this meeting. They begin objectively, almost casually, using journalistic jargon ("an immediate hit") about Humboldt's ballads. Then the tempo quickens to generate the excitement stirred up by Humboldt the poet, and Charlie takes over as narrator to communicate the growing eagerness that compels him to travel from the Midwest to meet his poet-hero. Charlie tries to be objective ("An avant-garde writer, the first of a new generation, he was handsome, fair, large, serious, witty, he was learned. The guy had it all"), but his language with its breathless commas, its run-on sentences, its colloquial ease, cannot check his mounting enthusiasm. He goes on to talk not about Humboldt, but about his own urgent desire to be near such a great poet. The continuous repetition of "I" and the odd mingling of factual detail (the fifty-hour Scranton-route Greyhound-bus trip, the job he got in New York as a Fuller Brush salesman) with the references to Beethoven's *Pastorale* and to a Marvellian green within him capture the intense, if slightly comic, ecstasy of that time. The reference to Humboldt's invitation allows Charles to reenter the narrative and recall not only the black coffee, and then the gin poured in the same cup, but the very words Humboldt had used to describe Charlie. At the end Charles and Charlie come together to make a joint avowal: "I always loved him." It is Charlie who says, "I loved him"; Charles supplies the dimension of memory and time, "always."

The opening paragraph establishes the ecstatic connection between Citrine and Humboldt, a relationship of love that even death will not destroy. At twenty-two,[2] Humboldt is at the height of his powers and his success, and he draws Charlie Citrine into his emotional and literary orbit. Charlie is in an eager, receptive state, ready to absorb everything he can from his friend and teacher. Humboldt's love and kindness manifest themselves in practical fashion: he introduces Citrine to the people in the Village and helps him establish his name as a reviewer. Humboldt knows his protégé is a kindred spirit, but he can detect early warnings of trouble: the hint of slyness with which Charlie disguises his inordinate ambitions, the tendency to baldness which the aging Charles will refuse to acknowledge, and the emotional handsome eyes which lead to his disastrous involvement with women. The seminal nature of the opening paragraph becomes clear only later, after one realizes that Citrine's account bursts out of its seemingly irrelevant details.

The opening paragraph also prepares the ground for Bellow's fictional strategies, especially his control of voice, time and narrative perspective. *Humboldt's Gift* is an account that is not written but told. The colloquial currents—"an immediate hit," "I can tell you that," "the guy had it all"—indicate that Citrine is speaking directly to his friends, desperately trying to tell all in order also to get rid of the tremendous pressure of a lifetime accumulated within him. He talks nonstop, allowing his memories, associations, thoughts, observations, all his literary and mental wealth, to pour out of him. That is why *Humboldt's Gift* is not divided into convenient, conventional chapters, but into forty-one unequal and unnumbered sections. Bellow, like the later Henry James, dictated *Humboldt's Gift* at the rate of five to twenty pages a day from notes scribbled the night before, occasionally departing from them to improvise.[3] The voice of Charles Citrine is that of a creator who has entered the very skin and being of his protagonist.

The many references to Proust (17, 23, 26, 31, 152, 275)[4] indicate an awareness of the Marcellian mode of controlling time and suggest that Bellow's strategy will be similar yet significantly different from that of his European precursor. Citrine, who has been trained to appreciate Proust by Humboldt himself (61), is not a single, contemplative, omnipotent consciousness who slowly conjures up a whole, lost world: he is a restless, multiple "I." He does not indulge in bouts of involuntary recollection, but is driven by a number of forces, within and without, that compel him to relive his whole life. He is not the ingenuous narrator Augie March was, one who had told the story of his adventures more or less chronologically. The process of recollection begins calmly and tranquilly enough (in the opening paragraph), but turns into a wild rush, Bellow employs a variation of the technique he had used in the first four chapters of *Henderson the Rain King* which erupt out of Henderson in chaotic fashion. In the first three sections (1–34) Citrine refers to almost every phase of his involvement with Humboldt in nonchronological fragments, darting from one event in the past to another, desperately trying to understand the strange reentry of Humboldt into his life. Humboldt "came from left field" (34), Citrine tells us, using the language of baseball. He invaded and changed Citrine's life and Citrine pours out all in order to understand how and why it all happened: "I wasn't doing so well myself recently when Humboldt acted from the grave, so to speak, and made a basic change in my life. In spite of our big fight and fifteen years of estrangement he left me something in his will. I came into a legacy" (6).

The first three sections display Bellow's superb control over his narrator and over narrative structure. The narrative appears to be hastily improvised and to move at a hectic and erratic pace, but it really departs from and returns to two major events—to the first encounter in May 1938 and to the Sunday in September 1952, when Humboldt drove Citrine to his home in New Jersey. Bellow makes Citrine convey a strong impression of Humboldt at the height of his poetic powers and his glory, just before decline set in. Both events celebrate Humboldt as poet and talker.

Humboldt's poems were "pure, musical, witty, radiant, human" (11). They were, Citrine tells us, Humboldt's "love-offering" to the modern world, his Platonic cry for the lost, original home world from which mankind has been cast away and to which it longs to return. As poet, Humboldt had a mission: he was to be the agent who would redeem and revive the human spirit exiled in the American wasteland. Bellow does not make Citrine quote any of Humboldt's poems as evidence of his poetic powers, but he allows his narrator to reenact Humboldt's spell-binding talk.

Humboldt was "a wonderful talker, a hectic nonstop monologuist and improvisator, a champion detractor" (4). He was the Mozart of conversation, a Haydn composing "an oratorio in which he sang and played all parts" (14). The theme of Humboldt's monologue on that May afternoon in 1938 was Success. Citrine convincingly recreates the manner in which Humboldt's talk spun round and round the topic, taking in the problems of modern poetry and of the poet in pragmatic, business America, darting to other topics but always returning to his basic theme, the fate of the poet in America: "In the midst of these variations the theme was always ingeniously and excitingly retrieved" (13).

Humboldt changed into a business poet in 1952. He cashed in on his reputation as a poet and put together intricate schemes to line up sinecures and foundation money. Physically he became thick and stout; signs of paranoia became evident; Humboldt kept himself going on pills and gin. The slow deterioration of Humboldt as poet and human being was offset by the golden brilliance of his conversation. All through that long Sunday of 1952 Humboldt displayed his literary and mental wealth. His encyclopaedic mind allowed him to range over all kinds of topics weaving together an intricate web of superb talk. His basic texts, Citrine informs us, were "Plato's *Timaeus*, Proust on Combray, Virgil on farming, Marvell on gardens, Wallace Stevens' Caribbean poetry" (17). Fascinated, Citrine listened and tried to join Humboldt in a duet, but was "fiddled and trumpeted off the stage." Not a mere soloist, Humboldt was a whole orchestra, a producer of conversational grand opera: "He passed from statement to recitative, from recitative he soared into aria, and behind him played an orchestra of intimations, virtues, love of his art, veneration of its great men—but also of suspicion and skulduggery" (30).

Humboldt's radiant presence almost prevents the reader from realizing that Bellow accomplishes other fictional tasks in the three sections. Citrine stood in the shadow of Humboldt, but Humboldt himself was aware that his "ingenu" friend had a secret mission and was bursting with a powerful ambition. Citrine put it colloquially thus: he "hoped to knock everybody dead" (12). To his beloved Demmie Vonghel, Citrine confessed that he had a funny feeling that he contained unusual information that people were waiting for him to deliver. Humboldt, with his prophetic soul, half-jokingly stated that Hegel's World Historical Individual might come from insignificant Appleton, Wisconsin (Citrine's birthplace), "from left field" (18).

The use of the identical baseball image for Humboldt and for Citrine

establishes the many connections that exist between them, connections
that develop into continuities. The voice of Charles Citrine, the narrator,
with its range and pace, is an astonishing extension of the talk
techniques and strategies of Humboldt that Citrine seems to have
appropriated and assimilated. Both have unfinished missions. During
the drive to New Jersey Humboldt held forth on a number of subjects; he
discussed "machinery, luxury, command, capitalism, technology,
Mammon, Orpheus and poetry, the riches of the human heart, America,
world civilization. His task was to put all of this, and more, together"
(21). Humboldt never did fulfill this task, but perhaps he bequeathed it
to Citrine, who will. Bellow announces here the major themes of his
novel which the rest of the sections will amplify and orchestrate.

The fourth section switches dramatically to the immediate present, to
December 1973, when Rinaldo Cantabile, a Mafia hoodlum, invades
Citrine's life. The story of Citrine's ordeals now begins. The "I" is now
the Charles Citrine of December 1973 who narrates all that happens to
him in chronological order. Blessed, like Herzog, with perfect recall, he
can shift effortlessly into the "I" of his earlier manifestations when he
chooses to evoke the past. Unlike Herzog's cramping time schedule of
five days, that of Citrine stretches to five months, which allows Bellow to
pack his fiction with action and event. The time pattern, which had at
first appeared bewildering, now slowly becomes clear.
   In September 1952 Humboldt wangled teaching jobs for himself and
for Citrine at Princeton. He maneuvered with Citrine's help to get
himself appointed to a Princeton Chair of Poetry, but in February 1953
the scheme fell through. In the fall of the same year Citrine's play, *Von
Trenck*, was a Broadway hit. Humboldt went into a decline and suffered
from depression and mania. He accused Citrine of betrayal and
treachery; they met as friends for the last time in May 1953 (147).
Citrine moved to Chicago, where he was rich and successful, winning
prizes and medals for his books on Wilson and Hopkins. In 1967/68, on
a journalistic assignment, Citrine was so shocked when he saw
Humboldt, a frightening apparition on a New York street, that he hid
from and avoided confronting his former friend. The sequence of events
from December 1973 to April 1974, noted in copious detail, poses no
problems. The real meaning of these events becomes clear only after one
has put together the fragmented constituents of Citrine's "I." For Citrine,
in December 1973, was falling apart. His life, in his own words, was in
great disorder.
   Physically, at fifty-five, Citrine appeared to be in good shape. To
Renata, his mistress, he reported his doctor's comments on his youthful

prostate and his supernormal EKG. He played squash and did yoga exercises to keep himself in trim, and he dressed up like a dandy. But his half-bald head (Denise, his ex-wife, noted that he combed his side hair over to hide his baldness), the bags under his eyes, his dewlaps and neck wrinkles (which Cantabile commented on to Polly), all told him that he "was getting that look of a badly stuffed trophy or mounted specimen that I have always associated with age, and was horrified" (171). Citrine was even more horrified after the pathetic end of Humboldt, but he refused even to contemplate the idea of death: "I continued to carry on as if it weren't yet time to think of death" (142). Financially, Citrine was in bad shape, having, as he put it, bungled the whole money thing. In 1970 he had an income in excess of a hundred thousand dollars. By 1973 most of his money had been drained out of him. The IRS, aided by Murra, Citrine's accountant, Denise, who filed endless ruinous lawsuits after the divorce, his own incompetent and exorbitant lawyers, Renata, on whom he spent lavishly taking her on trips to Europe, his friends, Szathmar and Thaxter, all combined to squeeze money, that vital substance for modern man, out of him. Intellectually, Citrine was stagnant, having drifted into the doldrums. His last book, *Some Americans*, subtitled *The Sense of Being in the USA*, was a failure. He owed publishers 70,000 dollars in advances, but felt too paralyzed to write anything. Emotionally, too, Citrine felt dissatisfied and empty, despite the "woman-filled life" (111) he has led and despite his current mistress, Renata.

Behind the facade of innocence and well-being, Citrine in December 1973 was in a state of near collapse. He felt that his brain was deteriorating (81). Shrewd Denise, with her huge amethyst eyes, noted the symptoms of his mental and physical decline and announced her diagnosis. "Sometimes I feel you might be certifiable or committable," she told him when they met in the county building (228). All Citrine's symptoms point to the fact that he was in the same condition that Humboldt had sunk to during his decline. The rot in Citrine was within, not as visible or as dramatic as Humboldt's, but just as deadly. Citrine would have gone the way of Humboldt had not help arrived in totally unexpected fashion.

Citrine summarizes how his life was transformed. Humboldt, his dead camerado, came at him

as in life, driving ninety miles an hour in his Buick fourholer. First I laughed. Then I shrieked. I was transfixed. He bore down on me. He struck me with blessings. Humboldt's gift wiped out many immediate problems.

The role played by Ronald and Lucy Cantabile in this is something else again. [110]

The reference to the Buick hurtling on to Citrine establishes the use of car imagery in the novel, and insists that Citrine could not run away from this experience in his usual manner. The verbs "transfixed," "bore down," "struck" reinforce both the intensity and the inevitability of what happened. The mention of the role of the Cantabiles immediately after the reference to the impact of Humboldt on Citrine's life is a significant juxtaposition despite the cryptically colloquial, "something else again."

Rinaldo Cantabile was a minor Mafia figure whom Citrine met at a poker game arranged by his friend, George Swiebel, to introduce him to the real Chicago. Outraged when Citrine (on the advice of his friend) stopped payment on a check for 450 dollars for his gambling losses, Cantabile avenged himself by indulging in acts of brutal and comic savagery. He battered Citrine's silver Mercedes, dragged him into the john of the Russian Bath and pushed him into a stall where Citrine had to hear his rumblings and smell his stink, got Citrine to apologize abjectly before witnesses, took him high up on the catwalk of an unfinished sixty-storied skyscraper, where he made paper planes of Citrine's fifty-dollar bills and sailed seven of them away.

With his thick, dark, minklike mustache, his elegant getup, his dagger brows, his white Thunderbird with its blood-red upholstery, his music-syllabled name, Rinaldo Cantabile is so extravagantly comic, dazzling, and realistic a character that his significance and function are not immediately apparent. A supernatural force, he has materialized suddenly in Citrine's life to move him from dead center. A mad and comic demon, he casts a fellow demon, who has adopted the protective disguise of an innocent, into a moronic inferno. The words he hurls at Citrine are edged with double meaning: " 'I'm not sleeping, why should you be?' " (37); " 'You don't know what you're into. Or who I am. Wake up!' " he shouts at Citrine over the telephone (46); " 'When are you going to do something *and know what you're doing?*' " asks Cantabile, spacing out the last words and heavily accenting them (86). Cantabile too has a mission: he has to rouse Citrine from the slumber that has sealed his spirit and get him to go about his proper business as a human being.

Cantabile, to put it directly, is a mysterious emanation of the dead Humboldt. Bellow provides many clues, hints and parallels that establish such a connection. Citrine feels, he knows not why, powerfully drawn to Cantabile. At their very first meeting he senses that "a natural connection" (91) exists between them. Later, he is aware that they are united by a "near-mystical bond" (177). Like Humboldt, Cantabile is a fanatical schemer whose face registers the turbulent emotions that boil within. Both drive elegant cars—Humboldt a Buick with luxurious upholstery, Cantabile a Thunderbird with blood-red seats upholstered in soft leather—and their driving habits are similar: Humboldt, a bad driver, drove fast and tailgated other drivers (21); Cantabile takes off at top speed and rides the bumpers of the car ahead, forcing the other motorist to chicken out (87). Humboldt carried a pistol, while Cantabile sports a Magnum, to exercise threats of vengeance. Both make use of telephone calls in the night to harass others (38). Both celebrate their triumphs in the same way, by rushing off to spend the night with girls (139–40, 170). The connection between Humboldt and Cantabile becomes clear when Citrine realizes that Cantabile is like Baron von Trenck, "demonstrative exuberant impulsive destructive and wrong-headed" (173). Humboldt had accused Citrine of stealing his personality and putting it into von Trenck. It is Cantabile who bears down on and transfixes Citrine, and later, strikes him with blessings.

All the stages of Cantabile's involvement with Citrine are significant. The poker game[5] indicates that Citrine's present friends cannot protect him, unlike Humboldt and Demmie Vonghel, on whom he had always relied for protection. George Swiebel, that self-designated expert on the Chicago underworld, did nothing to prevent his childhood friend from being cheated by the two hoodlums who crashed the party. Also, George underestimated Cantabile as a mere punk and a nobody. The poker game also reveals that Citrine, at fifty-five, is comically innocent, one who has so isolated himself from the rest of mankind that he does not know the brutal facts of life. One of the people at the party, a Sicilian undertaker, acts as a reality instructor for this educated nut: " 'That's not what a wife is about. And if you have a funny foot you have to look for a funny shoe. And if you find the right fit you just let it alone' " (63). Finally, the poker party allows Citrine to loosen his contracted psyche. Proud and self-contained, he never exchanged ideas with anyone but his intellectual friend, Durnwald, who is away. At the party Citrine talks away like a nine-year-old (105), pouring out everything about his life, his interests, his projects, even his relationship with von Humboldt Fleisher. "I never discuss these things with strangers," says Citrine (105). What Citrine does not realize is that Cantabile is not really a stranger to him.

The battering of the Mercedes is an attack, as Citrine recognizes, on himself, for the car was an extension of his foolishness and his vanity. He had bought it for 18,000 dollars when he met Renata. It was his "love-offering" to her (47); Humboldt's poems, too, were love offerings to the world, the use of the same term pointedly revealing the change in Citrine. Cantabile smashes this "shimmering silver motor tureen" (35) as if he wants to obliterate it and create something new. The results of the bashing are graphically presented in anthropomorphic terms. The protective shatter-proof windows are fractured; the beautiful metal skin looks corroded; the headlights are crushed blind and the doors are almost jammed shut. It had suffered, says Citrine, a kind of crystalline internal hemorrhage (36). He drives his mutilated car and himself to the shop where Fritz, who charges like a brain surgeon (71), will fix it.

Citrine suffers from internal shock when he sees his battered car. Like Tommy Wilhelm and Herzog, he feels a desperate craving for help, but he cannot locate George Swiebel, nor can the doorman or Vito Langobardi, a big-time hoodlum, help him. He does not go to the police, because he knows they cannot help him. Cantabile has "made a very peculiar and strong impression" on Citrine (89), who agrees to meet him at the Russian Bath hoping to get rid of his troubles in his usual fashion, "by submission and agreement" (55).

The taxi ride to the Russian Bath is also a trip back in time, a visit to the Chicago of his boyhood. As a kid Citrine used to visit the Russian Bath with his father. The landscape of his past, Citrine notes, has been destroyed: "The old boulevard now was a sagging ruin, waiting for the wreckers. Through great holes I could look into apartments where I had slept, eaten, done my lessons, kissed girls" (75). But it is still charged with memories of his parents' love for him and with his love of his childhood sweetheart, Naomi Lutz. Such memories are healing.

Cantabile tries to intimidate Citrine with threats, with baseball bats (which had been used to bash the car), and with the Magnum. Citrine wants to run off in the way he had done when a mugger had confronted him, but he can't escape from Cantabile. He then adopts the technique his brother protagonist, Mr. Sammler, had used: he switches himself out of the reality and the stink of the john by thinking of all that had been written about Cantabile-like ape behavior. He also dismisses Cantabile as a mere "actor" who is forcing him to be involved in a "dramatization" (89). Driven by some manic energy, Cantabile drags Citrine to the Playboy Club, where he has put together an intricate scheme in order to be mentioned in Mike Schneiderman's gossip column. Citrine has to make amends publicly in order to repair Cantabile's damaged reputation. Dissatisfied with Citrine's lack of sophistication (Citrine refers comically to the girl's bathing suit his mother had bought for him as a child), Cantabile takes him to the Hancock Building, where Citrine has to repeat his apology in front of an old fence, dressed up like a businessman.

Still dissatisfied with Citrine's reactions (he laughs, he does not shriek), Cantabile takes him to the sixtieth floor of an unfinished skyscraper. Here Citrine is really afraid and puts his arms around a pillar to keep himself from falling. Citrine cannot laugh off this situation, nor can he use it as an occasion for thought: the possibility of death is too stark a reality to be so easily dismissed. He watches his fifty-dollar notes sail away but cannot understand the significance of Cantabile's gesture. What he does realize at that moment is what Herzog came to acknowledge, that he has to "change everything" (102). The day of atonement ends with a request that Citrine supply Lucy, Cantabile's wife, with information and material about Humboldt, on whom she is writing her dissertation. Citrine forcefully refuses.

Citrine's whirlwind tour is also an impressionistic rendition of the sights, the sounds, and the smells of Chicago. In *Augie March* Bellow had heaped detail upon particular detail to convey Chicago's heavy and palpable density. The city scenes in *Herzog* were charged with electrical life to present a sense of nightmare, for New York was the City of Destruction. In *Humboldt's Gift* Bellow presents Chicago with effortless ease. Scenic details blend casually and vividly into the flowing narrative. From the top of the skyscraper Citrine has an overview of Chicago on a December afternoon: "A ragged western sun spread orange light over the dark shapes of the town, over the branches of the river and the black trusses of bridges. The lake, gilt silver and amethyst, was ready for its winter cover of ice" (97). The language has a delicacy and a lightness of touch, an ability to change pace and tempo with such rapidity that the details lose their thickness and become gossamer light. It is as if the perspective has changed. No longer oppressed by Chicago because he now understands it, Citrine can respond gaily to all it offers.

Citrine is as "minutely observant" (134) as Mr. Sammler (the same phrase is used for both protagonists), but his eyes are lit up with generous understanding. He notes the behavior of the grotesque lechers at the Downtown Health Club, but does not reduce it to an example of sex ideology. He can see the beauty of the commonplace even in a barbershop: "There, the usual busy sight—the three barbers: the big Swede with dyed hair, the Sicilian, always himself (not even shaved) and the Japanese. Each had the same bouffant coiffure, each wore a yellow vest with golden buttons over a short-sleeved shirt. All three were using hot-air guns with blue muzzles and shaping the hair of three customers" (70). Citrine makes use of vivid analogies. McCormick Place on Lake Michigan is like an aircraft carrier, moored at the shore (66). The taxi driver's hair "was wild-looking with an immense Afro like a shrub from the gardens of Versailles." On Division Street the double rows of silvered boiler-planters stand out like rivets against the blaring red of the brick and look "like the raised-skin patterns of African tribes" (71). Like most of his fellow protagonists, Citrine has an anthropologist's sensibility. He yokes strange associations together without any strain or effort. The white hot boulders in the Russian Bath "lie in a pile like Roman ballistic ammunition" (78). A Playboy bunny presents a peculiar mix: "Up to the chin she was ravishing. Above, all was commercial anxiety. My attention was divided between the soft crease of her breasts and the look of business difficulty on her face" (93). Above all, Citrine's wit and comic sense never allow him to be bitter. There may be something corrupt and foul about the huge nose of Bill, an acquaintance of Cantabile's, but Citrine's speculative slant makes it comic: "In a different context I would have guessed him to be a violinist who had become disgusted with music and gone into the liquor business" (92).

" 'My heart is breaking and I want to go home,' " Citrine tells Cantabile with an odd and uncharacteristic shift of tone at the end of their terrible day (106). His heart is breaking because a secret, inner wound has now opened up. And he wants to go back home to the world that Humboldt had revealed to him in *Harlequin Ballads*. Cantabile has somehow cracked open the protective and heavy armor that had weighed on Citrine's being. Citrine can now proceed on his journey to health and resume his quest for the human.

Cantabile's pointed though seemingly casual request for information about Humboldt triggers a huge reaction deep within Citrine. It allows him to release vital and detailed information about his emotional and intellectual problems which he did not supply Cantabile. It also enables him to recall and revalue his past, especially his involvement with Humboldt. The past can then be aligned with the present for both are vitally interconnected.

Charles Citrine now amplifies the fact that his condition in December 1973 is one of utter confusion. A ladies' man, as the doorman, Roland Stiles, characterizes him, Citrine has been emotionally involved with many women (Herzog, too, had shopped in vain from woman to woman) and has now reached a dead end. His childhood friend, whom he had loved deeply, had been Naomi Lutz, from whom he had borrowed thirty dollars in 1938 to go to New York. After that he was deeply involved with Demmie Vonghel, a self-styled "tiger-mother" (151) who acted as his protectress, his manager, his cook, his strawboss (163). She died in a plane crash just before Christmas in 1953, the year of Citrine's Broadway success.

In the middle 1950s Citrine married Denise, the script girl for the actor Verviger (who played Von Trenck), not because he loved her but, as Szathmar rightly pointed out, "because she talked like a syllabus, and you were dying for understanding and conversation and she had culture" (208). As he later tells Renata, he married Denise hoping she would act as his cultural adviser and protector (309). In 1959/60 they came back to settle in Chicago. The marriage fell apart in 1968/69 and in 1970, when Citrine was a defendant in a postdecree action filed by Denise, he met the voluptuous Renata, who became his mistress, hoping Citrine would marry her and make her respectable. Disappointed, she punished Citrine by inviting him to her apartment for dinner and then locking him out. The rich undertaker, Flonzaley, was with her. Citrine consoled himself by having an affair for a few months in 1972 with a young girl, Doris Scheldt, who introduced him to her father, an anthroposophist. But when Renata sent for him, Citrine rushed back to her. In December 1973 Citrine is, in the eyes of the world, "an old troubled lecher" (191); he however sees himself as "a person of frenzied longings" (190) which only Renata can elicit. As Citrine elegantly puts it, and he always puts it elegantly, Renata helps him consummate his earthly cycle (193). His relationship with her, however, is an unsure and emotionally insecure one.

Intellectually, too, Citrine is in the same state of terrible confusion that Herzog and Mr. Sammler had been in before their ordeals began. Mr. Sammler thought he had a handle upon the human situation, and wanted desperately to condense his vision of human life into a short statement. Herzog, wanting to change history and influence the development of civilization, aimed at solving the problem of the world's coherence. Citrine's intellectual ambitions are even more grandiose. The reader has to understand their origins, appreciate their inordinate range and realize how they've crumbled in December 1973.

Citrine carried his seething focusless intellectual ambitions with him when he went to New York, but he cleverly concealed them by wearing the mask of an ingenu. Only Humboldt could detect the slyness with which Citrine hid the aggressive forces at work within him. Citrine was deadly serious when he said he "hoped to knock everybody dead" (12). He wanted to challenge all the intellectuals of his time and stun the whole world by offering a new vision and reading of the human situation. Humboldt, too, had his intellectual dreams which he openly talked about. Having read Hegel's *Phenomenology*, Humboldt wanted to be the World Historical Individual that would manage the human enterprise. He considered himself an exceptional person and therefore an eligible candidate for power. At that time, Citrine tells us, "I was more or less a candidate myself. I, too, saw great opportunities, scenes of ideological victory, and personal triumph" (29).

Through the years Citrine secretly nourished his dream which acquired shape and direction from a note in a book by Valéry lent to him by Humboldt. Valéry had jotted down in the margin: *"Trouve avant de chercher"* (73). It led Citrine to take an intellectual path different from that of Humboldt who had explored the current ideologies, "Marxism, Freudianism, Modernism, the avant-garde" (158). Too proud to be guided by such ideologies, Citrine suffered from the delusion that he could "rise and dart straight to the truth." In the final Eisenhower years he abandoned New York (like Humboldt, who had betaken himself to New Jersey) and went back to Chicago in order to write his masterwork in secret. He thought he had found the ideal place to work in: "In raw Chicago you could examine the human spirit under industrialism." Also, he had, he thought, found his focus: his subject was to be "Boredom," a topic he had discussed with his friend, Humboldt. Over the years, Citrine worked a lot on this master essay but found that he "kept being overcome by the material" (108). He continued along the path of fame and success by writing biographies and superficial articles and essays published in *Life, Look* and *Esquire*. Gradually, however, he began turning out stuff that could not sell. His last book, which his publishers had begged him not to print, was quickly remaindered. As Denise rather bitingly put it, Citrine was sacrificing his mental life, which was drying out, to his erotic needs (43).

In 1970, urged on by his friend Pierre Thaxter, Citrine spent lavish sums of money as patron-editor of *The Ark*, a magazine which he hoped would allow him to realize his intellectual dreams. As its name implied, the journal was going to rescue mankind from the deluge of trivia that had descended upon the modern world and exercise a civilizing influence on mankind: "Everything possible must be done to restore the credit and authority of art, the seriousness of thought, the integrity of culture, the dignity of style" (249). The prospectus proposed a new task for America and the world. America had solved the old and painful problems of economic scarcity and of human freedom; now America had to formulate new basic questions for itself and for mankind.

Unfortunately, Citrine's dream never materializes. In 1973 *The Ark* was still in the planning stage. The total cost was enormous, for Pierre Thaxter's extravagant plans matched his friend's overambitious ideas. *The Ark* was to be produced on a new IBM machine, and it had to have new premises built and a special IBM operator-secretary. Pierre Thaxter did the whole thing in style, sending voluminous memoranda to Citrine together with the staggering bills which Citrine paid. The first number was yet to be published.

By December 1973 Citrine is in a state of intellectual torpor. He thinks of statements he has to make and of truths he has to proclaim to the world. But, shut up as he is within himself, he cannot summon up the energy required for this task. He keeps on doing "advanced mental work" (109) but feels a compelling desire to "lie down and go to sleep" (108). What prevents him from lapsing completely into lethargy is his recent interest in the ideas and writings of the anthroposophist Rudolf Steiner. Citrine has come to Steiner in two odd ways: through his affair with Doris Scheldt, and through his rationalist friend, Durnwald, who had kiddingly suggested that Steiner had much to offer on the deeper implications of sleep. On the morning after his terrible Cantabile day, Citrine decides to abandon thinking of everything that has made his life so complicated and burdensome—"Renata, Denise, children, courts, lawyers, Wall Street, sleep, death, metaphysics, karma, the presence of the universe in us, our being present in the universe itself" (110)—and meditate (in the fashion set down by Steiner himself in *Knowledge of the Higher Worlds and Its Attainment*) on Humboldt.

Citrine's day of remembrance is also a day of expiation, yet another day of atonement. Again and again he feels compelled to return to the moment when he committed the terrible crime against Humboldt, and he narrates everything that happened on that day, two months before his friend's death, in full detail. A crack journalist, grandly dressed, commissioned by *Life* to do an article on Robert Kennedy (Denise had arranged the whole deal), Citrine had spent the day with US senators and political bigwigs and was returning from a luncheon in Central Park when he saw his pal Humboldt with death written all over him, eating a pretzel stick. Citrine fled from his dying friend just as he had sped away from the Chicago mugger. So shocked was he that he fled all the way from New York to Chicago, hoping Denise would comfort his deathmood.

By setting down all the details Citrine conveys both to himself and to the reader the full significance of all that happened. The dandyish clothes and the trivial journalistic assignment reveal that Citrine still follows the primrose path of fame and success. The basketball match between Senators Kennedy and Javits (113–14), staged for publicity purposes, parallels and contrasts the innocent and human football passes Citrine had watched Humboldt and Kathleen throw in New Jersey (23). The scene with Denise in their bedroom in Chicago indicates that Denise cannot provide Citrine with the protection he needs and had married her for (115–16). Finally, Citrine's flight from Humboldt points to a basic weakness in his makeup: like all his fellow protagonists, he avoids reality instead of confronting it.

Citrine now acknowledges that he had sinned against Humboldt. It was a heinous sin because, as the postcard poem, which drops mysteriously out of his Humboldt collection of papers, reveals, Humboldt had regained some of his powers toward the end. The poem was a warning to Citrine, a reminder that he should use the powers of his imagination. Humboldt's message was that Citrine should cast away fear, which, according to Dahfu, was the ruler of mankind, and behave like the "heedless lions," those Blakean forms of that royal and redeeming human faculty, the imagination. By running away Citrine refused to help his blood brother; also, he lost the valuable insights that his friend might have provided him just before he died.

Citrine goes on to recall a crucial day in Princeton in 1952, on the morning after Eisenhower's landslide victory. Worried about his future (he had placed his hopes on being a cultural adviser for the Stevenson administration), Humboldt sought Citrine's aid in a peculiar scheme he put together to be appointed to a chair in modern poetry at Princeton. Their conversation on that day, recalled in minute detail, provides further insights into the makeup of Citrine. Living in the world of high consciousness, Citrine could not understand Humboldt's fears and did not realize why Humboldt had to go in for such a ridiculous scheme. Citrine lived an isolated existence, not bothering about human problems, leaving it to Humboldt to deal with practical matters like "money and status and success and failure and social problems and politics" (122). Also, the evil desires, suppressed by this innocent, were given expression through the medium of Humboldt. Citrine was like Herzog who refused to know evil and allowed others to experience it for him. The harebrained scheme filled Citrine with pungent delight which he refused to acknowledge: " 'You love intrigue and mischief. Right now your teeth are on edge with delight' " Humboldt had told Citrine (127).

Citrine's reluctance to enter wholeheartedly into the scheme drove Humboldt to a ritualistic dramatization of their interknittedness as brothers. He forced Citrine (who had a bank balance of eight dollars) to exchange blank signed checks with him. Humboldt called this exchange a covenant that made them blood brothers. The details that Citrine recalls indicate that they had taken an oath and signed a pact. Very moved, Humboldt had signed his name "with trembling force." Citrine's own arm "seemed full of nerves and it jerked as I was signing" (129). And Humboldt's slip of the tongue—" 'It's dangerous. I mean it's valuable' " (130)—indicated that any breaking of the oath would have dangerous consequences. At that time, Citrine did not realize the significance of this exchange. The meaning of this modern covenant will become clear only after Citrine has come to realize the relation between blood and money, and has discovered the role that money plays in the world today.

Citrine's recall of the decline and fall of Humboldt all through 1953 consists of a series of episodes both tragic and comic. He captures the mounting manic and clownish energy with which Humboldt worked out the Princeton scheme: "He was going to persuade Longstaff, do in Sewell, outfox Ricketts, screw Hildebrand, and bugger fate. At the moment he looked like the Roto Rooter man come to snake out the drains" (138). The disintegration of the Poetry Chair led in many ways to the collapse of Humboldt's marriage and to his growing paranoia, evident at the Littlewood party. Some episodes are hilarious: lesbians dressed as longshoremen rescue Magnasco from the clutches of Humboldt, while toilet paper streamers unroll all over the place. Others are sad and tragic, especially when the police handcuff Humboldt who has diarrhea on the way to Bellevue where they lock him up for the night. Citrine has to endure Humboldt's telephone threats: " 'I want you to know what it's like when the police come for you, and what a strait jacket is like' " (157). Citrine reenacts Humbolt's brilliantly crazy talk-sessions at the White Horse Tavern where Humboldt provided entertainment far into the night, uttering wisecracks—" 'I never yet touched a fig leaf that didn't turn into a price tag' " (159)—and coining epigrams—"Fidelity is for phonographs" (160). Citrine sums up Humboldt as performer: "he spilled dirt, spread scandal, and uttered powerful metaphors. What a combination! Fame gossip delusion filth and poetic invention" (161).

In the process of remembering the Humboldt of 1953 Citrine also evokes the warm, reassuring presence of Demmie Vonghel in his own life. Always in the background, Demmie Vonghel was a vital force for Citrine all through 1952 and 1953, one who provided the sustenance he needed at the time. Sketched with the lightest of touches, with facts, odd details and comments, and moments of comedy and delicate irony thrown in during the recall of Humboldt, Demmie emerges as a charming and lovable human being. Citrine notes the different planes on which she existed: there was "the primordial Demmie beneath the farmer's daughter beneath the teacher beneath the elegant Main Line horse-woman, Latinist, accomplished cocktail-sipper in black chiffon, with the upturned nose, this fashionable conversationalist" (147).

Like Rinaldo Cantabile, Demmie Vonghel is more than a brilliantly rendered character. With her innocence, she was strangely out of place in New York, as if she did not belong there but had been sent for a special spiritual purpose. Her beauty excited the demonic presences in the big city, stirring up the sexual passions of her dentist, her physician, her psychiatrist, all people "who were under oath, who were virtually priests" (165). Citrine speculates that the presence of Demmie answered the question whether "mania and crime and catastrophe were the destiny of mankind in this vile century? Demmie by her innocence, by beauty and virtue, drew masses of evidence from the environment to support this" (166). Her night voice, which arose after she fell asleep expressed her terror of "this strange place, the earth, and of this strange state, being" (147). Humboldt was prophetically right when he warned Citrine that Demmie had a lot of agony to get through (29). Demmie was prone to accident (153), as if she was driven to get out of this alien world and return to the spiritual home world to which she belonged.

When Demmie Vonghel died in a fatal plane crash in South America Citrine became vulnerable to the demonic forces that attack anyone who has attained fame, success, and wealth. After 1953 he lost his protectors, both of whom were aware of the evil lurking within Citrine. Humboldt had blurted out one day that Citrine was a real devil (18), while Demmie told him that there were "all kinds of sin" in him (167).

To prevent Citrine's meditation on Humboldt from becoming monotonous, Bellow inserts two interruptions that continue the action on the plane of the present. Renata promises to pick Citrine up at one o'clock so that he can meet with his lawyers and with Judge Urbanovich in the county building. Later, Polly Palomino and Rinaldo Cantabile provide a welcome interruption when they visit Citrine's apartment.

Cantabile's visit (168–87), brief though it is, is significant and reveals Bellow the craftsman at work. Seen through the eyes of an outsider, Citrine's apartment, with its Oriental carpets and the silk, plush bolstered sofa, reveals his way of life, one of soul-deadening comfort, of "whorehouse luxury," in the words of Cantabile (168). Surrounded by books (Citrine is an omnivorous reader), he lives a life of isolation, interested in spiritual matters, but also fascinated by fine clothes and by beautiful women. The conversation with Cantabile prepares the reader for three important events. Citrine is expecting his co-editor, Pierre Thaxter, from California. Wanting to help Citrine financially, Cantabile describes his business enterprises and mentions his connection with Stronson, an investment counselor. Thirdly, Cantabile suggests that they put a contract on Denise. Citrine rejects this criminal offer furiously. The conversation also reinforces Cantabile's connection with Humboldt. Like Humboldt, who had accused Citrine of provoking help by not giving a damn about his human problems, Cantabile says he feels compelled to help because Citrine is so innocent in practical matters: " 'You refuse to be alert about your interests. You let people dump on you. It starts with your pals' " (169). Determined to involve Citrine in his fanatical schemes, Cantabile fixes a strange look on his friend: the look is "tender concerned threatening punitive and even lethal" (186).

The half-hour ride to the county building (187–217), during which Renata suggests that Citrine tune out and meditate, allows Bellow to establish two interconnected items—Citrine's first encounters with Renata and the nature of his involvement with her.

Even before they met, Citrine tells us, there had been an "indirect connection" between him and Renata (194). Her ex-husband, Gaylord Koffritz, had an unusual encounter with George Swiebel's father, Myron, in the Russian Bath. Before offering his sales poetry on crypts, tombs, and mausoleums (was he the Humboldt of this death world?), Koffritz had let loose a torrent of talk about the terrible conditions in the new slum cemeteries, the ignominy and disrespect with which the dead were buried, their graves soon falling into ruin and decay so that after a time the dead were lost forever and forgotten. Myron Swiebel, who dreamed of living forever (194), was appalled. Citrine, who heard about Koffritz from his friend, George, and who had been brooding about death, began to suffer intense death anxieties. He had nightmares about being shut up in a coffin and suffocating under the weight of sand. In 1970, wanting desperately to escape from these death visions, he hunted for "salvation in female form," and thought he had found it on meeting Renata when they both had to be present for jury duty. Renata was "all woman, soft and beautifully heavy in a mini-skirt and nursery-school shoes fastened with a single strap" (203).

Their first rendezvous in the subcellar bar of an hotel, arranged by that bungler, Szathmar, Renata's divorce lawyer and Citrine's pal, was interrupted by Citrine's strange encounter with Naomi Lutz, and it ended not in the usual fashion, in bed, but with Citrine as art lover, admiring the naked beauty of Renata who has passed out (after downing five martinis) on the narrow sofa bed. For the first time in his career as an old sexpot (Cantabile's phrase), Citrine feels protective and sympathetic toward a lovely woman laid out before him on the white sheet as though on a mortuary slab. He sees an embodiment of beauty: "Every tissue was perfect, every fiber of hair was shining. The deep female odor arose from her" (217).

Citrine's involvement with Renata has to be regarded as more than just another affair. She is connected with the world of Maya, whose beauty she always directs Citrine's attention to (16, 202, 318). Having read Bacon, Citrine knows about and rejects the plastered Idols of the Appearances. But his senses are stronger than his mind and Renata makes a powerful impact on his senses. In *The Sense of Beauty*, which Citrine has read (19), Santayana writes about the strong hold which material beauty has upon the senses exercizing an effect that is primitive, fundamental, and universal. With her graceful feminine neck

(192), her incomparable hat and the suède maxicoat, her Hermes scarves, her elegant boots (378), her wonderful coloring (305), she caters to all the senses of Citrine, holds them in thrall, and provides him with wonderful extravagant comfort (350).

Bellow does not make the mistake of categorizing Renata as a mere beauty. Citrine is passionately attracted to her because she is what she is, Renata. He loves her for her wit and her rhymed sayings. She is one of the few people he can talk to about himself and about his strange ideas and views. Despite her intelligence, Denise was not a person with whom Citrine could exchange ideas. Renata, however, Citrine tells us, "was educated in the life and outlook of Citrine" (346). Both enjoy each other's company. By catering to her "hang-ups" and by insisting that she is not a dumb broad, Citrine reassures and consoles Renata. They complement each other. To use the words of the tuxedo-rental man, Citrine is a funny foot that needs a funny shoe. In Renata he finds the right fit.

Significantly, three persons, all associated with death, find themselves powerfully attracted to Renata: Koffritz, her first husband, who sold mausoleums, Flonzaley the undertaker, and Citrine, who thought Renata would assuage his anxieties about death. Beauty, it is clear, fascinates Death, who demands her complete and unconditional surrender.

By the end of section 20 (218), almost halfway through the novel, Bellow has made Citrine exhume almost every significant event in his past. The reader can now fully understand what Citrine meant when he said his life was in great disorder. It is as if all the asuric forces, within him and without, had been roused and were poised for a final assault. The only element that could repel these demonic forces was buried deep within his being. Citrine cannot describe it, but he knows he had it as a child, in the "first decade of life" (177). He calls it a "talent or gift or inspiration" (178). He has a metaphysical hunch that unlike other people, born oblivious to their immortality, he has not forgotten the soul world he came from. His fellow protagonists had intimations of the same kind: Joseph had felt that he did not quite belong to this world (DM, 21). Augie experienced the axial lines in his childhood, while Henderson, as a child, had sensed a pink light that was not quite human. Like Henderson and Herzog, Citrine uses the metaphor of a voice that speaks from deep within his being: "I had decided to listen to the voice of my own mind speaking from within, from my own depths, and this voice said that there was my body, in nature, and that there was also me. I was related to nature through my body, but all of me was not contained in it"

(186). He began to listen to these intimations of immortality in 1972 after he got involved with anthroposophy.

Citrine's fascination with the doctrines and methods of anthroposophy needs to be placed in perspective. As he himself confesses, he is still a novice and hasn't attained much (110); he is still in "theosophical kindergarten" (356). By December 1973 he has read a number of books and pamphlets by Rudolf Steiner and has had many heart-strengthening talks with Mr. Scheldt, whom he calls his "guru" but who is merely his adviser. Citrine is not an Initiate, one who has pursued and attained a knowledge of the higher mysteries. Not wanting to be "one of your idle hit-or-miss visionaries" (131), he practises the will-strengthening exercises recommended by Steiner. The technique of *dharana*, of focusing one's attention on certain objects so as to attain calm and inner contemplation leads to supersensible knowledge. According to Steiner, the disciple should "let his joys, his sorrows, his cares, his experiences, his deeds, pass in review before his soul; and his attitude should be such that he looks at everything else in his experience from a higher standpoint."[6]

Citrine's meditative technique is his idiosyncratic adaptation of techniques advocated by Steiner. Instead of achieving complete inner tranquility, he has moments when he loses a sense of detachment and begins to grieve, especially when he recalls the death of Demmie Vonghel. At other times, he propels himself out of his spirit of contemplation to think wicked thoughts (119). His meditation is really a release of memory, which, according to Plato, is a form of love.

All is now in readiness for an acceleration of action and event. The irruption of Rinaldo Cantabile into Citrine's life has set in motion certain forces that will change, and allow Citrine to change, everything. Equipped with an almost complete knowledge about Citrine's past and about the human arena around Citrine, the reader can now make the cross-connections that will allow him to "understand everything" as the dream manifestation of Humboldt had told Citrine (10). Equipped also with a knowledge of the preceding seven novels, the reader can now realize that Citrine is a composite and radiant fusion of all his fellow protagonists, one who has ventured further than any one of them into the craters of the spirit and has returned proclaiming: "Humanity divine incomprehensible!" (52).

The encounter with Denise in the county building reveals Citrine's changed perspective on people and events. With her huge eyes, her sibylline teeth, her tense martial voice, Denise is a more beautiful, a more civilized and cultured, and a more vampiric version of Margaret in

Seize the Day and of Madeleine in *Herzog*. She uses the legal system to drain all the money she can out of Citrine. Citrine, however, does not give in to the temptation to complain. Bellow makes him use the same language that Tommy Wilhelm had used, but changes its tone. "The weak at war never know how hard they are hitting you," observes Citrine (224), echoing Wilhelm's lament: "This is the way of the weak, quiet and fair. And then smash! They smash!" (STD, 112). Wilhelm had whined: "The Emancipation Proclamation was only for colored people. A husband like me is a slave, with an iron collar" (STD, 49); Citrine states matter-of-factly: "Since the Emancipation Proclamation there's been a secret struggle in this country to restore slavery by other means" (219). For Herzog, Madeleine was a bitch who had, as he complained to Edvig, stoned him out of his skull (H, 72), and provided him with an education. Citrine does not take Denise seriously and her words do not wound him. She is, as he tells Renata, a "comical not a tragic personality" (188). She may be a maddening pest, but, from the detached perspective of Citrine, she is merely a "marvelous lunatic" (232).

Not as detached or as objective is the perspective with which Citrine regards modern lawyers and their tribe. For his own lawyers he puts together a devastating oxymoron: they are "honest-looking deceitful" men (218). For the tribe, he invents a new category: "History had created something new in the USA, namely crookedness with self-respect or duplicity with honor" (221). The tribal gang decide among themselves how to "cut up" people so as to divide the money among themselves (219). Citrine uses images and metaphors from anthropology to characterize them and their actions. Pinsker, Denise's lawyer, is a beast, a cannibal. It is as if a fierce painted apparition had strayed from the primitive jungle into the modern world: "Cannibal Pinsker in a bright yellow double-knit jazzy suit and a large yellow cravat that lay on his shirt like a cheese omelette, and tan shoes in two tones. His head was brutally hairy. He was grizzled and he carried himself like an old prize-fighter" (228–29). Citrine does not want Pinsker (that man-eating kike, according to Cantabile) to tear at his guts (220) or to butcher and hack him to pieces (235). He is also afraid that his own lawyer, Billy Srole, would be ready to chop him into bits with his legal cleaver (222).

Citrine can, however, look at everything, at himself and at others, from an otherworldly perspective. That is why he remains calm and objective about his own plight: "Tomchek and Srole were just what I deserved. It was only right that I should pay a price for coming on so innocent and expecting the protection of those less pure, of people completely at home in the fallen world" (222). The inhabitants of this fallen world constitute what Humboldt had called a Cannibal Society

(14), consisting mainly of "successful, bitter, hard-faced and cannibalistic people" (118). Citrine wonders what Cannibal Pinsker might have been in an earlier incarnation (229). An answer will be provided later.

The letter from Kathleen informs Citrine about Humboldt's "gift" and is another confirmation of the fact that Humboldt was sane toward the end of his life.

The meeting with Thaxter allows Bellow to present one of the most flamboyant characters in *Humboldt's Gift*. Citrine pours out a torrent of detail about his exotic friend whom he has known for twenty years. Pierre Thaxter doesn't wear ordinary clothes: he garbs himself in such extraordinary outfits that he always stands out: "He would blow in from California wearing his hair long like a Stuart courtier and, under his carabiniere cloak, dressed in a charming blue velvet lounging suit from the King's Road. His broad-brimmed hat was bought in a shop for black swingers. About his neck would be apparently valuable chains, and also a piece of knotted, soiled, but uniquely tinted silk. His light-tan boots, which came up to the ankle, were ingeniously faced with canvas, and on each of the canvas sides there was an ingenious fleur-de-lis of leather" (246). Thaxter is at home in the world of international culture with his knowledge of Latin and Greek, his ability to pick up new languages, his views on art, architecture and music, and his mastery of the world of fashion. A fascinating and dazzling con artist and a connoisseur, Thaxter is irresistible to women. Citrine tries to sum up his friend: "But he was remarkably dignified, virtuous and faithful to his wife—to all his wives. He was warmly devoted to his extended family, the many children he had had by several women. If he didn't make a Major Statement he would at least leave his genetic stamp upon the world" (274).

Thaxter charms culture-obsessed Denise with his stylish airs and his lavish hospitality at Wimbledon. Renata knows instinctively that Thaxter is a phony, a charming, talented phony. Reluctant to pass judgement on anybody, Citrine cannot decide whether Thaxter is a crook or not. He is extremely fond of Thaxter and loves him. From the comic perspective Thaxter's personal foibles and eccentricities appear to be charming. Thaxter "was an excellent journalist. This was widely recognized. He had worked on good magazines. Each and every one of them had fired him" (252). Citrine knows instinctively that "something deep was at work and that Thaxter's eccentricities would eventually reveal a special spiritual purpose" (247).

Citrine's reactions to Pierre Thaxter and his notations about his friend indicate that human beings need to be understood rather than dissected and analyzed. A human being is a sacred riddle. Freudian and classical psychology does not provide an understanding of what a human being is, according to Bellow, for mysterious forces and elements are at work within and without. "What does clinical psychology know about art and truth?" asks Citrine (310). He could have extended the question to include Humboldt and human beings. For to know someone is to commit an act of reduction, as Herzog had discovered. Denise and Renata know Pierre Thaxter, but are finally limited in their assessment of him.

For Pierre Thaxter is more than Pierre Thaxter. He is, on one level, a continuation of Humboldt, as his broad-brimmed hat—Humboldt wore a "broad-brimmed hat" at Princeton (136)—his addiction to culture— Humboldt wanted to be the czar of culture for Stevenson—and his intense desire to be an exceptional person, all signify. Bellow adds an odd, minor touch of detail to underline the parallel: Humboldt's cottage in New Jersey had begun to tilt over because the crossroads had undercut the small bluff on which it sat (23); Thaxter's house in Palo Alto had its foundations undermined when a big hole was dug next to it to build a wing for *The Ark*. Humboldt, Citrine and Thaxter share a number of affinities. All three are excellent writers, all three fascinate and are fascinated by women, and all three aim at being cultural statesmen.

Pierre Thaxter is also an extension of Citrine. Thaxter's extravagant wardrobe exaggerates Citrine's dandyish tendencies. Thaxter's intense desire to make a Major Statement is a continuation of what Humboldt had wanted to announce to the world, and also an expression of Citrine's hidden yearning (now abandoned) to stun the world with an intellectual pronouncement. Thaxter has absorbed sustenance from his friend and teacher, Citrine, just as Citrine himself has been nourished by Humboldt. Thaxter confesses that he got his idea of writing about the leaders of the developing world from a casual remark dropped by Citrine; he is preparing to write about them by reading writers that Humboldt himself had mentioned to Citrine (275). Pierre Thaxter is more than Pierre Thaxter: he embodies and continues the forces, good and evil, present in Humboldt and in Citrine.

By hurling him into the moronic inferno of Chicago's underworld, Cantabile shocks Citrine out of his isolation and teaches him a number of lessons. Cantabile is clearly a *manic* manifestation of Humboldt, especially of the Humboldt who had concocted the Princeton scheme. In 1952 Humboldt had been all "asmolder" (127) as he planned his "putsch" (126). In December 1973 Cantabile's face steams with intrigue and judgements (256). Both their faces become fiercely white as they contrive their strategies: "Humboldt's big intelligent disordered face was white and hot with turbulent occult emotions and brainstorms" (125); Cantabile's face was "peculiarly white. He breathed the air as if he were stealing it. He had a look of eagerness and of distemper" (253). Cantabile hails Citrine as his "pal" (255), a term used by Citrine for Humboldt (8). Cantabile and Humboldt want to do Citrine some good, financial good, in both cases. Humboldt had warned Citrine of spending his whole life in the upper stories of higher consciousness (242), unaware of any evil in himself; Cantabile bluntly warns Citrine: " 'You're an isolationist, that's what you really are. You don't want to know what other people are into' " (256).

The kidnapping of Citrine and Thaxter, the strange happenings at the Western Hemisphere Investment Corporation, the ride in the police car and the strange rescue of Citrine from the police lockup are scenes brilliantly done, fast paced and extravagantly comic. Cantabile forcibly drags Citrine out of his isolation and compels him to experience the real world. Like Mr. Sammler, Citrine had been a voyeur, one who experienced the world obliquely through the medium of the mind: he had been "a fanatical reader, walled in by his many books, accustomed to look down from his high windows on police cars, fire engines, ambulances, an involuted man who worked from thousands of private references and texts" (280).

Cantabile's stratagem of passing Citrine off as his hit man to Stronson is a ludicrous travesty of Humboldt's absurd scheme of sending Citrine to Ricketts as his emissary. Citrine, as "Murder Incorporated" (277), is screamingly funny but, as Citrine realizes later, he was a "killer" in his own way. He was a kind of cannibal in that he did incorporate other people into himself and "consume them" (288). The ride to the police station[7] parallels Humboldt's ride to Bellevue in the police wagon. Citrine now realizes what it is like when the police come for him. His ordeal with Cantabile in the john of the Russian Bath was an experiencing of the stink of diarrhea that Humboldt had to endure at Bellevue.

The rescue by the daughter of Naomi Lutz (whose back curve this sex-pot notices, appreciates and compliments her on, conveniently forgetting that he had compared Demmie Vonghel's bottom to a white valentine greeting), like the letter from Kathleen, indicates that the forces of love, innocence, and goodness are mobilizing around Citrine waiting to repel the forces of destruction.

Both these forces battle each other for possession of Citrine's being. Citrine has, to use a Cantabile turn of phrase, come out of solitary confinement (172). Instead of merely listening to others he now begins to open up and talk to them. The talk sessions with Naomi Lutz (in Chicago), with Renata (on the plane to New York), with George Swiebel (before leaving Chicago), and with Huggins, Thaxter, and Kathleen (in New York), all reveal, among other things, what a brilliant talker Citrine has become, a magnificent extension of Humboldt as conversationalist.

Citrine is a fascinating talker. " 'All you have to do is ask him a question and he turns on,' " says Cantabile (176), who half-jokingly wants to book him as a nightclub act. Naomi Lutz gets Citrine to give her a sample of his higher talk and Citrine obligingly provides her with some insights into "sloth." He can talk on anything and everything. His language and its rhythms are so supple that they can take in an enormous range of topics, stretching from the trivial to the transcendent. Citrine has become the kind of talker Humboldt wanted to be: "magically and cosmically expressive and articulate, able to say *anything*" (119). Renata, who knows all about Citrine, testifies, though with a note of complaint, about the scale of his conversation: " 'Well, for a month now I've heard nothing but Humboldt and death and sleep and metaphysics and how the poet is the arbiter of the diverse and Walt Whitman and Emerson and Plato and the World Historical Individual' " (365). Citrine has, as it were, added Humboldt's voice to his own so that the range of his voice becomes truly cosmic.

The visit to Naomi Lutz releases memories of love. Citrine is sentimental but also absolutely serious about his love of Naomi. His declaration rings true: " 'I loved you cell by cell. To me you were a completely nonalien person. Your molecules were my molecules. Your smell was my smell' " (302). He also recalls his childhood love of his parents, of his whole family, their "primitive" (Naomi's term) love of each other (299) and their intense dependence on each other. Naomi's loving questions lead Citrine to realize that he generated an "utopian emotional love aura" which promised love but did not return it. His was a case of "longing-heart-itis," a form of potato love (299–300). Finally, their talk throws light on Citrine's love of Demmie Vonghel, a love so intense that Citrine went to the jungles of Venezuela to look for her and stayed there for a time with cannibals and missionaries.

The talk sessions allow Bellow to amplify one of the basic themes in *Humboldt's Gift*, one that Humboldt had talked about at their first meeting, the fate of the artist in America. Citrine talks freely about how and why both he and Humboldt failed as artists. Both had to confront that terrible and overpowering reality, America. Humboldt confronted this reality, an overwhelming world governed by the forces of money, politics, law, rationality, technology, head on. He abandoned the writing of poetry and set out to be rich and famous, but became instead "a hero of wretchedness" (155). Citrine now realizes that Humboldt's famous insomnia testifies to the inhuman power of this material world. Humboldt had been transfixed: "The world had money, science, war, politics, anxiety, sickness, perplexity. It had all the voltage. Once you had picked up the high-voltage wire and were *someone*, a known name, you couldn't release yourself from the electric current" (312).

The poet in America has always been an anomaly. America has never had a literary community that could sustain a gifted individual. Whitman and Melville, Citrine points out, were nineteenth-century solitaries who had to provide their own spiritual nourishment. In the twentieth century the predicament of the American artist has become even more acute. Not only does he lack the power to perform technological miracles, he also lacks confidence in his own spiritual powers and becomes a martyr, indulging in "childishness, madness, drunkenness and despair" (118). Like Poe, like Hart Crane, like Randall Jarrell, like Berryman, Humboldt finally succumbed to the pressures of this world and enacted "The Agony of the American Artist" instead of listening to the "essence of things."

Citrine, too, has not been able to listen to this Heraclitean essence. Instead of confronting American reality he shut his eyes and slunk away from it. He found the crisis of Western Civilization "identified by a series of dates (1789-1914-1917-1939) and by key words (Revolution, Technology, Science, and so forth)," so momentous, overmastering, and tragic that he refused to accept its challenge (108). Instead, he went to sleep. As he told Huggins, he affected a superior emptiness and considered himself more intelligent than others who tried to understand this crisis. He did become a biographer, a playwright and a winner of Pulitzer prices, but, as he confesses to Naomi, these activities were really a form of sloth: " 'As I was lying stretched out in America, determined to resist its material interests and hoping for redemption by art, I fell into a deep snooze that lasted for years and decades" (306). George Swiebel was right when he told his friend that he was damn clever and canny about his career (314). For Citrine did not destroy himself as Humboldt had done: he only went to sleep.

The trip to Coney Island is yet another return to the world of love. Citrine insists, he knows not why, that Renata accompany him despite the fact that homes for the aged depress her. Renata is horrified by the stark and naked reality of death and can only reconcile herself to it when it is disguised and decked out for presentation by people like Koffritz and Flonzaley. For Citrine, the trip marks the beginning of the process of freeing himself from Renata's erotic bondage.

The meeting with Menasha after fifty long years reestablishes a connection with someone whom Citrine had loved, in the phrase of a popular song, way back when. Menasha, the family roomer, was Charlie Citrine's childhood teacher and friend. Menasha had explained Darwin to Charlie, taught him astronomy, had taken him to the circus and bought him sodas and treats. Menasha had wanted to be a dramatic tenor, but his disfigured nose prevented him from becoming an opera singer. It was Menasha who used to take the six-year-old Charlie to grand opera in Chicago and explain to him the bel canto mode of singing in Aïda. Theirs was a relationship of love, with music creating a bond between them.

The meeting with Menasha and with Uncle Waldemar is not a mere coincidence but a miracle, a confirmation of certain truths that Citrine has now come to know. He realizes that human life is a mystery, that "there is far more to any experience, connection, or relationship than ordinary consciousness, the daily life of the ego, can grasp." Menasha and he, Citrine goes on, obviously "held permanent membership in some larger, more extended human outfit" (332). Human existence thus, cannot be perceived with the rational ego but has to be grasped by the soul. Bellow notifies us here that Humboldt's Gift has to be comprehended from an elevated perspective, or else the reader will be distracted by the many "cantankerous erroneous silly and delusive objects actions and phenomena" that are in the foreground (177). The coincidences in the novel are not illogical accidents but connections and relationships generated by the forces of love. It was their mutual bond with Humboldt that compelled Huggins to get in touch with Citrine through Kathleen. The presence of Kathleen in New York is yet another indication that the representatives of Humboldt are gathering around Citrine.

The renewed connection with Menasha tells Citrine that the mystery of human life cannot be exhausted by our senses and our judgment. The relationship between him and Menasha extends to other strange connections. Menasha and Uncle Waldemar are buddies, just as Citrine and Humboldt were friends. Menasha loved and looked after Citrine just as Uncle Waldemar loved his nephew, Humboldt, taught him football and baseball, and made an American boy out of him. All these cross-connections lead Uncle Waldemar, who is urged by his buddy, Menasha, and is aided by the sun that sends him a message (335), to entrust Humboldt's papers to Citrine.

Humboldt's letter to Citrine reveals Bellow at his fictional peak. Read against the accompaniment of the "racketing speed of the howling, weeping subway" (338), it captures the human accents of Humboldt as they shift from the sad to the comic, and from the witty to the tragic and the pathetic. It is quite literally (though Renata says this jokingly) a message from an old friend in the next world, for the dead, as Citrine suspects, are about us. It tells Citrine that Humboldt did make a Houdinilike escape from madness, proving once again that clinical psychology does not know the spiritual secrets of human nature.

The letter bares Humboldt's naked self, for toward the end he could observe some of his own symptoms with end-of-the-line lucidity. The writer of the letter is the lover of the *Phaedrus,* the poet who dreamed of redeeming mankind with his visions, the manic schemer of revenges, the envier of Citrine's success, the fierce driver of luxury cars, the quoter of Blake, the believer in the divinity of human beings. The letter's sentimentality and pathos are deliberately undercut by Humboldt's wit. Car-crazy Humboldt translates his breakdown and his weakening powers into car images: "My gears are stripped. My lining is shot. It is all shattered" (340). He uses the language of popular music to express his love of Citrine: "With all your faults, I love you still"; and then undercuts the emotion with a double pun, "you are a promissory nut," the term "promissory" pointing to the truth that Citrine promises love without delivering it. *Verbum sapientiae,* writes learned Humboldt, making yet another pun in Latin: for the dative and the genitive combine to imply that here is a message *of* the wise *to* the wise.

The letter also confirms the Humboldt/Cantabile connection. Humboldt accuses Citrine of having stimulated the blood-brother oath: "I was certainly wild, but I acted on a suggestion emanating from you" (339). Cantabile too had accused Citrine of having forced him to bash the Mercedes: " 'You made me. Yes, you. You sure did. . . . You forced me! You made me' " (45). Cantabile has roused Citrine out of his deep slumber; Humboldt's letter supplies him with the adrenalin he needs to be fully awake.

The quotation from Blake urges Citrine not to despair and to realize that "this World is a World of Imagination and Vision" (347). Above all, the letter is an act of love, a love offering, a reaffirmation of their covenant. "Be sure that if there is a hereafter I will be pulling for you," Humboldt assures his blood brother. And the letter ends with Humboldt's calm and confident proclamation: "We are not natural beings but supernatural beings" (347).

This long letter, which Citrine terms "the preface to Humboldt's gift," is a gift in itself. Humboldt "gives" Citrine a kind of self-awareness. Citrine can now acknowledge a spiritual deficiency in himself, the lack of love that prevented him from responding to his blood brother in time of need: "On that day I made a poor showing. I behaved very badly. I should have gone up to him. I should have taken his hand. I should have kissed his face." "But is it true that such actions are effective?" Citrine goes on to ask (341). He knows the answer now. He also knows that it was a "sin" to listen to the advice of Demmie, his protectoress, and not go to see Humboldt at Bellevue.

The gift is also a real bequest. Humboldt presents his friend with a film scenario as compensation for the "sin" of putting through Citrine's blank, signed check: " 'Charles, here is my gift to you. It is worth a hundred times more than the check I put through' " (346). The outline—which Renata terms "goofy" (342), which Humboldt claims "will be a fabulous legacy" (343), and which Citrine later refuses to develop into a screenplay (482)—communicates a number of things. Like the letter, it confirms the fact that Humboldt recovered his sanity toward the end. Humboldt's wit was "intact" (342) and allowed him to put together what Citrine later calls, a "burlesque of love and ambition" (374). Corcoran is obviously an extravagant caricature of Citrine, whose spirit Humboldt borrowed in order to create his protagonist. Citrine recognizes himself in Corcoran. As he tells Renata: " 'His scenario gives his opinion of me—foolishness, intricacy, wasted subtlety, a loving heart, some kind of disorganized genius, a certain elegance of construction' " (351).

What Citrine does not realize is that Humboldt's scenario is more than a mere retaliation against *Von Trenck*, the hit play in which Citrine had exploited Humboldt's personality. "You will make a good script of this outline," says Humboldt's letter, "if you will remember me as I kept remembering you in plotting this out" (346). What is implied is that Corcoran (the repetition of "cor" is significant) is a savage caricature of Humboldt himself. It is Humboldt who, "by wishing to play a great role in the fate of mankind . . . becomes a bum and a joke" (345). The scenario warns Citrine not to become a "farcical martyr" like Humboldt and to beware of "success." It also places before Citrine the deep humility that the true artist in modern America needs to practise before he can write magnificent poetry: "When the artist-agonist has learned to be sunk and shipwrecked, to embrace defeat and assert nothing, to subdue his will and accept his assignment to the hell of modern truth perhaps his Orphic powers will be restored, the stones will dance again when he plays. Then heaven and earth will be reunited. After long divorce. With what joy on both sides, Charlie! What joy!" (346)

Humboldt's "gift" has a profound effect on Citrine. Almost all the events that take place after Citrine gets Humboldt's gift prove that Humboldt is pulling for his friend. The meeting with Kathleen through the agency of Thaxter is another testimony that Humboldt's spirit is still

alive and active in a mysterious way. The death-threat note sent by
Cantabile, that manifestation of Humboldt, allows Denise to persuade
Judge Urbanovich to have Citrine post a bond. Two hundred thousand
poisonous dollars, money that would allow him to sustain his folly and
his vanity, are thus drained out of his system and hasten the process of
his separation from Renata. Thaxter, too, helps in his own peculiar way.
His phone call interrupts Citrine's love session with Renata who wanted
to store up a little comfort for their separation (358). Thaxter's proposal
that they do a cultural Baedeker of Europe together, and the false claim
that a publisher was prepared to stake him to a month at the Ritz,
deflects Citrine to Madrid and suffering instead of Milan and Renata.
The open heart surgery to be performed on his brother, Julius, forces
Citrine to take a trip to Texas, a trip that separates him from Renata who
flies to Milan. Citrine is now well on his journey to the human and
Bellow the artist now rounds off the many themes he has been developing
all through *Humboldt's Gift*.

Citrine can now understand, as the conversation with Kathleen
reveals (378), the role and significance of money, that potent and
dangerous force in the modern world. Most of Bellow's protagonists—
except Joseph and Mr. Sammler (who are supported by others) and
Henderson (who is a millionaire)—have had to come to terms with this
powerful phenomenon. Augie March, at the beginning, had thought
frivolously about money. Later, he realized how intricately money was
involved in the affairs of mankind and how much energy businessmen
devoted to the making of money. In typical long-winded fashion he had
explained: "Here was vast mankind that meshed or dug, or carried,
picked up, held, that served, returning every day to its occupations and
being honest or kidding or weeping or hypocritic or mesmeric, and
money, if not the secret, was anyhow beside the secret, as the secret's
relative, or associate or representative before the peoples" (AM, 359).
Tommy Wilhelm could not understand why money was adored by the
worshippers at the stock exchange. Both he and Herzog complained that
others compelled them to hemorrhage money.

In *Humboldt's Gift* the theme of money is presented in all its
complexity. Citrine did not at first understand Humboldt's obsessive
concern about money and its might. Humboldt had explained that "in
the unconscious, in the irrational core of things money was a vital
substance like the blood or fluids that bathed the brain tissues" (242). It
is because money is blood that Humboldt forced Citrine to sign and give
one another blank checks. The exchange was a modern form of
Blutbrüderschaft, the ritual practice of Teutonic knights of slashing
their wrists and pressing them against one another to swear brotherhood

and fidelity. That is why the breaking of this oath by Citrine (who did not go to visit his friend at Bellevue on the advice of Demmie Vonghel) and by Humboldt (who cashed Citrine's blood-brother check at a time when Citrine was in despair over the death of Demmie) proved so disastrous. Citrine becomes aware of the truth of Humboldt's theory of money as a vital substance only after he is forced to worry about it when it is steadily drained out of him. He feels a pressure on his chest as if he were deprived of oxygen (242–43).

Later, after almost all the poison is withdrawn from his system, Citrine realizes that Humboldt did not understand the higher significance of money. For money is not only a vital force, as Humboldt had claimed, but also a dangerous and destructive one. It was money that came between the two friends. Humboldt thought that money was freedom (159), but Henderson could have told him that money cannot bring about reality or freedom or love. Citrine gradually comes to know certain truths about money. Under the auspices of capitalism, money comically and irrationally begets itself. Citrine explains to Kathleen what happens when one achieves fame and money, twice remarking that Humboldt had not understood the price one has to pay for achieving success:

> "Hanging on to money is hard, of course. It's like clutching an ice cube. And you can't just make it and then live easy. There's no such thing. That's what Humboldt probably didn't understand. I wonder, did he think money made the difference between success and failure? Then he didn't understand. When you get money you go through a metamorphosis. And you have to contend with terrific powers inside and out. There's almost nothing personal in success. Success is always money's own success." [375]

In Citrine's own case money contributed to his prolonged lethargy. Humboldt wrestled with this terrible power and was overthrown by it. The letter to Citrine reveals that Humboldt, at the end, was aware of the overwhelming pressures of money on the human soul: "Oh! the might of money and the entanglement of art with it—the dollar as the soul's husband: a marriage nobody has had the curiosity to study" (340). "Don't get frenzied about money" (347) Humboldt warns his friend, proclaiming what Cantabile more gracefully demonstrated when he sailed away Citrine's clean (he significantly did not want any soiled notes) fifty-dollar bills. Money has become so potent a force that it has damaged the American psyche and interposed an immense barrier between man and his spiritual values.

The trip to Corpus Christi, Texas, appears to be a mere side-excursion, irrelevant to the main thrust of the narrative, but it is

both structurally and thematically essential. Not only does it separate
Citrine from Renata, it also makes Citrine return, yet again, to the world
of memory and love from which he has exiled himself. It allows him to
revisit "the conditions of childhood under which my heart had been
inspired. Traces of the perfume of that sustaining, that early and sweet
dream-time of goodness still clung to him [his brother, Julius]" (396).

Like Menasha, like Naomi, Julius is one of the secret forces in
Citrine's past. He is the only living embodiment of the love that the
Citrine family lavished on each other. Bellow found it difficult to
demonstrate this family love (it was easier to dramatize such family love
in the Montreal scenes in *Herzog*), though he does smuggle in some
references to Citrine's parents all through *Humboldt's Gift*. The brothers
have strong feelings toward each other. Charles's love of Julius is
extravagant and almost hysterical. With his alert eyes, his sharp face
and his business sense, Julius fights his attachment to his brother:
"Julius in fact loved me but affirmed and even believed that he didn't"
(354).

Julius, the latest incarnation of Amos (*Dangling Man*), of Simon
(*Augie March*), and of Will Herzog, the businessmen brothers of Bellow's
protagonists, provides more than a mere contrast. Bellow introduces
Julius casually and indirectly in the opening pages of the novel. For
Citrine comes to New York in 1938 wearing his brother's hand-me-
downs which were far too big for him. One of the first things that Julius
does in Texas is to tell Charles to get rid of his dandyish red shoes and
his checked "horseblanket" overcoat (382). Practical Julius gives him a
black vicuna coat and a pair of his own shoes which fit Charles exactly.
The fact that they have the same extruded eyes and straight noses
suggests, as Joseph of *Dangling Man* had discovered with regard to his
niece, Etta, a similarity of natures.

For Julius is like Charles in many ways. He has his share of sharp
wit: he characterizes Forrest Tomchek as "smoother than a suppository,
only his suppositories contain dynamite." Though afraid of impending
death, he can joke about wanting to be cremated rather than buried:
" 'Look for me in the weather reports,' " he says (387). He is intelligent,
as his reading of Toynbee and other historians reveals, only he
deliberately underplays his own intelligence by mispronouncing words.
He is proud of the fact that Charles's memory has been inherited from
their grandfather, "one of ten guys in the Jewish Pale who knew the
Babylonian Talmud by heart" (244). Julius, too, can remember the past,
as his effortless recall of Menasha Klinger suggests, but he prefers not to
do it in his brother's emotional manner, saying that he has no memory
except for business.

The outing to the property on the Gulf on the day before heart surgery

reveals Julius in action. He presents himself as an American millionaire
and a builder of genius. Charles can literally see the powerful forces at
work within his brother. His ferocious profile proclaims that he is a
fanatical schemer in ecstasy about transforming that dumping ground of
a peninsula into an urban paradise, "the towers in a sea-haze, the
imported grass gemmy with moisture, the pools surrounded by gardenias
where broads sunned their beautiful bodies" (395). Julius, who had
burned his adolescent brother's collection of Marx and Lenin pamphlets
(355), is Capitalism incarnate. Fully awake to money, Julius uses the
forces within him to build shopping centers, condominiums, motels,
contributing greatly to the transformation of Texas (245). The threat of
death slows Julius for a while, but after that danger is over, he is all
business again.

By sending his protagonist from New York and Chicago to Texas,
where there still is significant psychical and geographical space, Bellow
could demonstrate that the pioneering spirit is still alive in America. He
sends Citrine to Corpus Christi, the name suggesting the presence of the
old missionary spirit. By placing American materialism in the person of
Julius in the context of "the body of Christ," Bellow also evokes a
terrible irony. Citrine wonders about the spiritual career of his brother
and speculates that the heavy weight of American materialism and
prosperity has afflicted Julius's soul. America is a "harsh trial to the
human spirit" (383). But Julius's spirit is still alive, not completely
smothered by his involvement in big business. He speaks passionately
about Midwestern coal and its possibilities, about which, Citrine tells
us, Julius "was a romantic poet, a Novalis speaking of each mysteries"
(402), a Humboldt of the coal business, Citrine might have added. The
true implications of Julius's "spiritual" career become clear to Citrine
when he searches in Madrid for the marine painting Julius had wanted.

Julius had wanted a seascape, a painting of the ocean, pure and
elemental, not disfigured by any landmarks or human figures. Citrine
had had a glimpse of just such a scene on the plane flight from Chicago
to New York and it had given him a feeling of freedom (313). Julius's
renewed yearning (he had always wanted such a painting) intimates a
new Julius and the possibility of a new America. The America of Julius's
youth, that "materially successful happy land," had no energy to devote
to things of the spirit. Instead of high aspirations the people only asked
"for comfort and speed and good cheer, health and spirits, football
games, political campaigns, outings, and cheerful funerals" (421). Now
that practical desires had all been fulfilled, it was time to satisfy
metaphysical impulses. Charles interprets his brother's desire for the
water painting as implying a new hope for America and as signifying a

new trend, a desire perhaps for "elemental liberty, release from the daily way and the horror of tension? O God, liberty!" (422)

The trip to Texas allows Citrine to review and Bellow to present his views on America. All through the novel a stream of observations, comments and statements have poured out about America. Humboldt began it all when he stated that poets ought to figure out how to get around pragmatic America. Citrine goes a step beyond Humboldt in that he discovers that Chicago—which is the USA—"with its gigantesque outer life, contained the whole problem of poetry and the inner life in America" (9). Again and again Citrine refers to America's tremendous outer life. "The USA was a big operation, very big. The more *it*, the less *we*" (6); American poets testify that "the USA is too tough, too big, too much, too rugged, that American reality is overpowering" (118); to Naomi Lutz Citrine states, "America is an overwhelming phenomenon" (306).

Its technological miracles are omnipresent. In the Hancock Building, Citrine becomes aware that "architecture, engineering, electricity, technology" had brought him to the sixty-forth story (97). The Mercedes, with its "engines ticking like wizard-made toy millipedes and subtler than a Swiss Accutron" (36), the Playboy Club, set in one of the most glamorous parts of Chicago, the unfinished skyscraper swarming with lights, New York City's Fifth Avenue aglow with Christmas decorations and headlights, the marvelous teamwork and the medical technology that produce miraculous heart surgery—all illustrate the marvels of technology. According to Bellow, technology is "the product of science and capital." It is a triumph, he goes on, "of the accurate power of innumerable brains and wills acting in unison to produce a machine or a commodity."[8]

These wonderful works and magnificent achievements together with other factors like the rise of a capitalist society with its commitment to personal freedom for all (173). the banishment of hunger and scarcity, and the upsurge of mental consciousness because of widespread education have produced a glamorous and glittering outer life for America, but have serious damaged its inner life. What are the pains of plenitude, Humboldt had asked (162). What ugly monsters lurk beneath the swamp of prosperity?[9] America has arrived at an entirely new stage in the history of human consciousness (51, 59, 69). The spread of education has produced a world transformed by mind (74). Americans are living at a time when the mind "universally awakens and democracy originates, an era of turmoil and ideological confusion, the principal phenomenon of the present age" (59).

Humboldt had put forth the idea that America was God's experiment.

Her pains, unlike the old pains of mankind, were more peculiar and mysterious (162). Citrine uses subtle historical analysis to present the plight of America. No longer tormented by poverty, set free from some forms of anguish, Americans are afflicted with more subtle kinds of suffering. One of the deepest sufferings Americans have to endure, acccording to Citrine, is that of boredom, the pain caused by the wasted powers and unusable talents brought into being by the new developments in American society. Herzog and Mr. Sammler had seen the frantic actors on Broadway possessed by the terrors of freedom and modernity. Citrine presents a more abstract statement. America has "produced autonomous modern individuals with all the giddiness and despair of the free, and infected with a hundred diseases unknown during the long peasant epochs" (292).

Citrine does not set down all this abstract analysis about America and its condition in a coherent and logical manner. His views are scattered all through his account and, because they are spiced with wit and irony, they do not overburden the novel or slow its pace. He has a talent for the memorable phrase. Cantabile is one of "the new mental rabble of the wised-up world" (107). The awakening of the human mind is revealed by the fact that even policemen take courses in psychology. Mental currency abounds everywhere: "In the past, thoughts were too real to be kept like a cultural portfolio of stocks and bonds. But now we have mental assets. As many world views as you like. Five different epistemologies in an evening. Take your choice. They're all agreeable, and not one is binding or necessary or has true strength or speaks straight to the soul" (390).

Citrine's brilliant high-level analysis of the American predicament, like Herzog's and Mr. Sammler's views on the Broadway crowds, should not be regarded as a final assessment. They are products of a time when Citrine did believe, with Humboldt, in generating great thoughts and offering the world big ideas (Thaxter has now taken over this habit). Citrine fights the judgments he had made in his days of rashness (332). In his letter Humboldt had written that the mild lemon light of the sun that rinsed the streets of New York had suggested hope for the "wild combined human operation called America" (341). The trip to Texas sustains this hope. The gradual change in Citrine will lead him to a new perspective on America.

Citrine, another suffering joker, flies to Madrid and Renata. His sentimental longings are allowed to build up and are then deliberately undercut to provide hilarious comedy. Charlie dashes out of the 747, and is first at the passport window, first at the baggage counter, and then discovers to his dismay that his bag is the last one of all, coming "toward him like an uncorseted woman sauntering over the cobble stones" (406). Renata is not at the Ritz and Citrine, in a frenzy of apprehension that she was ditching him, finally falls asleep and is awakened by the operator, who tells him a lady is on her way up to his room. A fit of love madness seizes Charlie:

> A lady! Renata was here. I dragged the drapes aside from the windows and ran to brush my teeth and wash my face. I pulled on a bathrobe, gave a swipe at my hair to cover the bald spot, and was drying myself with one of the heavy luxurious towels when the knocker ticked many times, like a telegraph key, only more delicately, suggestively. I shouted, "Darling!" I swept the door open and found Renata's old mother before me. She was wearing her dark travel costume, with many of her own arrangements, including the hat and the veil. "Señora!" I said. [409]

Bellow's sense of comic timing and control of pace is superb. The operator's terse message triggers Citrine's adolescent yearnings, he drags the drapes open in order to provide more light for the glorious encounter, the colloquial "swipe" conveys the comic attempt of this dandy to conceal his age, the heavy, luxurious towels are a preparation for the luxurious beauty of Renata, the ticking of the knocker suggests the sensual feast he will enjoy, "Darling!" explodes out of him and then the sight of the medieval garments of the señora instead of the gorgeous crimson traveling costume of Renata leads him to squeak out, "Señora!"

Slowly, like a punctured balloon, Citrine is deflated of his need and craving for Renata. He sends a telegram to Milan asking her to marry him and buys an exotic and expensive red and black (colors that suited her best) cape for her. But he is outstrategied by the señora, who vanishes, leaving Roger, Renata's little son, with Citrine to prevent pursuit. Steadily going broke, Citrine has to move with Roger to a *pension*, a return in many ways to his 1938 boarding-house mode of existence. At the *pension* Citrine is rid of the many problems, sexual, financial, and intellectual, that nagged him in Chicago. He receives two letters, one from Renata, the other from George Swiebel. He rejects the advances of a Danish secretary. He looks after Roger and gets to know the little boy's desires and wants. He reads Steiner furiously. Though he is not aware of the fact, he prepares himself in this way for the arrival of Rinaldo Cantabile.

Renata's letter is, first of all, a cruel dissection of Citrine by a reality instructor. She tells him some home truths, accusing him of treating her as a "marvelous sex-clown" (429), warning him about his parasitic friends, telling him that to try to dope one's way out of the human condition is boredom itself (a telling hit, this), wondering why, if he believed he had a special mission on earth, he wanted a middle-class thing like marriage. The letter also reveals her warm affection for Charlie and for the delightful moments they had together. But, as a woman with a practical female-human outlook, she accepts the reality of the situation she finds herself in. The observation that the involvement with Humboldt had speeded the deterioration of their relationship (432) is yet another indication that Humboldt is pulling for his blood brother.

Citrine realizes that his passion for Renata involved him in the pursuit of physical beauty and perfection loved by the Greeks. His desire for this kind of beauty, Citrine suggests, is anachronistic because it belongs to the past when man was one with nature. But now, when man is entering a new stage in the history of human consciousness, now that the intellect and the spirit have awakened in man, one needs to seek out a new beauty, one that is internal, one that is "the result of a free union of the human spirit with the spirit of nature" (433). Citrine may be right about Renata but not about human nature: he cannot easily set aside his ingrained habit of heavy analysis.

"It's him you need not me," Renata wrote (432). Charles follows her suggestion and looks after Roger with tender affection, feeding him, walking the streets of Madrid with him, hand in hand. Citrine senses that Roger's spirit is at work within the little child, creating his own body: King Dahfu had told Henderson that the spirit of a person was the author of his body. Citrine, who had tried without success to enter the soul cravings of his eight-year-old daughter, Mary, intimates that Dahfu's belief may be true of early childhood: "In early childhood this invisible work of the conceiving spirit may still be going on" (442–43).

The letter from George Swiebel about his trip to Africa hunting for a berrylium mine with Louie, Naomi Lutz's son, appears to be a grotesque excrescence that violates narrative structure. It is only after the reader contrasts this journey with the adventures of Henderson that Bellow's fictional strategies become clear. For one thing, the trip is wildly comic. With his craving for bottled homogenized American milk, his total disbelief that the expression "mother-fucker" was not understood in primitive Africa, his love offering for his mother, a deadly, ugly Masai spear, Louie is both a caricature of the generation of the 1960s (its phoniness, physical weakness and stupidities, and its colossal ignorance) and a comic version of the American innocent abroad. The trip is also a highly affectionate parody of *Henderson the Rain King*. George's marvelous black man, Theo, with whom he develops a relationship quickly, and who, with Ezekiel, cons George, proves to be no Romilayu. Atti has been transformed into a lioness jumping on wild pigs in Nairobi's game park (447). The naked Arnewi now wear a nightgown-and-pajama type costume made on old foot-pedal Singer sewing machines that are in every African village.

George, that primitivist, who is always looking for something fundamental and primordial, believes with Henderson that Africa was the ancient bed of mankind, the original place where the human species got its start. The visit to Olduvai Gorge (the place that, according to Herzog, provided evidence that man has descended from a carnivorous ape that hunted in packs and crushed the skulls of its prey) and the meeting with Professor Leakey confirm George's belief that Africa is the home of man. Bellow slyly undercuts this idea by having George juxtapose in the same paragraph the news item that there were twenty-five murders in Chicago during a weekend. Savagery, murder, and violence appear to be accepted features of contemporary Chicago, not of the Africa scene (447).

George's trip to Africa indirectly affirms the truth Humboldt had proclaimed, that we are supernatural, not natural beings, that our home world is not Africa, but a glorious spiritual world that has been lost. In *Henderson the Rain King* Bellow had dramatized his belief that man was a noble savage who would be redeemed by the human imagination. Mankind, according to King Dahfu, will ultimately achieve nobility. *Humboldt's Gift* inverts such a belief. It assumes that mankind, originally noble and good, now inhabits a fallen world and has to seek for its home world of glorious origin.

The reentry of Cantabile into Citrine's life is timed so as to occur after ten weeks during which Citrine has bethought and becalmed himself. Cantabile tears down the dust-laden drapes of the chapel-like dark salon of the boarding house to let in the magic sunlight and to reveal religious pictures, bric-a-brac treasures and dried branches from Palm Sunday. The act is both dramatic and symbolic. The Mafia hoodlum provides the drama. The manifestation of Humboldt gives the act a symbolic dimension that Citrine immediately recognizes: "It all gave the effect of a period vanishing together with the emotions one had had for this period and the individuals who had felt such emotions. . . . My caller was still pulling at the drapes to let in more sun and he sent down the dust of a whole century" (451). It is as if this caller has brought down the dusty emotions and ideas of our time so as to reveal the religious sense they have hidden from us.

" 'You?' " exclaims Citrine (451). Citrine had earlier thought he would use this dramatic question when he met the woman who would relieve him of his intense death-anxieties: "On business errands on La Salle Street, zooming or plunging in swift elevators, every time I felt a check in the electrical speed and the door was about to open, my heart spoke up. Entirely on its own. It exlaimed, 'My Fate!' It seems I expected some woman to be standing there. 'At last! You!' " (197) Citrine was disappointed when the voice that said, "My Fate!" was silent when he met Renata, from whom he expected "salvation in female form" (203). It is Cantabile who *is* Citrine's "Fate" and brings him salvation.

As an agent of Humboldt, Cantabile is the one who strikes Citrine with blessings. As a messenger of good tidings, he is the one who brings the news about the sensational hit movie, *Caldofreddo*, based on the moviescript by Humboldt and Citrine. Humboldt had considered it too "chintzy" (342) to call this scenario a gift, but it is Humboldt's posthumous gift to his pal. Cantabile tells Citrine that Humboldt has "scored a success from the grave" (453). Humboldt took all the legal steps necessary to prove their authorship by mailing a copy of the scenario to himself by registered mail. Cantabile has now to rouse Citrine from his state of withdrawal from the world for Citrine has to complete some unfinished business.

Citrine has changed and Cantabile can no longer intimidate him. Bellow makes Cantabile gradually revert to a mere Mafia hoodlum. Citrine refuses to sign even to read the contract Cantabile places before him; he rejects the temptation of money that Cantabile dangles before him, refusing to leave Roger; he is not disturbed by the outrageous things that Cantabile says, especially about Humboldt, to provoke him. It is only when Cantabile refers to Humboldt's old uncle that Citrine remembers the plight of Uncle Waldemar in the nursing home and agrees to fly to Paris to see *Caldefreddo*.

The movie, whose story line Citrine had narrated to Polly and Cantabile, offers few surprises. One is that Otway, who plays Caldofreddo, strongly resembles Humboldt, yet another hint that the spirit of Humboldt is somehow alive, suggesting that (as Citrine later tells Kathleen) there is an "invisible link" between the two which will attract Otway to the *Corcoran* script (474). The end of the movie with its *Oedipus at Colonus* scene of reconciliation and forgiveness resolves the theme of cannibalism that runs all through *Humboldt's Gift*.

Cannibalism can be of different kinds. Modern cannibalism is of the ruthless variety, remorselessly devouring human beings as if they were objects and things. Pinsker and his tribe in Chicago are completely at home in this fallen world, having rejected and abandoned the inner life and the soul. The cannibals in South America are closer to our home world. They had eaten some of the missionary Vonghels, believing that such an ingestion would strengthen their inner selves. It did in a strange way, for the Vonghels forgave them and made them Christians. Caldofreddo, too, committed the sin of eating human flesh, but he confesses his sin in public and is forgiven at the end. Citrine, too, has partaken of Humboldt's spirit, but this "lunch of blood" is not an act of cannibalism, but an act of imagination and vision and love.

Citrine, who has never read a contract through in all his life, and who used to consider all business as fraud, can manage his business affairs quite efficiently, as his handling of the details about both film scripts testifies. He is, after all, the brother of Julius. He can now understand the Romance of Business, especially as handled by the polished Harvard business types and can sense its almost "transcendental" power over the modern world. But he knows that it has no real or enduring value, and cannot satisfy the soul.

The business of Thaxter's capture by the terrorists troubles Citrine. He is ready to help ransom his friend, as his letter to Stewart tells us, with the money from both movie scenarios. Stewart's letter suggests that the story of the abduction is phony, an ingenious publicity stunt staged by Thaxter. It is clear that Thaxter will write a book about his "experiences" and will undergo the pains of fame, money, and success. His Op Ed essay reads like the Major Statement he always wanted to make. He is on the way to become a version of the World Historical Individual Humboldt and Citrine wanted to become. As a continuation of Humboldt and Citrine, Thaxter will suffer the same pains they had to undergo.

Citrine's rejection of the Danish secretary indicates that he is rid of his obsession with sex. Like money, sex is a powerful and damaging force that has seized the modern world. The grotesque lechers at the Downtown Club, the tuxedo-rental man at the poker party, the Littlewoods, who want an Eskimo deal, Cantabile with his ideas about a sexual circus, Humboldt after the success of the Princeton scheme, Citrine himself, all testify that love manifests itself today mainly in the form of sexual degeneracy. "Ah, this sexually disturbed century!" (111) exclaims Citrine, that nymph-troubled man.

Citrine knows that deformity has overtaken love. In his own case he realizes that such emphasis has fallen on the erotic that all the eccentricity of the soul pours into the foot (190). His childhood love of Naomi Lutz, the daughter of a chiropodist, was pure and passionate. His love of Demmie was also pure: it is significant, however, that he first fell for her legs: "They were extraordinary. And these beautiful legs had an exciting defect—her knees touched and her feet were turned outward so that when she walked fast the taut silk of her stockings made a slight sound of friction" (19). As we have seen, Citrine married Denise not because he loved her but for cultural protection. When he first met the voluptuous Renata he noticed that she wore a miniskirt and nursery-school shoes fastened with a single strap. The basis for his attraction to Doris Scheldt was quite clear: her footwear was provocative, quite far out (14). Finally, Citrine does feel drawn, despite himself, to the Danish secretary, a gimpy blonde.

Bellow does not label Citrine a foot fetishist. He introduces a number of references to feet and presents the relationship between Citrine and Renata as the need of an atypical foot for an atypical shoe. Renata's use of Citrine's foot to make love to herself and her subsequent stealing of the shoe conveys the message that she needs Citrine to cater to her hangups and is a warning that he would have to hobble along without her. It is because they were so interconnected, or, as she puts it in her letter, "shoe and foot, foot and shoe together" (429), that it took so many powerful forces generated by Humboldt to separate them.

Citrine's ordeals are now over. The departure of Roger saddens him for a while. Our relationship has drawn to a close, he tells Cantabile, dismissing him. He has no long-range plans. He will go spend a week in Almería, acting as an extra (he is in no danger of becoming a Tommy Wilhelm) in a historical picture. He is in a transitional state, and people in a state of transition, he had earlier stated, "often develop an interest in the movies" (240). He will then go Chicago, from where he had run away, to settle some matters. He wants to talk to Humboldt's uncle and then come back to Europe to spend a month at Dornach, near Basel, at the Swiss Steiner Center, the Goetheanum. The novel does not end with Citrine at the Goetheanum, but Citrine's involvement with the ideas and teachings of Steiner needs to be examined and understood.

Citrine's fascination with the ideas of Rudolf Steiner has to be set against his intense dillusion with and rejection of the ruling premises of modern civilization. He is convinced that the ideas of the last few centuries have been used up and have lost their power. Mankind, consequently, cannot be sustained by them. He has had it, he informs us, with most contemporary ways of philosophizing. He cannot accept the common belief in the finality of death, a basic assumption of modern rationality and of the scientific world view.

In order to nourish his spiritual self which is in the process of awakening, Citrine reads Rudolf Steiner's works. His reading is erratic. He is familiar with *Knowledge of the Higher Worlds and Its Attainment*, with *Between Death and Rebirth,* and with the pamphlet, "The Driving Force of Spiritual Powers in World History." Dr. Scheldt gives him books to read "about the etheric and the astral bodies, the Intellectual Soul and the Consciousness Soul, and the unseen Beings whose fire and wisdom and love created and guided this universe" (260). On the flight to Texas he reads some occult books (380). Finally, in the *pension,* he reads a number of texts aloud to the dead, attempting to get in touch with them.

Citrine is clearly fumbling his way through the doctrines of anthroposophy. He is an explorer, setting out on a spiritual investigation. He is very serious about studying anthroposophy, as he tells Renata (349), but has not conducted a full and proper investigation of the subject. "I hadn't done my homework," he confesses (391). He is powerfully attracted to Steiner but also repelled by the more esoteric teachings. For Citrine cannot easily shed the skepticism that his rational and scientific training has fostered in him. He cannot accept certain occult peculiarities: "I couldn't make my peace with things like the Moon Evolution, the fire spirits, the Soma of Life, with Atlantis, with the lotus flower organs of spiritual perception or the strange mingling of Abraham with Zarathustra, or the coming together of Jesus and the Buddha. It was all too much for me" (263). Kafka's disgust with Steiner, noted in the *Diaries,* disturbs Citrine deeply. Outraged at times, he dismisses certain esoteric mysteries as "spiritual hokum" (288) and then hails others as "great vision" (439).

Citrine feels drawn to anthroposophy because it speaks to the deep needs of his own spirit, especially his sense of, to use a phrase from Delmore Schwartz, "the immortality of mortality." He is in search of a more spiritual and imaginative mode of knowledge; he senses ways of knowing that go beyond the human organism and its senses (228). The teachings of Steiner—that Scientist of the Invisible, according to Dr. Scheldt (260), a very rational kind of mystic, according to Thaxter (362)—make a profound impact on Citrine, especially when they reinforce his intimations about the self, about sleep, and about death (263).

Citrine has always felt oppressed by the heavy weight of his selfhood and by the "fatal self-sufficiency of consciousness" (417). The self-conscious ego is cold, unmoved, detached, unconcerned about others and their suffering, inviolate and, above all, inhuman. It is the seat of boredom (203). Another problem, a personal one for Citrine, is that there is no connection between this consciousness and the external world. The prevailing view has it that there is a dichotomy between subject and object, so that there is no bond between the two. According to Steiner, it is consciousness in the self that is responsible for this false distinction. Anthroposophy acknowledges the existence of the spirit, and maintains that there is a dynamic relationship not only between the physical body and the spirit but also between the outer world and the inner. Citrine, who cannot appreciate the world of maya, looks at anemones and senses that they "are capable of grace and they are colored with an untranslatable fire derived from infinity" (261). Pursing an idea out of Steiner, he develops a cosmological feeling for the sun, sensing a bond between the light within him and that of the sun. In the nursing home Uncle Waldemar had been profoundly moved by the light of the sun. In the Texas sunlight Citrine had felt a mass of love between him and his brother (398). The stability and inner peace, which he attains at the *pension,* allow Citrine to recover an Emersonian state, "an independent and individual connection with the creation, the whole hierarchy of being" (441).

Steiner's views on sleep fascinate Citrine. During sleep the soul goes off into the spiritual world where it can influence and be influenced by higher beings. Unfortunately, because the soul has become so debased in our time by being immersed in materialism and low preoccupations, it has forgotten its true language and cannot communicate its needs, so that the being of man is not refreshed. Citrine finds these views deeply moving because they allow him to understand Humboldt's insomnia, his own sloth and the condition of America today.

Humboldt couldn't sleep because the world, the human and American world with all its wonderful works, kept him awake. Maybe he was ashamed, speculates Citrine, because he had no words to carry into sleep (265). Citrine himself went to sleep in order to escape from the crises of American and Western civilization. Citrine is now awake. Like Citrine, America, too, despite being chloroformed by its technological advancement and by its desire to retain its "abominable American innocence" (209) will awaken from "the good liberal sleep of American boyhood" (396).

Steiner has, above all, confirmed Citrine's lifelong intimation that death is not the end and that the human spirit is immortal. Steiner's teachings about the spirit, the higher worlds and the invisible powers that inhabit those worlds free Citrine from the terror of the finality of death: "Under the recent influence of Steiner I seldom thought of death in the horrendous old way. I wasn't experiencing the suffocating grave or dreading an eternity of boredom, nowadays" (220–21). The awareness that the being-series does not end with man, and the fact that a human being is not confined to the span of one lifetime makes for a more spacious metaphysical situation (328).

Steiner's ideas excite Citrine's inner being which is now so open that he can respond extravagantly (as Henderson responded to the dreams and visions of King Dahfu) to the vision presented by a clairvoyant:

But what an object! Your eyes are now two radiant suns, filled with light. Your eyes are identified by this radiance. Your ears identified by sound. From the skin comes a glow. From the human form emanate light, sound, and sparkling electrical forces. This is the physical being when the Spirit looks at it. And even the life of thought is visible within this radiance. Your thoughts can be seen as dark waves passing through the body of light, says this clairvoyant. And with this glory comes also a knowledge of stars which exist in the space where we formerly felt ourselves to stand inert. We are not inert but in motion together with these stars. [394]

Citrine responds to this vision because it embodies what he has been in quest of: a connection between the spirit and the body, the bond between man and nature, and, above all, the dazzling inner beauty of the human spirit.

Citrine is no clairvoyant, but his adventures have equipped him with vision and insight. Humboldt had quoted Blake who had said that this world is a World of Imagination and Vision. Citrine now sees how wonderfully strange human life is. Humanity is both divine and incomprehensible. Human life is rich, baffling, agonizing, and diverse (251); it is also a dazing, shattering, delicious, painful thing (391). Life on earth is everything else as well, Citrine tells us, provided we learn how to apprehend it (350). One needs, above all, to recognize love as a powerful force in the universe, one that generates connections and relationships. Citrine's account is a celebration of love. The love between the two friends and their relationships with others have led to many cross-connections which will continue endlessly. We owe our very existence to acts of love performed before us, says Citrine (190). One needs only to think of young Humboldt (looked after by Uncle Waldemar), young Citrine (loved by his family and by Menasha) and young Roger (tenderly looked after by Citrine). Love, states Citrine, "is a standing debt of the soul" (190); it is gratitude for being (392). Demmie Vonghel had quoted from the Song of Solomon: "Many waters cannot quench love, neither can the floods drown it" (166). Henderson had discovered that it is love that makes reality reality. According to Simone Weil, those whom we love, exist. *Humboldt's Gift* maintains that those who love not only exist but help each other in mysterious ways.

Henderson the Rain King celebrated the powers of the Human

Imagination. In *Humboldt's Gift* the imagination and the soul fuse to form a new entity, the Imaginative Soul. Equipped with such a power, Citrine can now fulfill the cosmic destiny Humboldt had sensed that he himself would fulfill. He cannot put together a complete picture pattern of the world. For he is not a mastermind, or a world analyzer, or a Hegelian World Historical Individual. He can, however, complete Humboldt's mission and fulfill his own. Humboldt had wanted to drape the whole world with Wordsworthian radiance, but he lacked enough celestial material. His attempt, Citrine notes, ended at the belly (107). What Citrine implies is that it is not enough to capture that shaggy nudity below the belly, the sensual and sensuous world. Sensibility, Humboldt's favorite word, is no longer enough; what is now required is supersensibility. Humboldt had captured the old radiance. Now there is need for new vision. For, as Citrine has repeatedly mentioned, this is a dangerous moment both in human history and cosmic development (283). Mankind has been starved of the sustenance it needs for future development. It has "to recover its imaginative powers, recover living thought and real being, no longer accept these insults to the soul, and do it soon" (250).

It is up to Charles Citrine to accomplish this task. As an American who has been taught by Humboldt himself, he has to delve deep and uncover "the most extraordinary, unheard-of poetry buried in America" (407). Walt Whitman had said that democracy would fail unless its poets gave it great poems of death. Citrine has faced the terrible apparition of death and knows that it is just that, a mere apparition. He has awakened to a very big challenge and knows what he has to do:

> I had business on behalf of the entire human race—a responsibility not only to fulfill my own destiny but to carry on for certain failed friends like Von Humboldt Fleisher who had never been able to struggle into higher wakefulness. My very fingertips rehearsed how they would work the keys of the trumpet, imagination's trumpet, when I got ready to blow it at last. The peals of that brass would be heard beyond the earth, out in space itself. When that Messiah, that savior faculty the imagination was roused, finally we could look again with open eyes upon the whole shining earth. [396]

What Citrine has to do is to act not for himself alone but for the whole of mankind. Humboldt had written in his letter: we are supposed to do something for our kind. The theme of responsibility, sounded faintly in the Fanzel incident in *Dangling Man* is announced here in ringing tones. In the movie, Caldofreddo blows a trumpet whose key drives against his heart. The blast of Citrine's trumpet, with its keys held down against his heart and his imaginative soul, will be heard beyond this earth so that all mankind will open its eyes and be fully awake. And Citrine has both prepared himself and been prepared by Humboldt for this gigantic task. He has received Humboldt's gift or talent, absorbed Humboldt's voice, and developed the cosmic voice he needs to tell his tale.

Augie March was a puppet through which Bellow the ventriloquist had spoken. Bellow had to smuggle intellectual and literary references into Henderson's voice, for Henderson was not really an intellectual. Citrine's voice is his very own. He talks the way he talks because he is what he is: a Jew, an immigrant, an intellectual who has been brought up in the Western tradition (with some insights from the East), an American who has shuttled between the White House and Skid Row, a European Whitman who has absorbed the new and the old worlds into himself.

His language is racy, pungent, colloquial, of the streets of Chicago and New York. It is full of topical allusion for he is fascinated by the world he lives in: he refers to the Kennedys, to Senator Javits, to Vesco, to Gene Fowler, and to Harry Houdini. The history of Chicago is at his fingertips as the references to McCormick and the Capone days indicate. He is at home in the world of popular culture, sharing the American love of vaudeville, football, baseball, the funnies, popular songs, old movies, and boxing. George Swiebel's secretary looks like Mammie Yokum (46), while Renata at a London dinner is like Sugar Ray Robinson among the paraplegics (305). Death loses its terror when seen in terms of football and baseball: Humboldt "blew his talent and his health and reached home, the grave, in a dusty slide" (118); Papa Citrine is "brought down by the tackle of heavy death" (387).

Citrine is also familiar with the world of culture: references to Mozart and Verdi abound and there is mention of Goya, of Franz Hals and of Monet. Like the red and black cloak he bought for Renata, Citrine carries his learning lightly on his shoulders. He refers to almost all the major plays of Shakespeare, to the major philosophers, political scientists, psychologists, and thinkers of the Western world. It is as if he claims all the Great Books together with the *Syntopicon* as his rightful inheritance, and has absorbed them into himself and dissolved them into his account.

It is Bellow, of course, who has at last solved for himself the problem of language. Citrine can now perform his mission. He cannot write poems in the mode of Humboldt. Nor can he write the biographies he used to write. What he does is to venture into an art enterprise not undertaken in the old way (477), implying that it should not be read and interpreted in the old way. His first venture is the writing of this account.

But before Citrine can write such an account he has to participate in a ritual, not a grand Sophoclean choric scene of forgiveness and reconciliation, but an act of genuine and comic expiation. Uncle Waldemar had wanted to have a gathering of his dead. The three survivors (two old fuddyduddies and a distracted creature not far behind them in age, as Citrine puts it) come together for the reburial of Humboldt (who had been buried in a slum cemetery in Deathsville, New Jersey) and his mother in the Valhalla Cemetery, the name signifying the great hall of immortality in which the souls of warriors slain heroically were received by Odin and enshrined. It is an overwarm spring day in April 1974. Citrine, who never attended funerals (196), helps carry Humboldt's almost weightless casket. Even the bones, he surmises, which, according to Steiner, bear witness to the signature of the cosmos within a human being, no longer exist.

Citrine looks at the yellow compact machine that functions as bulldozer, crane, and digger. The result of the collaboration of the minds of many engineers, the machine conveys a message to Citrine, that "a system built upon the discoveries of many great minds was always of more strength than what is produced by the mere workings of any one mind, which of itself can do little" (486). Here is another of those technological marvels of America helping at Humboldt's funeral. The funeral director calls for a prayer. Instead of saying a prayer, Menasha, who has never sung on a stage but has always wanted "to stand in brocade and sing Rhadames in *Aida*" (332), announces, " 'I am going to sing a selection from *Aida*, "In questa tomba oscura" ' " (486), which he used to sing in Chicago in 1927 (329–30). Citrine mistakenly calls "In questa tomba oscura," which really is a concert arietta by Beethoven, an "aria" (486) from *Aida*. What Citrine (or Bellow) has in mind for Menasha is the tenor part of the "O terra addio" duet sung by Rhadames in the final scene of *Aïda*, a fact that can be confirmed by Citrine's recalling (five months ago in Coney Island) how Menasha used to tell him "about *Aida*, envisioning himself in brocade robes as a priest or warrior" (330). Menasha's stage is a cemetery. He does not have the brocade Rhadames should wear, but he prepares himself for the occasion and gives the greatest performance of his life. He raises his face, revealing his gaunt Adam's apple, clasps his hands and, rising on his toes, sings, with croaking voice, music from the final scene of *Aïda*. He follows this with a yelping out of "Going Home," a spiritual which, he announces, was used by Dvořák in the *New World* Symphony.

The crocuses that Menasha spots at the end are signs that the overdelayed spring will at last occur. They proclaim that despite technological devastation like the one in South Chicago, "certain flowers persist" (63) and tell Citrine that Humboldt's flowers had not been, as he had feared, "aborted in the bulb" (462). The crocuses also point to a change of fictional tactics. Each of Bellow's earlier novels had ended with a powerful resonant paragraph. The soft, relaxed ending is an essential part of Bellow's fictional strategy in *Humboldt's Gift*, which is a comedy about death.

For the real, climactic moment consists of the two songs of Menasha. Bellow projects a scene which combines elements of comedy with intimations of immortality. The comic pathos is essential for it mutes the powerful message of the scene and prevents it from becoming sentimental. Menasha's singing answers questions that the sight of the completely concrete enclosed coffins provokes. Citrine asks, "But how did one get out?," voicing his earlier fears of being suffocated under sand (197) and his horror of lying in the grave in one place (202). The voice of modern rationality immediately answers: "One didn't, didn't, didn't! You stayed, you stayed!" (487) But Menasha's feeble music had earlier affirmed "that the logically unanswerable was, in a different form, answerable" (332). As Rhadames he has already proclaimed in the words of the "O terra addio" duet not only that love will triumph but also that, despite imprisonment in a dark, sealed vault, heaven will open and errant souls will soar to the light of eternal day.[10] Menasha's singing reinforces Citrine's belief that he has "to help the human spirit burst from its mental coffin" (433).

The spiritual "Going Home" presents on the personal level Menasha's love of and longing for his dead high-school sweetheart wife to whom he will be returning soon. On another level, along with the marvelous technology embodied in the yellow machine, it blazons forth Citrine's faith in America. The fact that Dvořák had used the spiritual to compose his *New World* Symphony suggests that it is a call to America to awaken from the stupor of Big Business and return to its original dream of creating a new world. The spiritual also signifies that mankind will go back to the original world of light from which it has been exiled. Citrine's teacher and friend had the feeling that there was a glorious home world that was lost (24). For Citrine this is not a mere feeling but a truth. Death is no longer a terrible final reality but a threshold man has to step across to return to the spiritual world of his origins. Bellow's unerring fictional tact led him to use not the higher-thought clown, Citrine, but the Rouault-like clown, Menasha, to sing such cosmic truths.

NOTES

1. Saul Bellow, *Humboldt's Gift* (New York: Viking Press, 1975), p. 141. All subsequent references will be incorporated in the text.

2. We are told that Humboldt was twenty-two on p. 10.

3. An article by Karyl Roosevelt in the September 8, 1975, issue of *People* (p. 61) describes how Bellow dictated *Humboldt's Gift*.

4. According to Karyl Roosevelt, Bellow taught Proust twice a week by day, Melville and Defoe at night, in 1975.

5. In "Card Playing as Mass Culture," an article in *Mass Culture* (Bernard Rosenberg and David M. White, eds., Glencoe, Ill.: The Free Press, 1957), p. 418, Irving Crespi maintains that "in a representative American community, card playing is most typically an activity of families and friendship groups, meeting in their own homes, and playing either for no stakes or for only trivial sums."

6. Rudolf Steiner, *Knowledge of the Higher Worlds: How Is It achieved?* (London: Rudolf Steiner Press, 1973), p. 34.

7. The novel seems to have been published in a hurry. Cantabile is in the back seat of the police car on p. 286. On the next page we discover him in the front seat.

8. Saul Bellow, "Machines and Storybooks," *Harpers* 249 (August 1974): 50.

9. Bellow used the title "The Swamp of Prosperity" for his review of Philip Roth's *Goodbye, Columbus* in *Commentary*, July 1959, pp. 77–79.

10. I give below an extract from the libretto of the last scene of *Aïda* (Giuseppe Verdi, *Aïda*, translated and introduced by Ellen H. Bleiler, [New York: Dover Publications, Inc., 1962], pp. 139–40):

AIDA: O terra addio, addio valle di pianti . . . sogno di gaudio che in dolor svani . . . A noi si schiude, si schiude il ciel . . . si schiude il ciel e l'alme erranti volano al raggio dell'eterno di.
RADAMES: O terra addio, addio valle di pianti—
AIDA: O terra addio;
RADAMES:—sogno di gaudio che in dolor svani
AIDA:—a noi si schiude
RADAMES:—a noi si schiude, si schiude il ciel—
AIDA:—si schiude il ciel
RADAMES:—si schiude il ciel e l'alme erranti—
AIDA:—si schiude il ciel—
RADAMES:—volano al raggio dell'eterno di.
AIDA:—a noi si schiude il ciel.

Farewell, O earth, farewell vale of tears . . . dream of joy that vanished in sorrow . . . heaven is opening, is opening for us . . . heaven is opening, and our errant souls will soar to the light of eternal day.
Farewell, O earth, farewell vale of tears—
Farewell, O earth;
—dream of joy that vanished in sorrow—
—Heaven is opening—
—heaven is opening, is opening for us—
—is opening
—heaven is opening and our errant souls—
—heaven is opening—
—will soar to the light of eternal day.
—heaven is opening for us.

Works Cited

BY SAUL BELLOW

I. Longer Works

The Adventures of Augie March. Greenwich, Conn.: Fawcett Publications, 1965.
Dangling Man. New York: Signet, 1965.
Henderson the Rain King. Greenwich, Conn.: Fawcett Crest Book, 1959.
Herzog. Greenwich, Conn.: Fawcett Crest Book, Fawcett Publications, 1964.
Humboldt's Gift. New York: Viking Press, 1975.
Mr. Sammler's Planet. Greenwich, Conn.: Fawcett Crest Book, Fawcett Publications, 1970.
Mosby's Memoirs and Other Stories. New York: Viking Press, 1968.
Seize the Day. New York: Viking Press, Viking Compass Edition, 1961.
The Victim. New York: Signet, 1965.

II. Short Fiction, Reviews, Articles, and Lectures

"Bunuel's Unsparing Vision." *Horizon* 5 (1962): 110–12.
"Distractions of a Fiction Writer." In *The Living Novel: A Symposium*, edited by Granville Hicks, pp. 1–20. New York: Macmillan, 1957.
"Dreiser and the Triumph of Art." *Commentary* 11 (1951): 502–3.
"Gide as Autobiographer." *New Leader*, June 4, 1951, 24.
Translation of I. B. Singer's "Gimpel the Fool." *Partisan Review* 20 (1953): 300–313.
"Introduction." *Great Jewish Short Stories*, edited by Saul Bellow, pp. 9–16. New York: Dell Publishing Co., 1963.
"Henderson in Africa." *Botteghe Oscure* 21 (1958): 187–225.
"How I Wrote Augie March's Story." *New York Times Book Review*, January 31, 1954, pp. 3, 17.
"In No Man's Land." *Commentary* 11 (1951): 204.
"John Berryman, Friend." *New York Times Book Review*, May 27, 1973, pp. 1–2.
"Literary Notes on Khrushchev." In *First Person Singular*, edited by Herbert Gold. New York: Dial Press, 1963.
"Literature." In *The Great Ideas Today*, edited by Mortimer Adler and Robert M. Hutchins. Chicago: Encyclopaedia Britannica, 1963.
"Machines and Storybooks." *Harpers* 249 (1974): 48–55.
"A Personal Record." *New Republic*, February 22, 1954, p. 21.

277

"Skepticism and the Depth of Life." In *The Arts and the Public*, edited by James
    E. Miller, Jr., and Paul D. Herring. Chicago: University of Chicago Press,
    1967.
"The Swamp of Prosperity." *Commentary*, July 1959, pp. 77–79.
"A Talk with the Yellow Kid." *Reporter*, September 6, 1956, pp. 6–8.
"Two Faces of a Hostile World." *New York Times Book Review*, August 26,
    1956, pp. 4–5.

ABOUT SAUL BELLOW

I. Interviews and Biographical Material

Boroff, David. "The Author." *Saturday Review of Literature*, 19 September
    1964, p. 39.
Brans, Jo. "Common Needs, Common Preoccupations: An Interview with Saul
    Bellow." *Southwest Review* 62 (1977): 1–19.
Breit, Harvey. *The Writer Observed*. New York: World Publishing Company,
    1956.
Current Biography. New York: The H. W. Wilson Company, 1965.
Epstein, Joseph. "Saul Bellow of Chicago." *New York Times Book Review*, 9
    May 1971, p. 14.
Harper, Gordon L. "Saul Bellow—The Art of Fiction." In *Writers at Work: The
    Paris Review Interviews*. Third Series. Edited by Alfred Kazin. New York:
    Viking Press, 1967.
Harris, Mark. "Saul Bellow at Purdue." *The Georgia Review*, Winter 1978, pp.
    715–54.
Hobson, Laura Z. "Trade Winds." *Saturday Review of Literature*, August 22,
    1953, p. 6.
Howard, Jane. "Mr. Bellow Considers His Planet." *Life*, April 3, 1970, pp.
    57–60.
Kalb, Bernard, "Biographical Sketch." *Saturday Review of Literature*,
    September 19, 1953, p. 13.
Kazin, Alfred. "My Friend Saul Bellow." *Atlantic*, January 1965, pp. 51–54.
Kulshreshtha, Chirantan. "A Conversation with Saul Bellow." *Chicago Review*
    23, no. 4, and 24, no. 1 (1972): 7–15.
Kunitz, Stanley J. *Twentieth Century Authors*. First Supplement. New York: The
    H. W. Wilson Company, 1955.
Nash, Jay, and Offen, Ron. "Saul Bellow." *Literary Times*, December 1964, p.
    10.
Pinsker, Sanford. "Saul Bellow in the Classroom." *College English* 34 (1973):
    975–82.
Robinson, Robert. "Saul Bellow at 60—Talking to Robert Robinson." *The
    Listener*, February 13, 1975, pp. 218–19.
Roosevelt, Karyl. "Bellow." *People*, September 8, 1975, p. 61.

Steers, Nina. " 'Successor' to Faulkner?" *Show,* September 1964, pp. 38–39.
Stern, Richard, "Bellow's Gift." *New York Times Magazine,* November 21, 1978, pp. 12, 43–44, 46, 48, 50.

II. Selected Criticism

Allen, Michael. "Idiomatic Language in Two Novels by Saul Bellow." *Journal of American Studies* 1 (1967): 275–80.
Bradbury, Malcolm. "Saul Bellow's *The Victim.*" *Critical Quarterly* 5 (Summer 1963): 119–28.
Ciancio, Ralph. "The Achievement of Saul Bellow's *Seize the Day.*" In *Literature and Theology,* edited by Thomas F. Staley and Lester F. Zimmerman, pp. 49–80. The University of Tulsa Department of English Monograph Series, 7, 1969.
Clayton, John J. *Saul Bellow: In Defence of Man.* Bloomington: Indiana University Press, 1971.
Cohen, Sarah B. *Saul Bellow's Enigmatic Laughter.* Chicago: University of Illinois Press, 1974.
Dutton, Robert R. *Saul Bellow.* New York: Twayne Publishers, 1971.
Klein, Marcus. "A Discipline of Nobility: Saul Bellow's Fiction." In *Saul Bellow: A Collection of Critical Essays,* edited by Earl Rovit, pp. 135–60. Englewood Cliffs, N.J.: Prentice-Hall, 1975.
Opdahl, Keith. *The Novels of Saul Bellow.* University Park: Pennsylvania State University Press, 1970.
Rodrigues, Eusebio L. "Bellow's Africa." *American Literature* 43 (1971): 242–56.
————. "Bellow's Confidence Man." *Notes on Contemporary Literature* 3 (1972): 6–8.
————. "Koheleth in Chicago: The Quest for the Real in 'Looking for Mr. Green.' " *Studies in Short Fiction* 11 (1974): 387–93.
————. "Reichianism in *Seize the Day.*" In *Critical Essays on Saul Bellow,* edited by Stanley Trachtenberg, pp. 89–100. Boston, Mass.: G. K. Hall & Co., 1979.
————. "Reichianism in *Henderson the Rain King.*" *Criticism* 15 (1972): 212–33.
————. "Saul Bellow's Henderson as America." *Centennial Review* 20 (Spring 1976): 189–95.
Shulman, Robert. "The Style of Bellow's Comedy." *Publications of the Modern Language Association* 83 (March 1968): 109–17.
Sicherman, Carol M. "Bellow's *Seize the Day:* Reverberations and Hollow Sounds." *Studies in the Twentieth Century* 15 (1975): 1–31.
Stock, Irving. "The Novels of Saul Bellow." *Southern Review* 3 (Winter 1967): 13–42.
Wilson, Edmund. "Doubts and Dreams: *Dangling Man* and *Under a Glass Bell.*" *New Yorker* 20 (April 1, 1944): 70, 73–74, 78, 81.

MISCELLANEOUS

Agnon, S. Y. *Days of Awe*. New York: Schocken Books, 1948.

Arendt, Hannah. *The Origins of Totalitarianism*. New York: World Publishing Co., 1972.

de Bary, Theodore W., ed. *Sources of Indian Tradition*. New York: Columbia University Press, 1969.

Crespi, Irving. "Card Playing as Mass Culture." In *Mass Culture*, edited by Bernard Rosenberg and David M. White. Glencoe, Ill.: The Free Press, 1957.

Eisinger, Charles. *Fiction of the Forties*. Chicago: University of Chicago Press, 1963.

Ferenczi, Sandor. "Thalassa: Theory of Genitality." *The Psychoanalytical Quarterly* 3 (January 1934): 1–29.

Freud, Sigmund. *The Standard Edition of the Works*. London: Hogarth Press, 1958.

Gibson, James J. *The Perception of the Visual World*. Cambridge: The Riverside Press, 1950.

Hemingway, Ernest. *The Sun Also Rises*. New York: Charles Scribner's Sons, 1926.

James, William. *The Principles of Psychology*. Chicago: Encyclopaedia Brittanica, 1952.

Jean-Aubry, G. *Joseph Conrad: Life and Letters*. 2 vols. New York: Doubleday, Page and Co., 1927.

Lodge, David. *The Language of Fiction*. New York: Columbia University Press, 1967.

Lowie, Robert H. *The History of Ethnological Theory*. New York: Holt, Rinehart and Winston, 1966.

Malinowski, Bronislaw. *Sex and Repression in Savage Society*. London: Routledge & Kegan Paul, Ltd., 1953.

Marx, Leo. *The Machine in the Garden: Technology and the Pastoral in America*. London: Oxford University Press, 1967.

Poggioli, Renato. *Rozanov*. New York: Hilary House Publishers, 1962.

de Quincey, Thomas. *Confessions of an English Opium Eater*. Edited by Edward Sackville-West. New York: Chanticleer Press, 1950.

Reich, Wilhelm *Character Analysis*. 3rd enlarged ed. New York: Farrar, Straus and Giroux, 1971.

―――. *The Discovery of the Orgone: The Function of the Orgasm*. New York: Noonday Press, 1970.

―――. *The Invasion of Compulsory Sex-Morality*. New York: Farrar, Straus and Giroux, 1971.

―――. *Selected Writings. An Introduction to Orgonomy*. New York: Farrar Straus and Giroux, 1970.

Reik, Theodore. *Jewish Wit*. New York: Gamut Press, 1962.

Robinson, Paul A. *The Freudian Left*. New York: Harper Colophon Books, 1969.

Rosenfeld, Isaac. *An Age of Enormity*. Edited by Theodore Solotaroff. Foreword by Saul Bellow. Cleveland: World Publishing Co., 1962.

Rozanov, V. V. *Solitaria*. Translated by S. S. Koteliansky. New York: Boni and Liveright, 1927.

Rycroft, Charles. *Wilhelm Reich*. New York: Viking Press, 1972.

Schopenhauer, Arthur. *The World as Will and Idea*. Translated by R. B. Haldane and J. Kemp. Garden City, N. Y.: Doubleday and Co., 1961.

Steiner, Rudolf. *Knowledge of the Higher Worlds: How Is It Achieved?* London: Rudolf Steiner Press, 1973.

Sypher, Wylie. *Literature and Technology*. New York: Random House, 1968.

Verdi, Giuseppe. *Aida*. Translated and Introduced by Ellen H. Bleiler. New York: Dover Publications, Inc., 1962.

Index

Acting: in *Augie March*, 72, 78; in *Herzog*, 169, 171, 186, 191, 194, 195; in *Seize the Day*, 83, 85; in *The Victim*, 39, 40, 48, 52, 53

Adams, Henry, 110, 156

Adler, Dr. *(Seize the Day)*, 82, 85, 86, 89, 90

Adventures of Augie March, The, 57–80; historical time in, 62; Machiavellians in, 63, 64; Mexican adventures in, 68–70; structure of, 79

Africa: in *Henderson*, 121; in *Humboldt's Gift*, 265

Aïda, 274, 275

Allbee, Kirby *(The Victim)*, 39–41; encounters with, 39–41; significance of, 50, 51

America: *Augie March* as celebration of, 75; Bellow's views on, 261, 262, 270; effect of money on its psyche, 258; Henderson as, 113–15, 149, 152, 155, 156; main question for, 226; the poet in, 253, 256; new hope for, 260, 275

Animal references: in *Augie March*, 69; in *Dangling Man*, 42; in *Henderson*, 128, 147; in *The Victim*, 46–50, 52

Anthropological dimensions: in *Augie March*, 64; in *Dangling Man*, 19, 24; in *Henderson*, 122, 129; in *Humboldt's Gift*, 238; in *The Victim*, 46, 47

Arendt, Hannah, 190, 206, 215

Arnewi *(Henderson)*, 121, 122, 128

Baudelaire, Charles, 25

Bellow, Saul: challenges his fellow writers, 110–11; fictional universe of, 9, 10; on how people read, 9; on the act of creation, 10; on the art of the novel, 16; on the order of art, 10; on the writer as beginner, 32; Jewish heritage, 77, 78, 200, 201; reverence for life, 71, 72; use of language, 10; views on Freud, 174

Berryman, John, 74

Bhagavad Gita, 142

Bildungsroman: Augie March as, 60–61, 69; *Herzog* as, 161, 164, 165; *Mr. Sammler's Planet* as, 211

Blake, William, 52, 82, 98, 99, 101, 113, 126, 143, 144, 199, 200, 255, 271

Boehme, Jacob, 24

Breit, Harvey, 74

Brotherhood, 106, 126, 160, 201, 223

Bunam, the *(Henderson)*, 131–34, 144

Caligula (the eagle in *Augie March*), 68, 69

Cannibalism: in *Humboldt's gift*, 248, 249, 266, 267

Cantabile, Rinaldo, 232, 234, 236, 237, 238, 243, 244; as Citrine's teacher, 250, 258, 265, 266; as manifestation of Humboldt, 234, 235, 236, 237, 250, 251, 266

Chicago: in *Augie March*, 70, 74–77, 237; in *Dangling Man*, 25; in *Herzog*, 237; in *Humboldt's Gift*, 237, 238

Christian Scientist *(Dangling Man)*, 22, 29

Citrine, Charles *(Humboldt's Gift)*, as narrator, 230, 232; his comic sense, 238; his condition at fifty-five, 232–33, 238, 241; his involvement with Renata, 245,